DATE DUE

THE WILDERNESS REVOLT

Books by Diane Kennedy Pike

Search: The Personal Story of a Wilderness Journey
The Other Side (*with James A. Pike*)

Books by James A. Pike

The Other Side: An Account of My Experiences
with Psychic Phenomena (*with Diane Kennedy*)
If This Be Heresy
You and the New Morality
What Is This Treasure
A Time for Christian Candor
Teen-agers and Sex
Beyond the Law
A New Look in Preaching
Our Christmas Challenge
Facing the Next Day
Doing the Truth: A Summary of Christian Ethics
If You Marry Outside Your Faith
Beyond Anxiety
Cases and Other Materials on the New Federal and Code Procedure
Modern Canterbury Pilgrims (*editor*)

The
Wilderness Revolt

A NEW VIEW OF THE LIFE AND DEATH
OF JESUS BASED ON IDEAS AND NOTES
OF THE LATE BISHOP JAMES A. PIKE

Diane Kennedy Pike and
R. Scott Kennedy

DOUBLEDAY & COMPANY, INC.
GARDEN CITY, NEW YORK
1972

The authors are grateful to the following for permission to use copyrighted material:

Basil Blackwell, Publisher, London, for material from *Martyrdom and Persecution in the Early Church* by W. H. C. Frend and from *Theocracy and Eschatology* by Otto Ploger.

Cambridge University Press, New York, for extracts from *The Temple and the Community in Qumran and the New Testament* by Bertil Gartner.

The Clarendon Press, Oxford, for material from *Roman Society and Roman Law in the New Testament* by A. N. Sherwin-White, 1963. Used by permission of The Clarendon Press.

Columbia University Press and William R. Farmer for extracts from *Maccabees, Zealots, and Josephus* by William R. Farmer.

Doubleday & Company, Inc., for material from *The Ancient Library of Qumran,* copyright © 1958 by Frank Moore Cross, Jr. Reprinted by permission of Doubleday & Company, Inc.

Fortress Press and SCM Press Ltd. for material from *Jerusalem in the Time of Jesus* by Joachim Jeremias.

Harper & Row, Publishers, for extracts from *The Scrolls and the New Testament,* edited by Krister Stendahl, and from *Jesus and the Revolutionaries* by Oscar Cullmann.

Harvard University Press for material from Josephus, *The Jewish War, Antiquities, The Life,* and *Against Apion,* translated by H. St. J. Thackery, in The Loeb Classical Library.

Israel Exploration Journal, Jerusalem, Israel, for extracts from "Blessed Are the Poor in Spirit" by David Flusser, which appeared in Vol. 10, No. 1, 1960.

Judaism for extracts from "The Trial of Jesus in the Light of History" by Robert M. Grant, Vol. 20, No. 1, Winter 1971.

New American Library and Thames and Hudson Ltd., London, for material from *The Crucible of Christianity,* edited by Arnold Toynbee, Thames and Hudson Ltd. being the publishers in the United Kingdom, © 1969 Thames and Hudson Ltd., London.

S.P.C.K., London, for extracts as follows from *The Scrolls and Christianity* (S.P.C.K. Theological Collections 11), edited by Matthew Black: W. F. Albright and C. S. Mann, "Qumran and the Essenes: Geography, Chronology, and Identification of the Sect"; Matthew Black, "The Dead Sea Scrolls and Christian Origins"; Raymond E. Brown, "The Teacher of

Righteousness and the Messiah(s)"; F. F. Bruce, "Jesus and the Gospels in the Light of the Scrolls"; R. K. Harrison, "The Rites and Customs of the Qumran Sect"; John Pryke, "Eschatology in the Dead Sea Scrolls"; and Charles H. H. Scobie, "John the Baptist."

Stein and Day Publishers and B. T. Batsford Ltd., London, for material from the book *The Trial of Jesus of Nazareth* by S. G. F. Brandon. Copyright © 1968 by S. G. F. Brandon. Reprinted with permission of Stein and Day Publishers and B. T. Batsford Ltd.

Walter de Gruyter & Co., Berlin, Germany, for material from *On the Trial of Jesus* by Paul Winter, published by de Gruyter in 1961.

The Westminster Press and SCM Press Ltd. for extracts from *The Method and Message of Jewish Apocalyptic* by D. S. Russell. Published in the U.S.A. by The Westminster Press, 1964. Copyright © SCM Press Ltd., 1964. From *Interpreting the Resurrection* by Neville Clark. Published in the U.S.A. by The Westminster Press, 1967. Copyright © SCM Press Ltd., 1967. From *The Rule of Qumran and Its Meaning* by A. R. C. Leaney. Published in the U.S.A. by The Westminster Press, 1966. Copyright © SCM Press Ltd., 1966. All materials used by permission.

Biblical excerpts are from The Jerusalem Bible, copyright © 1966 by Darton, Longman & Todd, Ltd., and Doubleday & Company, Inc. Used by permission of the publisher. Also from the Revised Standard Version of the Bible. Copyrighted 1946 and 1952.

The authors would like to extend their special thanks to Justice Haim Cohn of the Supreme Court of Israel for material from his article "Reflections on the Trial and Death of Jesus," which first appeared in *The Israel Law Review* and was reprinted by *The Jerusalem Post* Press, 1967.

to
Mother and Dad
in love and gratitude

CONTENTS

SOURCES

Quotations from the Bible and the Apocrypha are from The Jerusalem Bible translation unless otherwise noted.

Quotations from the Dead Sea Scrolls are taken from the translation by G. Vermes, unless otherwise indicated.

Quotations from the writings of Josephus are from the Loeb Classical Library edition (see Bibliography under Thackeray).

Quotations from Bishop James A. Pike in the Preface and at the beginning of each chapter are excerpted and edited from transcripts of a seminar on Christian Origins given in May of 1969 for the Esalen Institute in San Francisco, by courtesy of whom they appear here.

ABBREVIATIONS

Dead Sea Scrolls

Blessings	Benedictions	IQSb
Com. on Hab.	Commentary on Habakkuk	IQpHab.
Com. on Is.	Commentary on Isaiah	4QpIs.
Com. on Nah.	Commentary on Nahum	4QpNah.
Dam. Doc.	Damascus/Zadokite Document	CD
Gen. Apoc.	Genesis Apocryphon	
Hymns	Hymns of Thanksgiving (Hodayot Scroll)	IQH
Is. Scroll	Isaiah Scroll	IQIs.
Man. of Disc.	Manual of Discipline (Rule of Community)	IQS
Mess. Coll.	Florilegium (a collection of Messianic passages with comments); fragments from Cave 4.	4QF1
Patr. Blessings	The Blessings of the Twelve Patriarchs	4QPatr. Blessings
Rule of Cong.	Rule of the Congregation (The Messianic Rule)	IQSa
Testimonies	Testimonies Scroll (a Messianic anthology of prooftexts)	4Q Testimonies
War Scroll	War of the Children of Light Against the Children of Darkness	IQM

Josephus

Ant.	*Jewish Antiquities*
War	*The Jewish War*

Bible Translations

RSV	Revised Standard Version
KJV	King James Version

ACKNOWLEDGMENTS

After Bishop Pike's death in Israel in the fall of 1969, we committed ourselves to the completion of his book on the historical Jesus. If then we had had any idea of the magnitude of the task we had undertaken, we would probably not have attempted it. Were it not for the help and encouragement of many friends, and the fact that we shared the burden, we could never have brought our resolution to fulfillment.

We are grateful to Kristin Champion, Arlene and Ed Kennedy, Tiralisa Kennedy, Mary Read, John D. Riley, John Rippey, Melinda Samis, Jean Sprague, and Eva Wilming for their help in proofreading and typing the manuscript at various stages.

To Alexander Liepa, our editor at Doubleday, go our thanks for his very specific and helpful editorial comments and suggestions.

The extraordinary flexibility and ongoing encouragement of several of the faculty at the University of California at Santa Cruz made it possible for Scott to work for nearly three years as an undergraduate student on the project brought to fruition here, and more especially their efforts enabled him to spend time in Israel for the writing of the manuscript during the fall and winter quarters of 1970–71. Special thanks are extended to Professors Page Smith and John Dizikes of Cowell College and Noel King of Merrill College for their guidance and support.

Our gratitude is also due to Bishop John A. T. Robinson and Professor S. G. F. Brandon of England for their continuing friendship after Bishop Pike's death, and for their encouragement and helpful criticism during the evolution of this manuscript.

Our sincere appreciation goes to Professor David Flusser of the Hebrew University in Jerusalem. Professor Flusser was a real friend to us in Israel at the time of Bishop Pike's death, and gave us many hours of his valuable time during our return trip to Israel a year later for the writing of this book. His profound appreciation of the historical Jesus and his deep insight into the origins of Christianity have contributed immeasurably to our understanding. We are not only indebted to Professor Flusser for his help with the book, but also for the kindness and friendship which he and his wife Hannah have shown us.

Finally, the book could not possibly have been completed without the patience, energy, and devotion of our good friend Mrs. Gertrude Platt of Santa Barbara, who did a yeoman's task in the typing and preparation of the various drafts of the manuscript.

We are glad to be able to present to a larger audience the fruits of Bishop Pike's treasured study of the historical Jesus. We hope our readers will find it rewarding and that Jim will be pleased.

Diane K. Pike
R. Scott Kennedy

Santa Barbara, California
Feast of Pentecost 1971

PREFACE

The one incontrovertible historical fact about Jesus is that he was crucified by the Romans as a political insurrectionist. The charge made against him, which was nailed to the cross for all to see, was that he was the "King of the Jews"—that is, a pretender to the throne of Israel at a time when Rome ruled. That a man who died as a criminal (in the eyes of Rome) and as a failure (in the eyes of his own followers) became the focus of one of the world's largest religions is, on the face of it, one of the most incomprehensible facts of history.

What, then, really happened? Why did the Romans execute a man whom the Gospels imply "did no wrong"? Why did they *crucify* him—the mode of execution reserved for rebels against the Empire? What did they mean when they accused him of being the "King of the Jews"? Why did his followers grow in number *after* his death? What meaning did this man's life and death have *in his own time and culture?*

The following chapters present a reconstructed picture of the complex culture and society in which Jesus lived. We have tried to make the period come to life—not just in its political dimension, not just in the religious realm, but in the fullness of the life experience of men of that age: devout adherents to the Covenant which Moses mediated between the God of Abraham, Isaac, and Jacob, and the People Israel.

These men—religious Jews of the first centuries B.C. and A.D.—constituted the circle of society in which Jesus moved. They studied and taught the Law of Moses. They worshiped in the Temple of Jerusalem. They meditated on the prophets and waited for the Messianic deliverer who would redeem Israel. They revolted against Rome's mighty Empire. To understand them, and Jesus, we must first grasp something of the history of the Jewish people.[1] In the context of that history, Jesus as an historical person comes alive.

BISHOP PIKE'S SEARCH FOR TRUTH

It is our conviction that Jesus cannot be understood properly except against the background of the Jewish nationalism of his day. His crucifixion is a direct result of his involvement in the Messianic activities of his people—activities aimed at establishing Israel as a free nation with God alone as King.

The late Bishop James A. Pike is primarily responsible for both this thesis and this book. His all-consuming interest at the time of his death was the writing of the book which you now hold in your hands. Bishop Pike intended to co-author the work with his wife, and together they had planned it in great detail, even though the manuscript itself had not actually been drafted.

It may be of interest to you to know something of how Bishop Pike became involved in the study which led to the book you are about to read.

In September of 1966 formal heresy charges were filed against Bishop James A. Pike by a group of his fellow bishops—the first time such a charge had been made against an Episcopal bishop since 1928.[2] Among the accusations made were that he denied the Virgin Birth of Jesus, the Doctrine of the Holy Trinity, the Holy Ghost, and the literal bodily Resurrection. Though Bishop Pike had never *denied* those doctrines (or any others) he had *questioned* many. He felt they were unnecessary stumbling blocks for twentieth-century man. Formulated in late Greek philosophical thought forms which are misleading (if not incomprehensible) in the context of our scientific world view, many of the Church's teachings seem irrelevant to Christian laymen in the "standard brand" churches, as Bishop Pike used to call them, and are either ignored or disbelieved.[3] Even though countless numbers of lay people, and many other clergy, shared his doubts, Bishop Pike was attacked as a "heretic" when he publicly voiced his reservations about creedal formulas.

It was out of his great love for the tradition of the Church and his deep conviction that the central meaning of the teachings was still relevant that Bishop Pike sought to update what he called the "packaging" (namely, the doctrines, creeds, and liturgical formulas) before all the "customers" turned completely away.[4] His concern began in

1960 while the churches in the United States were still enjoying the post-WWII boom. He felt then that the churches had "conformed to the world" rather than transforming it, that their statistical growth did not represent a real "advance," and that soon their hollow "foundations" would give way and decline would set in.[5] Though most thought him a prophet of doom in 1960, the decline of the Church was so rapid by the time of his death only nine years later, that even his harshest critics were alarmed at the growing crisis.

Bishop Pike's principal motivation for delving into the origins of Christianity, in the beginning, was a desire to answer the criticism leveled at him by his colleagues who, beginning in 1960, had been saying that his public questioning of the long-standing teachings of the Church was undermining "the faith once delivered to the saints." This barb set the Bishop researching, for he was certain that the "faith" delivered to the "saints" (believers) in the first century was not that which had been codified, canonized, and creedalized in the third, fourth, and later centuries. He hoped to beat his colleagues at their own "conservative" game.

Once launched on the study, however, he found that the need for ammunition with which to fight off heresy-hunters became a secondary impetus. In his study of the first century he discovered a more excitingly relevant Jesus than he had ever anticipated. To the surprise of many—not the least among whom were his fellow bishops —in 1966 James A. Pike resigned his highly prized administrative post as Bishop of California in order to devote himself to an intensive study of Jesus and Christian origins. He felt he could better fulfill his role as a bishop—that of being pastor to clergy and chief teacher and guardian of the faith—if he were not encumbered with so many meetings and fund-raising activities. He wanted to spend his time studying and learning and sharing his insights with others.

Perhaps because of their own disinterest in the subject matter he avowed he was studying, some of Bishop Pike's episcopal brethren doubted his motives, and it was soon after his resignation of his administrative post that they filed heresy charges against him. Thus his first "free" year was spent in a struggle with his episcopal colleagues which seemed to most church members, and certainly to secularists, like something out of the Middle Ages. In the fall of 1967 the Bishops of the Episcopal Church adopted a statement on theological freedom which made ample room for Bishop Pike in their denomination and declared the concept of heresy to be outmoded in our century, but they failed to deal with any basic questions about the reformulation of doctrines and creeds.

Bishop Pike found the victory a hollow one. His deepest desire was to be able to present the "product" of the church (i.e., Jesus) in "packaging" which would sell in the modern marketplace of ideas. In his three years as a "bishop at large" he spoke to thousands of people all over the United States, and to many in other parts of the world as well. He lectured on dozens of college campuses, preached in many churches of all denominations, addressed Jewish temples and synagogues, talked to secular groups of all kinds, and made hundreds of television and radio appearances.[6] No matter what his topic, he almost always found a way to use the historical Jesus and/or the history of Jesus' times as illustrative material. He felt both shed light on our contemporary scene and he wanted to share that light with others in his attempt to preserve the tradition which he felt "conservatives" would make obsolete within the century unless some drastic changes were brought about.

He also continued his research. By the time of his death he had accumulated a library of over eight hundred volumes in the field of Christian origins. His fascination with the subject was such that he read each newly published book or article on the day he received it. Those he found especially helpful he reread several times, and whatever new information he gathered or new insights he gained were shared with all who would listen. He was an impassioned and energetic man, and having found what he felt was the key to an understanding of the development of western culture and of the central insights of that culture regarding man in his universe, he fully intended to pursue his research indefinitely. He saw what he was doing as a kind of religious and cultural psychoanalysis which would enable many persons who were disturbed by the traumata of their religious heritage to understand the past, integrate it into the present, and move out unencumbered into an open future as persons of faith who believe the God of Truth is in the uncharted future as well as in the patterned past.

Bishop Pike had planned to write several books based on his research. He planned one on James, the brother of Jesus and the head of the Jerusalem Church; one on Paul, the founder of the movement we now call Christianity; one on the Jewish revolt against Rome in A.D. 66 and the fall of Masada; one on the growth and development of the Christian Jewish movement. At the time of his death, he was

ready to begin the writing of the first—and for him, the most important: an historical account of Jesus in the context of his times.

Perhaps the most poignant indication of the depth of Bishop Pike's
involvement in his study of Jesus' life was his eagerness to visit in
person all of the significant historical sites of the period 168 B.C. to
A.D. 135, and most especially the places associated with Jesus himself.
Bishop Pike had been to Israel five times. On his sixth, and last,
trip he visited the one area he had not yet seen—the wilderness. He
did not go there, as some have conjectured, looking for an undis-
covered scroll or other archaeological evidence. He sought a direct
experience of the wilderness in which Jesus had so often fasted
and meditated. Unfortunately, he did not live to tell about the experience he had there, nor to write the book into which the insights
from that journey would have been incorporated.[7]

"THIS RABBI JESUS . . ."

The thesis which follows is that which Bishop Pike developed over
the course of his four-year study. We have tried to present the
historical Jesus which so completely captivated and inspired Bishop
Pike. To use his own words:

"This is not just an exercise in primitivism. We have been very
interested in getting down to the first layer of historical tradition
insofar as possible. If we can find out who Jesus was, obviously we
want to. Getting close to him by finding out what the Jerusalem
Church taught—or Paul, or the early Church fathers—doesn't *necessarily* bring one closer to the Truth, but at least it is a place to
start to be honest.

"Any great figure who lives out a world view in zeal, in planning,
in wisdom, and in prudence—in the context of a corporate community—shows in the process who he is. He reveals what he's got,
how he responds to persons, how persons affect him, and how he
grows. So we will see a great deal, when we look honestly at the
Jesus of history, of that which we often call personal religion or ethics
or inspiration or mystical experience. We will see all these things.
The historical approach does not rob us of any of that. In fact, I
think it makes it clearer because it gives the real context in which
it's being displayed. Sheer abstractions arrived at by picking scriptural

texts or isolated parables out of context don't really give us much reality.

"The Church—or at least most of the Church—by moving past the somewhat existential script of the New Testament to the tired materials of late Greek philosophy for the construction of doctrines and definitions, ended up in a very arid place—at least three times removed from the reality of a Jesus who said, 'Sell your coats and buy daggers' [cf. Lk. 22:36]. Jesus affirmed Torah [the Law] more that anyone—'Not one jot or tittle shall pass away . . .' [cf. Mt. 5:17–19 and Lk. 16:17]—and yet in each instance where a person was involved, he leaped right over the fence of Torah to meet the needs of that person. But the kind of bloodless Jesus we get who is two natures in one person, three persons in one substance, and so on, is a long way removed from the one we discover in history.

"We have had some bad moments in our study when we really got a glimpse of what was underneath the tradition and were not sure we liked it. I'm not sure you'll like all of it. But I like it better the more I see of it, partially because I am reidentifying more and more with the period and with the man Jesus. I am finding that I have come to think so much of Jesus that words fail me. He is great. And I am not referring only—or even particularly—to a subjective experience of Jesus either. I mean that more and more real facts show that Jesus was a real man, *much greater* than the Church has appreciated. In fact, I'm not sure the Church really wants this one. I don't know what they would do with him. He's just fabulous.

"From the Jesus of history I get a clear image of a real flesh and blood person who was capable of a very big—perhaps total—dedication. He was acting on a premise which is not quite ours—that of an expectation of a literal breakthrough from outside of history—and yet it is not quite *not* our premise either. It is easy to put down that notion of history, and yet I have a concept of history which is an expectant one: which expects the new, the grace and freshness to break through. I don't really expect a legion of angels to arrive, but I have wondered if those people then really did either.

"I think God is for the freedom of all peoples, as individuals against churches that try to cramp their style, and as groups against cultures that try to dominate others. God is on the side of people who want their freedom, and so God was on the side of Israel against the Romans.

"Now, anyone who believes God is in some way going to make

manifest His sympathy with the cause of freedom will surely do his very best to create a confrontation which will enable the victory. Perhaps in Jesus' culture one had to talk about legions of angels led by some kind of divine figure or top angel, some commander who would come down with the angels. But the very fact that the images were ambiguous even then is perhaps an indication that they didn't consider it an either/or (divine or human) matter. They conceived of a man leading out as strongly and fully as he could toward the realization of the new, and of that which is divine merging with the human. Perhaps for that reason it is never quite clear in the New Testament whether it is 'just Jesus' who acts or whether it is the Son of Man.

"I am left with a wonderful sense of greater frontiers of understanding emerging from a study of the historical Jesus. I find myself not wanting to throw out any of the motifs or images. Certainly I want to speak out against the misapplication of them in institutional forms which repress people. I would be against myself if I misused some of these images to hurt a person.

"But I feel a little like Paul did when he wrote I Corinthians 3. He was writing when one of the big rows was going on among parties. Some were following Paul, some Apollos, some Peter; and some, who must have been the really irritating types, said, 'We just follow Christ.' (More churches get founded that way!) Some were terribly concerned with the here and now, and others about the next world.

"Paul said to them, *not* 'All you fellows get together and follow me.' No. He said, *'All things* are yours, whether Paul, or Apollos or Cephas or the world or life or death or the present or the future, *all* are yours; and you are Christ's; and Christ is God's' [I Cor. 3:21b–23]. There are diversities of concepts and images, and the more you know about the history of this period the richer the cafeteria of ideas and beliefs is—sometimes more rich than the stomach can take!—and *all things* are yours for the taking.

"As to Jesus himself, I do believe for a variety of reasons in what we call the resurrection, though I prefer to call it survival, or ongoing life. And I do believe in his communication with his disciples after his death. I believe that something very special happened that enabled his centrality to be maintained even though he had failed—as other Messiah figures had failed—to liberate Israel. He is a man in whom God breaks through in a big way. If this is less than classical Christian orthodoxy, it is *not* less than classical Christian Judaism of the first century, and it is to that Jesus that we give our attention in the full expectation that what we will discover there will be challenging, uplifting, and enlightening. This rabbi Jesus was the greatest—and is worth our coming to know."

In Quest of the Historical Jesus

The quest for the historical Jesus is a fairly recent phenomenon. It began only in the eighteenth century in the Age of Enlightenment when a new attitude toward history was born—a conviction that there was an objective point of reference called "historical fact" on which all interpretations of a given event were to be based. Historians sought to write purely objective accounts of the events of their time —devoid of personal and subjective interpretation—and theologians were naturally influenced by their approach. The new historiography was called the "higher criticism."[1] The methodology was highly rationalistic and positivistic, attempting to allow for no subjectivity.

It was in this context that the original quest for the historical Jesus arose. Nineteenth-century theologians thought it possible to discern objective historical fact in the gospel accounts of Jesus' life and teachings. James M. Robinson of the Southern California School of Theology in Claremont, California, states, "The *possibility* of the original quest resided primarily in its view of the oldest sources as the same kind of objective, positivistic historiography which the nineteenth century itself aspired to write."[2] This approach necessitated the drawing of a distinction between the original and authentic Jesus which the theologians sought to discover and the Christ of the Apostle Paul which they believed was being espoused by ecclesiastical authorities. Hence there developed a gap between the "Jesus of Nazareth" of historical research and the "Jesus Christ" proclaimed by the Christian Church.[3]

At the close of the nineteenth century the objection was raised that there had in fact been no life of Jesus which was really historical, since the participants in the so-called historical study failed to confine themselves to the search for a purely historical understanding. Instead, it was argued, they sought to define a new faith in the course of their study.

Indeed, historical theology sought to provide a new figure of Jesus which could serve as the basis for belief, replacing the dogmas of the Church. Scholars sought to give the personality of Jesus new life, but succeeded in doing so only by reading their own ideas into their accounts of Jesus' life and teachings. "Each scholar had created Jesus in the image of his own personality and his own ideals. And so Jesus had by turns been portrayed as an Enlightenment man, the genius of Romanticism, the moral example, the social crusader, etc."[4] Jesus as portrayed by nineteenth-century theologians was little more than their own creation. And this was the basic criticism underlying Albert Schweitzer's historical study of Jesus.

Albert Schweitzer's *The Quest of the Historical Jesus* is a classic example of the fact that most men who search for historical data about Jesus end up writing their own "gospel."[5] Although Schweitzer attempted a strictly historical analysis and understanding of the words and ministry of Jesus, and with devastating insight pointed out the flaws in earlier attempts to write lives of Jesus, he readily admitted the extent to which he himself was reflected in his life of Jesus. Schweitzer recognized, "There is no historical task which so reveals a man's true self as the writing of a Life of Jesus."[6] Despite his having written the work which founded a "new age" in historical theology's quest for the historical Jesus,[7] Schweitzer concluded that in such study "the guiding principle must ultimately rest upon historical intuition"[8] and that an honest historical methodology will result, as in his own case, in an understanding which transcends historical fact.[9]

Drawing conclusions from historical studies of the life of Jesus which go beyond those seemingly justified by the "objective" facts at hand has been a consistent practice of scholars searching for the historical Jesus. This has inevitably led to criticism of the perspective and motivation of any man who approaches the subject, whether from a sympathetic or critical viewpoint. It has often been said that the so-called historical lives of Jesus reveal more about the authors than about Jesus. This observation is as applicable to those men responsible for the earliest documents written about Jesus—the "gospels" as they are now known—as to the most recent scholars in the field.

Dr. Schweitzer endorsed the summation that "Jesus has been made the receptacle into which every theologian pours his own ideas."[10] He therefore began his own quest with the assertion that the Jesus of history cannot serve as a basis for a religion in the twentieth century, for "The historical Jesus will be to our time a stranger and an enigma."[11] Schweitzer believed that the historical Jesus who had been the object of the search of those who wanted to free themselves from the Church's portrayal of Christ, was even less acceptable to modern man than the figure of the Nicene Creed. Jesus, Schweitzer maintained, must be viewed as an historical figure in the context of his own times, who shared eschatological and apocalyptic ideas which are largely foreign to contemporary man. Schweitzer was critical of those studies of the life of Jesus which lifted him from his historical context—for Jesus, he felt, could only be understood in light of the ideas and practices of the period of first-century Judaism. He tried to give the full historical value and true historical setting of the preaching, teachings, and events of Jesus' life.[12] But Schweitzer eventually turned from his purely objective, historical approach to a subjective inference of meaning from the historical figure of Jesus. "Thus in debate over the historicity of Jesus in the second German edition . . . Schweitzer comes to the conclusion that 'religion by its very nature is independent of all history.' . . . in Schweitzer's mystical way he left behind him his original point of departure in historical research upon the quest of the historical Jesus . . ."[13]

A NEW QUEST

And it is precisely this observation which James M. Robinson of Claremont's Southern California School of Theology sees as the starting point for the "new" quest of the historical Jesus. This new quest began formally with the work of Ernst Käsemann, who in 1953 concluded that because something *can* be known about the historical Jesus, there must be a concern to *know* it in order to prevent the Christian faith from being a faith in a mythological lord.[14] This new attitude ended nearly half a century during which scholars, for scientific and theological reasons, had believed the writing of an historical life of Jesus impossible and illegitimate.[15] Dr. James M. Robinson attributes to the new quest the realization that there exists a "deeper level of the reality of 'Jesus of Nazareth as he actually was' which was not reached by 'the reconstruction of his biography by means of objective historical method.' . . . Quite apart from the assumptions of Christian faith, it is easy to see that all Jesus actually was is not likely to be fully grasped, objectively demonstrated, and definitively stated by historical research in any given period."[16]

The twentieth century has witnessed a shift in the perspective of the historian from that of the previous century, that is, from "cataloguing with objective detachment facts in sequence and with proper causal relationships." Instead, the historian's task has come now to be seen as that of seeking an understanding of the "deeplying intentions of the past, by involving one's selfhood in an encounter in which one's own intentions and views of existence are put in question, and perhaps altered or even radically reversed."[17]

The new quest of the historical Jesus is being conducted largely on this intuitive level—that is, in the subjective interpretation which goes beyond what may be *proven* by purely objective historical research. This historical intuition of which Schweitzer spoke is that which makes sense out of what is "knowable" in the study of the historical Jesus. This new perspective in the quest was not openly acknowledged in the last century though it was demonstrated by scholars in their works. All historical lives of Jesus are gospels—faith affirmations on the part of the specific scholar, based on what he has discerned to be the facts of the life and teachings of Jesus.

FACTS + FAITH

As participants in the new quest, the authors are not so pretentious as to state that all we have included in this book is "historical fact." The present work is a gospel in the sense that Mark's life of Jesus is a gospel: Mark attempted to make intelligible the meaning of the life of Jesus the Nazarene which he had discovered as relevant to his own life. We have tried to do the same, on the historical level, following the method of Bishop James A. Pike who began the quest which has come to fruition here and to whom we owe the basic thesis. That method, which he called "facts + faith," is carefully detailed in Chapter V of *If This Be Heresy* where Bishop Pike stated:

> A man can believe what is shown to emerge from the application of the very process that he uses in his workaday existence—the *empirical method*. This method, in brief, consists of
>   a. Examination of relevant data,
>   b. The drawing of a plausible inference from the data,

    c. Affirmation of the consequent hypothesis by faith, and
    d. Action based on this faith-affirmation.
Can any recognizably Christian conclusions be reached by this method? Or, to put it more broadly, can any religious truth emerge from this process? One thing seems fairly clear. None can be derived, plausibly, by any *other* method.

To put the matter descriptively, less and less will people believe conclusions reached by any other route. The only avenue open now is the faith-affirmation based on empirical data.[18]

Our practice has been to draw what we feel to be the most plausible inferences from the data available, and the present work is original only in that the basic hypothesis which gave direction and intention to our search—the outlines of the giant jigsaw puzzle, the last pieces of which we have been seeking—came intuitively to Bishop Pike in January of 1966. We have been fortunate to have at our disposal large numbers of documents from the period in which Jesus lived unknown to scholars prior to 1947. These have enabled us to put the puzzle together to our satisfaction.[19]

We have not addressed ourselves here to questions of personal faith or to dimensions of "eternal" meaning. We have limited our discussion to an attempt to restate the historical picture in such a way that Jesus can come into focus as a real person—a man who lived in first-century Israel, a great teacher and leader, an inspired and devoutly religious Jew, the symbol of his age: a rebel on a cross.

But the other levels of meaning are there. Jesus' teaching and preaching were directed toward individual men whom he hoped would see the historical moment clearly enough to want to change their lives radically and to begin to live lives of perfection and fulfillment at once. He believed the Kingdom of God was at hand, and that those who believed as he did could begin living in it without further delay. The cosmic, or eternal, dimensions of meaning are "beneath" or "in" and "throughout" the whole story. It is for that reason that the history which we recount here is shared by three major religions and has been the object of unending study by men who seek to know the deepest and highest truths about life.

It is our conviction that one of the great errors of the Christian Church is that of losing sight of its historical roots and its fundamental historical nature. Since the failure of the nineteenth century to recapture an historical basis for the Christian faith, many Christians in the twentieth century have tried to "save" the history by reading it principally as "myth." Then, because the "myths" seemed too airy and untenable, they were "demythologized" and laymen were offered, instead of an historically rooted faith, a dogmatic statement of the *meaning* of the history. We live in an age of science when truths are no longer accepted on authority alone, but are experimented with and either proven or discarded. Many would like to know if Christianity "works," but the Church has too often had neither the history nor the myths with which to communicate it—and the dogmas are not acceptable.[20]

We have tried to restate the history. We find that the myths (symbolic truth) emerge for us in the process and we hope that the same will be true for the reader. Jesus and the religious men of his age sought—perhaps as devoutly as men in any age known to man —to *live out* their understanding of the meaning of history and of life itself. Thus for them there was no distinction between myth and history. The "truth" was being acted out, lived out, in their midst. The very events of history (political history, if you wish) were the fulfillment of the words of prophecy, and God was being revealed in their time. They were being empirical and experimental in their approach to religious truth and this, we feel, can speak directly to modern man. At least half the battle in rediscovering the meaningful elements of the Christian heritage is won by gaining a clear picture of the history of Jesus' time. For those who have "ears to hear" and "eyes to see" and the will to seek the truth, the rest will follow.

FOR "THE LITTLE PEOPLE"

The present work is intended mainly for the lay reader, in whom the authors have a great deal of faith. It is our conviction that laymen, Christian, Jew, and agnostic, want to know what can be known about the historical Jesus. We do not believe they accept any longer the efforts of theologians who deny history and remove Jesus from his historical context, or of the apologists who attempt to salvage a first-century world view which modern man finds totally incomprehensible and inadequate to meet his needs. But we are confident that laymen are deeply concerned about the meaning questions of life and that, given the data with which to work, they will be capable of responding to first-century men, who were equally committed to the quest for truth, by making their own life commitments proper to and consistent with their scientific and pragmatic world.

Bishop Pike has recounted how, during the writing of his book *A Time for Christian Candor*,[21] an American bishop of the Episcopal Church wrote him requesting that he not write it. Fearing Bishop Pike's publication and his purpose of *"coming right out with it,* a bold statement of a post-Copernican theology—for lay people as well as for professionals . . . He said in effect: we know these things, Jim, but don't let 'the little people' know."[22]

William Stringfellow and Anthony Towne relate another such incident in *The Bishop Pike Affair:* "Bishop Hines opened the matter—speaking, Bishop Pike has said, for what was obviously by that time 'a group–mind'—with a question: had the Bishop of California [Bishop Pike] in what he had been doing and saying concerned himself with the effect this had on the little people? (The issue of the little people —presumably the ordinary churchgoing faithful—has frequently been raised by bishops who are critical of Bishop Pike's public comments. Thus, on another occasion, a bishop said to him: 'Look, Jim, we know what you've been saying is true, but you can't tell the little people all that.')

"Bishop Pike responded that, on the one hand, truth was truth and could not be made different for big people and little people, and, on the other hand, he didn't think that little people were all that little anyway. He pointed out that, as a result of education and mass communications and other modern phenomena, the little people were getting less little all the time, and knew, in fact, much more than some big people thought. He implied that *he* thought the little people would grow even bigger if the already big people would be more candid with them."[23]

The authors share Bishop Pike's conviction that "the little people are getting bigger all the time,"[24] and it is, therefore, for these "little people" who inspired and sustained Bishop Pike in his unrelenting quest for new and relevant information about the person Jesus, that this work has been completed.

THE WILDERNESS REVOLT

CHAPTER 1

The Freedom Struggle of the Jewish People

"Long since, my brave men, we determined neither to serve the Romans nor any other save God, for He alone is man's true and righteous Lord; and now the time is come which bids us verify that resolution by our actions." The Jewish War VII. 323

In the words of James A. Pike:

"The ceremony which celebrated the victory of the Maccabean revolt in about 164 B.C. was called the Cleansing of the Temple. It was celebrated by a feast of Dedication for the cleansing and re-dedication of the Temple. It is still celebrated by Jews today in the feast of Hanukkah.

"That same feast, according to the Fourth Gospel, marked a very important turn of events in Jesus' life, and Jesus himself is known to have sought to cleanse the Temple on an occasion which was probably one of the main events leading to his execution as an insurrectionist.

"Pompey had taken over Israel for the Roman Empire in 63 B.C. Later there began to develop a psychological need on the part of Roman emperors to be regarded as gods, with a kind of civic Shinto-type religion involving the offering of incense to the emperor to indicate respect for him as of the divine realm. This did not create a crisis for those belonging to most of the religions of the Empire, any more than it created a crisis for Christians in Japan at the time Japan was growing increasingly bellicose during the Second World War. Christians got in line. They were willing to regard the emperor as in some way divine. In fact, they were pretty much instructed by their respective churches to get in line: 'Don't

make a fuss over this; it's not worth it; it's really a matter of se-
mantics.' Very sophisticated.

"But this is *not* the way it was looked at during the first century
B.C. and A.D. by one group—and as far as we can see, by one
group only: that is, the Jews. The Jews in the Roman Empire felt
that they could not give this kind of recognition to the king or emperor, whereas most other people in the Empire did feel they could,
and still carry on with their own religious beliefs. If one did whatever was required in a religio-civic way, he could believe anything
he wanted. In fact, some people got initiated into two or three of
the mystery cults at a time, just to be sure.

"The response of the Jews, however, was to sustain a resistance
movement—which is natural to any subjugated people—with a particularly religious flavor, based on the idea that even if the Romans
let you worship God your own way you cannot have as king *anyone*
other than God. There cannot be any finalities—it was a theological point—no finalities other than God. This meant there had to
be some kind of theocracy.

"In their first attempt to have a theocracy, the Jews ran into difficulty. Obviously, some human beings had to run the government
for God. After the Maccabean Revolt, those persons were the
Hasmoneans. They set up a government for God, at least until
He sent a more perfect Governor. These human beings, however,
began to act very much like the aliens—the invaders, or the oc-
cupiers—who had been running the country for their own profit or
benefit. Religious Jews got fed up with Hasmonean rule for getting rather corrupt.

"So the Pharisees invited the Romans to come in under the
leadership of Pompey, saying they would rather have outsiders run
the country than have high priests and kings merge and then become corrupt, as the Hasmoneans had. For that leads to bringing
God down in people's eyes. When the government is bad, and it's
supposed to be *God's* government, then you don't like God either.
At least if the Romans run it, nobody will blame God for it, they
reasoned.

"But in spite of the compromise the Pharisees were willing to
make in this regard—that is, preferring to have the Romans run
the government until the Messiah came rather than their fellow
Jews so God wouldn't be blamed for the corruption—nevertheless,
devoutly religious Jews refused to honor the emperor as divine.
The resistance movement which resulted bears various names. Josephus calls the insurrectionists *lēstēs*, which appears in the King
James Version of the Bible as the description of the two persons
crucified on either side of Jesus. We translate it 'thieves.' That's not

inaccurate either: guerrillas are always thieves. How else could they survive?

"Another name of the movement is 'Zealots,' named after one Phinehas, found in the book of Numbers [25:6–13], who killed a man for having failed to keep an item of the Torah. It seems sort of narrow-minded, but nevertheless Phinehas' example gave the Jews the concept of being zealous for the Law. The resistance members were zealous for the way of life, for the distinct cultural forms, which were codified in Torah and took a highly religious form.

"Other names of the movement—which, in the time of Jesus, we find centered at Qumran where the Dead Sea Scrolls were found—are found not only in the literature of the Dead Sea Scrolls but also in the New Testament. They are the *Ebionim*, or 'the Poor'; 'the Many'; 'the New Israel'; 'the New Covenant'; 'the Way.' There was a direct continuity of resistance against foreign rule from the Maccabees, through the Zealots, probably through Qumran, to those who made the last stand at Masada. Jesus stands in the midst of this tradition."

———◆———

A COVENANTED NATION

The seeds of an apocalyptic revolution were sown "in the beginning" when the wandering Hebrew tribes first emerged as a nation. Israel's identity grew out of an uncompromising belief in One God. This radical monotheism made it impossible for the Jews to serve any king but God. In an age when large empires ruled the world, a religion which prohibited subservience to any king other than God could not help but lead to revolution.

Jesus lived in such an age. His nation, Israel, was under the dominance of the Roman Empire. His people were asked to render homage to Caesar as a divine ruler. He and other devout Jews of his time longed for Israel's deliverance from oppression, and for the liberation which living in the Kingdom of God on earth would bring.

At the time of Jesus, Israel had already been under foreign dominion for hundreds of years. First the Jews were conquered by the Babylonians. Then came the Persians, the Greeks, the Ptolemies, the Seleucids, and finally the Romans. The gradual assimilation of Palestine into the dominant Greek, or Hellenistic, culture of the time caused strain and discord between Israel and her rulers. The Jews felt the need to preserve their identity, and as Hellenistic influences grew, so did the Jews' emphasis on Torah and the Temple.[1] Torah was the Law of God which had been revealed to Moses on Mount Sinai and accepted by the People Israel as the basis of their social and political order. The Temple in Jerusalem was the external and visible symbol of the nation Israel and of the Jewish religion. It was the House of Yahweh, the One God of the Mosaic Covenant.

It was not until the reign of the Seleucid king Antiochus Epiphanes (175 to 164 B.C.), however, that the religious sensitivities of the Jews were grievously offended by a foreign ruling power. Antiochus issued a series of decrees which forbade compliance with the laws of the Torah. Jews were forbidden to observe the Sabbath, their holy day of rest, and to circumcise their children, the sign of entrance into the eternal Covenant with Yahweh. The Jews were instead compelled to take part in the worship of other gods, which was for them idolatrous, and to offer up sacrifices on pagan altars erected for that purpose. As the final insult, a graven image of the Greek god Zeus was set up on the sacred altar of the Temple, and all the heathen of the Empire were free to come to Jerusalem and pay homage to it.

While some Jews submitted to these decrees, many others fled to the desert or suffered martyrdom rather than violate the Torah. Those who fled into the desert wilderness and actively resisted the destruction of their religious and national tradition became prototypes for a long line of Jewish freedom fighters. Jesus stands in the tradition of those wilderness revolutionaries. Their history is his, and an appreciation of their struggle for freedom gives us a new perspective from which to understand the life and teachings of Jesus.

In the Gospel according to John (10:22) reference is made to the feast of Dedication as an important turning point in Jesus' life. It was at that feast that Jesus first began to be publicly recognized as the Davidic Messiah—the expected revolutionary leader of the Jewish nation. Since the feast of Dedication commemorates the victory of the first Jewish revolution, the Maccabean Revolt, the occasion for this clarification of Jesus' Messianic role was apparently chosen for its symbolic power. The feast of Dedication was central in the history of Israel's struggle for freedom; Jesus' disciples hoped he would be seen that way too.

THE RISE OF JEWISH NATIONALISM

By 168 B.C. the situation in Palestine had deteriorated to the point that conscientious Jews were compelled either to abandon Torah, to die as martyrs, or to resist the decrees of Antiochus Epiphanes by fleeing to the wilderness. Of necessity, a new spirit of nationalism was born. Until then, under the alien rule of the Persians, the Greeks, the Ptolemies, and the Seleucids, the Jews had concentrated on the consolidation of obedience to Torah as the rule of the land—including dietary rules, strict observance of the Sabbath, and proper worship in the Temple. They had been relatively content to spend their energies on the purification of the life of their own people and to tolerate the undesirable aspects of foreign rule, such as heavy taxation. They had made no concerted effort to regain the independence of Israel.

But the Jews believed that obedience to Torah in every regard was essential for the fulfillment of their holy Covenant with God. If Israel was not faithful, God would not keep His promises to His People, and therefore, to abandon Torah was to break the Covenant with God.[2] Since the Seleucids would no longer allow Jews the freedom to keep Torah, a surge of pietistic, nationalistic sentiment welled up across the land: Israel's independence would have to be won in order to preserve the Covenant relationship with God.

Open fighting began in the streets of Jerusalem and an underground resistance movement gathered in the hills of Galilee under the leadership of village priests and with the support of the agrarian population. In an attempt to enforce the decrees issued by Antiochus Epiphanes against the practice of Judaism, Seleucid soldiers went throughout the country setting up idols on village altars, compelling Jews to worship these pagan gods, burning copies of Torah, and forcing Jews to eat food, such as pork, which was prohibited by their Law (I Macc. 1:41 ff.). These offenses were so horrible that pious Jews reacted in violence against offenders—even against their fellow Jews.

It was just such an encounter which marked the beginning of the first genuine Jewish revolution. A priest and member of the Hasmonean family was offended by a fellow Jew who submitted under force to the Seleucid decrees, and called the people to rise up with him in revolt against their oppressors. The story is told in the first Book of the Maccabees:[3]

"As he [Mattathias] finished speaking, a Jew came forward in the sight of all to offer sacrifice on the altar in Modein as the royal edict required. When Mattathias saw this, he was fired with zeal; stirred to the depth of his being, he gave vent to his legitimate anger, threw himself on the man and slaughtered him on the altar. At the same time he killed the king's commissioner who was there to enforce the sacrifice, and tore down the altar. In his zeal for the Law he acted as Phinehas did against Zimri son of Salu. Then Mattathias went through the town, shouting at the top of his voice, 'Let everyone who has a fervour for the Law [or: 'who is zealous for the Law' RSV] and takes his stand on the covenant come out and follow me.' Then he fled with his sons into the hills, leaving all their possessions behind in the town . . . They organised themselves into an armed force, striking down the sinners in their anger, and the renegades in their fury . . . They wrested the Law out of the control of the pagans and the kings, and robbed sinful men of their advantage" (I Macc. 2:23–28, 44, 48).[4]

Because of the greater strength and numbers of the Seleucid forces, Mattathias organized the rebels for guerrilla warfare, taking advantage of their intimate knowledge of the land, instead of launching open attacks on the enemy. After Mattathias' death, the leadership of the revolt passed to his son Judas, known as Judas Maccabeus ("the hammer"), the greatest Jewish commander of the Second Temple period. This first Jewish Revolt, which has been known throughout history as the Maccabean Revolt, was named for Judas.

Judas Maccabeus and his zealous following succeeded in capturing Jerusalem in 164 B.C. and eventually were able to wrest control of the whole of Israel from the Seleucids. An independent monarchy was then established under the control of Judas' family, the Hasmoneans, and Israel was once again free.

When the battle for the freedom of Jerusalem had been won, Judas gathered his army together to ascend Mount Moriah, the site of the Temple, to give thanks and praise to God for the victory. The liberators found the Temple in ruins, the sanctuary desolate, the altar profaned, and the Temple gates burned. After a suitable period of mourning for the Temple's destruction, the Maccabees tore down the desecrated altar and built a new one in accordance with Torah. Then early the next morning, they offered sacrifice on the new altar, again according to the Law. They continued this celebration of thanksgiving in the Temple for eight days and "There was no end to the rejoicing among the people, and the reproach of the pagans was lifted from them" (I Macc. 4:58).

An ancient Jewish tradition has it that when the victorious guerrilla forces first entered the defiled Temple, they found only one small lamp there, containing scarcely enough oil to burn one day. When the Maccabees placed the lamp in the sanctuary and lighted it, the tradition says, God miraculously caused it to burn for eight days. It is in commemoration of the Maccabean victory, the rededication of the Temple, and the miracle of the oil that burned for eight days as a sign of God's favor that the Feast of Lights or Hanukkah is celebrated by the Jews each year—even today.

It is the feast of Hanukkah which is referred to as the feast of Dedication in John's Gospel, and it was apparently during that feast that the Temple hierarchy became outraged at Jesus' teachings, fearing that his popular support would lead to an insurrectionist uprising against the Romans.

APOCALYPTIC BELIEFS DEVELOP

For a brief period, the Jews were content with their newly won freedom and rejoiced in the Hasmonean rule, which they felt had been established with God's favor. Eventually, however, the Hasmoneans became Hellenized and corrupted by the tremendous power they wielded. Unrest began anew among pious Jews. That the Hasmonean dynasty which ruled in the name of God had become corrupt was worse than pagan oppression, for their rule dishonored God as well as themselves.

Some of the Jews sought assistance from the Roman Empire in their efforts to right the situation. The Hasmonean House eventually fell, but in the process Israel was once again absorbed into a pagan political framework—this time the imperial rule of Rome.

The logical expression of the religious and political tenets of Judaism was a theocratic ideal: the conviction that Israel was a nation of which God alone should be King.[5] This meant that Israel had to be free of servitude to foreign powers, and that all who adhered to the

Covenant were expected to work—fight, if need be—to bring about
the establishment of God's Kingdom on earth.

But disillusionment with the Hasmonean rule had led to the development of a second and complementary belief: that such a theocracy
would be established only when God Himself intervened in history
by sending a Chosen One, the Messiah, to establish His Kingdom
on earth.[6] Those persons who, from the time of the Maccabean
Revolt in 168 B.C. to the Fall of Jerusalem in A.D. 70, sustained
the expectation of God's intervention from outside of history are
called "apocalyptists." To these persons were "revealed" certain details
concerning the time and manner of God's intervention to establish
His Kingdom.[7]

A third important idea developed. It was the concept of a "holy
war." Apocalyptists believed that the forces of evil had God's people
temporarily under their control through the reign of foreign powers,
and that the latter would have to be overthrown for God's Kingdom
to be established. Such a revolutionary war, however, would have to
be fought at the moment of God's intervention, under the direction
of the Messiah and with the aid of God's angelic forces. It would,
in fact, be *God's* final war against evil, and righteous Jews would
only have the privilege of joining with God in accomplishing this
holy task. Preparation to take part in the Holy War became a major
goal of many religious Jews during the Roman period.

The conviction that God would fight on behalf of His People when
they were obedient to the Law and faithful to the Covenant sustained
the Jews during their oppression. The Maccabees were held in high
regard as prototypes of Jewish religious nationalists, and the tradition
of pious nationalistic resistance and revolt was perpetuated during
Roman rule by the "Zealots."[8]

It was into the context of these apocalyptic expectations that the
overthrow of Roman rule and the establishment of the Kingdom
of God on earth were imminent, that Jesus was born. The Romans
had conquered Israel in 63 B.C. under Pompey. Some twenty years
later a man named Herod was proclaimed King of Israel by the
Roman generals Antony and Octavian. Though the Jews objected, the
Roman senate confirmed Herod's appointment and the enlarged Roman
army in Israel forced the population to submit to Herod's rule. Against
the will of his subjects, then, Herod was established King of Israel.[9]
It was during King Herod's rule (37–4 B.C.) that Jesus was born.

RESISTANCE BECOMES INSURRECTION

An important incident occurred in 4 B.C., the probable year of Jesus' birth.[10] Two Galileans named Judas and Mattathias, who were descendants of the Maccabees, led an uprising in keeping with the tradition of that family. By order of the emperor, a large golden eagle had been erected over the main gate of the Temple in violation of Torah. Judas and Mattathias urged the people to join them in destroying the pagan figure. The Romans considered the Jews' action openly seditious, and intervened to prevent destruction of the eagle. Rioting broke out which was only suppressed after great bloodshed. Judas and Mattathias, the instigators of the revolt, were burned alive by the Romans.[11]

Shortly thereafter, King Herod died, and the Jews took advantage of the temporary absence of an imperial governor to strike back at the Romans. A rabbi named Judas[12] led a group of rebels in the ransacking of Herod's palace in northern Galilee. They seized property and arms which they planned to use against the Romans.

In addition, Jews rose in revolt in Jerusalem and in many other parts of the country. The rebels, according to the Jewish historian Josephus,[13] entreated the commander of the Roman troops assigned to keep peace in Palestine until a new governor could be appointed, "to depart and not to stand in the way of men who after such a lapse of time were on the road to recovering their national independence" (*War* II. 53; *Ant.* XVII. 267).

The insurrection was finally suppressed with the help of two additional legions of troops sent to Palestine by the Roman governor of Syria. The punishment inflicted on the insurgents was very severe: *two thousand* Jews were crucified around the walls of Jerusalem.[14] Death on the cross was chosen because the Romans felt this painful and visible mode of execution would be the most effective deterrent to further rebellions. The result, however, was that the atmosphere of oppression by the Romans became almost unbearable to the Jews, and they watched all the more eagerly for God's intervention through His Messiah. The crucifixion of these two thousand Jewish revolutionaries took place the year Jesus was born.

THE ZEALOT MOVEMENT GROWS

Instead of thwarting the rebellion, the Roman excess of cruelty helped to consolidate the resistance movement. The people could not soon forget two thousand crucifixions, and ten years later a new crisis occurred which gave them another opportunity to express their hatred of their Roman rulers.

In order to exact tribute from the Jews in accordance with the practice followed in all provinces of the Empire, Quirinius, the Roman legate of Syria in whose province Palestine lay, was instructed by the Emperor Augustus in A.D. 6 to make a census of the Jews in Palestine and to determine what level of taxes should be collected.[15] The issue of taxation by Rome had been avoided during the rule of Herod the Great; but in A.D. 6, Jews were faced with the prospect of paying tribute money directly to Caesar, the deified emperor to whom all imperial subjects offered tribute.[16]

Two pious Jews rose to meet this challenge to Yahweh's sovereignty, Zadok the Pharisee and the rabbi Judas of Galilee. As a rabbi, or teacher of the Law, Judas felt it his duty not only to point out the apostasy which paying tribute to Caesar represented but also to lead his people, in the tradition of his Maccabean ancestors, in resisting the census, and in refusing to pay tribute to Caesar. His rallying cry echoed the words of the Maccabees: "God alone is our sovereign Lord and we can call no man master or give him allegiance" (*Ant.* XVIII. 4–10; 22–23).[17]

The followers of Judas of Galilee armed themselves and took to the hills, launching a guerrilla campaign against the Romans and believing that if in good faith they resisted the tyranny of Rome in defense of the Law of Moses, the God of Israel would come to their aid as He had so often helped His People in the past. The Romans suppressed the revolt, and at the urging of the Jewish High Priest,[18] the people submitted to the census. But this temporary submission did little to dampen the people's resentment, and the matter of paying tribute to Caesar remained a critical issue of the day, as the New Testament accounts of the life of Jesus reveal.[19] Moreover, the followers of Judas the Galilean became known as the "Zealots," and their resistance was to continue for another sixty years.

The complimentary epithet "zealous," attributed to Judas of Galilee and his followers, was first used to describe one Phinehas who was accounted righteous because of his zeal for the Lord (Num. 25:6–15; Ps. 106:30–31). Phinehas had also been revered by the Maccabees, who were equally zealous for the Law.[20] The religio-nationalist freedom fighters came to be called "Zealots" because their motivating principle, like Phinehas', was an uncompromising allegiance to the God with whom the Jews had made their Covenant—the God whose will was revealed in Torah and to whom they owed their sole obedience. The Jewish historian Josephus dates the beginning of the Zealot movement in A.D. 6 with the uprising of Judas the Galilean and Zadok the Pharisee. But the Zealots were motivated by the same zeal for the Law which characterized the Maccabees (168 B.C.) and Judas and Mattathias (who died in 4 B.C.), and they were exponents of the same ideals of religious, cultural, and national independence. Thus not new was the movement which was to continue for over sixty years in its resistance to encroachments by the Romans on the integrity of the Jews' religious and national life. It represented a continuity of the Maccabean freedom struggle.

The most active members of the Zealot resistance movement probably did not constitute a very large numerical portion of the population of Israel, but the long years of activity, the remarkable persistence and the eventual success of the Zealots in the early stages of the Great Revolt against Rome make it clear that they enjoyed a wide range of support among the people. History has proven that guerrilla movements seldom succeed if they are without the sympathy and support of the people in whose land they fight. The 'am ha"aretz, or common people of the land of Israel, apparently sustained the Zealot resistance fighters during two thirds of a century of active rebellion against Rome—no small feat. Though such a resistance movement would undoubtedly have attracted a wide spectrum of sympathizers in various degrees of commitment, the popular base of the Zealots was among the rural, agrarian, and poor peoples of Israel, most of whom were centered in Galilee.[21]

A violent wing of the movement came to be called the *Sicarii*, or "daggermen." A *sica* was a curved dagger which these rebels carried concealed in their belts under their robes. Josephus reports that these daggermen managed to penetrate the innermost precincts of the Temple on several occasions, and even to assassinate a High Priest in A.D. 26 and a procurator in A.D. 46. The Sicarii were the extremist element among the Zealots, and were inclined to immediate and violent response to crises. They engaged in constant subversion, and their specialty was eliminating Jews in positions of responsibility who collaborated with the Romans.[22]

The majority of the freedom fighters were not so prone to take things into their own hands, at least in the manner of the Sicarii. They did feel, however, that man had to engage the foreign oppressors actively—as the Maccabees had fought the Seleucids—if God were to be expected to give assistance.[23] It was the conviction of the Zealots that if conditions became grievous enough in Israel, God would intervene to save His People. They advocated direct action as the mode of demonstrating their zeal for the Covenant and their unwillingness to compromise with foreign rule. They were confident that if their obedience to the Law were sufficient, God would come to their aid.

Disagreement frequently arose over tactics, since opinion always varied as to whether the time was right to strike out at the Romans. But the Zealots advocated unceasing protest and agitation against all forms of oppression and all manifestations of foreign rule until time for the final war came. They attempted to keep the pressure on the Romans by surprise attacks and quick retreats into the hill country, and they capitalized on any crisis to heighten the conflict and to bring more support to their cause by revealing the oppressiveness of Roman rule.

PONTIUS PILATE, PREFECT

In A.D. 26 a new Roman overseer, with the expanded responsibilities and authority which accompanied his title *Praefectus,* was appointed to the provinces of Judea and Samaria.[24] His name was Pontius Pilate. The powers of his office become especially significant when we consider the sentence he imposed on Jesus.

Pilate was particularly detested by the Jews because of his complete disregard for their customs and his harsh brutality. In contrast to the portrayal of Pilate in the New Testament Gospel accounts of Jesus' trial where he is pictured as a weak man, easily influenced by his wife, indecisive in his judgments, and eager to please the Jewish populace,[25] non-Christian historical accounts assert that he was harsh, cruel, and impulsive.[26]

One compromise which the Romans, prior to Pilate's appointment, had made in trying to appease the Jews and to avoid violation of their religious laws, was to prohibit display of the imperial standards bearing the Roman eagle within the city of Jerusalem. The standards violated the Mosaic injunction, "You shall not make yourself a carved image or any likeness of anything in heaven above or on earth beneath or in the waters under the earth; you shall not bow down to them or serve them. For I, Yahweh your God, am a jealous God . . ." (Deut. 5:8).

Soon after his appointment as prefect of Judea, Pontius Pilate sought to put an end to the "foolishness" which prevented the display of Roman standards in Jerusalem. At the normal time of replacing the Roman garrison in Jerusalem with fresh troops from Caesarea, Pilate ordered the troops with their standards bearing the eagle to enter the city at night so that darkness would conceal their act, and to station the standards at the garrison gate. When the Jews awoke, the standards would already be in place, and, Pilate reasoned, the Jews would submit to the change without protest.

He was wrong. Josephus reports that when the Jews saw what had been done upon the order of the new prefect, they went en masse to Caesarea where they presented Pilate with a petition to order the standards removed. When Pilate refused, they sat down in the palace courtyard declaring that they would not leave until the petition had been granted. The protest, one of the few examples of a nonviolent protest given by Josephus, lasted for six days. When Pilate announced that if they did not leave he would order them killed, the Jews knelt and stretched their necks out, saying they would prefer death to disobedience to God's commandments.[27]

Apparently Pilate was impressed by their tenacity, or feared the repercussions which such a slaughter might bring, and he ordered the standards removed. However, he did not give up his intentions to cure the Jews of their fanaticism. Later he ordered gilded shields, bearing a brief inscription, placed on the gates to Herod's palace in the Upper City. The Jews did not feel they could afford to let such an offense pass. When their peaceful petition for the removal of the shields was rejected, the Jews rioted in the streets of Jerusalem until they were put down by force.[28]

Another offense by Pilate was his attempt to defray the cost of an aqueduct by confiscating money from the Temple treasury. The uprising which this violation of Jewish autonomy provoked resulted in the slaughter of many Jews by the Romans.[29]

In the end, Pilate was removed from office because of an act of such enormous cruelty that the Roman authorities could not overlook it. The people of Israel were eager for a leader who would end their subjugation by the Romans and establish God's Kingdom on earth, and therefore followed any man who, by word or action, appeared to be the Messiah. Often such "Messianic pretenders," of which there were many during this period,[30] used "code" language to announce themselves. That is, they did and said what the Messiah was expected to do and say when he came.

The Samaritans, though a separate sect, were no exception with regard to these expectations and had to be watched by the Romans lest Messianic uprisings should lead to large-scale revolt. The Samaritans, because of the prophecy of Deuteronomy 18:15–18, expected a Messiah who would be Moses reincarnated. They believed that the Ta'eb or "restorer," would establish the Kingdom of God on earth by opening up Mount Gerizim, where they believed the "true" Jewish Temple had been swallowed up, and revealing the holy vessels hidden there.[31] The reappearance of the Temple and its holy vessels would be a sign to them that in fact the Messiah to be sent by God had come.

When a Samaritan, therefore, announced that he would reveal to his followers the vessels of their Temple on top of Mount Gerizim, his proffered identity was clear both to the Samaritans and to Pilate. Before the gathering multitude could begin their ascent, Pontius Pilate ordered his soldiers to cut them off. Josephus records that many Samaritans were slain and many of those taken captive were later executed. For this excessive repression, Pilate was punished by removal from office.[32]

It was Pilate who, as Roman prefect of Judea, ordered Jesus' execution as an insurrectionist. This judgment of his was in character with the general tone of his ten-year rule in Palestine.

THE GREAT REVOLT AGAINST ROME

The years following Pilate's term of office brought a succession of emperors in Rome and of procurators in Judea. Violations of the Torah similar to those which had given rise to the Maccabean Revolt recurred with increasing frequency, and the memory of the Maccabees' successes inspired the Jews to continued resistance. Many violent uprisings resulted.[33] Each repression of a revolt, or punishment of a Zealot leader by the Romans, seemed only to crystallize the anti-Roman sentiment among the Jews.

There arose also, during that period, numerous charismatic leaders. The historian Josephus terms them "Messianic pretenders," that is, men who by their words and actions offered themselves as potential Messianic deliverers. One Theudas, who is mentioned in Acts 5:36, promised to lead his followers dry-shod through the Jordan River to freedom, following the Exodus tradition. He was captured and executed by the Romans, along with many of his followers.[34] Later an Egyptian Jew gathered a group about him on the Mount of Olives and promised to destroy the walls of the city and the Romans. While the Egyptian escaped capture, many of his followers were killed or imprisoned.[35]

These are but two of many examples[36] which could be given to make clear the identification, by the Romans at least, of Messianic leaders performing—or purporting to—miracles, with anti-Roman agitation.[37] It was not unusual that the Romans viewed Jesus as an insurrectionist.

By A.D. 66, hostilities had reached the boiling point and Jews and Gentiles throughout all of Palestine and the Diaspora battled each other in bloody rioting. The Zealots captured the Temple mount, isolated the Romans in their strongholds, and then massacred them after the Romans surrendered.

Two of the Zealots' actions in the city of Jerusalem at the start of the revolt merit special attention. Following a power struggle in which a Zealot leader and his followers rejected the leadership of the High Priest Ananias and the priestly aristocracy, a new High Priest was elected using the ancient method of casting lots. The Zealots were concerned with preserving the continuity of Temple worship, and saw to it that a High Priest was properly selected according to the Torah. The rejection of Ananias as High Priest mirrored the twofold thrust of the Zealot movement: to overthrow the heathen Romans *and* the Jewish sacerdotal nobility.[38]

Another significant act in the initial stages of the fighting in Jerusalem was the burning of the public archives. Destruction of the public records, including records of debts, manifested the social aspect of the Zealot movement and, as Josephus observed, aroused the support of many of the poor.[39] The attention of the Zealots was not directed

solely at the occupying imperial forces, but also at the rich Jews of
the Herodian household, and at the Temple priests who collaborated
in maintaining Roman control of the country and grew rich in the
process.[40]

The imperial legate of Syria advanced on Jerusalem to suppress the
Zealots' revolt. After a short siege of the city, he withdrew unexplain-
ably, and, in retreat, his forces were decimated by the guerrilla tactics
of the Zealots.[41] The retreat became a rout and the legate succeeded
in escaping the country only after the loss of six thousand of his men
and all their equipment. Thus, in the fall of A.D. 66, the Jewish revolutionaries had finally pushed their country past the point of no return
in revolution against Rome.

In A.D. 67 the emperor Nero dispatched additional legions to Judea
in order to put down the revolt, and Vespasian headed the invading
army. Jewish defenses in Galilee were insufficient to meet the Roman
advance and one city after another went down in defeat. Then, after
the conquest of Galilee, the Roman forces took Transjordan and the
northern Judean hills.

Civil war in Rome in A.D. 68 and 69 gave a period of respite to the
Jews as the Roman siege was temporarily suspended. The defenders
of Jerusalem were bolstered by the remaining Galileans, but infighting
within the walls of the city weakened their defense and claimed the
lives of the High Priest Ananus and many others. The infighting was
primarily a struggle for the right to leadership—and over decisions
regarding tactics—not over the purpose of the revolt itself. But this
internal struggle considerably weakened the Jewish forces and contributed to their ultimate defeat.

Vespasian, who had been elevated to the position of emperor, renewed the battle by sending his son Titus to capture Jerusalem. In the
face of the Roman advance on the Holy City, internal differences
disappeared. Nevertheless, the vulnerability of the Jewish ranks had
been greatly increased. Titus' forces consisted of four legions (each
legion composed of ten thousand men plus auxiliary troops) and his
siege plan included a circumvallation wall four and one half miles
long around the city, designed to starve its defenders. Josephus, witnessing the siege, testified to its ferocity. It lasted five months and
included periods, according to Josephus' witness, when as many as
five hundred crucifixions per day took place. At times there were not
enough crosses for the bodies, and not enough room on the city walls
for the crosses.[42]

THE ZEALOTS' LAST STAND

During the fighting the Jews refused to compromise in any way with the Romans or to discuss terms for surrender. Josephus reports that any Jewish defenders who attempted to go to the Roman side, or to flee the city, were slain by the more zealous Jews. When Titus' troops breached the outer wall of the city, the Jews placed themselves between the invading forces and the Temple. After fighting back the first Roman onslaught, Titus' personal envoy entreated the Jewish defenders to abandon their cause in return for Titus' promise to spare the Temple. The offer fell on deaf ears: the Zealots scoffed at the thought of capture because of their belief that "the city was God's" (*War* VI. 93–99). In the ensuing battle the Temple was destroyed by flames.

The suicidal defense of the Temple is understandable, writes Professor W. R. Farmer of Drew University, because "the fanatic defense of Jerusalem was rooted in the belief that God was in his temple and would eventually destroy the Romans, if only a righteous remnant would fulfill Israel's part of the covenant and be zealous in keeping up the sacrifice, and in observing the Torah strictly."[43]

After the Temple was destroyed, the Jewish defenders remaining in the Upper City immediately sought terms from Titus, requesting to be allowed to leave the city freely and to emigrate to the wilderness. This request reflects their persistent hope that God would still see fit to deliver those who remained true to the Covenant—which had been received in the wilderness—even though the Temple had been destroyed. The Zealots knew the destruction of the Temple had not severed the relationship of God to His Chosen People, and hence they sought to return to the desert.

Titus, well acquainted through past Roman experience with Messianic movements associated with the desert wilderness, denied the request, and the defenders of Jerusalem died in one final battle. To this day in the Hebrew month of *Av,* religious Jews bewail the Fall of Jerusalem and the destruction of the Temple.

Proof that the destruction of the Temple and the Fall of Jerusalem did not destroy the hopes of the most fanatically religious of the Zealots is attested by the defense of Masada, the desert fortress built by Herod the Great and seized by Zealot forces at the start of the revolt.[44] Nine hundred and sixty Zealots—men, women, and children —defended Masada long after the Fall of Jerusalem, still awaiting God's intervention on their behalf. Outnumbered ten to one (twenty-five to one, counting support troops and auxiliaries) the Zealots held out for three years against the Tenth, and best, Roman legion. The Romans eventually succeeded in constructing a huge earthwork ramp which enabled their war machines to breach the casement wall of the otherwise impregnable fortress. Josephus records the words of Eleazar, the surviving leader of the Zealots, in convincing his compatriots to take their own lives rather than submit to capture and enslavement by the Romans. To the fateful end, the Zealots remained faithful to God and to their Covenant with Him.[45]

"Long since, my brave men, we determined neither to serve the Romans nor any other save God, for He alone is man's true and righteous Lord; and now the time is come which bids us verify that resolution by our actions. At this crisis let us not disgrace ourselves; we who in the past refused to submit even to a slavery involving no peril, let us not now, along with slavery, deliberately accept the ir-reparable penalties awaiting us if we are to fall alive into Roman hands. For as we were the first of all to revolt, so are we the last in arms against them. Moreover, I believe that it is God who has granted us this favour, that we have it in our power to die nobly and in freedom— a privilege denied to others who have met with unexpected defeat. Our fate at break of day is certain capture, but there is still the free choice of a noble death with those we hold most dear . . . while those hands are free and grasp the sword, let them render an honourable service. Unenslaved by the foe let us die, as free men with our children and wives let us quit this life together! This our laws enjoin, this our wives and children implore of us. The need for this is of God's sending, the reverse of this is the Roman's desire, and their fear is lest a single one of us should die before capture. Haste we then to leave them, instead of their hoped-for enjoyment at securing us, amazement at our death and admiration of our fortitude." (*War* VII. 323–88)

CHAPTER 2

Apocalyptic Nationalism

*"Hear, O Israel: The Lord our God is one Lord;
and you shall love the Lord your God with all your
heart, and with all your soul, and with all your
might."*   Deuteronomy 6:4, RSV

In the words of James A. Pike:

"The resistance movement as it developed, then, was religious
in its essential content. The distinction between sacred and secular
didn't exist. There wasn't anything that wasn't religious. To this
day the Torah rule about not eating pork is a very good rule to
observe in most parts of Israel. It will probably take another ten
or twenty years until they get enough refrigeration throughout
Israel to make you feel comfortable eating pork. We would think
of that rule as just good sense, good chemistry, good biology, or
good public health. But in the thinking of the Jews, at least at the
time we are talking about, this would have to have been a matter
of religion—or nothing. They just didn't have any other category.
What is good for the health of a person is a religious duty under
God—and that still kind of makes sense.

"When people say, 'Would Jesus have involved himself in something so secular as a revolution for the freedom of his country?'
it is a meaningless question. He involved himself, or he didn't.
But the question wouldn't have been secular vs. religious. Anybody
involved in the revolution was involved for religious reasons.

"There were some who were *not* involved in the revolution, and
some were *not* involved for other than religious reasons. For example, the members of the Sadducean party who were collabora-

tionists. They were the fat cats who had big houses in Jerusalem and other places, who ran the economic establishment, the banking finances, the animal business for sacrifices, and many other kinds of trade. The collaborationists had control of the Temple and they were hand-in-glove with the Romans. It would be hard for me to say that their affiliation or collaboration with the Romans had a religious basis. But those *involved* in the revolution were in it for *religious* reasons.

"The year Jesus was born (4 B.C., it is conceded to be) there were two thousand crosses around and in Jerusalem at the same time. *That many* of the revolutionaries were hung up at one time. When Jesus was ten years old, Judas of Galilee was killed, presumably by crucifixion, and then his partners who took over were also crucified. You can imagine the impression all of this must have made on a child of ten hovering near as the men in town talked excitedly about it.

"Jesus came from a religious family, from Galilee, and Galilee was the hotbed of sedition and insurrection among religiously motivated, Maccabean-minded people. He couldn't help but be tremendously influenced and affected by the resistance movement."

THE ZEALOTS AND RELIGION

"God only is our King," was the theme, or motto, for the Jewish nationalist movements from the second century B.C. to the first century A.D. Both the Maccabeans and the Zealots sought to preserve the Covenant relationship with Yahweh upon which their people's very existence and identity depended. They were zealous for Torah as the expression of their faithfulness to the Covenant, for, as W. R. Farmer writes, behind the zeal for Torah "lay the more fundamental and original zeal for the covenant God of Israel . . . a God who had chosen a peculiar people and who was, in his love for his people, exceedingly jealous of all other gods."[1]

Because of this absolute monotheistic faith, which made no distinction between politics and religion, or between sacred or secular, the Jews fervently resisted any Hellenization of their culture. The introduction of any pagan custom or institution in Israel was viewed as an incipient threat to Jewish identity and was greatly resented. Even the Greek gymnasium and the Roman games in the stadium were considered incursions upon the radical monotheistic beliefs and practices of the Jews and greatly increased tensions between the Jews and their overlords.

Only when their pagan oppressors committed overt acts in direct violation of the Torah did the Jews rise up in open revolt, however—uprisings which inevitably brought repressive retaliation. The long list of such incidents provides a chronology of the Jewish resistance movement and clearly reflects the religious motivation of the revolutionaries.

Both the Seleucids and the Romans, for example, burned copies of the Torah. We read in I Maccabees 1:56, "Any books of the Law that came to light were torn up and burned," and in Josephus' *War* II. 229, "On this occasion a soldier, finding in one village a copy of the sacred Law, tore the book in pieces and flung it into the fire." Such profanation of Torah was the worst possible offense to the Jews, and Josephus describes their reaction to the Roman's burning of the sacred book: "At that the Jews were roused as though it were their whole country which had been consumed in the flames" (*War* II. 230; *Ant.* XX. 113–17). Other direct offenses were decrees which compelled Jews to eat "unclean" foods, in violation of Torah, and to worship at pagan altars.[2]

In both periods religious Jews were prepared to fight and kill for Torah. Philo, a Jewish writer of the first century A.D. in Alexandria, wrote of the Jews: "They are men of great courage and spirit who are willing to die in defense of their national customs and laws with unshrinking bravery,"[3] and Josephus, in his later works, writes: "And from these laws of ours nothing has had power to deflect us, neither fear of our masters, nor envy of the institutions esteemed by other nations. We have trained our courage, not with a view to waging war for self-aggrandizement, but in order to preserve our laws. To defeat in any other form we patiently submit, but when pressure is put upon us to alter our statutes, then we deliberately fight, even against tremendous odds, and hold out under reverses to the last extremity."[4]

Further evidence of the Jews' remarkable zeal for Torah was their willingness to take their own lives rather than submit to or compromise with heathen who violated the Law. There is an account in II Maccabees (14:37–42) of one Razis who "finding himself completely surrounded" by the troops of Nicanor, "fell on his own sword, nobly resolving to die rather than fall into the clutches of these villains and suffer outrages unworthy of his noble birth," and we have already told of Josephus' account of the mass suicide at Masada in A.D. 73. Other cases of suicide in the Roman period are also recorded by

Josephus.[5] Such suicides spoke powerfully to the Seleucids and Romans as "incredible evidence that there was indeed no noble excess to which devoted Jews would not go out of zeal for their God and his Torah."[6]

Their zeal worked in the reverse when they were in a position to enforce their Law. Josephus records, for example, the policy of both the Maccabees and the Jews of the Roman period of encouraging, or even coercing, non-Jews to submit to circumcision in accordance with Jewish Law.[7] It was under such a policy of forced conversion that the Idumeans, Herod the Great's people, were circumcised under John Hyrcanus.[8]

One final evidence of the Jewish nationalists' pious zeal for the Law was their strict observance of the Sabbath.[9] Apparently it was only during the Maccabean period that the right even to defend oneself against attack on the Sabbath was established.[10] In the eyes of the Maccabees, and later the Zealots, the very survival of the Torah itself was at stake in such a case, thereby justifying violation of Sabbath restrictions: ". . . to compromise the Torah is not necessarily to abandon it [and] in the case of the Maccabees it was their zeal for the Law which sustained them even in those battles when they were transgressing the Law by fighting on the Sabbath."[11]

THE TORAH AND THE TEMPLE

The zeal for Torah was also directly related to devotion to the Temple. As W. R. Farmer, author of *Maccabees, Zealots and Josephus,* writes, "the Torah mediated God's revelation to his people, while the temple worship mediated the nation's devotion to its God."[12] The Temple was directly involved in the incidents which were the immediate causes of both the Maccabean and the Zealot revolts. It was Antiochus Epiphanes' "disastrous abomination," that is, defiling of the Temple, which touched off the Maccabean revolt; in Zealot times it was the refusal of the Temple priest Eleazar to offer the daily sacrifice to the emperor and the violation of the Temple's sanctity by the procurator Florus which brought the final break with Rome. The Temple was the central focus of Jewish nationalism.

Yet even such religious fervor does not make sense out of the Jewish nationalists' revolt against the invincible Roman Empire: "their apparently hopeless resistance to their heathen besiegers in the face of incredible difficulties must have been inspired to some extent by the faithful hope that God would intervene in some miraculous manner and deliver them from the hands of the Romans—as he had from the Assyrians in the days of pious Hezekiah, and from the Seleucids in the days of the pious and zealous Maccabees."[13]

Both the Zealots and the Maccabees assumed the absolute justice of their cause: that striking out against foreign oppressors who prevented their people from keeping faith with the Covenant was in accordance with God's will. To fight a pagan oppressor whose very presence violated the sanctity of both the Torah and the Temple was to participate in a *holy war,* and the notion of a holy war led the Jews to expect divine intervention on their side.

The Zealots stood in the long line of Jews who had trusted in God to intervene in their struggles against pagan oppressors, and by the Maccabean period it had become more or less normative for pious Jews to expect God to aid His People through the mediating agency of angels who would come to fight on their behalf.[14] Thus it is not surprising that the Zealots showed undying courage in the final stages of the Great Revolt against Rome. They looked for the momentary appearance of supernatural forces sent by God to aid them.

When the Temple had been destroyed, the Zealots sought to escape the city and retreat to the desert wilderness in order to preserve their covenanted relationship to God.[15] Most of them died in the suicidal effort to break through the Roman lines surrounding the city, but a few may have escaped and joined their brethren on the shore of the Dead Sea. The defenders of Masada withstood Roman attack for three more years against incredible odds, all the while sustaining their hope that God would send His angelic forces to rescue them.

It is probable that the Jewish nationalists interpreted the fall of the Temple as the judgment of God on the sins of His People—and perhaps even as essential to Messianic deliverance, as we will see later in discussing the Temple Scroll of the Qumran community. If so, the Zealots would have had more cause than ever to believe that, after such a severe chastisement, God would not delay long in sending His Messiah to rebuild the Temple and to establish His Kingdom on earth with the help of His People, Israel. The Zealots believed they could still be the faithful remnant spoken of by the prophets and therefore they had good reason to flee to the wilderness.[16]

There was a long association of the Jewish resistance movement with the wilderness. In the Maccabean period, as we have seen, such emigration was the first sign of nationalistic revolt.[17] In the Roman period, Josephus tells of the suspicion with which the Romans viewed any attempt to migrate in mass to the wilderness areas: "whether in the Seleucid or the Roman period, the crowds which went out into the wilderness were followed by royal [imperial] troops and put to the sword. Obviously the Seleucids and Romans regarded these religious gatherings as politically dangerous."[18] Josephus records that even the crowds which went out to hear John the Baptist in the desert were regarded as politically dangerous, and John's Gospel tells of an incident in the wilderness when Jesus had to leave a gathering of five thousand because they were about to declare him king.[19]

OTHER-WORLDLY OR THIS-WORLDLY?

Apocalyptic thought and religious nationalism developed simultaneously. "Apocalyptic" refers to the disclosure of some hidden truth, particularly about God or the divine purpose.[20] The concepts of divine intervention in history, of Messianic deliverance for the Chosen People, of the imminent arrival of the Kingdom of God and of the establishment of a Kingdom of righteousness at the conclusion of a holy war between the forces of light and the forces of darkness are all "apocalyptic" notions which permeated the thought of the religious nationalists.[21]

In fact, it is impossible to separate Jewish nationalism from Jewish apocalypticism during this period, even though such a dichotomy has been the basis of many studies of the life of Jesus.[22] The question often dealt with is, was Jesus an apocalyptist, or a nationalist? That is, was he concerned with the divine, or other-worldly, order of things, or was he related to the human, this-worldly, dimension? A survey of the history of the period in which Jesus lived and of the ideas of Jewish nationalists shows that religious nationalism and apocalyptic thought about God's intervention and rule were inextricably bound one with the other.

The most superficially apparent relationship between the two is the fact that the activities of apocalyptic writers and Jewish nationalists spanned the same period of history. The apocalyptists began their writing in the second century B.C. at the time of the Maccabean Revolt and continued writing during precisely the same period in which the predominant theme of Jewish history was nationalism, and resistance to foreign oppression and to Hellenization.

Dr. D. S. Russell, joint-principal of a Baptist College in Manchester, England, writes in his book about apocalyptic thought: "Not only did these apocalyptic books mirror the historical situation out of which they arose, they at the same time actually helped to create it. This was inflammatory material in the hands of those who wished to appeal to the religious fanaticism which became a feature of a particular section of the Jewish people. There can be little doubt that the Zealot party, for example, found in this literature just the kind of propaganda they needed to set alight the smouldering passions of their fellow countrymen. The Jewish War of AD 66–70 was fought in the confirmed belief that the people would witness the miraculous intervention of God as declared in the apocalyptic writings. Later still, in the revolt of AD 132–5 under Bar Kochba, it was again the apocalyptic hope which inspired the Jewish people to take up arms against their overlords. Both wars resulted in tragedy for the Jewish nation, and the apocalyptic literature was finally discredited in the eyes of all but a few.

"The apocalyptic literature is an example of the adage that 'man's extremity is God's opportunity.' It is essentially a literature of the oppressed who saw no hope for the nation simply in terms of politics or on the plane of human history. The battle they were fighting was on a spiritual level; it was to be understood not in terms of politics and economics, but rather in terms of 'spiritual powers in high places.' And so they were compelled to look beyond history to the dramatic and miraculous intervention of God who would set to rights the injustices done to his people Israel. The very urgency of the situation emphasized the nearness of the hour."[23]

THE KINGDOM OF GOD ON EARTH

Jesus' words "the Kingdom of God is close at hand" reflect the urgency of both the political and the apocalyptic emphases of his day. The apocalyptic writers "were convinced that God would make an end of evil and usher in his kingdom and that they themselves were soon to witness its appearing. The End might come at any moment and they were to see its coming with their own eyes. There was an air of eager, even desperate, expectancy that soon, very soon, God's rule would suddenly and devastatingly break in and God himself, either in person or through the Messiah, would right all wrongs and reward the patience and longsuffering of the righteous."[24]

The literature is filled with proclamations that "the end of days" was already upon God's people and that the "time of trouble" and of "woes and tribulation"[25] had already begun. To prove their case, the authors pointed to the "signs of the times" which could be read clearly in the events of everyday life around them: wars, earthquakes, famines, mysterious powers taking control of nature, fearful and mysterious portents for which there was no rational explanation, and omens in the heavens.[26] Closely associated with these "signs of the end" was the "Anti-Christ" who would appear in the last days to do battle with God.[27] The period of severe trial and tribulation which would ensue would end in the re-creation of the universe and the return of Paradise. The heavenly Jerusalem, prepared beforehand by God at the beginning of His creation, would be firmly established on earth.[28]

The concept of the ushering in of a heavenly Kingdom, that is, a kingdom in which God Himself alone would reign, is based on an understanding of history that holds God as the creator and controller of the ultimate outcome of all events. Man is held to be an important participant—largely by virtue of the Covenant—in the events of history in both its temporal and eternal aspects, and therefore man has a great responsibility to facilitate—even enable—the coming of the Kingdom. But the whole time-process is both determined and unified by the working out of God's eternal purpose.[29]

Man is not alone in his struggles. There are at work, *around* him and oftentimes *within* him, angels and demons—creatures of another order of being who are less than divine but more than human. This world of "spirits" will play an increasingly important role in the events of history as the Kingdom draws near, for the demons, under the rulership of Belial (or Beelzebub—commonly thought of today as Satan or the devil), will have to be defeated by God and His angels. Man can aid in this triumph by choosing "light," in which the angels dwell, as opposed to "darkness," in which the demons hide their evil deeds, but God alone can accomplish the final victory.[30]

The war between the forces of light and the forces of darkness first becomes manifest among men when the "children of light" cast out demons and restore order to the lives of men "disturbed" by the presence of demonic forces. The winning of such small "skirmishes" trains and prepares the holy "troops" for the final battle when the heavenly hosts will join the righteous children of light on earth and defeat the children of darkness once and for all. During the apocalyptic period belief in a whole hierarchy of angels grew up and the principal angels were given names. Thus Michael the Archangel emerged as the one who would command the heavenly forces in their final battle against evil.[31]

THE COMING MESSIAH

The ushering in of this "heavenly" Kingdom on earth was to be done by a Messianic figure, portrayed differently in the various writings, but always a specially chosen emissary from God. Often a temporary kingdom was anticipated as a first stage, an interim to be ruled over by the Messiah with the help of a "righteous remnant" of God's Chosen People who would bring the forces of evil under control. Then the "Day of Judgment" would come and the final victory over evil would be won by God with the help of his hosts of heavenly angels. The wicked would be cast out into darkness (or into the fires of Gehenna) and the righteous would enter the eternal Kingdom.[32]

Those who spoke of no intervening reign, or temporary kingdom, expected the Messiah to bring with him the Day of Judgment, and in all cases it was anticipated that the "righteous" would be made up first and foremost of God's Chosen People, Israel. Even the righteous dead would be raised up and given new life so that they could enter the eternal Kingdom.

Concepts of the Messiah had not crystallized in the apocalyptic period and descriptions of him varied from writer to writer. Some thought he would be from the House of Levi,[33] others from the House of David;[34] others believed there would be first a prophet and then one or two Messiahs, perhaps one a kingly Messiah and the other a priestly one.[35]

A new religious image emerged through the contributions of apocalyptic writers, and it is often confused with the Messianic figure. It is the concept of a "Son of Man."[36] The Son of Man is not a Messiah, however, but a corporate figure in which "the human and the humane triumph over the beastly and the bestial by the greatness and the power of God. It is a prophecy of the final triumph of God's people in God's kingdom in God's appointed time."[37] In later works the

figure is elevated to the status of a heavenly or divine being in whom
the mysteries of God's purpose are concealed and through whom what
is hidden will be revealed.[38] Not even then, however, should it be
confused with the Messiah, who is to be from "the human rather than
the divine side of the ledger," as Bishop Pike used to put it.[39]

THE RESURRECTION AND LIFE AFTER DEATH

One final and important idea which emerged in apocalyptic writings
and which was directly associated with the coming of the Messiah and
the establishment of the Kingdom of God on earth was that of a
general resurrection and a life after death. Until the second century
B.C. the only concept of a life after death in Hebrew thought was that
of Sheol, the abode of the shadow-like remains of human beings who
no longer have any vital personality.

In the apocalyptic literature, however, the dead are no longer referred to as "shades," but as "souls" or "spirits" who survive death
as conscious beings, thus indicating a radical change in belief about
the nature of survival in the life after death. "There is seen to be a
continuity between life on earth and life in Sheol in which the departed, as responsive and responsible 'souls' (or 'spirits'), can yet
maintain a life of fellowship with God whose jurisdiction is acknowledged beyond the grave."[40]

Moreover, men are seen as separated into two distinct categories in
death as in life: the wicked and the righteous. Man's destiny is determined by the life he has lived on earth and, though the full
results of his actions will not be determined until the final Judgment,
even in Sheol a separation is made.

Third, Sheol emerges as an intermediate state where the souls of
men await the Resurrection and final Judgment which will accompany
the coming of the Kingdom, and thus is only a foretaste of what is to
come.

Finally, the apocalyptic writings develop the idea of Hell as a place
of torment, though the word used is actually "accursed valley,"[41]
presumably the valley of Hinnon (Gehenna) west of Jerusalem, which
was a place notorious for idolatrous worship and the offering of child
sacrifices in earlier periods.[42] And, on the other hand, a paradise of
delights is envisioned for the righteous.[43]

Thus concurrent with the urgent teaching of the imminent establishment of the Kingdom of God *on earth,* we see the development of a rather comprehensive belief in life *after death* which included the resurrection of both the righteous and the wicked for the Judgment Day. The images related to both the afterlife and the Resurrection are diverse, but references to them occur in all but a few of the apocalyptic writings,[44] an indication of the extent to which both ideas were held by authors of the period.

APOCALYPTIC NATIONALISTS AND JESUS

It will be apparent to any student of the New Testament that Jesus taught many of the ideas which have just been attributed to apocalyptic thought. It is for that reason that Christian scholars have long insisted that Jesus was an apocalyptist and therefore not a nationalist, claiming his interests were other-worldly, not this-worldly: "Mine is not a kingdom of this world" (Jn. 18:36). However, a careful consideration of both the freedom movements and the literature of the day clearly indicates that the two cannot be separated.

For example, the first and greatest of all the Jewish apocalyptic writings, and the only one to be included in the regular canon of Old Testament books—the Book of Daniel—was apparently written during the reign of Antiochus Epiphanes, shortly after the outbreak of the Maccabean Revolt.[45] The historical events of the period are interpreted by Daniel, and in that book is to be found the famous passage in which the desecration of the Temple by Antiochus is referred to as the "disastrous abomination" (Dan. 11:29–31; 12:11).[46] The Book of Daniel, according to Dr. D. S. Russell, makes a great affirmation of faith in the abiding purpose of God which cannot and will not be frustrated by the devices of evil men, no matter how powerful they might be.[47]

In the Dead Sea Scrolls, we now have literature available to us that clearly reveals the inextricable unity of religious nationalism and apocalyptic thought. The Scrolls apparently belonged to a group who had gathered a vast library of manuscripts including not only Old Testament books but also many of the apocalyptic works of which we have just spoken. Among them were also apocalyptic writings authored by members of the Dead Sea sect itself.

It is helpful to take a closer look at the community made famous
by the discovery of the Scrolls, at their mode of life and at their
beliefs as revealed in their writings. They are the only group from the
period which we have been examining whose literature survives in
copies dating back to the first century A.D. and earlier. Therefore, the
Dead Sea Scrolls have been able to illuminate (and confound) much
that scholars had previously concluded about the period 168 B.C. to
A.D. 70, and particularly about the interrelatedness of the Zealot
movement and apocalypticism.

It will be apparent to the reader that Jesus must have been very
well acquainted with the scrolls discovered at Qumran—or other
scrolls expressing the same ideas—because his teachings as reported
in the Gospels reflect much of what can be found in them. It is
therefore reasonable to assume that we can learn a great deal about
Jesus by studying this sect of pious Jews who lived both before,
during, and after his lifetime and who did and thought many of the
same things as Jesus.

W. R. Farmer, who was fascinated by the common characteristics
which tied together the nationalists of the Seleucid and Roman periods,
writes: "There is a prevailing tendency among New Testament writers
to set Jesus against either one or the other of two false backgrounds.
On the one hand we have had the background of secular, this-worldly
nationalism, and on the other hand we have had the background of
religious, other-worldly apocalypticism. We have imagined the Zealots
to be this-worldly and activistic, and the apocalypticists to be other-
worldly and passive. The gospel portraits of Jesus have never really
come alive against either of these backgrounds. The reason for this is
plain to see. The Jesus of the Gospels is a real figure. However,
neither of the backgrounds against which we have tried to place him
is real. A real person does not come alive against an unreal background.
We must find for Jesus a real background, his true background, if we
ever expect him to 'come alive' as an historical person."[48]

CHAPTER 3

The Dead Sea Scrolls Community

"When these things come to pass . . . they shall be separated from the midst of . . . perverse men to go into the desert to prepare the way of Him: as it is written, 'In the wilderness prepare the way of [the Lord]. Make straight in the desert a highway for our God.'"

Manual of Discipline 8:12b–14;
A. Dupont-Sommer translation.

In the words of James A. Pike:

"It now seems clear that the headquarters of the Zealot resistance movement—at least during the Great Revolt of A.D. 66—was at Qumran, the site near which the Dead Sea Scrolls were found. In the literature of the Dead Sea Scrolls *and* in the New Testament we find the following names used to identify the movement: the '*Ebionim*,' or 'the Poor'—which meant 'poor' like the Franciscans are poor, a vow of poverty in the sense of sharing a common life, not in the sense of not eating well. 'Blessed are the *Ebionim*,' found in our Beatitudes, is from the Dead Sea Scrolls, as is the alternate form found in Matthew, the 'poor in spirit.'

"Another name found for the movement is 'the Many,' used frequently in the Dead Sea Scrolls and also found in the Book of Acts. In the Eucharistic prayer we use the phrase 'given for many,' referring to the body and blood. Now I always insert, when celebrating, the word 'the': '*the* Many,' that's what it means; a ransom for *the* Many, for the movement. Another name for the movement is 'the New Covenant,' or the New Testament. Other times it's called 'the Way.'

"It was thought, when the first Scrolls were found, that the

Dead Sea documents were Essene literature. We learn of this sect
from Josephus, from Philo, and from Pliny the Elder—all early
historians. The word 'Essene'—the origin of which is obscure—
is sometimes explained as meaning 'healer,' other times as 'pious,'
'righteous,' or 'holy.' The Essenes seemed to have spread throughout the entire region in which Jews were living—not just in Palestine. In Egypt they were called *therapeutae,* or 'healers.' Their
mode of living is described rather fully by Josephus. He seems
rather enthusiastic about the sect. He was trained by them at one
time, or was part of their movement.

"The historians describe the Essenes as both pacifist and celibate. Therefore, when so much of the Dead Sea Scrolls material
was found to be belligerent, and references to women and children were found—and skeletons of women and children were
found in the cemetery near Qumran, which was thought to be
the headquarters of the Essene sect—it seemed hard to reconcile
the evidence with the historians' accounts.

"Many scholars tried to reconcile the apparent contradictions
by saying, 'This is mythological, or picture language,' or 'It's
talking about the next world.' Take a book like the War Scroll,
called 'The War of the Children of Light Against the Children of
Darkness,' which tells how to run a revolution. You say, 'This
is just picture language about the ultimate issues of reality. It has
nothing to do with any earthly revolution, because after all Josephus said these people were pacifists.' But then other scholars began to say, 'Maybe the Essenes weren't pacifist after all.'

"Maybe the Essenes were pacifists, or maybe they weren't. Regardless of how we come out on that issue, opinion is sill divided
among scholars as to whether or not the Covenanter community
centered at Qumran (and also spread all over Israel in small communities) was the same movement as the Essenes. We have come
more and more to feel the Covenanters were part of the movement of Jewish nationalism, or resistance. Many of the documents
found there reflect very explicitly a revolutionary movement in
every respect. Other data supports this conclusion too—such as the
discovery on the top of Masada of the Qumran calendar for liturgical celebration, together, by the way, with a letter from one
John the Essene.

"What, then, is the relationship to the Essenes? Groups which
come together for a specific purpose, pool their resources, and
share a kind of communal life under discipline tend to develop
many of the same characteristics. Just because some of the features of the common life of Franciscans, Buddhist monks, communist cell block members, and hippie communes are the same

doesn't mean they all belong to the same movement. Therefore, we think that many of the features of the way of life of the Essenes and of the Qumran Covenanters are the same, but that they *may* not have been identical sects.

"The Qumran community seems to have been a kind of monastic, mutually committed movement like the Essenes—perhaps it could even be called Essenoid—but it had a very explicit revolutionary thrust. It seems *more* in line with the resistance movement, then, than with the Essenes—unless we use the term Essene in a very broad sense, referring to a general style of life, much as the word 'hippie' is used to describe a whole broad grouping of young people today who usually have only a few general characteristics in common: long hair, bare feet, a tendency to hitchhike carrying back packs, and maybe a communal style of living. It clarifies the issues more just to call these people 'Covenanters' and to leave the issue of the Essenes aside."

---◆---

THE DEAD SEA SCROLLS

The huge collection of manuscripts (now numbering over six hundred) which were uncovered near the Dead Sea in Palestine over a period of nearly ten years beginning in 1947 is apparently the fragmentary remains of what was once a very large sectarian library.[1] Scholars are still debating whether the library belonged to the sect known as the "Essenes," described by the ancient historians Josephus, Philo, and Pliny and said by Pliny to be located in the wilderness to the west of the Dead Sea between Jericho and Ein Gedi—a description which fits the place where the Scrolls were found. Most are of the opinion that the Qumran sect was almost certainly Essene.[2] Other scholars believe just as firmly that the Covenanters were *not* Essenes, but Zealots.[3]

Careful study of the fragments and scrolls found near Qumran during the more than twenty years since those first finds has made abundantly clear, no matter what specific titles are attached to the group, that the owners of the Dead Sea Scrolls belonged to the resistance movement. They were devout Jewish freedom fighters whose apocalyptic fervor manifested itself in a passionate religious nationalism.

The Qumran Covenanters had many characteristics in common with the Essenes, the Zealots, and the early Christians. It is therefore at least possible that "Essene" was a term applied to a broad category of desert-centered, apocalyptic nationalists rather than the name of a specific and narrowly defined sect.[4] The term "Essene" does not appear in either the Dead Sea Scrolls or the New Testament, and may have been used only by persons outside the movement. Both the Qumran Covenanters and the early Christians—and perhaps other groups as well—may have been called "Essenes" as a general description.[5]

There is no disagreement among scholars, however, regarding the importance of the Dead Sea Scrolls, which help us immeasurably to understand the historical period between the Old and the New Testaments.[6] But perhaps even more important for understanding Jesus is the interrelatedness of apocalyptic thought and the nationalist movements of the era which is made manifest in the Scrolls.[7]

The Dead Sea Scrolls fall into three basic categories: copies of Old Testament books, copies of apocryphal and pseudepigraphical works, and copies of sectarian works.

Documents which fall into the first category have been of particular interest to Biblical scholars because they are the earliest available copies of books from the Old Testament.[8] Most of the manuscripts with which scholars had been working until 1947 dated back only to the ninth or tenth centuries A.D.[9] At Qumran fragments were found of early copies of all of the books of the Old Testament except Esther. These fragments enabled scholars to determine with a large degree of certainty that the Old Testament canon was completed prior to the Maccabean period[10]—or at least by the earliest years of that period if the Book of Daniel is considered to have been written after Antiochus Epiphanes committed the offense of the "disastrous abomination."[11] Scholars have also utilized the Scrolls to verify that the textual tradition which has survived in the form of the traditional Hebrew Bible (the Masoretic text) is indeed antique and faithfully preserved.[12] But perhaps most important for Old Testament scholars is the information yielded by the Dead Sea Scrolls (together with other manuscripts such as those discovered at Wadi Murabba'at[13]) regarding the progressive development of the texts of the Old Testament over the course of the years.[14]

Of far more interest to us, however, are the apocryphal, pseudepigraphical, and sectarian writings which were discovered at Qumran, for these enable us to piece together the actual Jewish setting in which an apocalyptic understanding of history was essential and vital to the communal existence of groups of first-century Jews.[15] In this setting, the final war against the sons of darkness was expected every day and nationalistic fervor was very high.[16] Out of this setting grew the primitive Christian Church, which was the only continuation of this communal apocalyptic tradition to survive the Fall of Jerusalem with any vitality.[17]

THE FOUNDING OF THE QUMRAN SECT

It now appears that rather soon after the Maccabean Revolt—probably between 150 and 100 B.C.[18]—the *Hasidim,* or "pious ones," who had supported the Maccabeans in the early stages of the revolt and had even agreed to the principle of self-defense on the Sabbath, grew uneasy about the directions their new Hasmonean government was taking. It was in the early days of the Maccabean Revolt that the community of Hasidaeans was first mentioned (I Macc. 2:42) in literature of the times. Their support of the Maccabees was apparently a halfhearted one[19] and eventually they divided into two branches: the Pharisees who were unhappy with the Hasmonean rule but did not withdraw to the wilderness, and a desert wilderness sect called the Covenanters, who eventually came to be centered at Qumran.[20] The break appears to have come largely over the issue of whether the Hasmoneans could legitimately be regarded by the people as the new High Priestly family. Since the time of Solomon, the High Priest had always been appointed from among the descendants of Zadok, and the *Hasidim* believed the Zadokites to be the only legitimate priesthood. Many of those, therefore, who were devoted to the ancient Law and to the Zadokite priesthood withdrew to the wilderness and set up a communal life of their own.[21]

Both the information found in Dead Sea documents and the evidence uncovered by archaeological digs, including coins, graves, pottery, and strata of buildings,[22] lead most scholars to date the initial occupation of the center at Qumran between 135 and 100 B.C. The settlement of Qumran was built on the ruined foundations of an Israelite fortress which had lain deserted since the sixth century B.C. just to the south and west of the place where the Jordan River flows into the Dead Sea. The ruins can be visited today on top of a high terrace about midway between the rugged cliffs on the edge of the wilderness to the west, and the sloping plain which merges with the banks of the Dead Sea to the east. Only a short distance farther south along the shores of the

Dead Sea is Ein Feshka, a fertile desert oasis watered by fresh springs from the cliff rocks.

The community which began living at Qumran in the latter half of the second century B.C. apparently remained there steadily until its buildings were destroyed by an earthquake early in Herod's reign. According to Josephus the earthquake occurred in 31 B.C.[23]

After a gap of approximately thirty years, the site was reoccupied by the same group, and continued in use until the revolt against Rome, from A.D. 66 to 70.[24] It was during those years that many of the Scrolls were placed in large pots, sealed with wax, and carefully hidden in caves in the cliffs surrounding Qumran. Very near the community center itself, however, thousands of fragments representing more than a hundred manuscripts were apparently discarded in haste as the community fled from the Romans around A.D. 68.[25] These documents, torn up and hastily scattered in the nearby cave which has been designated Cave 4 by archaeologists, have proven the richest find of all, for they obviously were writings the Covenanters did not want to fall into the hands of the Romans. One would expect writings destroyed at the onset of the enemy to be seditious in nature, and this is precisely what the first reports of them indicate. Unfortunately, as of 1970 only the fragments entrusted to John Allegro for translation have been published.[26]

Thus the Qumran community came into existence, flourished, and died out during the very epoch of fervent Jewish nationalism of which we have been speaking—164 B.C. to A.D. 70. Because of the times in which they lived, the teachings of their first great leader, and the beliefs expressed in their sectarian writings, it seems that they were intimately related to the nationalistic movements of the day, probably with even greater fervor than most because of their ardent apocalyptic convictions.

BELIEFS OF THE QUMRAN SECT

The Qumran Covenanters based their beliefs on the ancient prophecies contained in the Old Testament, reinterpreted. Their first great leader, a man whom they never name but simply call the Teacher of Righteousness,[27] had reinterpreted all ancient Biblical prophecy and had shown them that the events of their own time were in fact the very circumstances which the prophets of old had predicted would accompany the "last days."[28] In their time, they came to believe, history as we know it was being brought to an end. It was soon to be transformed into a new age in which the original perfection and order of creation would be restored, and peace, harmony, health, and well-being would reign.[29]

Many of the writings authored by members of the sect are "commentaries" (*pesharim*) which explain the meaning of passages or entire books from the Old Testament, verse by verse, pointing out the contemporary events to which each verse refers. The Covenanters also collected what scholars call "Prophetic Testimonia"—that is, summary lists of prophecies being fulfilled in the end of time, sometimes with expository comments appended to each, sometimes without—and historical writings which utilize citations of Biblical passages to interpret in "prophetic" language the meaning and sequence of historical events of the past and future. All such writings were "revealed," they believed, through the special gift of interpretation which had been granted to members of the sect. They were convinced not only that the end of the age was upon them, but also that they, the Covenanters, had a special role to play in bringing it to its final culmination and fulfillment.

The tradition of the sect's interpretation was apparently set by the Teacher of Righteousness, who the Commentary on Habakkuk says spoke of "all that is to happen to the final generation," for God had set understanding in his heart "that he might interpret all the words of His servants the Prophets, through whom He foretold all that would happen to His people and His land" (Com. on Hab. 2:5–10). Another passage reads, ". . . this concerns the Teacher of Righteousness, to whom God made known all the mysteries of the words of His servants the Prophets" (Com. on Hab. 7:4–5). However, most of the commentaries and testimonies discovered are manuscripts written from the second half of the first century B.C. to the first half of the first century A.D., apparently after the Teacher's death.[30] They point to the events surrounding the formation of the sect—especially the persecution of the Teacher of Righteousness by the Wicked Priest—as evidence of the inauguration of the "end of times," and anticipate that the final war will be fought in the immediate future with the Romans, whom they call the "Kittim."

All of the convictions held by the Covenanters about the end of times are couched in a fundamental "Doctrine of the Two Ways" which is spelled in their Manual of Discipline:[31]

> He has created man to govern the world, and has appointed for him two spirits in which to walk until the time of His visitation: the spirits of truth and falsehood . . . For it is He who created the spirits of Light and Darkness and founded every action upon them and established every deed upon their ways (Man. of Disc. 3:17–19a, 25–26).

The sect taught, essentially, that in creating the universe, God released Power in two forms: the spirit of light and the spirit of darkness. Both are creative forces at work in all of us and in the world around us, as well as in the whole cosmos. The forces of light create all that is for the good and well-being of men and for the stability of the universe. They also serve as the source of understanding for men, leading to perception of the truth.[32]

The forces of darkness, on the other hand, release evil in the world, disrupting the harmony and balance of nature. They cause natural catastrophes, such as earthquakes, floods, and fires, create disease in men, and keep men bound by ignorance and separated from God, the source of all truth.

A further development of this doctrine is found in the Scroll The War of the Children of Light Against the Children of Darkness in which a detailed description of the final resolution of this duality is set forth. According to the War Scroll, God has appointed Belial as the Angel of Darkness to command the forces of evil and lead them into battle against good, and he has named the Archangel Michael as the Prince of Light. The Archangel Michael will command the angelic forces in their final battle against Belial—a battle in which all children of light will be able to participate.[33]

The Qumran community understood its decision to live in the desert in righteous perfection according to the Law to be a choosing to *walk in the light*.[34] The war between the forces of light and darkness, of good and evil, they believed, had first to be won in the lives of a faithful remnant of God's People Israel.[35] Then and only then would enough people be ready to fight on God's side in the final battle to enable Him to send His Messiah. Therefore the Covenanters chose a disciplined mode of life which would perfect and purify their own lives and give them the training needed to win the final battle.[36]

Victory in the war, then, as the Covenanters understood it, was being won at two levels. For those who entered the Community of the

New Covenant at Qumran, the war within their individual lives was fought and won by their choosing to walk in the light.[37] The power of the spirit of light filled them and healed them as they participated in the daily life of the community—a life which included prayer, worship, work, study, and living in love with their brothers. Though the gift of the spirit (or baptism by the spirit) could not be guaranteed through their joining the community,[38] it was far more likely to be granted under those circumstances than when living in the "world" where the forces of darkness still held sway. Among the Covenanters there were many who were already filled with the spirit of light. These members strengthened the manifestation of light in the midst of the community and made it easier, relatively speaking, for others of their company to enter that higher realm. When they did, their internal, or personal, "war" was won, and peace reigned in their own lives.

One of the manifestations of the power which the children of light possessed, according to the Dead Sea Scrolls and Josephus, was their ability to cast out demons. The Covenanters were exorcists. In a face-to-face confrontation, as the Covenanters understood it, the forces of darkness fled for fear of "exposure" by the forces of light. So when a child of light approached a man "possessed" by or "driven" by— that is, in the power of—a demon, or son of Belial, the presence of the light would cause the evil spirit to cry out and flee, leaving the formerly "possessed" person at peace, or at one-ness, or whole.[39]

Other manifestations of the power released by the baptism of the spirit of holiness, or light—in addition to the inner peace and physical health which the members possessed, and the power over demons— were the ability to remember and interpret dreams and visions (considered the primary modes of revelation by the Covenanters), the gifts of prophecy and foretelling the future, the talent of teaching, and the power to "do" the truth in specific acts of justice, mercy, and righteousness.[40] All of these "gifts of the spirit" were manifest in the "Congregation of the Poor" at Qumran, according to their literature and the early historians.

Since the children of light had already begun to partake of the heavenly characteristics believed to be manifest in the angelic beings who dwell perpetually in the presence of the Most High, they had in some sense already entered the anticipated Kingdom. As they saw it, they lived *in* the world but were no longer really *of* it, for the power of light and goodness, and therefore of Life, already held full sway in them, and the forces of darkness and evil, and therefore of Death, no longer had any power over them at all. They were the community of the final age—that is, the New Israel—living in the midst of the old age as a sign that the end of times was in fact at hand.[41]

According to this point of view, those persons possessed of demons were still under the power of Belial, or Beelzebub. Demons, the Covenanters believed, were the spirits (souls) of the fallen angels of whom the apocryphal Book of Enoch speaks.[42] Having been in the Kingdom of Light (heaven) and having learned some of the mysteries of eternity, they had nevertheless been enticed by the pleasures of the flesh. According to Enoch, deceived into feeling that earthly pleasures would give lasting fulfillment, these angels turned back from the path of understanding and wisdom and descended to earth to have intercourse with women who still lived in ignorance of the life-giving truth. The children they conceived were monsters born out of partial understanding who used those mysteries which had been revealed to the angels (enchantments, root cuttings, the resolving of enchantments, astrology, the constellations, the knowledge of the clouds, the signs of the earth, of the sun and of the moon)[43] to deceive the children of men, to hold power over them and to work evil among them.

The fallen angels, Enoch continues, were then chained by God in the shadowy nether regions of Sheol as their punishment. There they were to remain until the judgment day.[44] The spirits (souls) of the monstrous children which they had begotten, however, were allowed to continue to live on earth as "demons" who could only have life "in the flesh" by taking control of unwitting or misguided persons and "possessing" them.

The story in Enoch ends by asserting that the life of these evil spirits who continued to live on earth—because it did not acknowledge the true spirit of understanding and power as being from God—would ultimately be destroyed, for they could survive only in darkness. When the Kingdom of Light was established on earth, all demonic forces would be overcome and cast out into eternal darkness and into punishment in lakes of fire. The persons they held in bondage would then be set free.[45]

Because of a firm belief in the Enochian story, the Covenanters acknowledged daily that they were already in the Kingdom of Light— that they lived in "heaven" now, possessing the power and understanding of its spirit of truth. They were very careful, however, not to reveal the inner secrets of their understanding to persons who were not yet ready.[46] It would be too easy for others to use the powers revealed by the spirit for great evil and deception, they believed. Thus the mysteries were taught only to those with true understanding—that is, those who had been baptized in the spirit and in truth. Entrance into the Congregation of the Poor was gained only by going through a long and rigorous process, and no one outside their congregation was permitted to know the inner secrets of their teachings. In fact, we do not know if any of these secrets were ever written down. Scholars suspect they were not.[47] Let us look, then, at the style of life practiced by the Qumran Covenanters. The organization of their community and the activities in which they engaged were determined by the beliefs we have just outlined and were based on apocalyptic writings which describe the new age and the New Israel. An image emerges of a group which was preparing to share the ruling power with the Messiah once the Romans were overthrown, and we begin to see clearly how directly relevant to the "revolution" such apocalyptic beliefs were. That Jesus' teachings were very similar to the Covenanters', and that his style of life and the organization of the primitive Christian movement bear strong resemblance to those of the Qumran community, help us to understand why Jesus was crucified as an insurrectionist and why the Christians were later persecuted by the Roman Empire.

CHAPTER 4

The Style of Life at Qumran

"These twelve Jesus sent out, charging them, 'Go nowhere among the Gentiles, and enter no town of the Samaritans . . . preach as you go, saying, "The kingdom of heaven is at hand." Heal the sick, raise the dead, cleanse lepers, cast out demons. You received without pay, give without pay. Take no gold, nor silver, nor copper in your belts, no bag for your journey, nor two tunics, nor sandals, nor a staff; for the labourer deserves his food. And whatever town or village you enter, find out who is worthy in it, and stay with him until you depart.'"

Matthew 10:5, 7–11, RSV

In the words of James A. Pike:

"The hard-core revolutionary-minded members of the resistance movement, instead of being secular-minded, as we so often think, were even more religiously minded than the Pharisees. Their way of keeping their courage and boldness up in the face of Roman power was to exaggerate their Judaism—to exaggerate the ultimate importance of being a Jew and of keeping the Law.

"The version of the application of Torah which you find in the Dead Sea Scrolls and in the Damascus Document [discovered in a synagogue in Cairo in the eighteenth century] is much more strict than that of the Pharisees, much less accommodating to the way life is. A text you will recall as attributed to Jesus is interesting here. 'Unless your righteousness *exceeds* that of the Pharisees you shall in no wise enter the Kingdom,' which means the forthcoming kingdom to be established by the victory of Israel over the Romans. Another one of Jesus' teachings which appears to be a reaction against Pharisaic attempts to erode away the Torah by interpretation is, 'Heaven and earth may pass away, but not one jot or tittle of Torah shall pass away, and he who does not keep the slightest jot or tittle of Torah shall be the least in the coming Kingdom.' These teachings are typical of the desert movements and of the outlook of the men who lived at Qumran.

"The Judean wilderness was a kind of meditation ground for people functioning out of Qumran. The purpose of living in a cave, or in a tent out there, or just out on the ground, and of moving around, with no fixed place of your own, was twofold: to get used to hanging loose and not counting on a particular place to be, and second, to be alone for meditation. This group counted very much on meditation and quiet and aloneness, as well as on corporate activities, and Jesus is said to have fasted and meditated in this same wilderness for forty days after his baptism. We think he must have meditated not far from Qumran.

"The Poor at Qumran had a corporate liturgy—a kind of daily Mass. The principal meal each day was eucharistic. By eucharistic I mean more than just in the sense of giving thanks, but also in the fuller sense of celebrating that which is to be. Actually the Poor at Qumran awaited the Messiah. They had a chair for him because he might come at any moment and they didn't want to be inhospitable by not having set a place for him. So their meal had an eschatalogical note as well as the note of remembrance. That which was being remembered was, as is usual among Jews—and Christians, although they tend to forget it—the bondage in Egypt and the passage through the Red Sea waters: the Exodus. God saves. They looked toward the promised land, the thing being both remembered and celebrated as yet to come.

"So the people at Qumran had the liturgical dimension of life. They also believed in baptism, adult baptism by immersion in living, or moving water. The place of Jesus' baptism has traditionally been thought to be about a mile and a half from Qumran. John the Baptist functioned there.

"But the other side of their communal life was to have time for their individual quiet and meditation. The day was very carefully organized to provide opportunity for all of these functions. They also felt the importance of circulating the manuscripts of their own sectarian literature and of Biblical books, so they had a rather impressive scriptorium, or writing room, like the medieval monasteries. The writing desks, inkwells and pens have been found. They made scroll after scroll; many copies of the same books were found.

"The central figure of this movement—of Qumran, the resistance, the Covenanters—is the Teacher of Righteousness. He is unnamed, and there are some scholars who have speculated that he may have been Jesus because of the similarities between the two. But this is an open question. The important thing for us is that in this movement we find much that reminds us of Jesus and of the early Christians, as well as of the first-century Zealots, and it is all very interesting and very important for us today."

———————◆———————

ENTRY INTO A NEW COVENANT

The Qumran Covenanters were devout men (and some women) who withdrew into the desert wilderness in order to "separate from the habitation of ungodly men."[1] To that extent they constituted a protest movement against the faithlessness of all those whom they felt had broken the Covenant with God by their willingness to compromise with Hellenists, by their support of a kingdom which did not have God, and God alone, as king, and by their acceptance of a high priesthood which was not legitimate according to the Law.

But more important than the protest aspect of their withdrawal was the positive thrust of it. These devout men entered into a *New Covenant* with God.[2] Therefore, one of the names by which they are known is "Covenanters." They promised to keep the Mosaic Law in every regard, and to purify their own lives both ritually and in spirit so that they might serve as a ransom for the rest of Israel, for those who had gone astray. As a sign of the New Covenant, God, they believed, had granted them the gift of the spirit of holiness. Moreover, they believed God would soon fulfill the promise given to the prophet Isaiah, that for the faithfulness of a righteous remnant, Israel's enemy would be overthrown.[3]

The Covenanters understood themselves to be that righteous remnant of Israel, who, by their perfection according to the Law and by their ritual purity, were atoning for the whole People of Israel.[4] They felt they were facilitating the very process by which the whole People of God would be redeemed. They hoped their righteousness would enable God to send His Messiah and liberate His People from oppression. If so, the Covenanters would be the very ones who would help the Messiah to rule for the first thousand years. They would sit beside him as judges of the twelve tribes of Israel while the "mopping up" operations of the war went on, and until the trumpet was blown on the last day to raise the dead of Israel for judgment, along with men of all other nations.[5]

The Covenanters kept themselves in a perpetual state of readiness for that event. The priests at Qumran played an important role in the life of the community, for the original founders of the sect were direct lineal descendants of the Zadokite family. By association with this priestly group and as a way of asserting the legitimacy of the Zadokite priesthood as rightful heirs to the High Priest's office, the Covenanters often refer to themselves in their literature as "Sons of Zadok," even though not all of their congregation were priests.[6]

The priests said daily prayers on behalf of the community, had authority to interpret the Law, and had the responsibility to preserve the community in its purity.[7] Since the Covenanters believed the Temple priesthood was not legitimate, they did not go to Jerusalem to offer their sacrifices in the Temple. Instead they set up their own priestly organization and observed their feast days at Qumran. Moreover, they were prepared to step in and assume priestly duties in the Temple itself whenever the opportunity might present itself.[8]

OPPOSITION TO THE TEMPLE CULTUS

The Covenanters found fault with worship at the Jerusalem Temple on several grounds. The first, and most important, was their conviction that the High Priest should be a descendant of Zadok, who had been appointed the first High Priest by King Solomon. Since the Hasmoneans were not a priestly family and were not Zadokites, the Covenanters felt the High Priests appointed from Hasmonean ranks could not be worthy in the sight of God.

Second, the men at Qumran felt the wrong calendar was being used for feast days. During the rule of Antiochus Epiphanes a lunar calendar was introduced. This innovation, according to two of the favorite books of the Qumran group, Jubilees and I Enoch, was attributable to the evil influence of fallen angels and pagans, or Gentiles.[9] On the other hand, in those same books good angels are said to have taught Enoch (a prototype of the Son of Man) the solar calendar, which the Covenanters followed for their feast days.[10] They looked forward to the day when its use would be restored in the Temple.

Third, the Covenanters considered the Temple itself improperly constructed according to the prescriptions of the Law. The most recent Scroll to come into the hands of scholars (in 1967) has been tentatively named "The Temple Scroll" by Professor Yigael Yadin. Dr. Yadin is an Israeli archaeologist and former Chief of the General Staff of the Israel Defense Forces who directed the excavations at Hazor, headed the explorations of the Bar Kochba caves in the Judean desert, and led the international expedition which dug and partially restored Masada. According to Professor Yadin, who is working on its translation, the twenty-eight-foot-long Temple Scroll, the largest complete Scroll found to date, includes, among other things, precise measurements for the Temple which was to be built in the new Jerusalem. The Temple mentioned in the Scroll seems to be one that was to be built for use until the end of days when God Himself was to create a perfect Temple in the New Jerusalem. However, the sect apparently believed that the future God-built Temple would have the same plan and dimensions as this "interim" Temple, and in fact they seemed to feel the original Solomonic temple should have been built according to those prescriptions.[11]

The sectarians believed, as Jesus apparently did, that the Temple would have to be destroyed and a new one built in its place.[12] The sect apparently believed that the Temple of the newly found Scroll would be the one to serve until the one which would be the work of God Himself could be established.[13] That Temple, which was to come down from Heaven "ready-made," would be eternal.[14]

Because of these three major objections to Temple worship, the Covenanters had their own rota of priests, kept their feast days according to the solar calendar, and refused to send their sacrificial offerings to the defiled Temple cultus of Jerusalem.[15] The discovery of pits with the remains of burned bones suggests that the sectarians may even have offered their own sacrifices at Qumran.[16] Apparently the sect did pay Temple taxes—at least once in each sectarian's lifetime[17]—but they longed for the day when the Messiah would come and the Temple cultus and priesthood would once again be made to conform to the Law. As A. R. C. Leaney, a Reader in Theology at the University of Nottingham in England, has put it, "the sect arises

historically from a desire to replace both the defiled Temple and
the defiled priesthood, and the conception of [the Sect's] organization
derives directly from that of the priests organized for Temple duty."[18]

DAILY LIFE AT QUMRAN

Worship provided the framework for each day for the Covenanters.
They rose before dawn and, facing east, offered their morning prayers
to God. Apparently due to Zoroastrian influence (to which their Doctrine of the Two Ways, spoken of in the last chapter, can also be
attributed),[19] they felt their prayers helped strengthen the rays of
light which brought (or "pulled up") the sun.[20] They praised God
with hymns of thanksgiving for His gift of light at the beginning of
each new day of living in His Kingdom. At dusk, they again offered
prayers of thanksgiving and praise for the light of the day, and asked
God's protection during the darkness of the night.[21]

The day was divided into three parts.[22] One third of the waking
day was set aside for work, probably in the fields where they raised
the community's food. An irrigation system has been uncovered at
Ein Feshka, the oasis not far from Qumran, which no doubt fed water
to vegetable gardens and orchards cultivated by the sect. Other
archaeological finds at Ein Feshka which suggest that the oasis was
the site of the Covenanters' working day include remains of enclosures
for animals and what is thought to have been a tannery.[23] A tannery
would have been essential for the production of the numerous leather
Scrolls which were copied in the scriptorium and which have been discovered near Qumran.

A second third of the sectarians' day was spent in the study of
the Law. This was undoubtedly the reason the Qumran Scrolls library
was so large: each member of the movement would have spent a
great deal of time reading and studying the Biblical and sectarian works.
In fact, their Manual of Discipline provides that the Law be read
without ceasing; therefore, it is thought that one member of the sect
was always assigned, in a system of rotation, to read the Law on
behalf of the whole group so that there would be no gaps in the
study of Torah.[24]

The remainder of the day was spent by the Covenanters in prayer and meditation. The keeping of the prescribed calendar of prayers was essential to their life of righteous faithfulness to the Covenant.[25]

The men and women who lived at Qumran apparently constituted the headquarters of a larger network of communities scattered around Israel in or near villages.[26] Josephus estimates that there were about four thousand Essenes in Israel at that time (as contrasted with about ten thousand Pharisees, two thousand Sadducees, and one thousand Zealots) in a total population of about a half million.[27] Even if the movement centered at Qumran was not the Essenes referred to by Josephus, it nevertheless must have been large and significant. The long life of the sect, which persisted some two centuries or more; the fact that there were camps and settlements elsewhere in Israel which belonged to the same movement, as is indicated in the sectarian documents;[28] the size of the library accumulated at Qumran; the enormous number of writings authored by members of the sect; and the cemetery which contained graves of a thousand persons, all indicate that this was one of the major Jewish sects during the Hasmonean and Herodian eras.[29]

The Manual of Discipline, the document that guided members in their common life, indicates that those who took up residence at Qumran had to take the strictest vows of any in the movement.[30] They, in contrast to members of sister, or adjunct, communities, were to keep themselves entirely separate from "impure" men—that is, all those who did not adhere to the Law in its strictest interpretations and who had not entered the New Covenant.[31] Members of branch congregations were allowed contact with men of the world, but they were not permitted to eat with them or to do any business with them, except on "cash" terms, to minimize their association with such impure men.[32]

In addition, most members of the Qumran community were apparently celibate, though bones of women and children have been found in the nearby cemetery, indicating that there must have been some married members.[33] The latter undoubtedly had taken vows to abstain from sexual intimacy in accordance with rules for remaining ritually pure as "mustered troops" for the final war, since the men at Qumran were in a constant state of readiness for the Messiah's coming. In sister congregations, on the other hand, though celibacy was encouraged where possible, many—probably most—members were married.[34] In other regards the central congregation at Qumran differed from the branch communities only in the intensity of its communal life experience and in the fervor of its expectations and convictions.

THE COMMUNAL LIFE OF THE POOR

The buildings which composed the community's headquarters included facilities only for communal activities. There was a large room which was apparently used for meetings of the Assembly (as they called their gathered community) for deliberation, for judgment, and for their common meals.

Smaller rooms surrounding this hall were probably used for study and perhaps for the storage of the community's records. One was a large scriptorium, for the production of Scrolls: plaster tables and benches were discovered in the ruins, together with two inkpots. The members of the community must have spent a great deal of time there copying Scrolls for their own use and for distribution to sister communities.

Other facilities were a large kitchen and related storage rooms and a large pottery works where the pots in which the Dead Sea Scrolls were hidden were made, in addition to the community's other vessels and dishes. An elaborate water system had been worked out and included an aqueduct which brought water down from the cliffs above and several large cisterns for water storage. Much of this water was probably used for rites of maintaining ritual purity, stressed especially in the priestly practices at Qumran, and some baths seemed to be included.

There were no provisions in the communal buildings for lodging for the members. Archaeological evidence indicates that the members lived in tents and caves in the surrounding areas. Since their desert life seems in part to have been an attempt to return to the wandering wilderness life of their forefathers, permanence of residence could have no place in their style of life.[35]

The members of the movement held no private property. When they took their vows and entered the New Covenant, they turned over all their belongings to the overseer of the community, who was responsible for the care and distribution of all property and for regulating the work of the community.[36] Each member was given a robe to wear and a tool to use.[37] These, however, were also communal property and were only entrusted to him for his use. For this reason, another name of the community, used frequently in their literature, is "the

Poor." This did not mean poverty-stricken, but rather individually devoid of possessions.[38] The community may in fact have had considerable wealth as a group, which they were then able to share with others in need.[39]

Members were never allowed to carry money. When they traveled, they spent nights, insofar as possible, in sister communities and were fed by them. If it became necessary, traveling Covenanters were allowed to exchange services for food, but no other transactions with men of the world were permitted.[40]

Precautions for the protection of the community were taken. At Qumran a fortified tower provided some security against attack, as did the walls. The location, however, was poorly suited for defense, so the community would undoubtedly have been forced to flee under direct assault. Individual members carried daggers, or small swords (*sicae*), concealed in their robes when on the road, and they always traveled in twos for added protection.[41]

BROTHERS KNOWN BY THEIR LOVE

The Qumran Covenanters considered their relationships with each other to be of great importance to the righteous life they sought to lead. One of the functions of the meetings of the Assembly was to afford an opportunity to deal with injustices done within the community or with any unrectified wrong. Members were expected to admonish one another in the way of truth. If anyone had anything against a brother, or if a brother had done him any wrong, he was to go directly to his brother and tell him about it without delay. No man was to allow the sun to go down on his anger without telling the person concerned. If it was not possible for the two to settle the dispute, then the accuser was to confront the accused in the presence of a third person. If the matter still could not be settled, only then was it to be brought before the Assembly for their counsel. Another name of the community was "the men of God's counsel," for the members were eager for their brethren to give them evidence of any error. They sought to be perfect in their righteousness and wanted justice—that is, God's Law—to be done in every situation.[42]

Finally, the Covenanters sought in all these ways to "love one another." Loving mercy, one of God's characteristics in His dealings

with men, was a principal goal of their communal life. The love which
brothers in the congregation of the Poor had for one another served
as an important mark of their identity.[43]

THE RITES AND RITUALS OF QUMRAN

Entrance could be gained into the New Covenant only by a very long
and difficult process. Those who sought admittance went to Qumran
and expressed their desire. The head officer of the community—a
priest—examined them and if he found them to be sincere in their
desire to live in righteousness according to the Law, they then appeared before the Assembly. To the Assembly of "the Many" (perhaps
the most common name attributed to the Covenanters in their literature) they were asked to confess their own sins and the iniquity of all
the children of Israel, which they took upon themselves by entering the
New Covenant. If the Many saw fit to bless the novices and curse the
evil they confessed, they received them as provisional members of the
community for a year.[44]

During that first year, the novices were taught by a Covenanter
called the instructor. They were not allowed, however, to share the
congregation's ritual waters or to eat the common meal with them.
This was because they had so recently been "in the world" and might
contaminate the ritual purity of the Many by their unwitting defilement
through contact with wicked men.

At the end of a year's instruction in "the Way," as the Qumran
style of life was called, the novices were once again examined by the
Assembly. If found worthy to continue their association with the Poor,
the novices were then allowed to share the ritual baths, but not the
communal meal. Only after two trial years were they received into
full status. At that time they took vows to keep the New Covenant
and to strive to be perfect in doing the truth and in preserving their
ritual purity so they would at every moment be ready to receive the
Messiah. Their possessions were surrendered to the community at the
end of the second year and they were admitted to the common meal
at last.[45]

The meal seems to have been the most sacred aspect of the communal life of the Covenanters. Apparently it had an important function

in relation to the "end of days"—that of "rehearsing" the banquet at which the Messiah was to preside.[46] The ceremony was strictly designed and provided for members of the community to take their places at the banquet according to the rank assigned them by the Assembly. This rank was determined by the degree of righteousness and wisdom the member exhibited in his daily life. Before anyone ate, the priest stretched forth his hand to bless the bread and then the wine.[47] Their expectation was that when the royal, or Davidic, Messiah came he would sit beside the priest at the table at just such a banquet, and when the priestly Messiah arrived he would himself give the blessing and preside at the meal.[48]

The Covenanters practiced ritual baptism by immersion as a sign of entry into the New Covenant. Though baptism was required, they were under no illusions as to its effects. Members of the Many were admonished to manifest a righteousness which would exceed that of the "Pharisees" (who also taught that the Law should be kept in every regard). Their righteousness was to be in spirit as well as in truth (or in fact). External purity could be assured by the perfect fulfillment of the requirements of the Law. Inner purity, however, could only be guaranteed by the gift of the spirit of holiness. Therefore baptism by water alone, although necessary for ritual purity, was not sufficient. Baptism by the spirit was also essential and could only be acquired through the earnest seeking of a man's heart.[49]

A corollary to this baptism by the spirit would be an inner understanding of the Law which could not be taught by men—God's writing of the Law "on the hearts" of men. The spirit, they believed, was able to reveal secrets—depths of understanding and perception—which no teacher, no matter how excellent, could do.[50] For that same reason, though the Teacher of Righteousness had "revealed" many secrets to the Covenanters, only those who had received the gift of the spirit could truly *understand* those mysteries.[51]

The Poor entered the New Covenant, with its rigorous requirements, for only a year at a time. Each year, each man was examined by the Assembly and admonished in the way of truth by his brethren. If he was found to have been faithful to the Covenant and to have grown in righteousness, both in understanding and in deed, he was assigned his rank in the community for the coming year. If anyone had fallen back in his spiritual life, his status was reduced and, if necessary, a penalty prescribed in accordance with the Manual of Discipline. The penalties were very severe.[52]

Then a ceremony of the Renewal of the Covenant was held at which time all members renewed their vows and perhaps were even rebaptized.[53] This ceremony of the Renewal of the Covenant was held on the Feast of Weeks, or Pentecost—that is, seven weeks or fifty days after the Passover feast which commemorates the delivery of the children of Israel from Egypt. Pentecost (which in Greek means fifty days), or the Feast of Weeks, was the occasion for the Many to rejoice in the New Covenant into which they had entered with God, just as Moses had led the people to enter into the first Covenant with God at Sinai. The sign and seal of Moses' Covenant with God was Torah, the Law; the seal of the New Covenant was the gift of the spirit of holiness to the Poor.[54]

ANTICIPATING THE MESSIAH

The Qumran Covenanters lived a disciplined life of ritual purity and of righteous perfection according to the Law. Their desert headquarters was the home of the nucleus of the righteous remnant—a group which was organized and ready at any time to fight alongside the Messiah, to assume control over the Temple and its priestly office, and to reign in justice and mercy with the Messiah. Nonpriestly members of the Poor and all those who belonged to sister communities, both priests and laymen, were organized for battle according to the prescriptions of the War Scroll and had daily maneuvers in order to assure their readiness for the confrontation with the children of darkness. In fact, as A. R. C. Leaney, author of *The Rule of Qumran and Its Meaning,* points out, willingness to fight in the war of the sons of light against the sons of darkness was a specific requirement of membership in the Qumran community.[55] The only missing element of their apocalyptic scheme was the Messiah himself.

In the Qumran literature, Messianic expectations were nearly as diverse as—though perhaps more highly developed than—those of Jews in general during that period. In an age when the anticipation of the Messiah's advent was more intense and urgent than perhaps at any other time in the history of Israel before or since, all of the prophecies even remotely related to the end of days were studied, meditated upon, and applied to the events of their day. There were as many Messianic expectations as there were prophecies about the last days.[56] Some of the main currents of thought about, or images of, the Messiah held during that period from 165 B.C. to A.D. 70 were:

(1) That the Messiah would be a prophet like Moses.[57] This expectation was held most fervently by the Samaritans, but was among the threads of other tapestries of hope as well, including that at Qumran. The basic theme was that a prophet would arise who, like Moses, would give the people a new Law to inaugurate the new Kingdom. As far as the Samaritans were concerned, no man could be "like" Moses, for he had been the perfect lawgiver. They therefore expected the reincarnation of Moses himself—Moses "redivivus." Others were not so explicit about the image as the Samaritans were, but looked for a lawgiver who would be *the* prophet of Deuteronomy 18:15–18.[58]

(2) That the Messiah would be Elijah returned. A widely held expectation was that the prophet Elijah would return, as prophesied by Malachi, and, like "a voice crying in the wilderness," announce the imminent inauguration of the Kingdom.[59] He was sometimes identified with "the" prophet of Deuteronomy mentioned above.

(3) That a Davidic Messiah would come. In fulfillment of the prophecies in Isaiah, and Jeremiah, many expected a great leader from the house of David to rise up and lead his people to freedom over their oppressors.[60] The Davidic Messiah would be principally a military leader who would command the troops in the final war and accomplish the redemption of Israel by establishing a free nation once again. This would fulfill God's promise that He would establish the throne of David forever (II Sam. 7:11–17). The Davidic Messiah would be the lay head of the New Israel and would rule as universal king until the end of the age when either a priestly Messiah or the Son of Man would assume the throne in a Kingdom which would unite "heaven" and earth.[61]

(4) That an Anointed Priest would come. There was among many the expectation that the Messiah would be of the line of Aaron (or Levi), the faithful priest of prophecy, the Star of Jacob, and that he would be the mediator before God on behalf of His people to end all sacrifice because of the righteous fulfillment of the Law by all of God's People.[62] In the Qumran expectation this priestly Messiah was to come after the royal one. When the battle was over, he would reign alongside of the Davidic Messiah, apparently in higher rank since he was assigned a more important role at the Messianic banquet.[63]

(5)   That the Son of Man would come. The first mention of the Son of Man (in the apocalyptic literature) is by the prophet Daniel (7:13), and the concept is much elaborated upon in the apocalyptic work, the Similitudes of Enoch (I En. 37–71). This figure had the marks of a kind of prototype of humanity—the perfect image, or Second Adam, in whose likeness all men were made or would be made in the new Kingdom. The Son of Man when used in this way appears to be a corporate image of mankind in its perfection rather than an individual person. This heavenly figure was not expected until the warfare between the children of light and the children of darkness had ended, and thus is not usually considered a Messianic figure. We mention him here because the term is used frequently in the New Testament, often by Jesus himself, and because it is also confused with the concept of a Messiah.[64]

All the prophetic images of the Messiah listed above can be found in the Qumran literature. The Son of Man is not mentioned in the sectarian literature, but neither is it, properly considered, a Messianic image. The concepts which predominated in Qumranian literature are the Davidic (royal) and Aaronic (priestly) Messiahs, to be preceded by a forerunner, either "the prophet" (of Deuteronomy) or Elijah.[65] At Qumran, as elsewhere in Israel at this time, the object was not to restrict one's vision by making the expectation too precise, but rather to expand it by setting forth all the possibilities so that men would have "eyes to see and ears to hear" when the Messiah did appear.

There is some indication in the Qumran literature that the sect believed the Teacher of Righteousness to have been a kind of Messianic forerunner,[66] but evidently in the priestly rather than the prophetic tradition. He was a Zadokite priest and was given a special title by the sect, the Teacher of Righteousness, connoting neither a prophetic nor a Messianic function. Whether they expected him to return after death as prophet, priest, or king is an open question. A passage in the Damascus Document (6:2–10) which suggests that the Teacher of Righteousness will come, or "arise," at the end of days is not explicit enough to indicate whether it refers to his first appearance as their teacher (since they believed themselves to be already in the end of days) or to his resurrection after death.[67] But whether or not the Teacher of Righteousness was expected to return, that the Covenanters looked for a prophetic forerunner and both a priestly and a royal Messiah seems quite clear.[68]

QUMRAN AND THE GREAT REVOLT

It would not have been out of character, then, for the Poor at Qumran to have joined in full force in the Revolt of A.D. 66. If they believed, as apparently most Jews did, that the Great Revolt was the beginning of the final battle, they would certainly have fought with full vigor, expecting all the while that God would send his angelic forces, under the command of Michael the Archangel, to ensure the victory. Perhaps the Temple priesthood was entrusted into their hands in the Revolt when the provisionary government was set up. In any case, the destruction of the Temple and the Fall of Jerusalem, far from discouraging them, would have fired their expectation of an immediate and victorious culmination to the struggle, since those very events were essential to the establishment of the new Temple, the new Jerusalem, the new Israel: that is, the Kingdom of God.

It is not surprising, therefore, that the highly respected British scholar G. R. Driver and the late Cecil Roth, for many years a scholar of Jewish history, have each developed the thesis that the sectarians at Qumran were Zealots.[69] Surely their literature has nationalistic and warlike themes and overtones, and archaeological excavations at Qumran reveal that the headquarters was destroyed by the Roman legions in the second year of the Great Revolt. Moreover, the Qumran calendar was discovered in the storage room of the Synagogue on top of Masada where the last 960 defenders made their final desperate stand against Rome. It seems likely that by the time of the Revolt all apocalyptic and nationalistic revolutionaries would have been seeking "the" leader who could see them through to victory, and "philosophical" differences would have receded into the background.[70] The Qumran Covenanters could well have been among the "zealots" at Masada.

As Matthew Black, one of the leading Dead Sea Scrolls scholars, says: "No sharp line of distinction . . . can be drawn between an other-worldly eschatology and the political aspirations of the [Qumran] sect even in their wildest dreams of world dominion. The birth-pangs of the new age, the Kingdom of God, were to be the death-throes of the old age, the overthrow of the dominion of Satan represented by the kingdoms of this world . . . The Essene group who held the fort at Qumran at the outbreak of the First Revolt . . . had ceased, at least in their leadership and dominant elements, to be the pacific ascetics idealized by Josephus and Philo; they had by then thrown in their lot with Zealot and Pharisaic groups."[71]

A fragment discovered on Masada surely reflects the sentiment which must have prevailed both in the Temple, as thousands of Jews died in battle, and on Masada, where the last rebels committed suicide rather than submit to Roman slavery. Still strong in their conviction that God would save Israel and establish His Kingdom on earth, and confident that they had done their best to be faithful and righteous, they could well have cried out in perfect trust of God's plan that His Kingdom would be established on earth and the righteous dead would be raised up to share in it: "Son of Man, these bones are the whole House of Israel."[72]

It is this spirit of nationalism based on an intense apocalyptic fervor which permeates the New Testament, and it is only in this context that Jesus can be properly understood.

CHAPTER 5

Jesus and the Early Christians: A Continuity of the Qumran Tradition

"Is it possible that God has rejected his people? Of course not. I, an Israelite, descended from Abraham through the tribe of Benjamin, could never agree that God had rejected his people, the people he chose specially long ago. Do you remember what scripture says of Elijah—how he complained to God about Israel's behaviour? 'Lord, they have killed your prophets and broken down your altars. I, and I only, remain, and they want to kill me.' What did God say to that? 'I have kept for myself seven thousand men who have not bent the knee to Ba'al.' Today the same thing has happened: there is a remnant . . ."

Romans 11:1–5

In the words of James A. Pike:

"The narratives about Jesus' birth cannot really be called myth-making in the ordinary sense of the word. Matthew, for example, was trying to show that Jesus fulfilled all the possible prophecies about the Messiah, and he reached for it, really, for some of the prophecies don't necessarily have any Messianic connection.

"Take, for example, the prophecy 'He shall be called a Nazarene.' There is no prophet who said that, as far as we know. All of the other quotes can be found somewhere, but this one is not anywhere in the prophets. But Matthew thought there was, so he needed to have Jesus fulfill it. He solved the problem by having Jesus go to Nazareth to live.

"But he had to be from Bethlehem, too, because the prophet said, 'And you, O Bethlehem, in the land of Judah, are by no means least among the rulers of Judah; for from you shall come a ruler who will govern my people Israel.' Now that doesn't say very much, really, because it doesn't say the ruler will be the Messiah, but Matthew wanted to be sure it was fulfilled. So he had Jesus born in Bethlehem.

"In Matthew's account, then, Joseph and Mary seem to be from Bethlehem. They leave there to go into Egypt in order to get away from Herod who is trying to kill all the male children under two in order to be sure that he kills Jesus. Matthew seems to have included the story about the killing of the innocents in order to fulfill the prophecy about Rachel weeping for her children in Ramah, near Bethlehem. It is when Joseph and Mary and Jesus are returning from Egypt that they are warned in a dream not to go back to Bethlehem, and so they go up into Galilee and settle down for the first time in a place called Nazareth.

"In Luke's account, however, Joseph and Mary are from Galilee and only go down to Bethlehem for a census which was being taken by order of Quirinius, the governor of Syria. So that's a whole different approach, and it has its difficulties. Not only is it different from Matthew's story, but the census under Quirinius was not held until A.D. 6, and Jesus seems to have been born in 4 B.C. which was the last year of Herod's reign. It doesn't add up too well.

"There are other texts Matthew felt had to be fulfilled, such as the one from Isaiah, 'A virgin shall conceive and bear a son, and his name shall be called Emmanuel.' Now Matthew took the text from the Septuagint Bible that was used in Alexandria, Egypt —in fact, it was prepared there in Greek for Greek-speaking Jews and others—and there was a mistranslation of the Hebrew version which said, 'A young woman shall conceive.' Now 'young woman' and 'virgin' are not exactly opposites, but they are not actually identical either. If Matthew had had a Hebrew Bible to work with, he wouldn't have had to fulfill the prophecy of 'a virgin birth.'

"And so it goes, item after item. It is not mythological. It is seeing to it that prophecies are fulfilled. And Matthew says what he is doing each time: 'All this took place to fulfill what the Lord had spoken to the prophet'; and then the prophecy is quoted.

"I think the story can best be started by saying that Jesus was a Galilean. Mark begins by plainly stating that Jesus came from Nazareth in Galilee to be baptized by John. Jesus functioned in Galilee. It was an area that was more rebellious against Rome than any other part of the country, to the point that to be called a Galilean was to be under suspicion. This is revealed in the story about Peter warming himself by the fire outside Caiaphas' palace during Jesus' trial. They said, 'Isn't he a Galilean, too?' That was something like calling someone a communist back in the Joe McCarthy era.

"Jesus was from Galilee. He was a Galilean. He lived and worked in the heart of his country's breeding ground for revolutionaries. His followers later came to believe he was the Messiah, or 'deliverer' of his people."

QUMRAN AND THE CHRISTIAN CHURCH

The movement which centered around Jesus after his death—and later came to be called the Christian Church—was very similar to that which had its geographical center at Qumran. We cannot go into a detailed discussion of the similarities and differences here,[1] but it is important to sketch briefly the parallels between the two movements in order to round out our basic theme: that Jesus can only be properly understood when he is looked at in the context of apocalyptic nationalism, of which Qumran is an outstanding example.

As F. F. Bruce, Rylands Professor of Biblical Criticism and Exegesis at the University of Manchester in England, has said: "When any object is viewed against a new background, the object itself takes on a fresh appearance, and against the background supplied by the Qumran discoveries many parts of the New Testament take on a new and vivid significance."[2] Professor Bruce goes on to observe that those passages of the New Testament which reveal that the early Christians considered themselves to be the "righteous remnant" of Israel preparing the way for the final fulfillment of the promised Kingdom of God are much easier to understand when viewed in the light of the parallel beliefs of the contemporary Qumran community.

Frank Moore Cross, Jr., a Harvard professor and member of the international staff editing the Qumran manuscripts, has made a most interesting point in this regard. He is convinced that the primitive Christian Church must in some sense be considered a continuation of the style of life and beliefs of Qumran. "It is not merely by chance," he says, that so much of the apocalyptic literature "survived almost solely in a Christian milieu" and was suppressed in Rabbinic Judaism, which became normative after the Fall of Jerusalem.[3]

Professor Cross rightly observes that the New Testament and the sayings attributed to Jesus include too many parallels out of Jewish apocalyptic writings to allow any conclusion other than that Christianity represents a continuity of traditions.[4] Certainly there can be no question that the early Christian communities had a self-understanding which was essentially the same as that of the sect at Qumran: both believed themselves to be the "called and chosen Congregation of the End of Days."[5] As A. R. C. Leaney points out, the Qumran Covenanters' belief that they were the remnant of Israel to be established at the end of the ages was shared by both the Zealots *and* the early Christian Church.[6]

The parallels to, and antecedents of, Christian forms and concepts are of great significance, for between the Jewish apocalyptic communities such as that at Qumran and the early Christian Church stands Jesus—surely not outside the same tradition. Let us consider the similarities, then:

The self-understanding of the two communities was similar. Both the sectarians at Qumran and the early Christians believed they were living in "the last days" and that in some sense the new Kingdom was already being inaugurated. Both understood themselves to be the "new" Israel living in the midst of the events which would bring to a climax the "old" age. Both groups searched the scriptures for "signs of the times" and interpreted the events of their own age in the light of Old Testament prophecies.

However, the early Christians believed they were living in a "later" moment in the approaching of the end of days.[7] The Messiah expected daily by the Qumran community had already been revealed for the early Christians and his resurrection was evidence of the beginning of the "new creation." The Kingdom was closer to being fully established for the early Christians and they believed the whole process would be culminated quickly—within their generation. Therefore the Christians turned toward Gentiles to urge them also to repent. This attempt to redeem the whole world was anticipated by the Covenanters at Qumran,[8] but it was to take place *after* the appearance of the Messiah who would save Israel first, and only secondarily reach out to the "nations." Some of the early Christians, believing the Messiah *had come* in Jesus, moved to the second phase of activity by welcoming Gentiles into their movement.

Jesus himself stood more within the Qumran "moment," as is seen in his words: "I was sent only to the lost sheep of the House of Israel" and "The children should be fed first, because it is not fair to take the children's food and throw it to the house-dogs" (Mt. 15:24

and Mk. 7:27). But because of Jesus' death and resurrection, the timing of the final events had been advanced, his disciples believed. To quote again from Professor F. M. Cross:

> "We should emphasize that the New Testament faith was not a new faith, but the fulfillment of an old faith. The Church is precisely Israel in its own self-understanding. Jesus did not propose to present a new system of universal truths. He came to fulfill the past work of God, to confirm the faith of the fathers, to open the meaning of the Law and Prophets. The New Testament does not set aside or supplant the Old Testament. It affirms it and, from its point of view, completes it. Lines of continuity between Moses and Jesus, Isaiah and Jesus, the Righteous Teacher and Jesus, John the Baptist and Jesus should occasion no surprise. On the contrary, a biblical faith insists on such continuities. The biblical faith is not a system of ideas, but a history of God's acts of redemption.
>
> "It is not the idea of redemption through suffering but the 'event' of the crucifixion understood as the atoning work of God that distinguishes Christianity. It is not the doctrine of resurrection but faith in the resurrection of Jesus as an eschatological event which forms the basis of the Christian decision of faith. It is not faith that a Messiah will come that gives Christianity its special character, but the assurance that Jesus rules as the Messiah who has come and will come. It is not the hope of a New Creation that lends uniqueness to Christianity, but the faith that Jesus is the New Adam, the first of the New Creation. Finally, it is not a 'love ethic' that distinguishes Christianity from Judaism—far from it. The Christian faith is distinguished from the ancient faith which brought it to birth in its knowledge of a new act of God's love, the revelation of His love in Jesus' particular life and death and resurrection."[9]

In other words, the beliefs the Christians held were not different from those of the Poor at Qumran. The difference in the two groups lay solely in the fact that the Christians believed all the prophecies had been fulfilled in Jesus. That God had already acted to save His People Israel and that His Kingdom was already—in some sense at least—established on earth. The Christians were certain the time would be *very* short before the whole redemptive process would be completed.

The teachings of the two communities were similar. Both Qumran and the early Christians spoke of the war between the forces of light and the forces of darkness,[10] anticipating the final defeat of the forces of evil by God with the help of his angelic troops and the children of light, among whom both communities counted themselves.

Both groups attributed their ability to do righteousness, to walk in the way of truth and to love one another to the gift of the spirit of truth, or the spirit of holiness, or the holy spirit or "Christ's own spirit." The spirit of truth is in this view seen as a helper to the children of light, and the "children" are enabled by its mediation to live in the Kingdom even though the final victory has not yet been won and those who are under the devil's power still walk in ways of darkness.[11]

Both groups speak of the same Messianic expectations. However, by a process of Biblical commentary very much like that used at Qumran, in the New Testament Jesus is shown to have *already fulfilled* all the prophecies. He is principally identified as the Davidic or royal Messiah.[12] However, John's Gospel implies that Jesus is "the prophet" of Deuteronomy by reporting, for example, "Some of the people said, 'Surely he must be the prophet'" (Jn. 7:40).[13] And in Acts 3:22, Peter identifies Jesus precisely with the Prophet.

In the Epistle to the Hebrews an elaborate case is made for understanding Jesus to have been a priest according to the order of Melchizedek. According to the argument presented there, Jesus had fulfilled both the priestly and the royal Messianic expectations—an argument which could well have been designed to win over members of the Qumran movement who were expecting two Messianic figures.

In other words, both Qumran and the early Christian movement had highly developed Messianic expectations, the basic difference being that for the Christians those expectations had already been fulfilled in Jesus.[14]

The organization of the two communities was similar. Both the Qumran sect and the Jerusalem Church[15] led lives of communal sharing of property and both imposed punishments on those who deceived their brethren regarding their possessions.[16] Both had a democratic assembly (literally, "the Many" in both the Qumran literature and the Book of Acts[17]), a council of twelve (which seems related in both cases to the function of ruling over and judging the twelve tribes of Israel in the new Kingdom[18]), and an episcopal overseer, or "bishop."[19] Both had as their central rites, baptism and a communal meal.[20] Both saw repentance and entrance into a life of righteousness as necessary for participation in the New Covenant[21] and both felt the added gift of the spirit was a sign of internal purity and righteousness.[22] Both were associated with baptism by water *and* the spirit,[23] and the common meal had a Messianic significance for both.[24]

Both advocated a discipline appropriate to soldiers already mustered and prepared for the Holy War of the end of times—that is, keeping the "purity of their camps."[25] Therefore both advocated restraint from sexual intercourse and marriage—not as an expression of genuine asceticism but as what has been called an "interim ethic": their discipline was for the brief time remaining before Armageddon (the final battle) rather than an expression of the inherent evil of sexuality.[26]

These similarities make it quite apparent that the early Church stood in a direct line of continuity with the tradition represented by the sect at Qumran. Even the names used by the sectarians survive in the early Christian movement. The canon of scriptures, once put together, is called *The New Testament* (Covenant), and Paul reports Jesus as having initiated his disciples into the *New Covenant* at the last meal he had with them.[27] Jesus talks over and over again about *the poor* and there is reason to believe that many times he was referring to movements such as that at Qumran rather than to conditions of economic poverty. In the Book of Acts the young Church is called *the way,* as is Qumran, and even the word *church,* which in Greek (*ecclesía*) means "called out" or "called apart," gives a significance to the group's reason for being which is similar to the Qumran movement's having "separated itself" from evil men to become a righteous remnant.[28]

How then must Jesus have been related to the Qumran sect and how are his life, death, and resurrection to be understood in the light of the context in which he so obviously stood?

WHO WAS JESUS?

Once an understanding of the history of the Jewish people and the temper of the times in which Jesus lived gives us "eyes to see," it is not difficult to gather data from the Gospel accounts themselves with which to paint a vivid picture of Jesus and the movement he launched. The birth narratives and the genealogies in Matthew and Luke and the prologue to John's Gospel do not really concern us in a study of the historical Jesus, for all three are recognized by

Biblical scholars as interpretive appendages to the narratives added long after Jesus' death.[29]

Several elements of these "prefaces" to the stories of Jesus' life are of interest to us, however, because of what they tell us of the Gospel writers' understanding of Jesus. It should be noted, for example, that both Matthew and Luke go to great lengths, by means of genealogies which are inconsistent with one another (!), to prove that Jesus is a "son of David" and therefore of proper lineage to have been the long-expected Davidic Messiah.[30] In both genealogies Jesus' parentage is traced through his father Joseph,[31] even though the same authors also include the later strands of material attributing to Jesus a virgin birth by Mary and thus leaving Joseph out of the picture of Jesus' birth altogether as far as genealogy is concerned.

It is nevertheless apparent that it seemed important to both Matthew and Luke to establish Jesus' legitimacy as the Davidic Messiah, the primary image he is portrayed as fulfilling in the Gospels, and that the virgin birth narratives were added as a way of reading back into his very beginnings his special election by God. They are, as Bishop Pike used to say, larger frames put around the picture of Jesus to pay proper respect to it.

Second, it is of interest that woven into the Lukan birth narrative are two Maccabean war songs which apparently were adapted for the third Gospel from a first-century literary record called the "Baptist Document." Paul Winter, an eminent Jewish scholar whose personal suffering at the hands of anti-Semites during the German holocaust of the 1930s and 40s sparked particular interest for him in the development of Christianity, believes the original document dealt with the birth of John the Baptist.[32] Because of the close tie between John the Baptist and Jesus in their preaching and teaching, which is discussed in the following chapter, the origin of these songs merits special attention.

The hymns, which Christians have called the *Magnificat* (Lk. 1:46b–55) and the *Benedictus* (Lk. 1:68–75), resemble in form and phraseology other battle hymns which can be found in Biblical literature, such as those in I Chronicles 16:8–36 and I Samuel 2:1–10. They were, according to Paul Winter, first used by the author of the narrative of John the Baptist's birth as appropriate responses for John's mother and father to make on the occasion of John's birth. The author of the Baptist document, Winter believes, would have known them as Maccabean songs written and sung by a poet who had been one of a band of Jewish warriors and wanted to celebrate the fact that princes had been put down in the revolt and that the poor had been exalted.[33]

The songs would probably have circulated among the people for a period of several generations before they were finally written down as part of the Baptist document.

That these songs were later woven into the fabric of Luke's narrative of Jesus' birth suggests that the Gospel writer wanted to portray Jesus as a royal (Davidic) commander of the troops who "defeated" the enemies of Israel in the brave tradition of the Maccabean freedom fighters. When Zacharias and Elizabeth, parents of John the Baptist, speak the words of the hymns in the Lukan narrative,[34] the clear implication is that they apply to Jesus instead of to John. "He [God] has shown the power of his arm, he has routed the proud of heart. He has pulled down princes from their thrones and exalted the lowly. The hungry he has filled with good things, the rich sent empty away" (Lk. 1:51b–53).

These are the words of a psalm of thanksgiving which must have originally been sung after battle and which has clearly revolutionary overtones. As a part of Luke's narrative of Jesus' birth, the implication is certainly quite clear that Jesus would "lead a revolution."

"Blessed be the Lord, the God of Israel,
   for he has visited his people, he has come to their rescue
   and he has raised up for us a power for salvation
   in the House of his servant David,
   even as he proclaimed,
   by the mouth of his holy prophets from ancient times,
   that he would save us from our enemies
   and from the hands of all who hate us.
   Thus he shows mercy to our ancestors,
   thus he remembers his holy covenant,
   the oath he swore
   to our father Abraham
   that he would grant us, free from fear,
   to be delivered from the hands of our enemies,
   to serve him in holiness and virtue
   in his presence, all our days . . ." (Lk. 1:68–75)

This song of joyful praise originally sung before battle speaks clearly, in its new context, of the expectations of Jesus' followers that he would deliver them from their enemies in fulfillment of God's promise, as His part of the Covenant, and that He would establish Israel in freedom and in peace. The "enemies" spoken of should not be "spiritualized" as Christians have so often done, for to lift them out of the context of the history of Israel as a poor and subject people would be to alter the meaning of a whole tradition. It is clear that both Jesus and John the Baptist were seen by the Gospel writers as related to, and standing in the tradition of, the Maccabean rebels who fought for and won Israel's freedom.

GALILEE AND THE REVOLUTION

A third thing which we learn from the birth narratives is that Jesus' family, and therefore Jesus himself, was from Galilee.[35] This is significant since Galilee was the region in which the guerrilla activities of the freedom fighters were centered from the Maccabean Revolt through to that of A.D. 66. Being far to the north of Jerusalem and separated from the region of Judea by Samaria, the Galileans lived much more independently of the Temple cultus and of the authority of the High Priest and his associates than did other Jews. It was in Galilee that the tradition of the oral Law grew strong, a chief advocate of which was Rabbi Hillel (first century B.C.) who felt that the Law should be interpreted in such a way as to make it tolerable for the common people. It was also in Galilee that the synagogue movement flourished, for local priests had never really ceased their tribal-centered sacrifices there. Rabbi Hillel and others tried to help the local priests blend in with the Temple-centered cultus of Judea by encouraging them to develop centers of learning. These "synagogues" were not rivals of the Temple cult, but important interpreters of it.

The hasidic movement—that is, those pious ones who advocated a strict adherence to the spirit of the ancient Law and to the Mosaic Covenant—was very strong in Galilee, perhaps as a reaction to the fact that Hellenization had progressed much faster in Galilee than in other areas. The Sadducees, who kept only the external form of the Law and who were composed primarily of wealthy aristocrats who often collaborated with the foreign powers, not only had no foothold in Galilee, but were violently opposed by the Galileans.

The people in Galilee were on the whole much poorer, less educated and more rural, or agrarian, in their orientation than those who lived in Judea. At the time of Jesus, taxation in Galilee had risen to 40 percent of the earnings of the peasants—an intolerable burden for an already poor people. It is not surprising that out of Galilee came a movement of devout men who took religious vows of poverty. The *hasidim,* or pious ones, identified themselves by their very mode of life with their poor countrymen all around, and made a virtue of the life of poverty that most men lived of necessity. Nor is it surprising that the Galileans should have been more rebellious than the Judean Jews. Their devout adherence to Torah and the Covenant inspired a fervor for independence; their suspicion of the Temple priesthood and the Sadducean rulers, and their insufferable economic plight gave them a pragmatic impetus to revolt.[36]

No youth growing up in Galilee could have failed to have heard many stories of brave Galileans who fought for the freedom of Israel and for the sovereignty of God and God alone. Not only did the feast of Hanukkah celebrate the Maccabean revolt and victory, for example, but members of the Maccabean family were local heroes and near idols. A custom grew up in Galilee of naming one's children after the Maccabean heroes as a way of identifying with their revolutionary cause.[37]

A study of the names of all Jews mentioned by the historian Josephus in his accounts covering the period between 4 B.C. and A.D. 70 shows that Maccabean names (Matthias, Judas, Jonathan, Eleazar, Simon, John, and Mariamne) make up only 16 percent of the total. Of the names of all those actively engaged in the resistance of Rome, Maccabean names account for 54 percent, and of the actual leaders of seditious actions, 66 percent have Maccabean names.[38]

Since Galilee was a hotbed of seditious activity at the time of Jesus, it should not be surprising that Maccabean names were in abundance there. Yet it is still remarkable to most Christians to note that five, and perhaps six, of Jesus' twelve disciples had Maccabean names (Simon [2], Judas [2], John, and Matthew [?]), two of his brothers (Judas and Simon),[39] his mother (Mariamne is translated Mary in English), and several of his close friends.[40] It could also be mentioned that in the Book of Acts (1:23–26) a Matthias is chosen to succeed Judas among the twelve disciples—a clear echo, even if typological, of Judas and Matthias, leaders of the revolt against Rome in 4 B.C. (*War* I. 648–50). Thus Jesus is seen to have stood firmly in the tradition of Galilean veneration of the Maccabean heritage.

No doubt the crucifixion of two thousand Galileans for their uprisings against the Romans following Herod's death in 4 B.C., just about the time of Jesus' birth, would have been remembered in Galilee with great bitterness and resentment. Perhaps it is this event to which Matthew alludes in his account of the "slaughter of the innocents"

(Mt. 2:13–18) according to which Herod the Great ordered killed all the male children in the region of Bethlehem who were two years of age and younger in order to stamp out the threat of a leader arising from the House of David. The fact that Bethlehem is the "house of David" from which the Messiah was expected to arise, and the fact that the slaughter of innocents and the crucifixion of the two thousand Galileans in a Messianic uprising both occurred around the time of Jesus' birth, may be more than coincidental.[41]

Jesus would have been a young and impressionable boy of ten when the founder of the Zealot movement, the rabbi Judas of Galilee, was killed because of his attempt to convince the people not to submit to Quirinius' census. He could not help but have been influenced by the death of such a local hero. In fact, the growth of the Zealot resistance movement in the hills of Galilee must have deeply influenced and affected all young men who grew up there.

JESUS, THE NAZARENE

It is reported in the Gospels that Jesus grew up in Nazareth.[42] There is very little evidence, either archaeological or literary, of a village in Galilee named Nazareth at the time of Jesus. Even Josephus, who describes the life of Galilee and names its towns and villages in great detail, omits the village of Nazareth.[43] We can assume, then, that Nazareth was an extremely small village at the time of Jesus. Its insignificance is suggested in John's Gospel where Nathanael is said to have asked, "Can anything good come from Nazareth?" (Jn. 1:46).

Matthew associates the name of Jesus' family's village with a prophecy: "There he settled in a town called Nazareth. In this way the words spoken through the prophets were to be fulfilled: 'He will be called a Nazarene'" (Mt. 2:23). Though scholars have never discovered the prophecy to which Matthew was referring,[44] it is true that throughout the Gospels Jesus is referred to as "the Nazarene." In fact, translations which read "Jesus of Nazareth" are in error in their rendering of the Greek; they should read "Jesus the Nazarene." But perhaps the fact that Jesus was from Nazareth served to reinforce the memory of both names, even though they are not derived from the same Hebrew root and therefore "the Nazarene" does not mean "the one from Nazareth."[45]

Yet Jesus was called the Nazarene (*ha noṣri*), the early Christians were called Nazarenes (*noṣᵉrim*), and in Hebrew the name for Christians is still the same today: *noṣᵉrim*. Why would this have been so if the name "Nazarene" is not derived from "Nazareth"? The Hebrew root *nṣr* means to "keep" or to "guard." *Noṣᵉrim,* therefore, can be interpreted to mean "keepers of secrets" or "guardians of special usages or doctrines."[46] St. Paul corroborates this interpretation by referring to Christians as "stewards of the mysteries of God" (I Cor. 4:1), which were undoubtedly the "mysteries of the kingdom of heaven" referred to by Matthew (3:11). Those secrets or mysteries of the Kingdom have to do with when and how it is to come, what the signs of its approach are, who will "inherit" it, etc. Another "secret" which is kept by the Christians, according to Paul, is the "mystery of the gospel" (Eph. 6:19) or the "mystery of Christ" (Col. 4:3)—that is, who the Elect One is, what he will do and suffer, how we can know him, how the Christ saves us, etc.[47]

Secondly, that which the *noṣᵉrim* "observed" may well have been special rites of purification, baptism in particular, for the liturgical language of the Church seems to suggest this. A beatitude in the *Acts of Paul and Thekla* reads: "Blessed are they who keep the baptism," and the Church father Origen says, "And blessed is he who hath part in the first resurrection, who kept the baptism of the Holy Spirit."[48]

Finally, it appears that the ancient Rekhabites, the "caravanners" or "wayfaring people"—the various itinerant craftsmen mentioned in the Old Testament—were also known as *noṣᵉrim,* and that this "keeping" and "guarding" of secrets and special usages referred to the preservation of technical or magical "knowledge": the craftsman's secrets and tricks of his trade.[49] It may be of special significance, then, that Jesus was known as a Nazarene and that his father was a *carpenter,* for the Rekhabite (*noṣᵉrim*) craftsmen included in particular *carpenters,* along with boatbuilders, smiths, locksmiths, and gold- and silversmiths.[50] Jesus may well have been raised in a family which preserved and guarded "secrets," both of the craft of carpentry and of the Kingdom of God.

In any case, the fact that Jesus was known as "the Nazarene," or "keeper of secrets," provides further grounds for associating him with movements such as that centered at Qumran. After all, the Covenanters guarded such secrets too, and their Teacher of Righteousness had "revealed" the meaning of the secrets to them.[51]

Though we do not deal with the inner, or "hidden" meaning of

Jesus' teachings in this book nor with the "secrets" of the Qumran sect—both of which had to do with the coming of the Kingdom—it is important to take note of this aspect of Jesus' life. Certainly the most profound significance of everything we are recounting is to be found at the level of the "mysteries." A thorough grasp of the historical dimension of the life and teachings of Qumran and of Jesus introduces one to all the secret teachings but does not "reveal" them.

The Covenanters, Jesus, and the early Christians all saw themselves as living in the midst of and acting out the teachings which they held, and they believed the mysteries were being unfolded in the events of their day. Therefore a study of their lives and the history of the period should give one the basic information out of which a deeper understanding of the inner "mysteries" would grow. Any subsequent depth study of the teachings will then be grounded in reality. The writings of the Qumran community, in which the teachings revealed to them by the Teacher of Righteousness are expounded, and of the early Christians, in which Jesus' teachings are recorded, touch on the "secrets." But generally speaking, as both Jesus and the Covenanters taught, only those who have grown to a certain level of spiritual perception by their own experience—that is, those who have been baptized by the spirit of holiness—will have the inner knowledge and true understanding which will enable them to comprehend the mysteries.

Though we do not deal with the timeless, spaceless, "cosmic" dimension of the meaning of the historical events here discussed, in fact all of the events of which we write, and all of the teachings mentioned, point to a higher, or deeper, truth and reality which is "kept" for the inner circle of those baptized by the spirit of truth and of holiness. Jesus the Nazarene was one of the prime revealers of those "mysteries,"[52] and he taught that anyone who was ready to acknowledge that the Kingdom was in fact at hand, and to live as though it were true, could know the truth: "If you continue in my word . . . you will know the truth, and the truth will make you free" (Jn. 8:31b–32, RSV).

JOHN AND JESUS

Even in the narratives which developed late in the first century— long after Jesus' death—about his birth and early years, and which were largely *a*historical, we see much that indicates the revolutionary context behind the expectations which filled the minds of Jesus' followers as they interpreted Jesus' teachings and activities. The stage was clearly set for the Gospel narratives of Jesus' life.

Jesus emerges at a given point in a drama which re-enacts, to a large extent, the theme of the great Exodus from Egypt. As the apocalyptic nationalists saw it, Israel had once again sold herself into slavery. Israel lived in the midst of a pagan Hellenistic culture and served rulers and leaders who had betrayed her Covenant with God. Her only salvation, as they saw it, was for the People to withdraw to the wilderness and re-establish their Covenant with God. Many had done just that, as the tradition centered at Qumran shows. God had provided them with a leader, the Teacher of Righteousness—a kind of "new Moses"—who had revealed to them the "new" Covenant by reinterpreting the words of the prophets of Israel in the light of contemporary events.

The people of the "new Israel" devoted themselves to fulfilling the new Covenant in every regard in order that God might "lead them to the promised land." But this time, in contrast to the first Exodus, they did not expect God to provide them with a new land but rather with a transformed Israel—an Israel freed from oppression and transmuted into the Kingdom of God on earth. The historical process, they believed, was to be brought to an end in their time, and a new age inaugurated. The new creation would begin when the way of the Lord had been prepared in the wilderness. God would send a prophet, who would be (or be immediately followed by) a royal Davidic Messiah who would liberate Israel. A priestly Aaronic Messiah would then preside over the establishment of God's Kingdom on earth.

John the Baptist and Jesus appear on the scene just at the Messianic high point. According to the New Testament, John is the prophetic "voice crying in the wilderness, preparing the way of the Lord"; Jesus is the Davidic Messiah who redeems, or liberates, Israel; and the final consummation of the Kingdom (that represented by the priestly Messianic expectation) is coming in the immediate future.

In the words of the Qumran Manual of Discipline, "This is the time for the preparation of the way into the wilderness, and he shall teach them to do all that is required at that time and to separate from all those who have not turned aside from all ungodliness" (Man. of Disc. 9:19b–21a).

CHAPTER 6

John the Baptist: A Voice in the Wilderness

"A voice cries, 'Prepare in the wilderness a way for Yahweh. Make a straight highway for our God across the desert.'"   Isaiah 40:3

In the words of James A. Pike:

"John the Baptist, without any doubt, stemmed from the Qumran tradition. But he didn't dress in a white robe like the Essenes did; he dressed like the prophet Elijah. Perhaps here we are getting near to myth-making, but John is portrayed as having acted out the role of Elijah. Just as Elijah came out of the desert dressed in camel's hair, so did John. John does all the things that Elijah did, as though he were Elijah returned. Elijah was supposed to come back, in the Judean tradition, before the Kingdom could be established.

"John the Baptist's approach was, if you announce the coming of the Kingdom, it will come. You baptize like mad—you get a lot of people in on the right side, among the elect, by having them repent and be prepared for it—prepared as God's agents.

"But John the Baptist did not succeed, as you know. He had his head cut off. John was written up by Josephus as being killed as a rebel. The New Testament didn't put it quite that way, but the fact that he raised the issue of Herod's marriage to his brother's wife was sufficient to show that he was a rebellious fellow! And then the fact that he was preaching the coming of the Kingdom of God as against the oppressors was certainly seditious.

"Then along comes Jesus, doing the same thing: announcing the Kingdom; even using John the Baptist's words. The two obviously had a lot in common."

JOHN THE BAPTIST AND QUMRAN

The accounts of Jesus' life given by the Gospel writers assume a background and an understanding of the traditions we have been describing. They are not designed to give the reader textbook coverage of the history of the Jewish people and their beliefs. Rather, they interpret the life of one man—Jesus—in the light of scriptures which include, it must now be acknowledged, not only the canonical Old Testament but also the Apocrypha, the Pseudepigrapha, and the sectarian writings of the Qumran Covenanters, plus, perhaps, other writings of which we do not yet have copies.

The Gospel writers begin, then, by introducing us to John the Baptist who, they explain, was preaching in the wilderness of Judea (the home region of the "new Israel," the Qumran sect) saying, "Repent, for the kingdom of heaven is close at hand" (Mt. 3:1–2). In fulfillment of the prophecy of Isaiah 40:3, John was, the Synoptic Gospel writers make clear, "The voice of one crying in the wilderness: Prepare the way for the Lord, make his paths straight" (Mt. 3:3, RSV). Many people went out to hear him and he urged them to change their ways, to begin to bear fruits of righteousness, and to be baptized as a sign of repentance, for "one" was coming after him who would baptize with the spirit and with fire.[1]

How are we meant to interpret this portrayal of John and his teachings? We should first notice that what John announced publicly by his preaching was essentially the meaning and significance of the Qumran sect. Their Manual of Discipline (7:13–16) says:

> They shall separate from the habitation of ungodly men and shall go into the wilderness to prepare the way of Him; as it is written,
>> "Prepare in the wilderness the way of [the Lord];
>> make straight in the desert a path for our God."
> This path is the study of the Law which He commanded by the hand of Moses, that they may do according to all that has been revealed from age to age, and as the Prophets have revealed by His Holy Spirit.

Moreover, John's style of life bears strong resemblance to that of the Many at Qumran. He lived in the wilderness, dressed in a simple garment of camel's hair with a leather girdle around his waist, and ate only food which grew naturally on the land—locusts and wild honey.[2] Not only the locale and the simplicity of dress are reminiscent of the Many, but even the food.[3] The Damascus Document (12:12–15) mentions three kinds of food eaten by the sectarians—honey, fish, and locusts. This may mean nothing more than that such food was typical of the wilderness area, but by maintaining such a diet John would have kept himself pure even by the food laws of Qumran.

In not eating bread and not drinking wine,[4] however, John would have differed from the Poor at Qumran where bread and wine were regularly included in their communal meals.[5] It may be, therefore, as is suggested by Charles H. H. Scobie,[6] professor of New Testament Literature and Exegesis at the Presbyterian College in Montreal, that John had taken a vow of abstinence and was trying to demonstrate by his fasting the repentance and humility before God which he demanded in his preaching, rather than simply reflecting background with or training by the Covenanters. Nevertheless, he would not have made himself unacceptable to the Many by his life style and habits, since they conformed, even if incidentally, to the Qumran Rule. Therefore, it is at least possible that John was, or had been, in some way associated with Qumran.

The Many at Qumran did not recruit members from the masses. Rather, they were highly selective and gave their teachings only to those who were willing to spend two years in preparation for initiation into the New Covenant. Therefore, it would appear that if John was associated with Qumran, he had embarked on a venture which was a kind of "missionary arm" of the movement of which Qumran was the center. He stood apart from the community and declared that the way of the Lord was to be prepared in the desert and that the Kingdom was in fact at hand. By this message he seemed to be affirming the role of the Qumran sect and others like it, implying that they had successfully "atoned" for Israel so that the Kingdom could in fact come. John warned all those who were not yet prepared, to repent and to cleanse themselves both ritually (by baptism) and actually (by deeds) so that they too could enter the Kingdom which was about to be established. Presumably he and his followers felt they were already living in that Kingdom.

We cannot know, of course, whether John ever belonged to the Qumran sect. There are many scholars who believe he must have at least been closely associated with them,[7] but our information about his life is very limited. What we do know is that he grew up in the wilderness (Lk. 1:80). Since the Rule of the Congregation (1:7–22)

of Qumran makes provision for the training of those who came as
children for instruction, and for their assimilation by stages as adult
members, and since according to Josephus the Essenes "adopt other
men's children, while yet pliable and docile, and regard them as their
kin and mould them in accordance with their own principles" (*War* II.
120), it is possible John was raised by the Covenanters. He later
emerges in the wilderness of Judea preaching a message steeped in
the thought which is expounded in the writings collected at Qumran.
It would not, therefore, seem unlikely that John grew up at Qumran
and perhaps was even a full-fledged member of the sect until he felt
called to publicly announce the Kingdom and to baptize the masses so
that they might also be prepared.

JOHN'S MESSAGE AND BELIEFS

Whether or not John was raised by the Covenanters or ever belonged
to the movement in the formal sense, it cannot be doubted that he
was strongly influenced by them. In fact, his style of life and his
preaching, which formerly seemed eccentric and ascetic to Christians,
now can be seen to have belonged to a major stream of first-century
Judaism—the very stream out of which Christianity must also have
emerged. The Dead Sea Scrolls have given us the background we
needed to understand John's message and his customs. As Dr. Scobie
has put it, "the Scrolls support the view which sees John in the context
of a number of roughly similar groups active in the Jordan valley area
and making up a non-conformist, baptist, sectarian movement within
the Judaism of the period. This movement forms the background of
John's ministry, and undoubtedly influenced his thought at many
points. It is from this movement that John emerges as an independent
and individual figure with a highly distinctive message of his own, a
message which in its simplicity and prophetic urgency, in its call for
repentance and cleansing, in its confident proclamation of a new age
about to dawn was used, in the providence of God, as the starting
point for the mission and ministry of the historical Jesus."[8]

As Professor Scobie indicates, John was not alone in the wilderness.
There were many devout Jews who sought to prepare a way in the
wilderness by repenting of their sins and being baptized into a life of
righteousness.[9] John stood in that tradition and he, like the Covenant-

ers, regarded persons who had not so repented and been baptized as utterly defiled and belonging to the realm of Belial, or Satan. Therefore, "when he saw a number of Pharisees and Sadducees coming for baptism he said to them, 'Brood of vipers, who warned you to fly from the retribution that is coming?'" (Mt. 3:7).[10] And John, again like the Covenanters, considered that only those who in spirit and in truth were righteous could be considered the true Israel: "But if you are repentant, produce the appropriate fruit, and do not presume to tell yourselves, 'We have Abraham for our father'; because, I tell you, God can raise children for Abraham from these stones [i.e., out here in the desert]" (Mt. 3:8–9).[11]

John believed, as the Covenanters did, that when the Messiah came to establish the Kingdom there would be a judgment day and only the righteous would be saved. The children of Belial would be cast out into darkness where they would suffer and burn in the eternal fire. Perhaps he differed in his degree of urgency, however, in that he seemed to feel the Messiah was at hand and the judgment imminent: "Even now the axe is laid to the roots of the trees, so that any tree which fails to produce good fruit will be cut down and thrown on the fire" (Mt. 3:10).[12] He advocated, therefore, that his listeners share their possessions (Lk. 3:10–11), imitating to at least that degree the communal commitment of the Covenanters, and make the best of the other circumstances of their lives (Lk. 3:12–14) since the end was coming soon.

But more than that, John also required "righteousness" on the part of those who received his baptism. "The 'way of the *torah*' leading to 'liberation from many tyrants,' as inculcated by John, demanded then of the people a complete fulfillment of the law alike in its moral and in its political aspect. From the moral point of view it required 'perfect justice toward men and piety toward God';[13] in the political sphere obedience to the law concerning the Israelitish monarchy, i.e., the installation of a native king chosen by God, non-recognition of foreign rule, refusal of the oath of allegiance, and perhaps also a refusal to pay taxes to foreigners such as was required of the Jews by Judas the Galilaean."[14] In this regard John also resembles the Covenanters.

It was not, therefore, in his message or demands on the people that John differed from the Poor of Qumran, but rather in extending a public invitation for all to repent and be baptized, without requiring a lengthy period of preparation for vows of communal life.[15] The baptism of fire and spirit which would follow at a later stage of the unfolding of the Messianic promise were a part of the expectation of the Covenanters as well, as we have seen,[16] but John's baptism in water as a sign of repentance appears to have been a one-time affair. Though John himself may well have practiced regular washings, as the Covenanters did, his appeal to others appears to emphasize a once-and-for-all decision to turn from sin and be cleansed.[17]

Bishop John A. T. Robinson of England, author of *Honest to God,* and a New Testament scholar who has given considerable attention to the study of John the Baptist, has observed that John did not really modify or change the baptismal customs of Qumran. Rather, he merely gave a new emphasis to one element: the initial baptism of repentance. Bishop Robinson suggests that John's emphasis on the one-time baptism for cleansing may have come about because he was not gathering a community around him, but rather sending men back, "as Israelites purified for the coming judgment, to their ordinary occupations."[18]

Robert Eisler, late Fellow of the Austrian Historical Institute at Vienna University, was perhaps the first scholar to fully appreciate the political context of the life of Jesus and John the Baptist. In his major work, *The Messiah Jesus and John the Baptist,* Dr. Eisler offers an alternative explanation for John's baptism, but one which is not inconsistent with the apocalyptic Messianist expectations outlined above. He suggests that John's baptism may have represented a special rite of washing for purification preceding the march to war, which, as on the Day of Atonement, took the form of a purification of souls from every offense through a public confession of sins. In the same spirit, he suggests, the Israelites of old, at Mizpah, before the decisive battle against the Philistines, "drew water and poured it out before Yahweh. They fasted that day and declared, 'We have sinned against Yahweh'" (I Sam. 7:6).[19]

On such an occasion, Dr. Eisler suggests, the soldiers would declare their allegiance to the kingship of God and His chosen representative, and be baptized. The entire rite, he explains, had a significance analogous to that of the ordinary soldier's oath in the Roman army, "an oath taken in the name of the emperor by the commanders immediately before marching out."[20] It is only through this oath that the soldier's service becomes a solemn and sacred military duty. The Jews also had rites for the sanctification of war. If John's baptism were in some way analogous to the Roman army's oath of allegiance, Dr. Eisler believes we would have the explanation for why baptism is so often called a "sacrament," a word which in Latin (*sacramentum*) means primarily and essentially the soldier's oath of allegiance. What Robert Eisler is suggesting, then, is that John the Baptist's baptismal confession is the soldier's oath of allegiance in the army of those who fight with and for the Messiah.

JOHN AND THE REVOLUTION

For the most part, the Gospel accounts obscure the revolutionary character of John's activities. There are, however, two references which associate John with anti-Roman agitation and which, interestingly enough, are reported to have been spoken by Jesus. In Matthew 11:12, Jesus says, "Since John the Baptist came, up to the present time, the kingdom of heaven has been subjected to violence and the violent are taking it by storm." In Luke 16:16 he says, "Up to the time of John it was the Law and the Prophets; since then, the kingdom of God has been preached, and by violence everyone is getting in." Both statements imply that John was associated with the beginning of the violent Zealot revolution in some way.[21]

Robert Eisler says that according to Josephus' references to John in both the Halosis document and the *Antiquities,* John was involved in the uprising of 4 B.C., which followed the death of Herod the Great, and was arrested and executed in A.D. 35 by Herod Antipas. During the entire period, Eisler believes, his preaching was thought to have been revolutionary in character. "The 'men of violence' are the champions of the guerrilla war of independence[22] against the Romans, dwelling as 'outsiders,' 'outcasts' (*barjonim*), in the mountains and deserts, and called by their opponents *lestae . . .* bandits or plunderers."[23] Eisler believes that Jesus lauded the Baptist as the greatest of all men yet born because before his time Moses and the prophets had only *spoken* and prophesied of the Kingdom of God, whereas John had been the first to attempt a realization of the idea, to "prepare the way."[24]

To substantiate the plausibility of this assertion, Eisler points out that the Gospel of Luke reports what must have been a sort of field sermon delivered before the march into battle. The crucial passage reads, "Some soldiers asked him in their turn, 'What about us? What must we do?'" (Lk. 3:14a). But Eisler suggests that the Greek word does not mean "soldiers" but rather "persons on the warpath" or "going to war" or "engaged in war."[25] In view of the contents of the sermon preached, Eisler suggests that these could not have been Roman troops as Christians have usually taught, but rather would have been the "revolutionary champions of liberty,"[26] that is, members of the Zealot freedom movement. He also suggests that John's answer: "No intimidation! No extortion! Be content with your pay!" (Lk. 3:14b) bears strong resemblance to the exhortations to military discipline which Josephus claims to have delivered himself to the volunteers and insurgents, the so-called "robbers" (*lēstēs*), whom he recruited in Galilee at the time of the Revolt of A.D. 66:

> And he collected a hundred thousand young men, armed them and taught them the art of warfare . . . And he said to them, "If you thirst for victory, abstain from the ordinary crimes, theft, robbery, and rapine. And do not defraud your countrymen; count it no advantage to yourselves to injure another. For the war will have better success if the warriors have a good name and *their souls are conscious of having purified themselves from every offence.* If, however, they are condemned by their evil deeds, then will God be their enemy and the aliens [will] have an easy victory."[27]

Dr. Eisler's point about the importance of the purity of the lives of the "soldiers" which John was recruiting is significant, for the same emphasis on the "purity of the camp" was stressed by Qumran, by Jesus, and by the early Church.[28] Since the war to be fought was a holy war to establish a Kingdom in which God, and God alone, would be King, the soldiers who fought the battle had to be worthy of the Kingdom in their own right: they had to be righteous and prepared to enter it even by virtue of their actions in the war itself. As A. R. C. Leaney has written, "The war of the sons of light against the sons of darkness . . . is but the terrestrial and visible part of a war in the whole universe."[29] But the war against the forces of evil here on earth is actually one and the same as the celestial, or cosmic war, so that it is possible to imagine angels and man (that is, the children of light) fighting side by side. For that reason, men had to purify their behavior so that they could conform to the standards set by the angels in their midst.

If all of the instructions given by John on this occasion are seen, as Dr. Eisler suggests, as a simple address delivered on a very definite occasion to the combatants for freedom, they take on an import and a clarity which are lacking if one understands the "soldiers" to be Romans. This is an army with no regular military supplies and they naturally ask the Baptist, "What must we do?" (Lk. 3:10). He replies that they should as far as possible, as comrades-in-arms, help each other out:[30] "If anyone has two tunics he must share with the man who has none, and the one with something to eat must do the same" (Lk. 3:11). In response to the tax collectors, Dr. Eisler assumes that John was advocating that they continue to collect the moneys which until then had gone to the Romans—presumably so that they could be used to support the war of liberation—but that the tax collectors should be careful not to continue the illegal collection of amounts over and above what was due. In this way, even though taxation would continue, the people would still obtain considerable relief.[31]

We believe it is not unlikely that Dr. Eisler's theory comes close to the truth of the situation, with regard both to John the Baptist's activities and to this particular "sermon." Not only does it make sense out of the particular incident, and give added meaning to John's baptism, but it also fits in with the rest of the data we have regarding the period in which John lived, the obvious association he had with the desert Messianic movements, the anti-Roman climate, and the manner of John's death. Moreover, what the historian Josephus wrote about John adds weight to Eisler's thesis:

> Now at that time there walked among the Jews a man in wondrous garb, for he had put animals' hair upon his body wherever it was not covered by his (own) hair; and in countenance he was like a savage. *He came to the Jews and summoned them to freedom,* saying: "God hath sent me to show you the way of the Law, whereby ye may free yourselves from many masters; *and there shall be no mortal ruling over you, but only the Highest who hath sent me.*" And when the people heard that, they were glad; [and there went after him all Judaea and the (region) around Jerusalem]. And he did nothing else to them, save that he dipped them into the stream of the Jordan and let (them) go, admonishing them to desist from evil works; (for) *so would they be given a king who would set them free* and subject all (the) insubordinate, but he himself would be subject to no one—(he) of whom we speak. Some mocked, but others put faith (in him).[32]

But to some of the Jews the destruction of Herod's army seemed to be divine vengeance, and certainly a just vengeance, for his treatment of John, surnamed the Baptist. For Herod had put him to death, though he was a good man and had exhorted the Jews to lead righteous lives,

to practise justice towards their fellows and piety towards God, and so
doing to join in baptism. In his view this was a necessary preliminary
if baptism was to be acceptable to God. They must not employ it to
gain pardon for whatever sins they committed, but as a consecration
of the body implying that the soul was already thoroughly cleansed by
right behaviour. When others too joined the crowds about him, because they were aroused to the highest degree by his sermons, Herod
became alarmed. Eloquence that had so great an effect on mankind
might lead to some form of sedition, for it looked as if they would be
guided by John in everything that they did. Herod decided therefore
that it would be much better to strike first and be rid of him *before
his work led to an uprising,* than to wait for an upheaval, get involved
in a difficult situation and see his mistake . . . Though John, because
of Herod's suspicions, was brought in chains to Machaerus . . . (*Ant.*
XVIII. 116–19. Italics ours)

In the Gospels, Herod Antipas is reported to have imprisoned John,
hesitating to kill him because the people believed him to be a prophet,
for an offense which does not at first appear at all political in nature:
John criticized Herod for his marriage to his brother's wife.[33] However, the Slavonic version of Josephus gives a fuller version of the
incident and sheds light on why such criticism by a "prophet" would
have bothered Herod so much.

According to that version, though all who respected the Law of
Moses were shocked and offended by Herod's marriage to Herodias,
John alone had dared to criticize him, saying, "You have married
your brother's wife in defiance of the Law, and just as he [i.e.,
Herod's brother Philip] died a cruel death, so will divine vengeance
bring your life to an end. The judgment of God is inexorable, and
you are doomed to die miserably in exile . . ." This attack, Josephus
reports, infuriated Herod, who ordered John flogged and thrown out
of his palace. But John persisted in waylaying the tetrarch, reiterating
his accusations, until Herod "grew furious, and gave orders to slay
him."[34]

Since John had accurately predicted the death of Philip and the
loss of both his wife and his kingdom,[35] his words to Herod constituted a grave threat, or an invitation to bring about a coup d'état;
for John, whom the people believed to be a prophet, predicted that
Herod's life would be brought to a miserable end in exile. Herod
was well acquainted with the tradition of the prophets, and he also
knew the temper of the Jewish people at the time: that they were

prone to revolt and eager to follow any man who would lead them in the struggle for their freedom. He could not have been expected to take such a "prophecy" lightly and certainly would not have allowed John freedom to continue publicly making such incendiary statements. Today John would have been arrested for "inciting to riot" or "threatening the life of the president."

WHO WAS JOHN?

How then do the Gospel writers intend us to understand John? The Synoptic Gospels identify him as the prophet Elijah returned—not only by the writers' use of the prophecy of Isaiah and that from Malachi 3:1, "Look, I am going to send my messenger to prepare a way for me,"[36] but also in the words of Jesus himself who is reported to have said, "Because it was towards John that all the prophecies of the prophets and of the Law were leading; and he, if you will believe me, is the Elijah who was to return" (Mt. 11:14).[37]

The fact that John emerges from the wilderness and does his preaching there is certainly in the desert tradition of Elijah, and there is also a certain parallel in John's criticism of Herod and his wife Herodias (Lk. 3:19) to be found in Elijah's faultfinding with Ahab and Jezebel (I Kings 21:17–24). Nevertheless, the Dead Sea Scrolls now make it seem likely that the Fourth Gospel is closer than the Synoptics are to the sectarian apocalyptic tradition in which both John and Jesus stood and therefore may well have a more accurate record of the understanding of John's role which prevailed during his lifetime. Bishop John Robinson of Trinity College, Cambridge, England, writes, "I believe that the fourth Evangelist is remarkably well informed on the Baptist, because he, or at least the witness behind that part of his tradition, once belonged to John's movement. . . ."[38]

It has long been assumed by Biblical scholars that the writer of the Fourth Gospel presented a somewhat distorted view of John the Baptist in an attempt to prove that John played only a minor role as a forerunner to Jesus as Messiah.[39] An argument in reverse was often used, saying that if John had to be downgraded by the Gospel writers with such vehemence, he must have, in fact, been very important. The Scrolls, however, have enabled scholars to reinstate the Fourth

Gospel as a basically authentic source concerning the Baptist,[40] since it probably reflects one of the earliest traditions about the significance of Jesus' life—a tradition which was in close continuity with the wilderness sect movements like that at Qumran. Perhaps the attitudes and ideas attributed to the Baptist are not, therefore, totally the result of a Christian bias. Perhaps instead they indicate that John was himself an apocalyptic Messianist in the Qumran tradition, as some scholars suggest.[41] And perhaps all four Gospels can be harmonized by seeing them in the context of "Essenoid thought" and considering them as fragmentary bits of information which are essentially supplemental in character.[42]

According to the author of John's Gospel, John the Baptist denied that he was either *the* prophet of Deuteronomy or Elijah and claimed to be only "the voice" of Isaiah 40:3 (Jn. 1:19–23). It is possible that John believed, as the Covenanters may have,[43] that the prophet had already come in the person of the Teacher of Righteousness. Or, as Bishop John Robinson suggests, it may be that John fervently believed it was *Elijah* to whom he (John) was the forerunner.[44] Or perhaps, as Dr. Charles Scobie postulates,[45] John merely preferred not to identify himself with any specific Messianic expectation in order to have the widest possible appeal because of his fervent conviction that the time was very short before the Messiah's appearance. None of the Gospels suggest that John believed himself to be the expected Messiah, or even that his followers believed him to be. It may well be, therefore, that John sought to make clear that he was only announcing the coming of the Kingdom and did not seek recognition as a prophet himself. Thus his message would have been in harmony with that of the Qumran sect and his statements about himself would not have been out of deference to Jesus' importance so much as out of his understanding of the moment of Messianic history in which he stood.

At the least it can be said that the similarities between John's Messianic expectations and those of the Covenanters are sufficient, as Professor W. H. Brownlee of the Duke University Divinity School demonstrates,[46] to enable us to affirm that John's message would not have been offensive to the Qumran sect. In fact, Bishop Robinson makes a good case for the fact that Jesus was the first person to assign any Messianic role to John. Perhaps neither John nor his disciples would have seen John as "Elijah" if it hadn't been for Jesus. Dr. Robinson feels that it was difficult for everyone—John, John's disciples, and Jesus' disciples—to accept Jesus' judgment that *John* was Elijah since all of them had thought of *Jesus* as fulfilling that role.[47]

JOHN AND JESUS

That John the Baptist had a very large following is amply indicated in the Gospels as well as by Josephus. Not only did thousands go out to the wilderness to be baptized by him in the river Jordan[48] but John's disciples appear to play a significant role throughout the Gospel narratives.[49] After Jesus began his public work, at least some of John's disciples decided to follow Jesus[50]—presumably thinking that he might be the Messiah—and John apparently did not oppose this. But the fact that at least one sect survives until today (the Mandaeans[51]) which claims John the Baptist as its founder, is a strong indication that John was an influential leader and dynamic preacher and teacher in his own right.

It is possible that John's attitude toward Jesus was like that of many other devout men of his day—that if Jesus could show by what he was able to accomplish that he was in fact "the one" for whom they were waiting, John too would rejoice in him and acclaim him as Messiah.[52] Nearly all the Jews were fervently awaiting the Messiah at that time. There were many Messianic images to be drawn on in Old Testament prophecy and all were current in the teachings of the period.[53] The People, therefore, watched for signs that the Messiah had come. Christians have usually been taught that the Jews' frequent requests that Jesus show them "signs" revealed their lack of faith. But to the contrary, their eagerness for evidence of the Messiah's appearance was due to the People's fervent desire not to miss the crucial moment of his coming.

Likewise, men who believed themselves to be the Chosen One, or Messiah, sought to "act out" the role prophesied. They believed that if God had indeed chosen them, He would fill them with His power *in the midst* of their Messianic activities (as foretold by the prophets) and would send His legions of angels to accomplish the final act of redemption. Therefore, a man of faith *acted,* in the sincere conviction that if God found favor with him He would *meet him in the act* and, by the victory accomplished for the freedom of His People, confirm His choice of the Messiah.

For both the Messianic "pretenders,"[54] as they are often called— that is, those individuals who offered themselves as the Chosen One of God—and for the People as a whole, the test of the "true" Messiah would be the manifestation of God's power in the works ("signs") and in the victory over Israel's oppressors ("redemption," or liberation of God's People) which under His leadership would be granted. God acts in the midst of history: His Messiah, therefore, will do mighty acts and will succeed in freeing God's People and in establishing the Kingdom of God on earth.

It should be noted that Jesus was only critical of persons who asked for signs but *did not believe* that the Kingdom was at hand, and therefore would not repent. Thus, when the scribes and Pharisees asked for a sign as a way of testing him or finding something about which to challenge him, Jesus said that their generation would not be given any sign other than the sign of Jonah: that is, they were being given the opportunity to repent.[55] The story of the rich man and Lazarus (Lk. 16:19–31) indicates how little chance Jesus felt there was of those who were unrepentant being convinced by signs. In the story the rich man asks that Lazarus be sent to his brothers to warn them to repent so that they could enter the Kingdom: " 'They have Moses and the prophets,' said Abraham, 'let them listen to them.' 'Ah no, father Abraham,' said the rich man, 'but if someone comes to them from the dead, they will repent.' Then Abraham said to him, 'If they will not listen either to Moses or to the prophets, they will not be convinced even if someone should rise from the dead' " (Lk. 16:29–31).

It is clear from many passages that the people believed in Jesus largely because of the signs he did: "There were many people in the crowds, however, who believed in him; they were saying, 'When the Christ comes, will he give more signs than this man?' " (Jn. 7:31).[56] And toward the end of Jesus' public teaching it was the "signs" that most troubled the authorities: "Then the chief priests and Pharisees called a meeting. 'Here is this man *working all these signs,*' they said, 'and what action are we taking? If we let him go on in this way everybody will believe in him, and the Romans will come and destroy the Holy Place and our nation' " (Jn. 11:47–48. Italics ours.).

John's disciples obviously believed that the Kingdom was indeed at hand and they had repented and been baptized by John. Therefore, Jesus' response to John's disciples, who were sent to ask if Jesus was "the one" who was expected,[57] probably reflects quite accurately the attitude Jesus had toward those who *did* believe—those for whom signs would be the means of their recognizing the Messiah.

John is reported to have sent his disciples to Jesus to ask, "Are you the one who is to come, or have we got to wait for someone else?" Jesus answered by pointing to "signs" which were manifest in the works he was doing: "Go back and tell John what you hear and see; the blind see again, and the lame walk, lepers are cleansed, and the deaf hear, and the dead are raised to life and the Good News is proclaimed to the poor" (Mt. 11:2–5). The evidence Jesus gave would have been clear to John, who was familiar with the Messianic prophecy which it fulfilled[58] and who would thus have been able to "believe" because of the signs.

Jesus did not define his own Messianic role, however. Perhaps he was leaving John the freedom to draw his own conclusion in that regard; perhaps Jesus himself was not yet certain if he was the Messiah or simply another "voice" in the tradition of John; or perhaps, as Bishop John Robinson suggests, he was indicating to John that he was not "the one" to which John was referring (i.e., Elijah), but another (i.e., in the tradition of the prophecy of Isaiah).[59] But the signs of the Kingdom were clear to Jesus, and would have been to John and his disciples as well.

JESUS' ASSOCIATION WITH JOHN'S WORK

The Gospels indicate that at the start of his public preaching Jesus was associated with John the Baptist. Not only did he receive John's baptism, but he preached his message: "The time has come and the kingdom of God is close at hand. Repent, and believe the Good News" (Mk. 1:15). Or simply, according to Matthew, "Repent, for the kingdom of heaven is close at hand" (Mt. 4:17). In addition, Jesus and his disciples administered a baptism of repentance like John's, and the Fourth Gospel reports that John's disciples were alarmed by the numbers who were being baptized by Jesus, intimating that they thought there was a kind of rivalry between the two.[60] However, the Baptist's response showed that he did not feel them to be in competitive roles and Jesus obviously respected John and considered him to be playing an important role in the Messianic drama. It seems more likely, therefore, that the two shared a kind of partnership in preaching and baptizing in the early part of Jesus' public work.[61] Their messages and acts pointed to the same imminent establishment of the Kingdom.

In fact, Professor David Flusser of Hebrew University in Jerusalem believes, as do other scholars, that Jesus' exposure to the apocalyptic nationalism of the Qumran sect may have been mediated by John the Baptist.[62] Certainly Jesus was "initiated" into the gospel of John by being baptized by him. To that extent, at least, he can be considered a disciple of John at the beginning of his public work.

There are indications in the Fourth Gospel that the two preached and baptized for a time in a cooperative fashion: "Jesus went with his disciples into the Judaean countryside and stayed with them there and baptised. At the same time John was baptising at Aenon near Salim" (Jn. 3:22–23). Herod evidently found them to be so much alike in their preaching and style that he wondered if Jesus was not John the Baptist raised from the dead (Mt. 14:1f.). Jesus is reported to have told his disciples that John was in fact Elijah returned— indicating a genuine appreciation for the importance of John's preaching and implying, by Matthew's use of the statement, that John was the forerunner for Jesus (Mt. 17:11–13).

Jesus remained associated with John and the traditions and memories surrounding him throughout his teaching and preaching,[63] and even after John's death (according to the Gospels) he refused to tell the chief priests, scribes, and elders where he got his authority because they would not acknowledge John's as being from God.[64] Thus it seems clear that Jesus' work was closely tied to John the Baptist. Perhaps he was a student, or disciple—in which case he may have learned much about the ways and teachings of the Qumran community from John. Probably they were associates in preaching and baptizing.

JOHN'S INFLUENCE ON JESUS

Just how much influence John would have had on Jesus depends not only on the prominence of John but also on the extent of contact they would have had with each other. The Lukan birth narrative suggests that John and Jesus were born within six months' time of each other (Lk. 1:5–80). If this was the case, they would have been contemporaries. Robert Eisler, author of *The Messiah Jesus and John the Baptist,* has argued that John had preached for at least a generation before Jesus' baptism. Such a theory would enhance the significance of John's mission and increase the probability of his influence on Jesus.[65]

In the first two Gospels we are told that Jesus did not begin the major part of his public preaching and teaching until after John's arrest,[66] and that John was executed before Jesus.[67] But even with the limited contact suggested by the Synoptic Gospels, it is apparent that John (a) had enough in common with the Qumran sect to suggest that he was either trained by them or had been in close contact with them, (b) was closely associated with Jesus, at least in the early period of Jesus' public activities, (c) and therefore may well have been the mediating influence between Jesus and the Qumran Covenanters.

Whether the latter is true or not, it is clear that Jesus' teachings and his life style reflect a strong influence from the sectarian apocalyptic and nationalistic movements represented by both Qumran and John. In our concluding chapters we illustrate those apparent influences and parallels. We hope thereby to illuminate Jesus' role and teachings, making them more comprehensible and more relevant to twentieth-century men who have too often found him ethereal and unfathomable.

CHAPTER 7

Jesus: A Teacher of the Law

"Do not imagine that I have come to abolish the Law or the Prophets. I have come not to abolish but to complete them. I tell you solemnly, till heaven and earth disappear, not one dot, not one little stroke, shall disappear from the Law until its purpose is achieved." Matthew 5:17–18

"You must therefore be perfect just as your heavenly Father is perfect." Matthew 5:48

In the words of James A. Pike:

"What is interesting about Jesus is that though he seems to have insisted that every jot and tittle of the Law had to be kept, when it came to personal confrontations, or personal relationships, he acted out of an almost naïve compulsiveness. He leaped right over the fences around the Law to respond in love to a person's needs. And he viewed this as a *fulfillment* of the Law, not an abrogation of it.

"For example, Jesus saw a man lying by the Pool of Bethesda in Jerusalem waiting to be healed. The man had been there for years, and could never get into the water quickly enough to be able to be healed. Jesus was there on a Sabbath day, but when he saw the situation he cured the man.

"There were two schools of thought regarding such healings. The Shammai school of Pharisees taught that *any* healing on the Sabbath was a violation of the Torah. The Hillel Pharisees taught that if it was a matter of life or death, you could heal—or even save an animal, for that matter: pull an ox out of the ditch. But the Hillel people were something like modern physicians in that regard. Just try to get yourself healed on Saturday today if your illness is chronic and not acute! 'I'm very sorry,' the answering service will say, 'the doctor can be reached on Monday.' The Shammai people would have been shocked that Jesus healed at all on the Sabbath, but even the Hillel people would have been disturbed that he had violated the union rules! There was no excuse for that. What was the rush? The man had been there for years.

"This same spontaneous response is characteristic of Jesus in many other instances. He saw the situation and leaped right over the careful restrictions around the Law. He didn't *break* the Law, but neither was he constricted by it. In order to relate to certain types of people, he had to be more liberal in his interpretation of the Law than other teachers. He couldn't have related to prostitutes and tax collectors and other 'unclean' types if he had been rigid about it.

"This reaction is very interesting in Jesus. It is a beautiful compulsion to respond in love to people. It is quite different from Paul who later said, 'The Torah is over.' And yet oddly enough you don't see in Paul the same kind of fresh love and directness that you see in Jesus who thought he was constrained by the Law, and yet was very loving."

JESUS IS BAPTIZED BY JOHN

We know almost nothing about Jesus' childhood and youth. What few inferences can be drawn about those early years are of a most general nature and of little help in determining what specific influences might have been brought to bear on him.

We can assume that Jesus was raised in a devoutly religious Jewish family. We are told, for example, that he was circumcised according to the Law eight days after his birth (Lk. 2:21). Second, we know that he must have been well trained in Torah, for his parents were able to take him as a child of twelve to Jerusalem and present him, according to the custom of the times, to the teachers of the Law in the Temple as a promising student of Torah. Jesus was able to engage in the discussions, "listening to them and asking them questions" about the interpretations of the Law, with such skill that "all those who heard him were astounded at his intelligence and his replies" (Lk. 2:42–47).

Third, Jesus must have been taken to the synagogue regularly as a child, for Luke records that "He came to Nazara, where he had been brought up, and went into the synagogue on the sabbath day as he usually did" (Lk. 4:16). As an adult, he not only continued this custom of regular attendance at the synagogue, but he frequently taught there as well.[1] Fourth, we are told by Luke that "every year [Jesus'] parents used to go to Jerusalem for the feast of the Passover" (Lk. 2:41), a religious duty for devout Jews. Jesus, therefore, began the practice of making pilgrimages to Jerusalem for feast days early—at least by the time he was twelve—and evidently continued it during his adult years. The Gospel writers give several examples of feasts he attended in Jerusalem and of his teaching in the Temple.[2]

Finally, when Jesus taught, he spoke with the authority of one who had a thorough knowledge of the Law gained at an early age, and a deep understanding of its meaning and application developed over the years. As Luke says, "his teaching made a deep impression on them because he spoke with authority" (Lk. 4:32).[3]

What Jesus did during the interim years, from the time of the interchange in the Temple with the teachers of the Law at twelve until the occasion of his baptism by John, we cannot really know. Since he was a Nazarene, we may assume that he was being trained in the "secrets" of his father's craft—carpentry—as well as in the mysteries of the Kingdom of God, but it is impossible to determine with certainty whether or not he received all of that training in Galilee. We are told by both Matthew and Mark that Jesus came down from Galilee to the Jordan to be baptized by John (Mt. 3:13; Mk. 1:9), but whether that was meant to imply that Jesus had remained in Galilee all those years of his youth and early manhood is, of course, impossible to know.

Luke says that Jesus was a young man "about thirty years old" when he began his ministry (Lk. 3:23). All three of the Synoptic Gospels imply that he was baptized by John not long before he began his public ministry. Therefore, we can infer that when he presented himself for baptism Jesus was already a mature young man with a rich background in the Law and in the apocalyptic teachings upon which John based his preaching.

Christians have often been mystified by the baptism, wondering why Jesus, whom they have been taught was "without sin," underwent a baptism of repentance. If, as we have suggested, John's baptism was the occasion of throwing in one's lot with the holy army of liberation which was being gathered in the wilderness, Jesus' baptism becomes

more comprehensible. In order to declare himself a part of the apocalyptic freedom movement, Jesus would have had to make a public
confession of sin, for both at Qumran and in John's baptism that
confession included not only one's personal guilt (if such was appropriate) but also the guilt of the whole People Israel. It was a
confession on behalf of *all* those who had gone astray, and constituted
an expression of the willingness of the one being baptized to atone
for the sins of all by his own life of righteousness.

Bishop John Robinson has suggested that John's baptism was specially designed *to force* the inauguration of the final events related to
the establishment of the Kingdom of God on earth. Though the identity of the Messiah was as hidden from John as it was from everyone else (Jn. 1:26, 31, 33), Dr. Robinson believes that John the
Baptist was different from other apocalyptic Jews of his time in that
he was certain that the Messiah was *already among them* and was
only waiting to be revealed (Jn. 1:26). John the Baptist emerged,
Robinson postulates, in response to a call from God (Jn. 1:33),
in order to set the last things in motion by his baptism by water.
Since baptism by water was necessary before baptism by the spirit
could come, and since the "one to come" would be consecrated for
his mission in part by receiving the baptism of the spirit (Jn. 1:31),
John hoped his work would enable the Messiah to be revealed.[4]

If, then, we picture Jesus going into the wilderness in order to
throw in his lot with the apocalyptic freedom movement, and John
baptizing people in the full expectation that the one who would lead
his people to freedom and establish the Kingdom of God would soon
appear, we can begin to understand the significance of what is described as having happened on the occasion of Jesus' baptism.

Both John and the Covenanters taught that after the baptism by
water, the baptism of the spirit would come to those who were pure
within and worthy of receiving it. Immediately after being baptized
with water by John, Jesus, we are told, received the baptism of the
spirit in such a dramatic way that John himself saw it.[5] Jesus "saw
the Spirit of God [the spirit, the Holy Spirit] descending like a dove
and coming down on him" and heard a voice from heaven [of God]
say, "This is my Son, the Beloved; my favour rests on him" (Mt.
3:16–17). John is reported to have borne witness to this event saying,
"I saw the Spirit coming down on him from heaven like a dove and
resting on him. I did not know him myself, but he who sent me to
baptise with water had said to me, 'The man on whom you see the
Spirit come down and rest is the one who is going to baptise with

the Holy Spirit.' Yes, I have seen and I am the witness that he is the Chosen One of God" (Jn. 1:32–34).

Through the ages mystics, saints, and other great religious leaders have reported that their profound religious, or spiritual, experiences have been accompanied by external, or seemingly external, phenomena like the voice and the dove mentioned in connection with Jesus' baptism by the spirit. Moses' encounter with God on Mount Sinai and Paul's experience on the road to Damascus are familiar examples from the Bible of similar religious experiences in which voices were heard and phenomena seen (Ex. 3:1–6; Acts 9:3–7). Our scientific knowledge is too limited at this stage in our development as a human race to be able to "explain" such events, but we would be less than scientific if we did not report the observable data regarding such experiences so that scientists can begin to probe and analyze them in order to discover the natural laws at work in them.[6] As historians we would likewise be negligent not to record and take note of such a key event for, even though we might not fully understand the accompanying phenomena, we can see the impact it had on Jesus' life.

The most obvious result of the baptismal experience was that Jesus received the assurance that he had been accepted as one of God's children. His internal purity matched the external purity which resulted from John's ritual act, and God had granted him the baptism of spirit along with that of water. He was thereby fully received into the Kingdom of Light because God had found his life of righteousness pleasing.

It is important to recognize that this experience of Jesus' was not unique in kind, though it was of course uniquely his experience and came to him in an individualistic way, as all personal experiences do. The Covenanters taught that when any man had purified his inner soul, he would receive the spirit of holiness which would reveal to his inner heart the "truth" of the mysteries which the Teacher of Righteousness taught.[7] We have reason to believe that many of the Covenanters had been baptized with this holy spirit since they were known as healers, prophets, and exorcisers, manifesting the same "gifts" of the spirit mentioned by Paul.[8]

And certainly Jesus' disciples received the baptism of the holy spirit: "When Pentecost day came round, they had all met in one room, when suddenly they heard what sounded like a powerful wind from heaven, the noise of which filled the entire house in which they were sitting; and something appeared to them that seemed like tongues of fire; these separated and came to rest on the head of each of them.

They were all filled with the Holy Spirit, and began to speak foreign languages as the Spirit gave them the gift of speech" (Acts 2:1–4). In fact, Jesus promised them that they would receive the baptism of the spirit and told them to wait for it, for "John baptised with water but you, not many days from now, will be baptised with the Holy Spirit" (Acts 1:4, 5).

The "descent of the holy spirit" on Jesus should not, therefore, be regarded as a *unique* sign of God's favor. The singularity of its impact was due to the degree of Jesus' dedication and preparation. His righteousness enabled him to receive the spirit in fullness at his baptism by water, and then to bear the fruit of it to a much greater degree than others around him.

JESUS IN THE WILDERNESS

In the Gospel accounts, Jesus' baptism is followed by his temptation in the wilderness. With the gift of the spirit, Jesus must also have received fuller understanding, at the deepest level, of the "secrets" of the Kingdom. Not only did the Qumran Covenanters teach that the spirit would reveal the truth to the inner man, but Jesus himself told his disciples, "When the Spirit of truth comes he will lead you to the complete truth" (Jn. 16:13a). Surely Jesus' own experience of the baptism of the spirit cannot have been *less* profound than that. As a child of light, or son of God, power would have been released in him to overcome the forces of darkness which surrounded him, and he, like the Covenanters, would have had power to cast out demons, to heal, to prophesy, and to perform miracles from that time forward.

It is no wonder, then, that Jesus was "led" or "driven" by the spirit into the wilderness to fast and to wrestle with the possibilities now open to him. Many temptations are inherent in such powers, the greatest being to use it for one's own gratification and acclaim. In the story told in the Book of Enoch, discussed in Chapter 3 above, the children of the fallen angels were severely punished for refusing to give credit and praise to God for the power and knowledge which they had, and for deceiving men into thinking that the power was their own. For Jesus to have chosen such a course would have been to fall into the service of the devil (Beelzebub), for he would have been using the power and knowledge given him as a child of light to strengthen the forces of darkness in the world. This would have been a sin against the holy spirit.[9] As Jesus later warned his disciples, the state (or condition) of a man who commits a sin against the spirit is worse than before he received the baptism of the holy spirit—before he was first cleansed and purified.[10]

Thus for forty days and forty nights (a Biblical phrase meaning "a long time"), Jesus was tempted by the devil in the wilderness. If he had this power, why did he not use it for his own gratification? ("If you are the Son of God, tell these stones to turn into loaves." Mt. 4:3.) If he had this power, why did he not use it to give spectacular demonstrations in order to impress men; even the scriptures say that God would not allow harm to come to him. ("If you are the Son of God, throw yourself down [from the pinnacle of the Temple in Jerusalem], for Scripture says, 'He will put you in his angels' charge, and they will support you on their hands in case you hurt your foot against a stone!'" Mt. 4:6.) And again, if he had this power, why did he not take over as ruler of the world; all he would have to do would be to change his allegiance from light to darkness. ("I will give you all these [kingdoms of the world and their splendour] if you fall at my feet and worship me." Mt. 4:9.)

Jesus was able to overcome the temptations largely because his profound knowledge of scripture had led him to anticipate such temptations. In each instance a passage came to mind which sustained him in the truth and the devil was not able to lure him away from the light: "Man does not live on bread alone but on every word that comes from the mouth of God" (Mt. 4:4), "You must not put the Lord your God to the test" (Mt. 4:7), and "You must worship the Lord your God, and serve him alone" (Mt. 4:10).[11]

Jesus' priorities remained clear: he had chosen the path of righteousness and truth which characterized the children of light. He would have no other king than God. He would not try to take things into his own hands or to set his own pace for the unfolding of the plan for the end of days. He would trust in God, and God alone.

When this first victory over the forces of darkness had been won, the Gospels report that he was ministered to by the "angels," heavenly beings who dwell only and for always in the presence of God. Only after such a victory could he emerge from the wilderness, ready to preach and teach and heal as part of the army of the children of light who were preparing the way for the final victory over the forces of darkness and for the establishment of the Kingdom of God on earth.

THE WILDERNESS IN ISRAEL'S HISTORY

Jean Daniélou,[12] well-known Roman Catholic New Testament scholar recently made a cardinal of the church in France, sees in Jesus' going out into the wilderness a repetition of the theme of the great Exodus by the Israelites from Egypt through the desert. Just as the people spent forty years in the wilderness, Jesus spent forty days and forty nights. Just as the Israelites got hungry and doubted God, so Jesus was tempted to test God by asking Him to provide food when he was hungry. Just as the Israelites worshiped the golden calf at Mount Sinai, Jesus was tempted to worship Satan on a high mountain. Thus Jesus emerged from the wilderness, prepared to help inaugurate the "new Israel," perhaps the first evidence of his fulfillment of the Deuteronomic prophetic image of the "new Moses."

Bishop John Robinson also sees the temptation stories as a typological re-enactment of the Exodus from Egypt. Though he believes that Jesus may well have been tempted in the wilderness, Robinson suggests that the Gospel writers, in telling the story, deliberately selected three (out of what were undoubtedly, says Dr. Robinson, many) temptations which would parallel the experiences which the "old" Israel had in the wilderness.[13] Dr. Robinson points out that all of Jesus' scriptural answers to the temptations can be found in the Exodus story in the context of incidents where the Israelites *failed* to make the proper response and then were found to be unfaithful to God.[14]

Bishop Robinson believes the Gospel writers intended to show that Jesus had been faithful in the very ways the "old" Israel had failed to be. The Israelites wandered in the wilderness forty years before they learned that "man does not live by bread alone," and the first generation—those who had murmured, complained, and mistrusted— were not allowed to enter the promised land. The Israelites *did* tempt God by asking Moses to give them signs to prove that God was in fact with them. Though Moses did not turn stones to bread, he *did* strike rock to get water. And finally, the People wandering in the Sinai wilderness *did* turn away from God to worship an idol—the golden calf which they had created themselves.[15]

The Gospel writers portray Jesus, Bishop Robinson believes, as undergoing the same kinds of temptations as the Israelites of old, but he emerges victorious, having conquered the temptations by faith in God. Thus he is proven worthy to be the representative of the "new" Israel. In his forty days and nights in the wilderness Jesus even repeats Moses' forty-day, forty-night retreat to the top of Mount Sinai (Ex. 34:28). Jesus thus emerges as "the one" to lead the People out of bondage into freedom, partners in a New Covenant with God.[16]

Jesus' wilderness experience, then, can be understood in the Exodus tradition, and the temptations and Jesus' victory over them can be viewed as a "sign" that he was the "new Moses"—the prophet of Deuteronomy that so many of his people expected to come to redeem them.

Withdrawal into the wilderness had been an important part of Israel's history in other ways, too. It was a place of refuge for David and the Maccabees and a place of turning back to Yahweh in penitence and for restoration to the Covenanted relationship for Elijah, the Qumran Covenanters, and John the Baptist.[17] In fact, the very roots of monotheism—the throwing off of false idols and pagan ways and the affirming of one's utter dependency on God, and God alone—are to be found in the wilderness. The tests to which the wilderness puts one, and the hardships which it imposes, are "designed to burn into Israel's heart the secret of her election with which she stands and falls—the first requirement for a life in the strength of God's election is the understanding that the elect people are completely and continually dependent on God."[18]

The desert wilderness strips away all false securities. In the barrenness of the wilderness, all other supports fall and one is laid bare to the One God, the Power, the constant source of all life, and the root of all security. Thus by remaining steadfast in his commitment to serve the One God, Jesus confirmed his "election" to the "new Israel" and no doubt greatly heightened and deepened the power of the spirit which he had received at his baptism.

JESUS' MESSAGE

At the outset of his public preaching, Jesus adopted the style and message of John the Baptist with very little variation. He believed, as John did, that announcing the Kingdom and calling people to repentance would speed, and perhaps enable, its coming. Through his baptism by John, Jesus had identified himself with the nationalistic and apocalyptic thrusts of the desert Messianic movements, and what he preached and taught and did were further confirmations of that association. In fact, Bishop John Robinson believes that Jesus began his work by accepting the Malachi role which John had prepared for him—that of the prophet Elijah returned.[19]

Not only was Jesus' message like that of John the Baptist, but it was in keeping with the Qumran tradition as well. All were proclaiming: "The kingdom of God is close at hand. Repent, and believe the Good News" (Mk. 1:15).[20] Jesus' message was good news to his people, for it promised their imminent deliverance from their Roman oppressors and the fulfillment of all their hopes and aspirations by the establishment of the Kingdom of God on earth. The People Israel were to be admitted first to that Kingdom and by their lives of perfect righteousness in harmony with the will of God, who alone would rule in the new Kingdom, they were to serve as witnesses to all other peoples—"a light to the nations"—that the forces of evil, of darkness, and of death had been overcome, and that the Kingdom of Light had been established. The announcement of the Kingdom's coming brought great joy and a promise of peace to all who believed it to be so: to those who "had ears to hear."

But Jesus' message was "bad news" to the Romans, for it had insurrectionist implications. It pointed to an impending revolution in which the Roman rulers would be put down from their positions of power and thrown "into the blazing furnace" (Mt. 13:42, etc.) and the Jews would gain their freedom. The Romans, therefore, were very sensitive to Messianic preaching. They knew the restlessness—and sometimes desperation—of the people, and they could not afford to allow a charismatic leader to arise and his movement to gather momentum. Such a leader could easily incite the people to revolt as Judas of Galilee had done in the recent past.[21]

But neither could the Romans afford to be careless about the manner in which they eliminated any apparent opposition to their rule. First of all, their legal system was highly developed and insofar as possible they treated even subject peoples with a degree of fairness and due process. Administrators of occupied regions were expected to adhere to Roman law in their dealings with subject peoples. And secondly, an uneasy peace could be maintained in Israel only when large numbers of Jews of the Sadducean and priestly classes were willing to collaborate with the Romans. Wealthy and influential Jews made administration of the region much easier and the Romans tried to maintain a congenial relationship with them. Rash and unjustified murders which might offend even the collaborators—or on the other hand, which the collaborators themselves might commit, thus offending their own people—were detrimental to the Roman cause and were therefore to be avoided.[22]

From the other perspective, it is understandable that Jesus should at first try to keep his message as quiet as possible—speaking only for those who had "ears to hear" (e.g., Mt. 13:13–17) and were ready to join his movement—for he was not ready for a public confrontation with the Romans. Whenever anyone openly identified him with the Messianic role, or the fulfillment of Messianic promises, or when he performed signs and works, he urged people to "take care that no one learns about this" (Mt. 9:30), or ordered them "not to make him known" (Mt. 12:16).[23] Only later, when plans for a public confrontation with the authorities in Jerusalem had been carefully laid, did Jesus begin publicly to acknowledge himself as having a special role in Messianic history.

It is also understandable that Jesus' disciples should have feared Roman detection of their movement and that they should have been suspicious of those Jews who held positions of high authority and who could, if they chose, act as informers to the Romans—or who could even get rid of Jesus themselves in order to avoid the outbreak of open conflict with the Romans. The Gospel accounts are filled with insinuations that many were "out to get" Jesus: the Pharisees (the liberal, or "middle of the road," group of religious Jews, but when used derogatorily, the hypocritically religious), the chief priests (collaborators with the Romans), and the "Jews" (used in the Fourth Gospel to refer to Jews from Judea, large numbers of whom were collaborators, or at least cooperators, with the Romans, as contrasted with those from Galilee and Samaria[24]).

The Pharisees were seen to be in league with the Romans, as in Mark 3:6, which reads, "The Pharisees went out and at once began to plot with the Herodians against [Jesus], discussing how to destroy him." The Herodians were a political group which did not exist, as far as we know, until after the Fall of Jerusalem in A.D. 70, if at all.[25] The term is undoubtedly used to indicate persons directly tied into Roman rule, for Jesus is reported to have cautioned his disciples against the leaven of the "Pharisees" and of the "Herodians," or Herod (Mk. 8:15), as though that "leaven" were the same—perhaps "against" him.

Other passages reveal the disciples' anxiety that they were being "watched." "At this the Pharisees went out and began to plot against him, discussing how to destroy [Jesus]" (Mt. 12:14). "But [the scribes and Pharisees] were furious [at what Jesus had said and done], and began to discuss the best way of dealing with Jesus" (Lk. 6:11). And "The scribes and the Pharisees began a furious attack on him and tried to force answers from him on innumerable questions, setting traps to catch him out in something he might say" (Lk. 11:53–54).[26] It is apparent that the disciples knew that Jesus' life—and theirs— was in danger the moment he began to teach authoritatively about the Kingdom of God.

JESUS ORGANIZES A MOVEMENT

Jesus set up his own "organization." That is, he called together a council of twelve, reminiscent of the twelve of Qumran, and told them they would judge the twelve tribes of Israel when the Kingdom was established (Mt. 19:28 and Lk. 22:30), just as the Manual of Discipline of Qumran indicates the Covenanters' inner circle will, in the last days, "pay to the wicked their reward."[27] Within the twelve, there were three who were particularly close to Jesus. Though at Qumran there were an *additional* three who were priests and who ruled *with* the twelve, nevertheless, the positions of special responsibility, privilege, and trust assigned to Peter, James, and John[28] may well reflect Jesus' awareness of the Qumran 12+3 pattern. Since priests played no special part in Jesus' movement, he did not *add* three to the twelve, but merely set three apart from the group.[29]

It seems from the Gospel accounts that Jesus was preparing the twelve to take over and/or carry on after the Messiah's appearance, for he not only indicated that they would act as judges over the twelve tribes, but he gave them special instructions regarding the inner meaning of his teachings. He explained with great care even those parables which he gave to the masses without interpretation. "The mysteries of the kingdom of God are revealed to you," Jesus told his disciples; "for the rest there are only parables, so that they may see but not perceive, listen but not understand" (Lk. 8:10).[30]

During his last weeks with them, Jesus gave his disciples as much instruction as he felt they could absorb and then promised that when they, too, received the spirit of holiness, all they would need to know would be revealed to them. "I have said these things to you while still with you; but the Advocate, the Holy Spirit . . . will teach you everything and remind you of all I have said to you" (Jn. 14:25–26) and "I still have many things to say to you but they would be too much for you now. But when the Spirit of truth comes he will lead you to the complete truth" (Jn. 16:12–13a). This expectation, as we saw in Chapter 3, was also part of the Qumran teaching, and just before Jesus was crucified, he initiated the twelve into the New Covenant through a meal very much like that used at Qumran (I Cor. 11:23–29), indicating that they were now prepared to receive the gift of the spirit.

Thus it would seem that from the beginning Jesus saw himself either as functioning independently of John the Baptist and other established groups such as that at Qumran, or as the leader of a subsidiary group acting in harmony with the other desert movements. Since the roles Jesus envisioned for himself and for his disciples were so much like those which the Qumran Covenanters had earlier defined for themselves, it would seem that Jesus' movement was an outgrowth of theirs in some way, or that it was a kind of Galilean branch of it. Or, perhaps Jesus' movement could be seen as a "reform" movement of the Qumran sect, if, as some scholars have suggested, we interpret his apparent references to their teachings as polemics against them rather than simply indications of both his and his listeners' familiarity with those teachings.[31]

It may be that Jesus had been closely associated with the Covenanters (whether through John the Baptist or directly) but had decided that their approach, though basically sound, was lacking in some ways. His basic difference with them seems to have been his belief that the masses needed to be reached with the message of the Kingdom. That conviction alone would be sufficient to account for the things he did which seem out of character for one influenced by the Covenanters: his baptizing of the masses in the tradition of John; his more "liberal" interpretations of the Law—in the tradition of Hillel Pharisaism—enabling thereby everyone, regardless of his station in life, to be obedient within the spirit of the Law; and his association with men who were not "pure" by Qumran standards.

To view Jesus' movement as a "reformed" or missionary branch of the Qumran community is not implausible in the light of the many similarities and parallels between the Dead Sea sect and Jesus and the early Christian movement, but such a view must remain only a conjecture. What we can be sure of, as a result of the discovery of the Dead Sea Scrolls, is that Jesus' movement in its early stages was by no means unique in kind, and that the people to whom he preached had enough background to be able to understand his message and his actions.

With special attention to the historical setting of the first-century Judaism in which he found himself, then, let us consider Jesus as a teacher, as a preacher, and as a prophet during the brief period of his public activities.

JESUS AS TEACHER

The forceful statements by Jesus quoted at the beginning of this chapter regarding his attitude toward the Law of Moses have often puzzled Christians who have been taught that Jesus, like Paul, no longer believed the Mosaic Law to be in force. Paul's belief that the Law had been superseded, however, was based on the "later" moment in the events of the end of days which was discussed in Chapter 5. Because Jesus had been raised from the dead and the disciples had received the spirit of holiness promised as a confirmation of the New Covenant, Paul believed the Kingdom was in the process of being established and that the Law had been "written on men's hearts," as the Qumran sect also anticipated would happen at the end of days.[32]

Jesus, however, lived and taught in the "earlier moment" shared by the Qumran Covenanters. He announced the coming Kingdom, but for him it had not yet been established. He spoke of the time to come and taught his disciples what it would be like. For Jesus, the Law was still in full force and none of the commandments could be done away with until all were fulfilled in the Kingdom. In his urging that the Law must be kept to "perfection," and that the spirit as well as the letter of the Law was essential, Jesus was like the Covenanters.

In spite of Jesus' conviction that the Law had to be kept in every regard in both spirit and truth, in which he was like the Covenanters—

the most "conservative" Jews—Jesus' *interpretation* of the Law followed that of the Hillel, or "liberal," school of Pharisaic thought. For this reason Jesus' approach might at first seem to be contradictory. But Jesus was faithful to the letter of the Law while giving it a broader, or more liberal, *application* and *interpretation* than others who shared the same literal approach.

Because of Jesus' frequent criticism of the Pharisees, Christians often assume that he was not a "legalist," or did not subscribe to the Mosaic Law as other Jews did. But Jesus' criticism was leveled at the Pharisees' *hypocrisy* in keeping the Law, not at their subscribing to it or even necessarily at their interpretation of it. Such criticism as Jesus leveled at the Pharisees was common among the Pharisees themselves and later got recorded in the Mishnah and the Talmud. Jesus is reported to have told his disciples, "Unless your righteousness *exceeds* that of the scribes and Pharisees, you will never enter the Kingdom of heaven" (Mt. 5:20, RSV).

In other words, he did not give *less* importance to the Law than the Pharisees did, *but more*. Professor David Flusser, who as a Jew respects Jesus as a great teacher of the Law, points out that "All the motifs of Jesus' famous invective against the Pharisees in Matthew 23 are also found in rabbinical literature. Both in Jesus' diatribe and in the self-criticism of the rabbis the central polemical motif is the description of the Pharisees as being prone to hypocrisy. Jesus says that 'they make up heavy loads and lay them on men's shoulders, but they will not stir a finger to remove them' (Mt. 23:4). In the Talmud we read about five types of Pharisaic hypocrisy: the first is to 'lay the commandments upon men's shoulders.' "[33]

Thus it is fair to say that Jesus stood *within* the "Pharisaism" of his day, rather than outside of it, or in opposition to it. In fact, as Professor David Flusser has pointed out to the authors, the term "pharisee" has a very negative connotation in Hebrew and was never used by anyone as descriptive of himself. Rather, it was always applied *to others* in a critical or derisive fashion.

When Jesus, or any other rabbi, began his remarks with: "Woe to you, Pharisees" (Mt. 23:13, etc., RSV), by his very use of the term he implied the word which followed—"hypocrites!" As Professor Flusser noted, the only persons on record who ever called *themselves* "pharisees" were St. Paul and the Jewish historian Josephus, both of whom were writing in Greek. The Greek word for "pharisee," however, does not have the same negative connotation as the Hebrew.[34] Therefore, Jesus was a rabbi among other rabbis of his day, teaching the Law according to his own understanding and *criticizing* those "pharisees" whom he felt to be hypocritical.

Jesus' arguments with those who criticized his disciples for not observing the Law always involved questions of interpretation, not disputes over the Law per se, and were in keeping with the best rabbinical traditions of legal debate. The underlying assumption by both parties was that the Law should be kept. The issues raised were over what the Law meant and in what manner it was to be kept. It is just such a tradition of debating the meaning and interpretation of the Law, of which the arguments reported in the Gospels provide good examples, that became the main core of what is now called Rabbinic Judaism. Once the Temple had been destroyed, the sacrificial and priestly practices centering in the Temple at Jerusalem were of necessity dropped from Jewish tradition in its active expression. The Law became the sole focus and expression of religion for the Jews. It was felt, therefore, that it would be helpful to Jews, especially those in the Diaspora—that is, dispersed throughout the Empire— if the oral traditions regarding the interpretation of the Law were put into writing.

The Mishnah and the Talmud, initiated in the Councils in Javne after the Fall of Jerusalem in A.D. 70 and completed in Galilee in the third and fifth centuries A.D., are records of the opinions of authoritative rabbis regarding the meaning and interpretation of passages of the Law. The opinions of two of the leading authorities during the time of Jesus are recorded in the Mishnah. They are the Rabbis Hillel and Shammai, both of whom lived and taught in the first century B.C. Hillel believed the Law should be interpreted in such a way that its spirit could be kept by all men. Shammai was what might be called a "strict constructionist"; he taught that the Law should be kept to the letter and that no new "interpretations" should be allowed. Interpretations are what have been recorded, however, and continue to be expanded by Jewish scholars of Torah even in the present day.

It was in the style of Hillel Pharisaism that Jesus interpreted the Law. Thus Professor Flusser is able to state, "When we compare Jesus' words and actions in the synoptic Gospels with the rabbinical prescriptions of his time, it becomes clear that, *even in his most revolutionary actions,* he never transgressed the bounds of the contemporary interpretation of the Mosaic Law."[35]

KEEPING THE SABBATH DAY HOLY

The major point of contention between Jesus and the "Pharisees" regarding the Law arose from their differing views on keeping the Sabbath. Many Christians have been taught that Jesus violated the Pharisaic understanding of keeping the Sabbath,[36] but Professor Flusser argues that Jesus' attitude is *consistently* Pharisaic—that is, within the norm of rabbinic interpretation in his day. Even his oft-quoted "the sabbath was made for man, not man for the sabbath" (Mk. 2:27) has a close parallel in rabbinical literature.[37]

It will perhaps be helpful to illustrate this point with a few familiar incidents from the New Testament. On several occasions Jesus was criticized for healing on the Sabbath. Once he healed an invalid who had been lying by the pool of Bethesda for thirty-eight years (Jn. 5:1–18). Another time he straightened a man's withered hand (Mt. 12:9–14; Mk. 3:1–6; Lk. 6:6–11). On still another occasion he restored sight to a man who had been born blind (Jn. 9:1–41). A fourth incident involved his straightening a woman's back which had been stooped for eighteen years (Lk. 13:10–17). And finally, he healed a man of dropsy (Lk. 14:1–6).

Professor Flusser says, and other scholars agree,[38] that it was the fact that the diseases were in no case critical and could have waited for treatment on another day that aroused the anger of the "Pharisees." The latter maintained that "Every question of danger to life takes precedence over the Sabbath,"[39] but prohibited the curing of nondangerous illnesses *by physical means.* Dr. Flusser observes that even though Jesus treated nondangerous illnesses, he did not do it physically, but rather healed by the spoken word.[40] Therefore, though the Pharisees objected, Jesus was not actually in violation of their interpretation of the Law. The critics no doubt represented the more conservative wing of Pharisaic teaching, and were perhaps offended because Jesus "appeared" to be violating the Law even if he was not literally doing so.

The Covenanters were more strict than the Pharisees regarding Sabbath observance, but even their Scrolls indicate that they permitted the saving of a man's life on the Sabbath: "But should any man fall into water or fire, let him be pulled out with the aid of a ladder, or a rope or [some such] tool."[41] But they were not allowed to remove an animal which had fallen into a pit on the Sabbath—either with or without the use of devices.[42]

The Pharisees, as Jesus' rhetorical questions in Luke 14:5 and Matthew 12:11 indicate, allowed even the saving of animals: "Which of you here, if his son falls into a well, or his ox, will not pull him out on a sabbath day without hesitation?" Jesus implies his agreement with that interpretation and uses it to bolster his own opinion that healing (by words) should be considered even more justifiable: "Now a man is far more important than [an animal], so it follows that it is permitted to do good on the sabbath day" (Mt. 12:12). Jesus was concerned to make clear not that the Law was no longer valid or that he had broken the Law, but rather that his act was perfectly lawful by the Pharisees' own standards.

It was the objection that Jesus' disciples were "picking ears of corn, rubbing them in their hands and eating them" (Lk. 6:1) that gave rise to Jesus' statement about the Sabbath being made for man (Mt. 12:1–8; Mk. 2:23–28; Lk. 6:1–5). David Flusser points out that variant texts of Jewish Christian origin and the *Diatessaron* suggest that the disciples only rubbed the ears in their hands and were not plucking them.[43] While most rabbis did not even permit rubbing the ears of corn, let alone the picking of them, there were rabbis like Jesus who, according to Professor Flusser, permitted the rubbing of ears of corn on the Sabbath. Thus the only apparent example of Jesus' condoning a violation of the Sabbath arises from a mistranslation: if the disciples did not actually *pick* corn on the Sabbath, then they were within the bounds of at least one Pharisaic interpretation of the Law according to which *rubbing* ears of corn was not a forbidden act.[44] And even in this incident, Jesus was not himself accused of violating the Law, but only his disciples.

Another supposed departure from Pharisaic interpretation is found in Mark's account of the issue over the washing of hands (Mk. 7:1–9). "They noticed that some of his disciples were eating with unclean hands, that is, without washing them . . . these Pharisees and scribes asked him, 'Why do your disciples not respect the tradition of the elders but eat their food with unclean hands?'" (Mk. 7:2, 5). Actually, the Pharisees did not consider the washing of hands before their meals an element of the oral Law during Jesus' lifetime. As a "tradition of the elders" it was a matter of choice, a voluntary act.[45]

It may be that this passage reflects an issue between Jesus and the Qumran sect, who *did* observe very strict rules regarding washing before meals.[46] If so, we would have to assume that after the Fall of Jerusalem, when the "Pharisees" would have been the opposition party to the Christians, the name was changed in the story. But in actual fact, had it been the Pharisees who raised the question with Jesus it would not have been the Law but rather a custom that was at stake. His response to them indicates as much: "You put aside the commandment of God to cling to human traditions" (Mk. 7:8).

Jesus' position seems again to have been within the Law as interpreted by many Pharisees in his day. But once more, even if such a "breach" of the Law were proven, it was only some of Jesus' disciples, and not he himself, who were reported to have violated the custom.

Thus it would seem that Jesus required of his disciples that they, like he, fulfill the Mosaic Law in every regard.[47] What are recorded in the Gospels as issues over the Law serve as examples of cases in which Jesus' interpretation of the Law brought criticism from teachers who did not, as he seems to, fall within the "liberal" camp of Hillel Pharisaism. Such fine points of the Law would have been of great interest to early followers of Jesus who were devout Jews with great reverence for the Law. Today most Christians know very little about the Mosaic Law and jump to the incorrect conclusion that because there were disputes over the interpretation of it, therefore Jesus did not advocate keeping the Law.

DIVORCE AND PROSELYTISM

There were two issues on which Jesus appears to have adopted strict interpretations of the Law. With regard to divorce, Jesus agreed with the Shammai, or conservative, school's interpretation rather than with either Qumran or the Hillel Pharisees. He said, "It has also been said: 'Anyone who divorces his wife must give her a writ of dismissal' [Deut. 24:1–4]. But I say this to you: everyone who divorces his wife, except for the case of fornication, makes her an adulteress; and anyone who marries a divorced woman commits adultery" (Mt. 5:31–32). This extremely strict interpretation of the Deuteronomic law appears to go beyond even that of the Covenanters, who did not forbid divorce but only required a man seeking to divorce his wife to first clear it with the overseer of his "camp."[48]

Jesus referred to the Genesis stories of creation (Gen. 1:27 and Gen. 2:24) to demonstrate that marriage is a permanent state and divorce is forbidden.[49] "Have you not read that the creator from the beginning made them male and female and that he said: 'This is why a man must leave father and mother, and cling to his wife, and the two become one body'? They are no longer two, therefore, but one body. So then, what God has united, man must not divide" (Mt. 19:3–12, esp. 5 and 6).[50] The Qumran literature, on the other hand, combined those same citations with Genesis 7:9, "two of each kind boarded the ark with Noah, a male and a female, according to the order God gave Noah," to prove that a man should have no more than one wife *at a time*. Thus their Scrolls make reference to "whoredom by taking two wives during their lifetime."[51]

Jesus was also like the Shammai school of Pharisaism in his opposition to proselytizing. The first century A.D. was a period of very avid missionary zeal for Jews, who were hard at work converting Gentiles throughout the Empire. Jesus was apparently opposed to this, for he is reported to have criticized the Pharisees involved in proselytizing by saying, "Alas for you, scribes and Pharisees, you hypocrites! You who travel over sea and land to make a single proselyte, and when you have him you make him twice as fit for hell as you are" (Mt. 23:15). This reflects Jesus' great concern for the purification and redemption of the people of Israel first, before reaching out to the Gentiles (Mt. 10:5–7), and in this emphasis he was like the Covenanters. Jesus' statement may also reflect, however, his awareness that for a Gentile to take on the Mosaic Law voluntarily was an even heavier burden than for a Jew who had been born into the Covenant tradition.[52]

When Jesus spoke about adultery, he said, "You have learnt how it was said, 'You must not commit adultery' [Ex. 20:14]. But I say this to you: if a man looks at a woman lustfully, he has already committed adultery with her in his heart" (Mt. 5:27–28). Many passages in the Qumran Scrolls suggest a similarly strict interpretation with regard to adultery: for example, "stubbornly follow a sinful heart and lustful eyes," "folly and brazen insolence," "they have not lusted after their eyes," and "thoughts of the guilty inclination and after eyes of lust."[53] To interpret the Law with attention to the inner thoughts and feelings of a man was in keeping with the emphasis which both Jesus and the Covenanters put on purity of the "spirit" as well as of the Law.

There are other parallels which can be drawn between Jesus' interpretation of the Law and that of the Qumran sect, some of which have parallels in Pharisaic teaching and some of which do not. For example, both forbade taking oaths of any kind.[54] But the important thing to recognize is that all of Jesus' teachings and interpretations regarding the Law fell *within* the bounds of Pharisaic Judaism. Even the two great commandments Jesus used to sum up the Law are found in the Torah (Deut. 6:5 and Lev. 19:18); Jesus was, in an insightful way, quoting Scripture he knew intimately when he said: "This is the first [commandment]: 'Listen, Israel, the Lord our God is the one Lord, and you must love the Lord your God with all your heart, with all your soul, with all your mind and with all your strength.' The second is this: 'You must love your neighbour as yourself'" (Mk. 12:29–31. Cf. also Mt. 22:36–40). Moreover, Jesus' famous "Golden Rule," "So always treat others as you would like them to treat you" (Mt. 7:12a), was said to be the essence of Judaism by the sage Hillel in the first century B.C.[55]

LOVE AND HATE FOR ENEMIES

It is a common misunderstanding to view Jesus' moral teachings as opposed to the Judaism of his time. They were not unique or exceptional as is often thought. The most nearly original teaching of Jesus—and certainly not an insignificant or unimportant one—was his commandment to his disciples that they should love their enemies. The standard Jewish law of the time, instituted in an earlier period as a corrective to excessive vengeance against the enemy and therefore an ethical advancement in its own right, was "an eye for an eye, a tooth for a tooth." There are passages in the Qumran Scrolls, however, which are much stronger than that, suggesting that the Many should "hate" their enemies. Christian scholars often point this out as evidence that Jesus was obviously ethically superior to the Covenanters.

For example, Krister Stendahl of the Harvard Divinity School has explored the ideals of hate, nonretaliation, and love found in the

Scrolls and in the New Testament writings. He maintains that "at Qumran 'love' is confined to the community and . . . the attitude of nonretaliation [towards those outside of the sect] is by no means a type of love."[56] Yet in the Manual of Discipline we read: "I will pay to no man the reward of evil; I will pursue him with goodness. For judgement of all the living is with God and it is He who will render to man his reward . . . I will not grapple with the men of perdition until the Day of Revenge, but my wrath shall not turn from the men of falsehood and I will not rejoice until judgement is made" (Man. of Disc. 10:17–20).

This seemingly awkward juxtaposition of hatred and nonretaliation in the sect's writings is, in Dr. Stendahl's view, explained by the sharp line which the Covenanters drew between men of the spirit of light and men of the spirit of darkness. Vengeance toward men of darkness is foregone on a personal scale for it is left to be meted out by God on the final Day of Revenge. In Stendahl's words, therefore, for the Covenanters, "To pursue outsiders with good is a special case of 'the eternal hatred' [Man. of Disc. 9:21 f.: 'Everlasting hatred in a spirit of secrecy for the men of perdition!'], not of love."[57]

Yet the Gospels contain certain passages which record that Jesus shared an attitude very similar to the Covenanters' concerning vengeance. After being rebuked by a Samaritan village and certain villages in Galilee, Jesus forestalled the rage and vengeance of the disciples by explaining to them that the fate of those villages on the Day of Vengeance would be worse than that suffered by Sodom and Gomorrah[58] (Lk. 9:51–56; 10:1–16).

Raymond E. Brown, S.S., of St. Mary's Seminary in Baltimore, has suggested, however, that the formula of hate, found in the Qumran initiation ceremonies in the Manual of Discipline, may be stylized and ancient, while the hymns which conclude that same work and convey quite another impression may express a later ideal of personal piety.[59] If this be true, then perhaps we should not so easily dismiss the Covenanters as "ethically inferior" to Jesus. After all, Jesus also advocated "hatred"—not of *enemies,* but of *family*—for those who sought to follow him: "If any man comes to me without hating his father, mother, wife, children, brothers, sisters, yes, and his own life too, he cannot be my disciple" (Lk. 14:26).

It may be that such eschatological hatred "for the sake of the Kingdom" of those who had not chosen the way of truth, who were enemies because they were still "children of darkness," was characteristic of both Jesus and the Covenanters, and that in personal relationships both advocated love rather than hate. With this as the interpretation of the "hatred" of which both the Covenanters and Jesus spoke, the seeming contradiction would be resolved. By becoming a "child of light" and despising "evil ways and all those who walk in them," one is freed in his personal life to walk in the way of truth and light. In "the light," one is able to love even one's enemies.

Moreover, there are passages in writings from the time which approach the ethical level suggested in Jesus' instruction to love one's enemy.[60] For example, Jesus' injunction in Matthew 5:38 f. to resist not evil, but rather to turn the other cheek, has an interesting parallel in this passage from the Scrolls: "I will pay to no man the reward of evil; I will pursue him with goodness. For judgement of all the living is with God and it is He who will render to man his reward."[61] This passage reveals an attitude suggested when personal forgiveness of "men of power" was appropriate, whereas the attitude of hatred toward enemies discussed above "had an eschatological character."[62]

Furthermore, David Flusser points out that the concept of not repaying evil with evil found expression not only in the Qumranic literature, but in "pietistic" Pharisaic literature as well. It was an important element of the teachings found in the Testament of the Twelve Patriarchs, copies of which have been found at Qumran.[63] The following passage from the Testament of Gad, for example, though not an exact parallel of Jesus' commandment to "love your enemies," nevertheless reveals a high level of ethical—and even psychological—sophistication:

"And now, my children, hearken to the words of truth to work righteousness, and all the law of the Most High, and go not astray through the spirit of hatred, for it is evil in all the dealings of men . . . Beware, therefore, my children of hatred; for it works lawlessness even against the Lord Himself. For it will not hear the words of His commandments concerning the loving of one's neighbor, and it sins against God . . . For as love would quicken even the dead, and would call back them that are condemned to die, so hatred would slay the living, and those that had sinned venially it would not suffer to live. For the spirit of hatred works together with Satan, through hastiness of spirit, in all things to men's death; but the spirit of love works together with the law of God in long-suffering unto the salvation of men . . .

"And now, my children, I exhort you, love you each one his brother, and put away hatred from your hearts, love one another in deed, and in word, and in the inclination of the soul . . . Love one another from the heart; and if a man sin against you, speak peaceably to him, and in your soul hold not guile; and if he repent and confess, forgive him. But if he deny it, do not get into a passion with him, lest catching the poison from you he take to swearing and so sin doubly. And though he deny it and yet have a sense of shame when reproved, stop reproving him. For he who denies may repent so as not again to wrong you; yea, he may also honor you, and be at peace with you. And if he be shameless and persist in his wrongdoing, even so forgive him from the heart, and leave to God the avenging." (Test. of Gad 3–6 passim. Our modification of R. H. Charles's translation.)

It is worth taking note, finally, of David Flusser's view of Jesus' commandment to love one's enemies: "Jesus added an important corollary to the theses of his Jewish predecessors. The Judaism of his time, or at any rate certain circles in it, forbade people to hate their enemies and required them to behave in the same way towards sinners as towards the righteous. Jesus called for love even of one's enemies and even of sinners. This demand of Jesus was evidently too radical for the young Church. In the New Testament love of one's enemies is mentioned only in Jesus' teaching in the synoptic Gospels. The requirement that one should love the sinner became known later through the synoptic Gospels, but it was not always practised by Christians."[64]

"WALK IN THE LIGHT"

Perhaps the most striking parallel, in the ethical or moral realm between Jesus' teachings and those of Qumran are those found in the Gospel of John. In the Manual of Discipline the sectarians are urged "to *practice*" or "to *do the truth*."[65] Jesus is reported in John to have said, "But the man who *lives by the truth* comes out into the light, so that it may be plainly seen that what he does is done in God" (Jn. 3:21). Compare also this statement from the Scrolls, "Truth abhors the works of falsehood, and falsehood hates all the ways of truth. And their struggle is fierce for they do not walk together,"[66] with these words spoken by Jesus, "And indeed, everybody who does wrong hates the light and avoids it, for fear his actions should be exposed; but the man who lives by the truth comes out into the light, so that it may be plainly seen that what he does is done in God" (Jn. 3:20–21).

In the Manual of Discipline the sectarians are called "witnesses of truth."[67] Only in one other document does this phrase occur, and that is in the New Testament's Fourth Gospel, where it is used both of John the Baptist and of Jesus: "You sent to John, and he has borne witness to the truth" (Jn. 5:33, RSV) and, "Yes, I am a king. I was born for this, I came into the world for this: to bear witness to the truth" (Jn. 18:37).[68]

"BLESSED ARE THE POOR . . ."

It was principally in his thought and teaching about the events that would accompany the end of the age that Jesus was most strongly influenced by Qumran, or most fully shared their teachings and world view.[69] As Krister Stendahl points out, Albert Schweitzer's *The Quest of the Historical Jesus* marked the beginning of fifty years of Biblical studies for which "eschatology," or the doctrine of the end of days, was the key word. With Schweitzer "eschatology" was discovered to be the climate and the frame of reference for the appearance and the teaching of Jesus from beginning to end.[70] But it has only been since the discovery of the Scrolls that we have been in a position to compare "the Messianic expectation of the Jewish sect called the Christians with another Jewish sect, already on the scene at the time of Jesus."[71]

Take, for example, Jesus' most famous set of teachings, delivered in the "Sermon on the Mount." Because Jesus is said to have gone up onto a mountain to deliver his message to his followers, many scholars have seen these teachings as a kind of "new Law" given to Jesus' disciples, paralleling the "old Law" delivered by Moses at Mount Sinai.

We have seen that the Qumran community believed it had entered into a New Covenant with God—a Covenant that was a new commitment to the Mosaic Law and added the promise of the gift of the spirit of holiness as a sign to those who entered into it. The interpretations of the Law and the prophets given to the Covenanters by the Teacher of Righteousness were comparable to the Law given by Moses to the Israelites.

Thus it is possible that the collections of teachings gathered by Matthew and Luke (Mt. 5:1 to 7:29; Lk. 6:20–49) were their understandings of the "new Law" according to Jesus. We have no way of knowing, however, if Jesus' *intention* was to deliver such a "new Law" or if instead the "Sermons" in the Gospels represent later collections of some of Jesus' most famous and profound teachings.

It is not without interest to note, however, that the sermons according to both Matthew and Luke begin with a series of three "blessings" which have striking parallels in the Qumran sectarian writings. Not only are blessings as a literary form to be found in the Qumran materials—for example: "Words of blessing. The Master shall bless them that fear God and do His will, that keep His commandments, and hold fast to His holy Covenant, and walk perfectly in all the ways of His truth; whom He has chosen for an eternal Covenant which shall endure for ever"[72]—but the actual pattern of content is found in the Hymns of Thanksgiving Scroll, where the sectarian author thanks God: "To have appointed me in Thy truth a messenger of the peace of Thy goodness, to proclaim *to the meek* the multitude of thine mercies, and to let them *that are of contrite spirit* hear salvation from the everlasting source, and to *them that mourn* everlasting joy."[73]

Jesus, in the spirit of this psalmist of the Qumran community, *proclaims* God's mercies to the same people mentioned in the hymn, promising them everlasting salvation and joy: "Blessed are *the poor in spirit,* for theirs is the kingdom of heaven. Blessed are *those who mourn,* for they shall be comforted. Blessed are *the meek,* for they shall inherit the earth" (Mt. 5:3–5, RSV). Professor David Flusser, in his essay "Blessed Are the Poor in Spirit . . ." says, "The addressees of both passages are the same: in both the good tidings are promised to the poor in spirit (Hymns: 'to them that are of contrite spirit'), to the meek, and to them that mourn. *Such affinity cannot be accidental:* both 'tricola' [groups or collections of 3 sayings] are based on the same combination of Isaiah 61:1–2 and Isaiah 66:2 . . ."[74]

Jesus appears to be speaking out of, and probably to, a familiarity with the Qumran community and its teachings. The terms "poor in spirit" and "the poor," which is used by Luke (Lk. 6:20b, KJV), were used by the Covenanters, as we have seen, to identify themselves.[75]

Jesus was probably addressing himself to persons who identified themselves with that desert movement, or at least were highly sympathetic to it. As Professor Flusser says, the "connection between the beginning of the Sermon and the ideology of the Sect must have been clear to the hearers of Jesus' words. It is therefore probable that in his opening words Jesus deliberately alluded to the doctrines of the Sect with the intention to stress the points of contact between his message of love and the radical social claims of the Sect, the promise of eschatological salvation of the poor, the afflicted, and of them that suffer persecution and despair."[76]

Second, Jesus makes clear that the blessing conferred on the members of the movement—"the poor" or the "poor in spirit"—is that they will inherit the Kingdom. This of course was the whole thrust of the Qumran sect's teaching and their very *raison d'être* was to live in such a state of righteous perfection that they would be worthy of inheriting the Kingdom of God, or of heaven, when it was established *on earth.* This latter point is brought home in verse four when Jesus makes clear that the "meek" will also inherit the *earth.* That is, the heavenly or "otherworldly" realm will enter, merge with, and transform the earthly or "this worldly."[77]

Third, the very fact that he opened his address with the theme of inheriting the Kingdom stresses Jesus' identification with the desert tradition to which John the Baptist belonged and of which Qumran is representative. He promised that those who became "poor" in order to hasten the coming of the Messiah would inherit the Kingdom with him. The theme of the coming Kingdom is predominant throughout Jesus' teaching. He used many parables to describe it and to try to indicate what his disciples could do in order to inherit it.

Two parables can serve as familiar examples:

"The Kingdom of heaven is like treasure hidden in a field which someone has found; he hides it again, goes off happy, sells everything he owns and buys the field." (Mt. 13:44)

"A man had two sons. He went and said to the first, 'My boy, you go and work in the vineyard today.' He answered, 'I will not go,' but afterwards thought better of it and went. The man then went and said the same thing to the second who answered, 'Certainly, sir,' but did not go. Which of the two did the father's will? 'The first,' they said. Jesus said to them, 'I tell you solemnly, tax collectors and prostitutes are making their way into the kingdom of God before you. For John came to you, a pattern of true righteousness, but you did not believe him, and yet the tax collectors and prostitutes did. Even after seeing that, you refused to think better of it and believe in him." (Mt. 21:28–32)[78]

Furthermore, the prayer which Jesus taught his disciples and which has been universally prayed by Christians ever since, stresses the same theme:

"Our father, who art in heaven, hallowed be thy name. *Thy kingdom come, thy will be done, on earth as it is in heaven"* (Mt. 6:9–10, RSV).[79]

It does not take a stretch of the imagination to see the rest of the Beatitudes as derived from beliefs, teachings, and attitudes of the Qumran sect, even though their precise parallels as literary forms have not been found as yet in the sectarian writings. The Beatitudes give expression to the following concepts and beliefs held by "the poor."

"Blessed are those who hunger and thirst for righteousness, for they shall be satisfied" (Mt. 5:6, RSV): the Qumran sect sought to be perfect in their righteousness; surely when "God only" was established as King, this desire would be fulfilled. "Blessed are the merciful, for they shall obtain mercy" (Mt. 5:7, RSV): the Covenanters sought to be merciful to one another, expecting that God in His mercy would save them in the last days. "Blessed are the pure in heart, for they shall see God" (Mt. 5:8, RSV): the poor at Qumran did not believe it was sufficient to follow the letter of the Law; they sought an inner purity of the spirit (the heart was the symbolic seat of man's spirit) and they believed if they were perfect in both ritual and spiritual purity they would "see God" on the judgment day.[80]

"Blessed are the peacemakers, for they shall be called sons of God" (Mt. 5:9, RSV): the Covenanters believed themselves to be the children of light (sons of God), who, by winning peace in their own lives and by throwing in their lot with the forces of light, would help to bring lasting peace on earth in the form of God's eternal Kingdom.[81] "Blessed are those who are persecuted for righteousness' sake, for theirs is the kingdom of heaven. Blessed are you when men revile you and persecute you and utter all kinds of evil against you falsely on my account. Rejoice and be glad, for your reward is great in heaven, for so men persecuted the prophets who were before you" (Mt. 5:10–11, RSV): the Many had a strong tradition recalling the persecution of their sect and their Teacher of Righteousness, all of which they identified as "signs of the time" indicating that the coming Kingdom was imminent.[82]

Luke follows the "blessings" with a series of "woes": "But woe to you that are rich, for you have received your consolation. Woe to you that are full now, for you shall hunger. Woe to you that laugh now, for you shall mourn and weep. Woe to you, when all men speak well of you, for so their fathers did to the false prophets" (Lk. 6:24–26, RSV).

Although these "woes" are missing in Matthew, Professor Flusser points out that it is likely they would have formed the counterpart of the preceding Beatitudes in the original teachings of Jesus. For not only is there a strong dualistic trend in the beliefs of the Qumran sect to which the Beatitudes seem to be connected, but also there is what Dr. Flusser calls the "social pathos" of all the Beatitudes. He points out that in the Book of Enoch (94:6–103) woes against the wicked rich are mingled with words of hope and promise of eternal bliss to the righteous poor.[83] One example of the dualistic "positive" and "negative" thrust of the attitudes and teachings of the Covenanters can be found in the ritual for admittance to the Qumran movement, where the priests *bless* those who keep the Covenant and will thus enter the Kingdom, and *curse* those who have fallen away.[84]

THE RESURRECTION OF THE DEAD

One last element indicating an influence by Qumran on Jesus' teaching regarding the coming Kingdom is found in his descriptions of the after-life. Not only did the Covenanters envision a judgment day such as that which Jesus describes in his parable of the talents and in his description of the great separation of sheep and goats (Mt. 25:14–46), but also they anticipated the enjoyment of a kind of angelic existence after the judgment day, an idea very similar to that expressed by Jesus when he says, "Those who are judged worthy of a place in the other world and in the resurrection from the dead . . . are the same as the angels, and being children of the resurrection they are sons of God" (Lk. 20:35–36).[85]

Belief in the resurrection was not peculiar to Jesus and the Poor of Qumran, however. The majority of Jews had come to accept the resurrection of the body as part of the general scheme of redemption which would follow the Messiah's advent. Only a few Jews did not believe in a general resurrection on the judgment day. Jesus is reported to have chided the Sadducees, who did not believe in the resurrection of the dead, for their lack of understanding of both the Scriptures and the power of God.[86] Not even a belief in immortal men and in ascensions was as alien to ancient Judaism as it is to modern men. Melchizedek was thought to be immortal, Elijah had an ascension attributed to him, and Enoch is, like Melchizedek, a kind of angelic and thus immortal figure.[87] Therefore, Jesus' teachings about the resurrection, and the disciples' experiences of Jesus after his death, were not without a context of thought and expectation. However, as we shall see in Chapter 13, the fact that Jesus' resurrection was not followed by the general resurrection and the judgment day turned out to be one of the crucial factors in the development of Christianity.

As we have seen, then, Jesus' teachings were in every regard within the "boundaries" of the thought of his day. In the words of the Jewish scholar Joseph Klausner, "throughout the Gospels there is not one item of ethical teaching which cannot be paralleled either in the Old Testament, the Apocrypha, or in the Talmudic and Mishnaic literature of the period near to the time of Jesus."[88] Moreover, the striking similarities between Jesus and the Qumran sect in their teachings about eschatology—the coming Kingdom and the events which would accompany it—make it clear that Jesus was in the mainstream of Messianic apocalyptic expectation of first-century Judaism.

Christianity did not develop into a predominantly Gentile movement until after the Messianic, or nationalistic, hopes of the Jews were quite thoroughly dashed in the Great Revolt of A.D. 66–70.[89] If one were to define a "normative" or "orthodox" Judaism which enjoyed the widest possible support before that devastating event, it would be the apocalyptic nationalism of which Jesus distinguishes himself as an example, rather than an exception.[90]

CHAPTER 8

Jesus: A Preacher of the Kingdom

*"Do not suppose that I have come to bring peace
to the earth: it is not peace I have come to bring,
but a sword. Anyone who does not take his cross and
follow in my footsteps is not worthy of me."*

Matthew 10:34, 38

In the words of James A. Pike:

"In the Judean tradition, Elijah was expected to return before
the Messiah, to prepare the way for the coming of the Kingdom of
God. In the Samaritan tradition there was no Elijah expected; they
were waiting instead for Moses to reappear, or reincarnate. You
will notice that on the Mount of Transfiguration Jesus and his
disciples had a visionary experience which couldn't have been better
staged. On either side of Jesus were Moses and Elijah. Prizes for
everybody. If you look at it from the Samaritan standpoint, your
expectation is fulfilled. If you look at it from the Judean point of
view, you're satisfied, too.

"The Qumran or Covenanter pattern was that Elijah the prophet
would appear first, and then two Messiahs—one priestly and one
kingly. You will remember that since the early Christian teaching,
Jesus has been called priest, prophet, and king. He is seen to be
all of these things. There was to be a prophetic forerunner and
then the priest and king. The priestly Messiah was to be tops over
the kingly one, however.

"The problem of the early Christian Jews was that they claimed
Jesus was one of these figures—the Davidic, or kingly, Messiah.
But a Covenanter would have asked, 'Then where's the priest?' So

the Epistle to the Hebrews—according to Father Jean Daniélou, a Roman Catholic who works in this field—was written for Essene-minded Christian Jews—those who came out of the Essene, or Qumran tradition. The Epistle to the Hebrews shows that Jesus was a priest according to the order of Melchizedek, even if he couldn't be traced back to Aaron or Zadok. He was a higher priest —or perhaps even Melchizedek himself, who had already become a heavenly figure very much like the Son of Man.

"Jesus sent his disciples out two by two to the villages and towns, saying, 'Skip the Samaritans and skip the Gentiles and by the time you come back the Kingdom will have come.' They did get back, but nothing happened. The Kingdom did not come. After about three days had gone by, I am sure some polite disciple must have said, 'What's new, Jesus?'

"Albert Schweitzer, without benefit of the Dead Sea Scrolls, saw this point and figured out that Jesus must have decided then that there had to be a confrontation. Talking about it was not enough; words were not enough. Action was needed.

"Now the confrontation was never meant to be the victory in itself. It was designed to be the catalyst for opening the heavens for the forces of light to come. It was like the expectation of the Zealots on Masada from A.D. 70 to 73. They felt if they held out long enough against the Romans, and kept up the tension, God would intervene and send His heavenly troops.

"Jesus planned the confrontation carefully. He went down to Jerusalem for the feast of Hanukkah—secretly, by himself—and laid the plans. He had connections with a man with a house in Jerusalem. To have a big house in Jerusalem was like having a house in Manhattan today. Jesus knew a person of great prominence, then, who was known as the beloved disciple, but who was not one of the twelve, and was not a Galilean.

"He also had become friends with Joseph of Arimathea, a member of the Sanhedrin, but not one of the central group of Jesus' disciples, obviously. He also had someone handy—doubtless Lazarus—to take care of the donkey on which he was to make the entry into Jerusalem. The donkey was the sign of Bar David, the son of David. He arranged for a hideaway in Bethany: he never spent the night in Jerusalem, though he was determined to have the Seder [Passover meal] in Jerusalem. He had all of this lined up, with plans for the palms to be waved, the right words to be used, so everything would be right."

—————◆—————

JESUS ORGANIZES A COUNCIL OF TWELVE

Jesus launched his teaching and preaching activities in Galilee and kept them centered there, even though he is reported to have preached and baptized from time to time in the part of Judea where John was accustomed to work, in the region of the Jordan River.[1] Jesus apparently recruited his disciples in Galilee. In fact, the Synoptic Gospels give the impression that the disciples may even have been ready and waiting for Jesus to "return" and give them leadership. Luke 4:14 f. says, "Jesus, with the power of the Spirit in him, returned to Galilee; and his reputation spread throughout the countryside. He taught in their synagogues and everyone praised him."

It is not inconceivable that Jesus had been sent by his fellow Galileans to be trained by John the Baptist at Qumran or to be a leader in the revolution of which Galilee was the principal breeding ground. It is not hard to believe that he was their most promising teacher and leader. If this was the case, then the twelve may have been among the local leaders in Galilee who were ready to assist Jesus upon his return. If they had made all the necessary preparations so that they could leave their work and go with him as soon as he came back, the stories of their "callings" in the Gospels would certainly be more comprehensible, and plausible. But such a theory must remain only speculation since very little data is given in the New Testament about the background of the disciples.

We are told in the Synoptic Gospels that Jesus went walking along the shore of the Sea of Galilee, saw Peter, James, Andrew, and John fishing, and called to them, promising to make them "fishers of men" (a code phrase worked out ahead of time, perhaps) if they would join him. They "immediately" left their nets and followed him.[2] This would seem very irresponsible behavior for men who were undoubtedly supporting families, if they in fact went off with Jesus with no more thought or planning than that. Moreover, considering the cool reception given Jesus among the people of his family's synagogue,[3] it is doubtful that hardworking fishermen would have gone off with Jesus on a whim or even on a strong intuition unless they had in mind something that they felt it was very important to "catch" men for.

If, however, the twelve were already part of a kind of underground revolutionary Messianic movement, such ostensibly erratic or impulsive behavior would make real sense. In fact, John's Gospel says that two of the first men to follow Jesus were disciples of John the Baptist (Jn. 1:35–37). One of the two was Andrew and it was he, John records, who recruited Simon Peter for Jesus' discipleship (Jn. 1:40–42). The implication in the Fourth Gospel is that Andrew and Peter —and perhaps one other disciple—were recruited while Jesus was still near the Jordan River following his baptism, and it was only the "next day" that he went up to Galilee where he found Philip and Nathanael (Jn. 1:43 ff.).

The Fourth Gospel, then, seems to make even more clear than the Synoptics Jesus' association with the desert sect movements such as that of John the Baptist. Indeed, if some of Jesus' closest disciples were trained first by John the Baptist, then it is easier to understand why they would have been ready to follow Jesus "immediately." If as John's Gospel reports, they believed they had "found the Messiah" (Jn. 1:41), then they would have known at once that the moment they had been preparing for—that time when the Messiah would come and the Kingdom would be established on earth—had arrived.

Matthew seems also to have been prepared one way or another for he would not likely have risen up and followed Jesus without hesitation[4] unless he had been in training for the apocalyptic events at the end of the age and believed Jesus to be the one who could lead them through these events.

On the other hand, that the "underground" would have had members holding posts in all walks of life is not surprising, but to be expected, for that is the way it has been with all revolutionary movements throughout history. And that the time for Matthew to leave his position as a tax collector and withdraw with Jesus for intensive training and preparation could have been prearranged also seems quite plausible. What does not seem likely is that anyone would walk away from such a lucrative post to go with a man of whom he knew nothing as part of a high-risk movement in which he had not up till that time been involved.

We are not told much more about the recruitment of the disciples. The Fourth Gospel indicates that Philip was from Bethsaida, "the city of Andrew and Peter" (Jn. 1:44), implying some link between the three. Philip was apparently the one who notified Nathanael that their "leader" had arrived—in language which only a Messianist, or apocalyptist, would have understood: "We have found the one Moses wrote about in the Law, the one about whom the prophets wrote: he is Jesus son of Joseph, from Nazareth" (Jn. 1:45).

Jesus had not met Nathanael before, according to the story, but is said to have recognized him even before Philip approached him and called him (Jn. 1:45–51). This seems to be further evidence that Jesus' selection of his disciples was not a random process, but rather that he knew before his return to Galilee who had been prepared to share his leadership so that all he had to do was gather them together when he got back. The groundwork had been laid. Nathanael, for example, was well versed in apocalyptic literature even before he went with Jesus. The initial conversation reported between the two gets right to the heart of the movement's goals: "You are the King of Israel!" Nathanael said to him. Jesus replied, "I tell you most solemnly, you will see heaven laid open and, above the Son of Man, the angels of God ascending and descending." These are words which a man who had read the Qumran Scrolls and the apocalyptic writings could not misinterpret: Jesus was saying to Nathanael in scriptural language what he preached more directly to the masses, "The kingdom of God is at hand."

Of the other disciples we know only that they were chosen to be among the twelve[5] and that they were apparently not averse to violence or "revolutionary" acts. Among them were Simon, a Zealot (Lk. 6:15; Acts 1:13);[6] James and John, two hotheads, or "Sons of Thunder" (Mk. 3:17);[7] Peter, an "outlaw" or "rebel" (Barjona; Mt. 16:17, RSV);[8] and possibly a member of the "daggermen" or Sicarii —Judas Iscariot (Mt. 10:4; Mk. 3:19; Lk. 6:16).[9] Moreover, as we have already mentioned, at least five of the disciples had Maccabean names, indicating their strong association with the nationalistic or Zealot (in the broad sense) movement.[10]

Though the twelve were often slow, according to Gospel accounts, to comprehend the deeper meanings of Jesus' apocalyptic teachings, they did not seem slow to take action when action seemed to them to be needed. For example, when a Samaritan village failed to respond to Jesus, James and John were ready to bring fire down to consume the village right then (Lk. 9:54)[11]—a kind of immediate "judgment" instead of waiting for the final day. And in the Garden of Gethsemane, when the soldiers came to arrest Jesus, Peter drew his sword and struck.[12] James, John, and Peter were the inner circle of the disciples.

Thus it would seem that the disciples Jesus chose to share his leadership were men prepared for the revolution—men who under-

stood what Jesus meant when he said, "Do not suppose that I have
come to bring peace to the earth: it is not peace I have come to
bring, but a sword" (Mt. 10:34).[13]

THE NATURE OF THE TASK

Jesus demanded a discipline of his disciples which was not unlike
that undertaken by the men at Qumran. They apparently gave up all
their property, quit their work, and left their families in order to
follow Jesus.[14] Though Jesus promised them "riches" both in the
immediate future and in the age to come,[15] their life in the interim
was not easy. "For the sake of the Kingdom of God" they had no
possessions and no regular homes to live in,[16] and those who were
able to, remained unmarried.[17] Jesus' words about the "cost" of
discipleship were harsh:

> "Do not suppose that I have come to bring peace to the earth: it is
> not peace I have come to bring, but a sword. For I have come to
> set a *man against his father, a daughter against her mother, a daughter-
> in-law against her mother-in-law. A man's enemies will be those of his
> own household.* Anyone who prefers father or mother to me is not
> worthy of me. Anyone who prefers son or daughter to me is not
> worthy of me. Anyone who does not take his cross and follow in my
> footsteps is not worthy of me. Anyone who finds his life will lose it;
> anyone who loses his life for my sake will find it." (Mt. 10:34–39)[18]

Jesus asked of his disciples total commitment to the cause. He
urged them to count the cost ahead of time so they would not regret
their decision:

> "And indeed, which of you here, intending to build a tower, would
> not first sit down and work out the cost to see if he had enough to
> complete it? Otherwise, if he laid the foundation and then found
> himself unable to finish the work, the onlookers would all start
> making fun of him and saying, 'Here is a man who started to build
> and was unable to finish.' Or again, what king marching to war
> against another king would not first sit down and consider whether with
> ten thousand men he could stand up to the other who advanced
> against him with twenty thousand? If not, then while the other king

was still a long way off, he would send envoys to sue for peace. So in the same way, none of you can be my disciple unless he gives up all his possessions." (Lk. 14:28–33)

A part of what they had to take into account was that they might well die on crosses for following Jesus, for he told them they must be willing *each day* to take up their crosses (Lk. 9:23). This appears to be a reference to the fact that those who were crucified were forced to carry their own crossbars to the place of execution. It also reflects the danger any group ran which came together in the wilderness tradition of protest, as has been noted several times before.

Jesus was obviously not calling his disciples for a simple "preaching mission" or there would have been no such danger involved in it. He demanded a rigid discipline of them, comparable to that of soldiers of righteousness in training for war—the final battle against the forces of darkness. It is not surprising, therefore, that Jesus refrained from marriage himself, and that he urged his disciples either to leave their wives for the period of preparation for the end of days, or to remain unmarried: the abstinence from sexual relations during a time of preparation for war and during the war itself is one of the laws of purity for a holy war, as we pointed out in Chapter 4. As F. M. Cross, Jr., the Harvard scholar and member of the Dead Sea Scrolls team, says in speaking about the Qumran community, "Theirs was not a genuine asceticism, but an eschatological asceticism. They did not, it seems, reject marriage as such, but marriage in the present circumstances."[19]

The same seems to have been true of Jesus and his disciples, for the style of life they chose was for an expressed purpose and did not cause them to shy away from persons who had possessions and homes or who were married. Neither did they condemn such persons or the state of matrimony itself. Jesus did say, however, that it would be very difficult for a rich man to get into the Kingdom of God, apparently because attachment to material goods made it hard to put the Kingdom first.[20]

Paul later explained this "interim ethic" to new members of the movement. After Jesus' death and the resurrection experiences, the followers of Jesus believed the time before the final battle to be upon them, and expected Jesus' coming "in power" at any moment. Therefore Paul said in his first letter to the Corinthians: "Brothers, this is what I mean: our time is growing short. Those who have wives should live as though they had none, and those who mourn should live as though they had nothing to mourn for; those who are enjoying life should live as though there were nothing to laugh about; those whose life is buying things should live as though they had nothing of their own; and those who have to deal with the world should not become engrossed in it. I say this because the world as we know it is passing away" (I Cor. 7:29–31).

SIGNS OF THE KINGDOM

Jesus' teaching and preaching seem to have been very effective, for he developed a wide following from Galilee and from the surrounding areas of the Decapolis and Tyre and Sidon.[21] He not only taught but *acted* with authority, casting out demons,[22] healing the sick,[23] forgiving sins,[24] raising people from the dead,[25] and performing other miracles, such as changing water into wine, calming a storm, walking on water, and multiplying fish and loaves.[26] His fame spread largely because of the works that he did,[27] but he was careful only to perform such miracles when the persons who received the benefits had faith[28] that the Kingdom was indeed at hand so that they would give the praise and thanks to God and not to him.[29] Moreover, he withdrew when people came to him solely because of the "signs" that he did, since his major purpose was to announce the imminence of the Kingdom.[30] In these ways he sustained the commitment not to use the powers he had received for any other purpose than to facilitate the establishment of God's Kingdom on earth—a commitment which had been tested in the wilderness—and insured that he would not fall into temptation again.[31]

It is significant that the demons, the children of darkness, were the first to recognize his power.[32] They would shout out when they saw him coming, saying, "You are the Son of God!" (Mk. 3:11; Lk. 4:41), or, "What do you want with us, Jesus of Nazareth? Have you come to destroy us? I know who you are: the Holy One of God" (Mk. 1:24; Lk. 4:34), or, "What do you want with us, Son of God? Have you come here to torture us before the time [i.e., before the final judgment day]?" (Mt. 8:29), or, "Swear by God that you will not torture me!" (Mk. 5:7; Lk. 8:28). By his very presence Jesus announced the arrival of the Kingdom, for light began conquering darkness at his approach, and the evil spirits, or children of darkness, were the first to acknowledge their inability to live in the light. They were, therefore, the first to acknowledge Jesus' power over them as a child of light, or a son of God.

THE DISCIPLES TEACH, PREACH, AND HEAL

In spite of the wide following he had attracted, however, Jesus became increasingly sensitive to the crowds of people who he felt were "harassed and dejected, like sheep without a shepherd" (Mt. 9:36), and he had compassion for them. So he called his disciples together and said, "The harvest is rich but the labourers are few, so ask the Lord of the harvest to send labourers to his harvest" (Mt. 9:37). Then he gave his disciples power and authority over unclean spirits, to cast them out, and to heal every disease and every infirmity, and he sent them out to announce the coming Kingdom.[33]

Jesus' instructions to the disciples suggest a strong association with the Qumran style of life. By casting out demons and healing, the disciples were to announce the approaching Kingdom by their presence as well as by their words, as is characteristic of children of light. He told the seventy, gathered to spread the word of the coming of the Kingdom even faster, "Whenever you go into a town where they make you welcome, eat what is set before you, cure those in it who are sick, and say, 'The kingdom of God *is very near to you*'" [italics ours]. This is precisely within the Qumran tradition, for they too believed the *presence* of the children of light gave witness to the imminence of the Kingdom.

Jesus sent them out two by two, and told them to take nothing with them beyond what they wore: "Take nothing for your journey, no staff, nor bag, nor bread, nor money; and do not have two tunics." The message he told them to preach was simply, "the Kingdom of God is at hand." He urged them to find out the "worthy" or "sons of peace" and to stay with them. He assured them that they would be able to tell whether or not the members of a household were "worthy" by whether the peace which they brought with them (that peace which is the result of the internal war between light and darkness having been won)[34] rested on the household or returned to them. If it returned, the disciples were to move on and to find a household where men of peace abided and to stay with them.

All of these instructions were like those given members of the Qumran community when they traveled. They too were to travel in twos, carry no money and no change of clothes, and stay with members of their sister communities where they could enjoy the companionship of others who walked in the light and could eat the food which was served without fear of defilement.

It appears that even though Jesus extended his preaching to the masses, he still did not want his disciples to mix with company which could defile them or lead them astray. Thus he urged them not to go anywhere among the Gentiles and to enter no Samaritan towns. He himself went with them through Samaria on other occasions and seemed to have no fear of defilement from Gentiles, but as far as we know he did not carry on any preaching or teaching among them. The one, apparently ad hoc, exception is that related by John. After Jesus' lengthy conversation with the Samaritan woman at the well (Jn. 4:1–26), Jesus stayed on in that Samaritan village for two days and "spoke to them" (Jn. 4:40–43).

His strict instructions to his disciples, however, and to the seventy later recruited to go out on a similar mission, probably revealed Jesus' concern for their spiritual welfare, a concern at least equal to his sense of urgency regarding the announcing of the Kingdom. In other words, only if his disciples remained strong in their own dedication and perfect in their own righteousness by the Law, would they be worthy to enter the Kingdom themselves. Moreover, only through such worthiness were they able to cast out demons and heal, aiding the establishment of the Kingdom by their own lives and presence. Jesus, therefore, gave instructions to them which would help them maintain their own state of spiritual readiness while out on their preaching mission and not in his presence.

It is also possible that Jesus' caution about the "houses" to which he sent his disciples was an indication that he had given them instructions to go to those sister communities of the Qumran (or desert) movement with which he was familiar, and that he feared some would not be willing to receive his disciples because he had begun a kind of "branch" movement. If that was the case, it would be easier to understand why Jesus told the disciples to go to only one house in each village and to stay there the whole time: there would not likely have been more than one branch of the Many in any village or town, nor would such branch houses be likely to have been found among Gentiles or in Samaritan villages. Therefore, if his disciples were not received in the house, or sister community, to which Jesus had sent them, they would not have been able to stay in that village but would have had to move on until they found a safe place to stay.

Jesus' admonition that his disciples "shake off the dust" that was on their feet "for a testimony against them" when they were not received in a given village reflects both his sense of urgency (there is no time to discuss fine theological points now!) and his earnest conviction that all issues of justice and truth would soon be settled. "I tell you solemnly, on the day of Judgement it will not go as hard with the land of Sodom and Gomorrah as with that town" (Mt. 10:15). And, "you will not have gone the round of the towns of Israel before the Son of Man comes" (Mt. 10:23b).

Seeing that the harvest was plentiful and the laborers few, Jesus had decided to send out his own disciples to reap the ripe grain. He was aware, however, that to do so was to run a great risk, for it would be easy for the Romans and their Jewish collaborators to detect the growth of his movement. He feared for his disciples, knowing that they could be captured and persecuted in this final hour by the "forces of darkness" were the latter to learn of the disciples' revolutionary talk. Thus he cautioned them, "Remember, I am sending you out like sheep among wolves; so be cunning as serpents and yet as harmless as doves. Beware of men: they will hand you over to sanhedrins and scourge you . . . You will be dragged before governors and kings for my sake" (Mt. 10:16-18a. Cf. Lk. 10:3).

But Jesus seems to have decided it was worth the risk of persecution because the time was so short. "Do not be afraid of them therefore. For everything that is now covered will be uncovered, and everything now hidden will be made clear. What I say to you in the dark, tell in the daylight; what you hear in whispers, proclaim from the housetops. Do not be afraid of those who kill the body but cannot kill the soul; . . . but the man who stands firm to the end will be saved . . . I tell you solemnly, you will not have gone the round of the towns of Israel before the Son of Man comes" (Mt. 10:26-28a, 22b, 23b).

Jesus, then, in the early part of his public work, seems to have done essentially what John the Baptist did. He preached the coming of the Kingdom and baptized people with water so they would be prepared when the Messiah came and the Kingdom was established. Later, apparently feeling the need to get the word around even faster, he sent out his twelve disciples to preach and teach and heal—also with the intent of announcing the imminence of the Kingdom. Still later, he sent an additional seventy with the same message, appointed to the special task of preceding him in the towns where he would go and preach.

In all cases, the missions seemed to be successful in terms of the response of the people to Jesus and his disciples. The seventy were reported to have returned with joy, saying, "Lord, even the devils submit to us when we use your name." And Jesus was pleased, though he encouraged the disciples not to rejoice in their powers but rather in the fact that those powers were a sign that the disciples would be admitted to the Kingdom (Lk. 10:17–20).

Nevertheless, the major thing was still lacking: the Messiah had *not* come before the mission was completed.[35] Simply announcing the Kingdom had *not* accomplished what Jesus had hoped. According to Mark and Luke, after the disciples returned from their mission and made their reports, Jesus indicated they would withdraw from the public for a time: "The apostles rejoined Jesus and told him all they had done and taught. Then he said to them, 'You must come away to some lonely place all by yourselves and rest awhile': for there were so many coming and going that the apostles had not time even to eat" (Mk. 6:30–31). They "withdrew to a town called Bethsaida" (Lk. 9: 10), the home town of Peter, Andrew, and Philip, located on the northernmost shore of the Sea of Galilee.

Matthew associates that same withdrawal to the wilderness with Jesus' receipt of the news that John the Baptist had been beheaded by Herod (Mt. 14:13). We cannot know, of course, whether Jesus had in fact learned of the Baptist's death on that occasion, or whether the delay in the Kingdom's establishment was the sole cause of his withdrawal. But it seems clear that Jesus felt the need to reassess his approach and to seek God's guidance as to the next step he should take. Soon, if not immediately, thereafter he began to change his tactics.[36]

WITHDRAWAL TO THE WILDERNESS

Though it would appear that Jesus wanted to withdraw to the wilderness in order that he and his disciples might reassess their mission, they could not escape the crowds. Their preaching, teaching and healing had attracted many followers who apparently not only believed them when they said that the Kingdom was at hand, but who must also have begun to believe that this Jesus was "the one" they had been expecting.

When Jesus and his disciples withdrew to the wilderness beyond Bethsaida, the crowds preceded them (Mt. 14:13b–14a; Mk. 6:33–34a; Lk. 9:11a; Jn. 6:2). As we have seen, withdrawal into the wilderness was usually a "sign" to the people that a given man was about to declare himself a candidate for the Messiahship—that is, that he believed God had called him to play a special role in his people's history and was therefore willing to act out a Messianic role to see if God, by granting His power, would confirm his "election" as Messiah. So much was this the case that, as we saw in Chapter 1, for a charismatic leader to withdraw to the wilderness with a "multitude" of people was sufficient provocation for the Roman governors to order the participants put to death. The Romans were quite certain that such a withdrawal would soon lead to a revolution.

Christians have usually focused on the wilderness event traditionally known as "the Feeding of the Five Thousand" purely as a miracle. In the light of the history of such wilderness gatherings, however, this occasion needs to be re-examined and perhaps even reinterpreted.

No doubt Jesus withdrew into the wilderness in order to reassess his own role in the unfolding of Messianic history in the light of the delay in the establishment of the expected Kingdom. If in fact he had also learned of John the Baptist's death, then certainly that would have been one of the factors to be taken into consideration. John's death would have been a great loss to Jesus personally because John had played a very important role in his life. But it would also have been a blow to the future of the New Israel, for the Baptist had been a prophetic voice instrumental in preparing the people for the Kingdom. What must Jesus do now to further the cause he had shared with John?

John Robinson suggests[37] that Jesus had first accepted the role of Elijah the prophet, fulfilling the Baptist's words: "This is the one I spoke of when I said: A man is coming after me who ranks before me because he existed before me" (Jn. 1:30). Jesus' activities following his baptism by John certainly suggest that this was the case. He seems to have understood himself to be preparing the way for "that great and terrible day" (Mal. 3:23) by announcing its imminence and urging people to repent and change their ways while there was still time. As Elijah returned, or reincarnate, he would have had the task of hastening the baptism of fire: "He [the 'messenger' of God] is like the refiner's fire . . . He will take his seat as refiner and purifier:

he will purify the sons of Levi and refine them like gold and silver, and then they will make the offering to Yahweh as it should be made. The offering of Judah and Jerusalem will then be welcomed by Yahweh as in former days, as in the years of old" (Mal. 3:2b–4). When Jesus said, "I have come to bring fire to the earth, and how I wish it were blazing already!" (Lk. 12:49) he could well have been speaking out of an understanding of himself as Elijah, seeing a part of his function to be that initiation of the baptism of fire.[38]

In the wilderness, however, Jesus appears as the prophet of Deuteronomy—the new Moses.[39] According to the Gospel accounts, the people went ahead of Jesus and his disciples into the wilderness without his inviting them. However, there is every indication that the group which gathered was no casual crowd. They obviously went because they knew Jesus and because they knew he was withdrawing to the wilderness: "When Jesus received this news he withdrew by boat to a lonely place where they could be by themselves. But *the people heard of this* and, leaving the towns, went after him on foot" (Mt. 14:13). "So they went off in a boat to a lonely place where they could be by themselves. But people *saw them going,* and *many could guess where;* and from every town they all hurried to the place on foot and *reached it before them*" (Mk. 6:32, 33). "But the *crowds got to know* and they went after him" (Lk. 9:11a). "And a large crowd followed him, *impressed by the signs he gave* by curing the sick" (Jn. 6:2). [Italics ours.]

The clear implications are that (1) the "crowds" were persons who knew Jesus and his work well, and that (2) they knew *where* he was going, for they were able to arrive there *before* he did. "As [Jesus] stepped ashore he saw a large crowd" (Mt. 14:14a; Mk. 6:34a). Therefore, it seems likely that Jesus had met in that same wilderness location with the same crowd—or at least many of the same people— on other occasions.

Moreover, though Jesus had gone there to be alone with his disciples, when he saw the people "he took pity on them" (Mt. 14:14b; Mk. 6:34a) and "made them welcome" (Lk. 9:11b). Mark says Jesus felt the people "were like sheep without a shepherd" (Mk. 6:34b), so he taught them (Mk. 6:34b) and "talked to them about the kingdom of God" (Lk. 9:11b) and healed the sick (Mt. 14:14b; Lk. 9:11b). Jesus does not appear, therefore, to have been displeased with the gathering of the people. It seems reasonable that he had taught, preached, and healed there on other similar occasions.

In fact, when it got late Jesus, instead of dismissing the crowd as his disciples wanted him to do, insisted that they be fed (Mt. 14:15, 16; Mk. 6:35–37a; Lk. 9:12–13a). Since there were only a few fish and barley loaves available, Jesus took it upon himself to "feed" the multitudes. The Gospels imply that he caused the loaves and fishes to multiply so that there was more than enough for all (Mt. 14:17–21; Mk. 6:38–44; Lk. 9:13b–17; Jn. 6:8–13).[40] In other words, Jesus gave the people bread in the wilderness, just as Moses had given them manna.

THE NEW MOSES?

John very significantly introduces the whole incident with the words "It was shortly before the Jewish feast of Passover" (Jn. 6:4). Passover is the feast at which the deliverance from Egypt is recalled and the People remember their forty years in the wilderness when God provided for their needs. By Jesus' action, he was, like Moses, "feeding the people" in the wilderness and thus in effect announcing himself as their "deliverer." The sign was so clear to the crowd that John records, "The people, seeing this sign that he had given, said, *'This really is the prophet who is to come into the world!'*" (Jn. 6:14b. Italics ours). That is, they recognized that by the feeding of the multitudes in the wilderness Jesus had announced himself to be the prophet like Moses promised by God in Deuteronomy 18:15–18: the deliverer.

Jesus cannot have been unaware of the impact which his actions in the wilderness would have on the multitudes. He knew and shared their eager anticipation of the Messiah's advent and was obviously steeped in Messianic prophecy and sought to act out his role in relation to it. He would have been perfectly aware that the "sign" he had performed would be understood by them to mean that he was God's Chosen One. In other words, the "miracle" of the multiplication of the loaves and fishes could not have had, for the crowds, other than political, even revolutionary import. It is no surprise the people immediately "recognized" him as "the prophet" of Deuteronomy.

In fact, the Gospel accounts make it appear that Jesus had organized the crowd in conformity with the Qumran War Scroll. That is, the *men* ("to say nothing of women and children"; Mt. 14:21)[41] were divided into companies, by hundreds and fifties (Mk. 6:39–40; Lk.

9:14),[42] and it was Jesus who asked his disciples to have them seated "by companies" (RSV). Again, the implication is clearly revolutionary: Jesus had instructed the people and organized them as troops mustered for the final battle of the holy war, just as John the Baptist had done before him.

It would seem, then, that the stage was set for Jesus to make a move as the People's new deliverer. If John the Baptist had been killed, that would surely have heightened the tension which so frequently led to revolts against Rome. Yet Jesus does not appear to have withdrawn from a situation in which (1) he met with a gathering of five thousand in the wilderness, (2) he taught and preached about the Kingdom of God, (3) he healed the sick, a sign that the Kingdom was already in their midst, (4) he acknowledged the military organization of the group by seating the men by companies, and (5) he "fed" them as a sign that he was the new Moses. All five of these actions were revolutionary in import according to the tradition of apocalyptic nationalism in which Jesus stood.

In spite of all this, however, Matthew and Mark report that Jesus immediately "made the disciples get into the boat and go on ahead to the other side while he would send the crowds away" (Mt. 14:22; Mk. 6:45). And John says, "Jesus, who could see they were about to come and take him by force and make him king, escaped back to the hills by himself" (Jn. 6:15). These responses seem to contradict the motivating force and direction of Jesus' previous responses and actions. The crowds cannot be blamed for misinterpreting such clear Messianic acts. What, then, was his reason for refusing to lead a Messianic uprising at that time?

Hugh Montefiore, recently elected Suffragan Bishop of Kingston in England, has argued that the "many" (members of the movement?) who were coming and going (Mk. 6:31) were engaged in preparations for a Messianic uprising, and that Jesus and his disciples withdrew from the scene of that activity to a favorite rendezvous they had in those parts.[43] It is possible that the disciples' mission had been so successful that thousands of people had gathered in Capernaum (or thereabouts), where Jesus seems to have centered his Galilean movement, in readiness for the coming of God's Kingdom.

Jesus' withdrawal to a place in the wilderness with which the crowd was already acquainted suggests either that the same group had met there with him before or that on this particular occasion it was a planned gathering. Otherwise it is not likely that so large a group would have found their way there *before* Jesus arrived.[44] This gathering, then, would seem to have been in the tradition of other Messianic movements organized in the wilderness.

Bishop Montefiore calls attention to the fact that the phrase " 'sheep without a shepherd' means, according to Old Testament usage, not a congregation without a leader but 'an army without a general, a nation without a national leader' . . . Jesus was very sorry for them, for *he deeply sympathized with their need.* Possibly," Bishop Montefiore continues, "Jesus went out into the desert precisely because he was as yet undecided whether or not to associate himself with this Messianic movement."[45]

Jesus' teaching on that occasion, Dr. Montefiore postulates, may have been his attempt to explain to the crowd why he could not be the kind of military leader they sought.[46] What he "fed" them could well have been his teaching regarding how the Kingdom would have to be established and what role the Messiah would have to play. He appears to have wanted to avoid—in this incident as in others— striking a military blow without some clear sign from God that the time for the final battle was upon them.

Finally, the fact that Jesus could not trust his disciples in this situation, but had to dismiss them first and only afterwards was able to dispatch the crowd, suggests that "the real sympathies of the disciples were with the hopes and wishes of the five thousand rather than with the purposes of Jesus."[47]

After the pressures and tension of such a highly inflammable situation in which Jesus resisted a deliberate attempt on the part of five thousand enthusiastic followers to draft him as their military leader for a revolt, Jesus was in particular need of time alone. He withdrew into the hills to pray (Mk. 6:46).[48]

Jesus obviously believed that he had been chosen by God to fulfill a special role in Messianic history, but he was not prepared to have his followers establish him king by force. He needed instead to have some confirmation *by God* that he was indeed the Chosen One. It was, after all, *God's* final war against the forces of darkness, and *God's* Kingdom which would be established. It had, therefore, all to be done according to God's plan—by the power of the forces of light and righteousness.

It was not that Jesus did not want to be king, but rather that he wanted to be king *only if that was God's plan for him.* When he said, "My kingdom is not of this world," he did not mean that he would *not rule* in this world, but rather that his kingdom (if, indeed, God chose to make him king) would not be established by the ordinary processes of this world of overthrows by violence and of rule by suppression. His kingdom here on earth—which was God's promise to His People—would be established by God Himself through the power of His armies of angels. "Mine is not a kingdom of this world; if my kingdom were of this world, my men would have fought to prevent my being surrendered to the Jews. But my kingdom is not of this kind" (Jn. 18:36).

THE BREAD OF LIFE

It is because Messianic acts are so directly related to God's acts of intervention to save His People that apocalyptic teachings were so important. Unless one understood that God was acting in the midst of history to bring His promise to fulfillment, one could easily miss the significance even of "miracles" like Jesus' feeding of the five thousand. An understanding of the events of their day as the fulfillment of ancient prophecies was essential for all those who wished to enter the New Covenant with God.

It was in an attempt to stress the importance of apocalyptic teachings for comprehending the signs of the time that Jesus apparently interpreted that wilderness incident for the disciples.[49]

The people asked him, "What must we do if we are to do the works that God wants?" (Jn. 6:28). He answered, "This is working for God: you must believe in the one he has sent" (Jn. 6:29). So they asked him again, *"What sign will you give* to show us that we should believe in you? What work will you do? Our fathers had manna to eat in the desert; as scripture says: 'He gave them bread from heaven to eat' " (Jn. 6:30, 31). Then Jesus said to them, "I tell you most solemnly, it was not Moses who gave you bread from heaven, it is my Father who gives you bread from heaven, the true bread; for the bread of God is that which comes down from heaven and gives life to the world" (Jn. 6:32, 33). In other words, Jesus wanted the people to acknowledge their utter dependence on God for their life and not on him. Neither he nor Moses gave the "bread of life"; only God Himself could give that.

Jesus then explained that man does not live by bread alone—a perception and a conviction which had been tested out in his own life while fasting in the wilderness—but that the spirit gives life. His teachings, Jesus explained, were intended to lead them to life in the spirit. He told them that he would give his own body in order that they might have life, and that if they believed he was the one to deliver them, they would be able to enter the Kingdom and have eternal life (Jn. 6:35–71).

He then made clear the distinction between the old and the new Covenants: "Your fathers ate the manna in the desert and they are dead; but this [Jesus' teachings] is the bread which comes down from heaven, so that man may eat it and *not die*" (Jn. 6:49, 50). And again, "This [Jesus' teachings] is the bread come down from heaven; not like the bread our ancestors ate; they are dead, but anyone who eats this bread will live for ever" (Jn 6:58). Eating the bread which Jesus provided clearly meant committing their lives to live in the light; that is, joining the movement of those who were seeking by their own righteousness to atone for all of Israel and to enable the establishment of the Kingdom of God on earth. By beginning now to walk in the light they could have the eternal life which the gift of the spirit confers.

To his disciples, when they were alone, he said, "Men of little faith, why are you talking among yourselves about having no bread? Do you not yet understand? Do you not remember the five loaves for the five thousand and the number of baskets you collected? . . . How could you fail to understand that I was not talking about bread? What I said was: Beware of the yeast of the Pharisees and Sadducees." Then they understood that he was not warning them about the yeast of bread, but "the *teaching* of the Pharisees and Sadducees" (Mt. 16:5–12).[50] Since the Pharisees and Sadducees did not stand in the same tradition of apocalyptic teaching, Jesus' disciples could not trust their interpretations of the events of their times. Instead, Jesus was saying, only his teaching in the desert apocalyptic strain would lead them surely to eternal life—that is, life in that dimension of experience in which God and God alone is King. He therefore urged them to believe what he taught.

Some of them did not believe; others were unable to promise to give their lives for the Kingdom. Those withdrew (Jn. 6:64–66). But the disciples believed Jesus' message and also believed that Jesus had a special role to play in bringing it to fulfillment (Jn. 6:67–69), so the core of his group remained strong. Those who remained with Jesus were ready to lose their lives for the Kingdom, if need be,

when God gave a sign that the time was right. That is, they were
ready to fight the revolutionary, Messianic battle, using the force, or
power, of light and righteousness to defeat the forces of darkness.

A DEVOUT JEW

Thus a clear picture of Jesus emerges. He was a devout and practicing
Jew who had been circumcised according to the Law; who was
trained in Torah so that by the age of twelve he was able to engage
in discussions regarding the interpretation of the Law with the scribes
in the Temple and hold his own ground; who attended the synagogue
regularly and often taught there; and who went to Jerusalem for
feast days according to the custom of his people, and there taught
in the Temple. He taught the Law with an authority which came
from deep understanding, and earned the title of "rabbi"—or teacher
of the Law. He had a large following, mostly from Galilee and the
surrounding areas of the Decapolis and Tyre and Sidon. He urged
his disciples to keep the written Law in every regard, and those who
he felt were ready, he urged to be filled with the spirit of holiness
so that even what they thought would be pure.

As a teacher of the Law, Jesus stood within the Hillel tradition,
the broad (or liberal) interpretation of the Law, with the exception
of only two teachings. This in no way relieved his followers of the
responsibility to *keep* the Law, however. It meant only that the *manner*
in which they kept it was sometimes not as strictly defined as by
certain other rabbis of his time.

As a preacher, Jesus stood within the framework of the teachings
of apocalyptic Messianist groups such as that at Qumran. In the
beginning his message was simple, as was that of John the Baptist.
As the prophetic figure of Malachi, Jesus announced that the Kingdom
of God was at hand, calling all Jews to repent and be baptized in
preparation for their inheritance of the Kingdom. He urged the people
to be perfect in their obedience to the Law.

By his actions, Jesus showed himself to stand within the Law, and
yet not to be so bound by it as to be incapable of engaging in personal
encounters which to other Jews would have seemed questionable. He
did not hesitate, for example, because of laws of purity, to speak to
the Samaritan woman at the well, with whom he ended up having

a deep theological discussion which led her to believe him to be the prophet who was to come, and which in turn brought many of the people of her village to believe in him (Jn. 4:1–42). Nor did he remain restricted to his own understanding that he was sent only to the people of Israel when he healed the daughter of the Syrophoenician woman (Mt. 15:21–28; Mk. 7:24–30). Neither did he hesitate to do good on the Sabbath, especially by healing, even when he knew that many would criticize him and accuse him of violating the Sabbath Law. In these instances he leaped over the fence of the Law in order to meet the needs of persons in love and compassion. But he obviously did not feel that such actions in any way abrogated the Law, but rather fulfilled its spirit.

By the same token, Jesus saw all the works he did—including the "miracles"—to be evidence that the Kingdom of God was at hand. Jesus was only able to effect mighty acts, and to cast out demons (the children of darkness), and heal, because he had already entered the Kingdom through his decision to walk in the light. Like the Qumran Covenanters, John the Baptist and his followers, and Jesus' own disciples, Jesus believed that the spirit of holiness which he had received at his baptism had given him the power to do mighty works as "signs" that the Kingdom was at hand. His disciples, like the Covenanters, were able to perform the same "miracles" which Jesus performed, according to the degree of power which each of them had received. All such manifestations were proof that God had power to overcome evil, and were to be expected as part of the new creation —the new order of things being established. Those persons who saw the "signs of the times" and understood their significance, were moved to change their ways and to live in righteous expectation of the Messiah's coming.

Gradually, however, Jesus came to believe something further was expected of him. He had trained and organized a council of twelve and had a following the equivalent size of a legion of five thousand soldiers. He and his disciples had gone throughout all of Galilee and through parts of Samaria and Judea announcing the Kingdom. Yet still God had not intervened by sending His Messiah and the host of angelic troops under the command of Michael the Archangel to redeem Israel and establish the Kingdom of God on earth. Something more must yet be required.

It was possible that in spite of the large numbers of persons who had followed him, there had not yet been enough to enable the Messiah to come. Jesus' "woes" to Chorazin, Bethsaida, and Caper-

naum (Mt. 11:20–24; Lk. 10:13–15), which had been the centers
of his teaching, reflect his feeling that somehow his mission had
fallen short, and he is reported to have told the disciples at one
point that the Son of Man would have to be "rejected by this generation" (Lk. 17:22–30). Perhaps he feared that the Kingdom could
not be realized in his time after all because of the lack of faith of the
people.

But principally it appears that Jesus began to re-examine his role
in Messianic history to see if something more were required of him.
He asked his disciples not long after the incident of the feeding of the
five thousand in the wilderness, "Who do people say that I am?"
And they told him what is reiterated elsewhere in the Gospels:[51]
John the Baptist, Elijah, one of the prophets. Then Jesus asked, "But
you, who do you say I am?" Peter's response must have confirmed
what Jesus had begun to suspect about himself, as the feeding of the
five thousand indicated: "You are the Christ [the Greek word for
Messiah]" (Mk. 8:27–30).[52] But he told the disciples that they
were not to tell anyone that he was the Messiah (Mk. 8:30; Mt. 16:
20; Lk. 9:21), apparently not wanting to head up any Messianic
demonstration that might be initiated by men rather than by God.[53]

THE TURNING POINT

Soon thereafter, according to our Gospel writers, an event took place
which dramatically changed the course of Jesus' life and the future
of the movement he had organized. Jesus took the inner three, Peter,
James, and John, and went up on a high mountain where they could
be entirely alone. According to the Gospel accounts,[54] as Jesus was
praying, his entire appearance was transformed by a tremendous white
light shining on him, in him, and through him—"like the sun" (Mt.
17:2), "dazzling" (Mk. 9:3), "brilliant" (Lk. 9:29). Then two men
appeared and began talking to Jesus. They were Moses and Elijah
(Mt. 17:3; Mk. 9:4; Lk. 9:30).

The disciples were very sleepy and seemed not to comprehend
what was happening. They made a rather childish response, which
might even have led to idolatry: they wanted to build three booths,
simple shelters made of the branches of trees used for shade or rest

(Mt. 17:4; Mk. 9:5, 6; Lk. 9:32, 33). They apparently hoped that Jesus, Moses, and Elijah would want to remain on top of the mountain. But then the power of the experience seemed to overcome the three disciples as well. "A cloud came and covered them with shadow; when they went into the cloud the disciples were afraid. And a voice came from the cloud saying, 'This is my Son, the Chosen One. Listen to him'" (Lk. 9:34–35).[55] The disciples were understandably awestruck and afraid, and they fell on their faces as a sign of great respect. When Jesus spoke to them and they looked at him again, Elijah and Moses had gone and Jesus stood alone (Mt. 17:6–8; Mk. 9:8; Lk. 9:36).

This crucial experience was not spoken of until after the resurrection had occurred,[56] and therefore its interpretation must have been colored by the disciples' later experiences and reflection. In fact, some scholars believe the whole transfiguration event should be considered post-resurrection.[57] But even though the interpretation may reflect post-resurrection insight and understanding, we do not believe the experience itself need necessarily be removed from the story of Jesus' life, for we know from the accounts of other persons in other times and places that experiences of "transfiguration" do take place.[58] Rather, it seems the task of one seeking to examine the event as history is to determine what happened and what the results of it were. For the account of what happened, we must rely on the report of the disciples as it is related to us in the Gospels. Even though we may suspect that it was altered somewhat by the telling of it over a period of years and by the experiences of the disciples in the interim, it is all we can know of the event itself. As for what the results of the transfiguration were, those can be perceived in the change of Jesus' course of action which followed.

Here we have, it would seem, the culmination of the process of change and re-evaluation which Jesus had been undergoing since the return of his disciples from their preaching mission. He had fully expected that before they got back the Son of Man would have arrived: that is, the final events leading to the founding of the Kingdom of God on earth would have been in process, if not accomplished. The fact that it had not all happened as he anticipated must have been a great disappointment, not only to the disciples, but to Jesus himself.[59] It was apparently at this time that John the Baptist, whom Jesus believed to be performing a vital role in preparing the way for the Messiah, was killed. The harsh reality of the unexpected turn of events must have forced Jesus to do a great deal of searching for his own role. He had lived in righteousness, taught many people, done "great works," preached with authority, and announced the coming Kingdom. But somehow none of it had been enough.

With the transfiguration experience Jesus entered a whole new dimension of insight and understanding. Two of the most important Messianic figures are reported to have appeared and talked with Jesus: Moses and Elijah. The coming of both a prophet like Moses and Elijah reincarnate were devoutly anticipated by most Jews, and we have shown that there is reason to believe Jesus first saw himself as Elijah and then at least acted out the role of Moses. It was apparently only in the transfiguration experience that Jesus perceived that those two promises had *already been fulfilled*—in John the Baptist (Mt. 17:10–13; Mk. 9:11–13), and perhaps, though the Gospels do not report it, in the Teacher of Righteousness.[60] Almost the only conclusion Jesus could have drawn, if he believed the prophecies regarding Moses and Elijah to have been already fulfilled, was that the time was right for the appearance of the Messiah himself. But the question remained as to who was the Messiah. After the transfiguration, Jesus must have been almost certain it was he. However, the only way for him to prove it would be to go to Jerusalem and present himself as Messiah in order for God to be able to reveal His will.

Jesus told his disciples that he would have to go to Jerusalem and possibly suffer many things from the authorities there in order to determine at last whether he had been "chosen" by God to fulfill the Messianic role (Mt. 17:22, 23; Mk. 9:30–32; Lk. 9:43b–45). Only in such a confrontation with the forces of darkness, which had dashed so many Messianic hopes in years past, would the final test be made.[61]

PREDICTIONS OF SUFFERING AND DEATH

Jesus began to prepare his disciples for a confrontation[62] with the Jewish and Roman officials (the forces of darkness), which he hoped would "force the issue" and heighten the tension in the conflict between the children of light and their enemies so that the Messianic drama would begin. Jesus' predictions of suffering and even death seem to reflect the suffering servant image of Isaiah 53. But the passage in Isaiah refers to the whole People of Israel,[63] and while the Qumran community had developed a self-understanding that as the "new Israel" they would be able to be a "living sacrifice" for the redemption of their people, suffering as a ransom for Israel, there is no evidence that any of the Jewish sects in Jesus' day expected the Messiah himself to suffer, and certainly not to die.[64]

Rather, there was the anticipation of a general suffering associated with the Messianic drama (the woes and tribulations of the last days), and it must have been this suffering and persecution at the hands of the forces of darkness that Jesus foresaw for both himself and his disciples. Certainly many other devout apocalyptic nationalists had died before them, including John the Baptist. Jesus is reported to have asked James and John, whose mother sought an important place for them in the coming Kingdom, "Can you drink the cup that I must drink, or be baptised with the baptism with which I must be baptised?" (Mk. 10:35–38; Mt. 20:20–22). When they replied that they could, he answered, "The cup that I must drink you shall drink; and with the baptism with which I must be baptised you shall be baptised, but as for seats at my right hand or my left, these are not mine to grant; they belong to those to whom they have been allotted" (Mk. 10:39–40; Mt. 20:23).

In other words, Jesus seemed to feel that both he and his disciples had to be willing to commit themselves totally—perhaps even unto death—but that the determination as to what roles each would have in the establishing of the Kingdom was God's choice, and God's alone.

Only in retrospect did the Evangelists *personalize* Jesus' anticipated suffering of all creation and make it apply to himself, as they attempted to show that Jesus had fulfilled all the Messianic expectations including that of the suffering servant figure in Isaiah. As participants in the death throes of the old order which was soon to pass away, Jesus saw that he and his disciples would have to undergo suffering. Perhaps he even hoped that he (and they) could be a "ransom for [the] Many" (Mk. 10:45),[65] that by their own suffering and deaths, if need be, they might prevent other brothers in the cause from needing to undergo similar trials and tribulations.

However, only in the final test—only by directly confronting the forces of darkness in a Messianic demonstration—could God's will in the matter be revealed. If God had chosen Jesus as His Messiah, then He would intervene on behalf of the forces of light and establish His Kingdom on earth. Jesus believed fervently that God would act, and thus was certain that his disciples would "not taste death" before they saw the Kingdom of God "come with power."[66]

Once the decision to seek a confrontation had been made, the whole tone of Jesus' teaching and preaching changed. He tried to prepare his followers for the suffering and the struggle ahead, focusing his attention on Jerusalem where the confrontation needed to take place, and he began to speak more openly and more boldly. For example, when some Pharisees tried to warn him that Herod wanted to kill him,[67] he said, "You may go and give that fox this message: Learn that today and tomorrow I cast out devils and on the third day attain my end. But for today and tomorrow and the next day I must go on, since it would not be right for a prophet to die outside Jerusalem . . . Yes, I promise you, you shall not see me till the time comes when you say: 'Blessings on him who comes in the name of the Lord!'" (Lk. 13:31–35). Since this salutation was intended for the Messiah, this was a clear and open indication that, when the time was right, Jesus intended to allow himself to be proclaimed the expected deliverer.

Apparently Jesus made his plans for those final events which would bring the Messianic issue to a head with persons *other* than his disciples. Of course we can only speculate as to who those other persons might have been. We are told of a man who owned a house in Jerusalem, who agreed to host Jesus and his disciples for the meal which became his "last supper." We are told also of Mary, Martha, and Lazarus who provided refuge for Jesus and his disciples during that long week. Joseph of Arimathea is mentioned as one who got permission to take Jesus' body down from the cross. But we have no way of knowing whether Jesus was in touch with these persons, or with leaders of other Messianic groups, or with branch houses of Qumran, or with whom. What we are told is that Jesus went up to Jerusalem alone, apparently to make the arrangements, and that his disciples remained ignorant of the specific plans right up to the last.

John tells us (Jn. 7:1–15) that when it came time for the Feast of Tabernacles (Succoth), Jesus' brothers urged him to go to Judea, to Jerusalem, for the feast and to let people see the great works he was doing. "If a man wants to be known he does not do things in secret; since you are doing all this, you should let the whole world see." Jesus told them, however, that it was not yet his time and that he would not go to the feast—that they should go on without him.

But after his brothers had gone, Jesus also went up to Jerusalem to the feast, "quite privately, without drawing attention to himself." For several days Jesus did not appear among the crowds. Then about the middle of the week (the feast lasts seven days) he "went to the Temple and began to teach." The people were amazed at his teaching. It must have been quite revolutionary, for they said, "Isn't this the man they want to kill? And here he is, speaking freely, and they have nothing to say to him! Can it be true the authorities have made up their minds that he is the Christ (i.e., the Messiah)?" (Jn. 7:25–26). And a dispute is recorded among the chief priests and Pharisees as to whether Jesus might not in fact be the Messiah (Jn. 7:40–52).

Jesus stayed on in Jerusalem for some time—a month or two—teaching openly in the Temple. The Pharisees spent a great deal of time putting questions to him and watching and listening to him, trying to determine if he was the expected Messiah or not,[68] for they too awaited the deliverance of Israel promised by the prophets.

THE ISSUE OF TAXES PAID TO CAESAR

Some of the collaborating Jews watched for a cause to arrest Jesus but were understandably reluctant to do anything which might incite the crowds—who believed Jesus to be a prophet—to open riot and rebellion. From time to time they posed questions which they hoped would cause Jesus to give an answer which would alienate the crowd.

> "Master, we know that you are an honest man and teach the way of God in an honest way, and that you are not afraid of anyone, because a man's rank means nothing to you. Tell us your opinion, then. Is it permissible to pay taxes to Caesar or not?" But Jesus was aware of their malice and replied, "You hypocrites! Why do you set this trap for me? Let me see the money you pay the tax with . . . Whose head is this? Whose name?" "Caesar's," they replied. He then said to them, "Very well, give back to Caesar what belongs to Caesar—and to God what belongs to God." This reply took them by surprise, and they left him alone and went away. (Mt. 22:16–22)

This famous encounter[69] is generally cited by Christians to prove that Jesus urged his disciples to cooperate with the Romans and not to resist governmental authority. Such an interpretation, however, is due to a misreading of the historical situation and of Jesus' answer.

The tribute paid to Caesar was a burden on the Jews which they could hardly bear. The Jews in Galilee suffered more than those in

Judea because they were poorer to begin with, and their rate of taxation had risen to 40 percent by the time of the events we are describing. But more than the economic factor, a deep religious principle was involved: the question of the sovereignty of Yahweh. The great rabbi Judas of Galilee had urged the Jewish people to revolt over the issue of taxes in A.D. 6, teaching them that to pay taxes to Caesar was to become subservient to him, and that Jews could serve none other than God. This had given rise to the burning issue of the paying of tribute, and that issue continued to be a focus for the larger question of the Jews' posture vis-à-vis the imperial occupation of Israel.

The Gospel of Mark makes it clear that the question posed to Jesus in the above exchange was of a critical nature (Mk. 12:13) and Luke mentions that spies who were sent out to catch Jesus had asked the question (Lk. 20:20). As Oscar Cullmann, the famous New Testament scholar, has observed, the tribute issue was *the criterion* of loyalty toward Judaism in the eyes of the zealous Jews, and also *the criterion* of loyalty to the Empire in the eyes of the Romans. The atmosphere of the encounter in the Temple courtyard, highly charged since the country was brimming with anti-Roman agitation, placed Jesus in a dilemma: "If he answers yes, he will be shown up as a collaborationist and will disillusion the majority of the people; for it is precisely in this connection that these have rested such great hope in him. If he answers no, this is an avowal that he himself is a Zealot, and indeed a leader of the Zealots; and we know what that meant to the Romans."[70]

At face value, Jesus' statement "Give back to Caesar what belongs to Caesar, and to God what belongs to God" has an obvious note of ambiguity, which enabled him to avoid the entrapment planned by those who raised the question. Yet it is difficult to accept that such ambiguity would have been allowed to pass. As Professor S. G. F. Brandon of Manchester University in England has written, no Messianic character could have evaded an issue of such fundamental importance to his countrymen.[71] If, as most scholars accept, the words actually spoken by Jesus have been preserved in the Gospels, then the people must have had some basis for understanding what are the things of Caesar and what are the things of God.[72]

Dr. Brandon asserts that to the religious Jews of that day, who were caught up in the national resistance to Roman rule, the definition of "things" and the meaning of Jesus' response were clear—that the "things of God" meant the resources of Israel and they were *not* to be given to a heathen lord. "Jesus' pronouncement, therefore, was wholly in line with Zealot teaching, and so it must have been understood by those to whom it was originally addressed. In other words, Jesus ruled decisively against the payment of tribute. Caesar could, ironically, have what was his; but the Holy Land of Judaea, and its resources, were emphatically not his but God's."[73] The fact of Jesus' denunciation of paying tribute is corroborated, in Brandon's view, by Luke's listing it among the charges against Jesus presented to Pilate. In fact, Luke's account suggests that such pronouncements against Caesar were a general feature of Jesus' teaching. "We found this man inciting our people to revolt, opposing payment of the tribute to Caesar and claiming to be Christ, a king" (Lk. 23:2); "He is inflaming the people with his teaching all over Judaea; it has come all the way from Galilee, where he started, down to here" (Lk. 23:5).

Oscar Cullmann disagrees with Dr. Brandon, and states that the complexity of Jesus' "intentionally ambiguous" response left room for misinterpretation. According to Cullmann, it was only through misinterpretation that the charge was made before Pilate that Jesus forbade his followers to pay tribute to Caesar, a charge which means, in other words, "he is a leader of the Zealots."[74] Cullmann emphasizes the irony in Jesus' statement by comparing it to his earlier statement about serving both God and mammon, or money. In Cullmann's view, Jesus "recognizes that within its sphere the State can demand what belongs to it: money, taxes. But it is not placed on the same level as God . . . do not give Caesar *more* than his due! Give him nothing that belongs to God!"[75]

While Professor Brandon views Jesus' response as entirely consistent with Zealot principles, Dr. Cullmann believes it would have appeared to them a "deplorable compromise."[76] W. R. Farmer concurs with Cullmann, stating that Jesus' answer was certainly not that of a Judas Maccabeus.[77] And Professor David Flusser writes: "Once again Jesus had succeeded in evading capture, while at the same time making his meaning unmistakably clear. One cannot serve two masters, God and mammon. Money comes from Caesar, and so it must be handed over to him. Quite certainly the saying did not express friendship with the Romans, but it showed also that Jesus was no supporter of revolt against the Romans."[78]

All such opinions must be taken into account in assessing Jesus' attitude toward the payment of tribute to Caesar, but an important factor which is omitted in the explanations above, is the immediacy with which Jesus saw the Kingdom's coming. Dr. Paul Winter's rhetorical question takes the eschatological setting of Jesus' statement into account: "It is all very well to say 'Render unto Caesar what belongs to Caesar'—but what belongs to Caesar at a time when the Kingdom of God is expected to break in any day, any hour?"[79]

What belongs to Caesar? Nothing!

In the final stages of history all of one's personal resources and the whole of the nation of Israel are to be dedicated totally to the realization of the Kingdom. Jesus' statement concerning the tribute was not intended to give guidelines to Christians in all ages regarding the question of their attitude toward the state. Rather, it was comparable to his statements regarding chastity and marriage, that is, it was another example of an interim ethic defining what the attitude of religious Jews should be in the short time before the Kingdom is established.

THE LIFE OF THE POOR

As a reinforcement of this interpretation, it is well to remember that the Zealot guerrilla fighters who lived in the hills of Galilee and Judea, the wilderness sects such as that at Qumran, the followers of John the Baptist, and the disciples of Jesus, had *all* expressed by becoming voluntarily "poor" their contempt for the edicts to bow to Caesar. That is, none of them worked for wages nor carried on their person, nor had in their possession Roman coins. By not possessing or carrying money, these nationalist resistance members automatically exempted themselves from taxes: they had no income on which to be taxed.

The Zealot freedom fighters did rob or steal from the Romans or from the collaborators in order to maintain their movement. For this reason they became known as "thieves" or "brigands" to those who opposed them, and the Jewish historian Josephus applies the term "robber" (*lēstēs* in Greek) indiscriminately when speaking of the Zealots. They *were* robbers, but their cause was the freedom of Israel and the establishment of a theocracy, *not* their own welfare.

The Covenanters managed without money by pooling all their resources and putting them under the management of the Overseer in each community, and by raising their own food insofar as possible. John the Baptist lived off the land, eating only what was found growing naturally. It is possible that some of his disciples did likewise.

Jesus' disciples also pooled their resources, giving their communal purse to Judas Iscariot to manage (Jn. 12:6; 13:29),[80] and they depended at least partially on funds received from wealthy Jews sympathetic to their cause. We have a story in the Gospel of Luke, for example, about a Jewish tax collector in Jericho named Zacchaeus (Lk. 19:1-10). Jesus, to the surprise of many who criticized him for being the guest of a "sinner," stayed in Zacchaeus' home on one occasion. As a result of his visit, Zacchaeus evidently threw in his lot with his people, for Jesus said, "Today salvation has come to this house, because this man too is a son of Abraham." But in addition to gaining his sympathy, Jesus secured a sizable gift for the movement: "Look, sir, I am going to give half my property *to the poor,* and if I have cheated anybody I will pay him back four times the amount" [italics ours]. There were undoubtedly other such "conversions."[81] We know, for example, that one of the twelve, Matthew, had been a tax collector. Large contributions to Jesus' movement by wealthy "converts" must have helped considerably to sustain it. Other passages indicate that Jesus' followers were accustomed to giving whatever surplus they had to the poor, that is, to the movement.[82]

JESUS OUTWITS HIS CHALLENGERS

When Jesus was asked whether or not it was lawful for Jews to give tribute to Caesar, the "spies" who put the question hoped that Jesus would be placed in an impossible position. If he said yes, the crowds would turn against him as a traitor to his people; if he said no, he could be arrested for resisting Roman authority. But Jesus outwitted those who sought to trap him. First, apparently neither Jesus nor his disciples were carrying any Roman coins, for he had to ask his interrogators to hold up one of the coins paid for taxes—to use for an illustration. The reply he then gave was clear: only those who served Caesar as their king had anything which "belonged" to Caesar; those who served God, and God alone, knew that all belonged to Him.

Jesus was merely stating in another way what he had said on other occasions: "No one can be the slave of two masters . . . You cannot be the slave both of God and of money" (Mt. 6:24). "You must love the Lord your God with all your heart . . . This is the greatest and the first commandment" (Mt. 22:34–40; Mk. 12:28–34).

To pay taxes to Caesar was to acknowledge him as king; no son of Abraham who subscribed to the Mosaic Covenant and was faithful to it could have any other "god" before the God of that Covenant. Jesus was advocating noncooperation by a self-imposed state of poverty —a form of "passive resistance" to Caesar's rule. While nothing in the form of his answer could be used against him as grounds for arrest, its import was clear to those who "had ears to hear."

On another occasion the chief priests and scribes asked him openly in the Temple by what authority he did the things he did, again hoping to trap him.[83] If he claimed any authority other than that delegated by the Romans, he would be guilty of treason. Yet they knew he could not claim Roman authority. Again Jesus outwitted them. Knowing that they did not want the crowds to turn against *them,* and knowing also the people's belief in John the Baptist as a true prophet of God, Jesus replied: "'And I will ask you a question. Tell me: John's baptism: did it come from heaven, or from man?' And they argued it out this way among themselves, 'If we say from heaven, he will say, "Why did you refuse to believe him?" and if we say from man, the people will all stone us, for they are convinced that John was a prophet.'" Since the chief priests and scribes refused to answer, so did Jesus (Lk. 20:3–8).

Finally it came time for the feast of Dedication, or Hanukkah— the feast which celebrates the rededication of the Temple after the Maccabean Revolt. It was then that Jesus was approached in the Temple and asked, "How much longer are you going to keep us in suspense? If you are the Christ [the Messiah], tell us plainly." Jesus answered them, "I have told you, but you do not believe. The works I do in my Father's name are my witness . . . If I am not doing my Father's work there is no need to believe me; but if I am doing it, then even if you refuse to believe in me, at least believe in the work I do" (Jn. 10:22–42).

David Flusser believes that Jesus avoided using the word "Messiah" with reference to himself because of the political potency of the term.[84] But it is possible that in addition he felt the decision as to who was to be the Messiah was God's, and God's alone. All he could do was point to the works he did as signs of the Kingdom of Light in their midst. He could offer himself to be used by God as God saw fit, but it was not his place to claim God's election. He did imply, however, that his words and deeds had Messianic import, and he chose to make his acknowledgement of Messiahship at a most appropriate time: the feast for remembering and celebrating the Maccabees' revolt and victory.

Then Jesus again withdrew to the wilderness[85]—this time to make his final preparation, undoubtedly through fasting, meditation, and prayer. His disciples joined him there, and for nearly three months he taught them, preparing them for their final initiation into the New Covenant and their entry into the Kingdom. He did not return to Jerusalem again until he went up with his disciples for the final Passover feast.

Some members of the Sanhedrin, however, after Jesus' words and actions during the feast of Dedication, were determined that something had to be done about him. "Here is this man working all these signs . . . If we let him go on in this way everybody will believe in him, and the Romans will come and destroy the Holy Place and our nation" (Jn. 11:47b–48). They could see another revolt coming on—the predictable outcome of the People's believing Jesus to be the Messiah who would liberate them from their oppressors. It was then that the High Priest Caiaphas first suggested that it would be better that this one man die than that the whole nation should perish at the hand of the Romans (Jn. 11:49–50).

Jesus' preparations were made, and the stage was set for the final confrontation. Albert Schweitzer describes this change in mood and how Jesus' understanding of what was required of him had evolved. He sought to make real the eschatological hope for which he had taught his disciples to pray: "Thy Kingdom come."

"Jesus' purpose is to set in motion the eschatological development of history, to let loose the final woes, the confusion and strife, from which shall issue the Parousia [the coming of the Son of Man and the dawning of the Kingdom of God], and so to introduce the supramundane phase of the eschatological [final] drama."[86]

Jesus "lays hold of the wheel of the world to set it moving on that last revolution which is to bring all ordinary history to a close. It refuses to turn, and He throws Himself upon it. Then it does turn; and crushes Him."[87]

CHAPTER 9

Jesus: A Prophet of the End of Days

*"Blessings on him who comes in the name of the
Lord! Blessings on the coming kingdom of our father
David!"*   Mark 11:9–10

In the words of James A. Pike:

"Someone has used the word 'reckless' with reference to Jesus' activities during that last week in Jerusalem. In one sense I suppose Jesus was reckless. And yet when it came to the big thing, it was quite well planned. At least it was not haphazard recklessness. We were taught in Sunday School, for example, that Jesus used whips against the money changers in the Temple, knocking over a card table or two and causing one or two doves to fly away. When we would ask, 'How could Jesus, the peaceful, calm, serene, perfect son of God, get mad like that?' we would be told that it was righteous indignation—a kind of anger which only God can rightly exercise.

"Well, I don't think Jesus was angry at all, frankly. This cleansing of the Temple was carried out with the care of a man who knew what he was doing and why. The operation seems to have gone off without a hitch. No one interfered, or was able to stop him. He used the whip to cause a stampede—used it on the animals, not on people, and was therefore nonviolent. The animals did the rest, knocking over booths and tables and stalls and preventing the Temple police from stopping him. He stayed around and taught in the Temple court. He slipped out of town at night to his hideout in Bethany. He slipped back into town for the *seder* [Passover meal/last supper] with his disciples in a location previously arranged so that no one would know where they were.

"No, neither the Temple scene nor the entry into Jerusalem
were casual, spontaneous events. Both were carefully planned. But
there *was* a grave risk involved—of that there can be no doubt.
In that regard, and in that regard alone, could Jesus be called
'reckless.' He was, like Paul, 'not counting the cost.' "

————————◆————————

THE TRIUMPHAL ENTRY

What has traditionally been called the Triumphal Entry of Jesus into
Jerusalem is well named, for it is not the story of a humble figure
submissively coming to meet his death, but of the triumphant arrival
of the Son of David, organized so as to make Jesus' Messianic role
obvious to the Jewish pilgrims gathered for the feast day. Its every
element reveals that Jesus cast himself in the line of Jewish resistance
leaders dating back to the Maccabees, choosing actions which could
not have had other than political impact of considerable proportions
on Jewish and Roman authorities. The German scholar Paul Winter
correctly assessed the situation when he wrote, "The description in
each of the four Gospels has the features of a political demonstration.
It is obvious that tradition saw Jesus' entry into the capital city of
Judaea as a symbolical seizure of the reins of government. He is
hailed by the masses as king."[1]

Jesus and his disciples approached Jerusalem from the wilderness
to the east, where they had been "in retreat" since the feast of
Dedication, and went up to the city via Bethpage and Bethany.[2]
There Jesus' party was buoyed by the numerous Galileans—notorious
for their seditious activities—who, for the feast days, camped near
Bethany on the east side of the Mount of Olives in Jerusalem.[3]
According to Joachim Jeremias, Professor at the University of Göt-
tingen, Germany, and prolific writer in the field of New Testament
studies, "Each group of festival pilgrims had its fixed quarters for the
feast, in conformity with the distribution of different sections of the
population in different quarters of the town . . . From the fact that
Jesus used to spend his nights at Bethany, we may presume that the
quarters for Galilean pilgrims were to be east of the city."[4]

As previously mentioned, most of Jesus' followers were from Galilee,
the main seat of anti-Roman feeling and Messianic ideas. Conditions
in Galilee were desperate enough that agitation during the Passover

festival was almost inevitable. For the Jewish masses, journeys to Jerusalem for the feast days were the accepted means of contact with the Holy City,[5] and Jerusalem was (and is) the object of every Messianic movement's zeal. That Galileans had caused uprisings in the city before is attested to in the Gospels themselves: "Some people arrived and told [Jesus] about the Galileans whose blood Pilate had mingled with that of their sacrifices" (Lk. 13:1). Moreover, the Jewish historian Josephus fully documents the participation of Galileans in Messianic revolts in his accounts of Zealot activities in Jerusalem, as we saw in Chapter 1.

It would not have been surprising, therefore, that zealous Galileans would have rejoiced in the opportunity to proclaim Jesus king. Surely all of them would have heard reports of him even if they had not yet had opportunity to see and hear him personally. Their enthusiasm for Jesus would have been great both because of the remarkable healings and miracles he was known to have performed and because of their deep need for a deliverer. These things could not have been far from their minds as they welcomed Jesus as their anticipated king.

Even though Galileans were very poor, many of them would have been in Jerusalem for this particular feast. The Passover celebration was the one occasion for which the poorer people of the country made a special effort to travel to Jerusalem if financial limitations made it impossible for them to make the journey for the other feasts.[6] The influx of poor and rebellious Galileans would have added to the volatile situation in the already crowded capital.

Jerusalem was a city of about twenty-five thousand at the time of Jesus (with twenty thousand living within the walls of the city and some five thousand to ten thousand outside), but it swelled to several times that number at the time of the Passover feast.[7] In addition, Josephus records that in times of national agitation the number of Passover pilgrims rose enormously because it was at that time of the year that the Messiah was expected to manifest himself.[8] It was because of the influx of pilgrims that the Roman governor further buttressed the Roman garrison in Jerusalem for Passover and other high feast days and transferred his own headquarters from Caesarea Maritime (on the Mediterranean coast) to Jerusalem, where he could closely watch any new development in the city.[9]

Jesus' entry into Jerusalem would have represented to his contemporaries a self-declaration of his Messiahship. "As recounted in the Gospels, the event has the appearance of an unmistakable messianic demonstration. As such it would have been open defiance of imperial authority—a proclamation of the will to national independence from Roman rule . . ."[10]

> The next day the crowds who had come up for the festival heard that Jesus was on his way to Jerusalem. They took branches of palm and went out to meet him, shouting, "Hosanna! Blessings on the King of Israel, who comes in the name of the Lord" (Jn. 12:12–13).[11] "Blessings on the coming kingdom of our father David!" (Mk. 11:10).

Jesus' riding on the foal of an ass had Messianic significance, because the Book of Zechariah records an oracle which says: "See now, your king comes to you; he is victorious, he is triumphant, humble and riding on a donkey" (Zech. 9:9). The arrival of the King of Israel in Jerusalem is pictured as a triumphant entry of one who has already achieved victory over the nations and now rules from Sea to Sea.[12] The oracle describes a war between the Sons of Zion (i.e., Israel) and the Sons of Greece (i.e., Israel's pagan rulers) in terms not very different from those of the War of the Sons of Light Against the Sons of Darkness.[13] Moreover, the king is portrayed as the one who will "proclaim peace for the nations" after God has put an end to all war (Zech. 9:10).

Jesus obviously considered this particular Messianic prophecy appropriate for his own entry to Jerusalem: he had made arrangements ahead of time for an ass to be made available for his use.[14] Perhaps Jesus chose this style of entering the city because of the subtle balance of meaning which such an entry would have—a meaning which would be particularly appropriate for one who stood in the desert wilderness tradition in which nationalistic and apocalyptic themes were inextricably bound together. "On the one hand, this symbolic act of riding into Jerusalem on the back of an humble ass, placed Jesus in position to be hailed as the conquering king of the Jews whose dominions would stretch from sea to sea. On the other hand, this king was to be humble, and he was to declare peace among the nations."[15]

Some Christian apologists lift the fulfillment of Old Testament prophecy completely out of its historical context of Jewish Messianism, which had strong nationalistic overtones, in order to "explain away" Jesus' apparent political involvement. For example, J. C. McRuer, Chief Justice of the High Court of Justice in Ontario, Canada, says that the Jews "came to proclaim a king, but Jesus came to Jerusalem not as a conquering king but as a servant riding on the colt of an ass, the dual symbol of peace and humility,"[16] implying that Jesus would not have wanted to be king. However, Jesus' entry into the city—viewed in the context of the Jewish peoples' Messianic expectation and in the light of the symbolic meaning which the prophecy of Zechariah gave it—cannot be seen as other than a self-assertion of his identity with the Son of David, a figure neither intended nor received as one of "peace and humility" in the sense implied by McRuer.

Nevertheless, we also believe that Jesus hoped his kingship would bring an end to violence and bloodshed. God, according to the beliefs of the apocalyptic nationalists, would confirm the election of the chosen Messiah by enabling a victory over the forces of darkness in the world. When the children of light had triumphed and God alone ruled on earth, then peace would reign at last and all manifestations of war would cease. This could only happen, however, when the present world order had toppled, including the reign of Rome, and the heavenly Kingdom had in fact been established.

SYMBOLS OF LIBERATION

Other aspects of Jesus' Triumphal Entry would have had for his fellow Jews a significance quite different from that traditionally associated with Palm Sunday. For example, the very palm branches of John 12:13 were a sign of the Jewish resistance movement.[17] Coins minted in the Maccabean period and during the Jewish Revolts of A.D. 66 and 132–135 were stamped with the inscription "For the Redemption of Zion" and pictured a palm tree as a symbol of the liberated nation. The victorious Judith of the Old Testament is said, in Judith 15:12, to have taken branches in her hand and distributed them among her suite as part of her victory celebration. The victory of Judas Maccabeus and the rededication of the sanctuary after its desecration by a "blasphemous and barbarous nation" were observed by festivities and rejoicing, with branches, leafy boughs and palms (II Macc. 10:1–8); and the conquest of Acre by Simon the Hasmonean was also celebrated with palm branches, according to I Maccabees 13:51.

If, therefore, John has preserved an historical fact, omitted by the Synoptists, in referring to the use of palm branches, their presence "would seem to indicate that there may well have been within the rejoicing crowd those who looked to Jesus as one who, following in the footsteps of the Maccabees, would lead the nation to victory in its struggle to throw off the 'yoke of the heathen' and reassert the sovereignty of God over Israel."[18] For "the branches of a palm tree were in ancient times employed as a symbol of triumph, and were presented to honour victorious conquerors. The branches thrown under the feet of Jesus, and particularly palm branches, would signify the celebration of victory over the pagan oppressor."[19]

In order for palm branches to be used, previous arrangements would have to be made. Palm branches are very difficult to cut, as anyone who lives in an area where they grow can attest, and palm trees are not plentiful in Jerusalem. It appears, therefore, that the palm branches, like the ass, were a part of the plan made by Jesus for the entry. It is even possible they were cut in Jericho and Ein Feshka, desert oases near Qumran where date palms were to be found in abundance, and brought up to the city for the occasion. This would explain why John states so simply that the crowd "took branches of palm and went out to meet him": the branches must have been cut and ready when the time came.[20]

The cries of "Hosanna" which greeted Jesus as he entered Jerusalem might more appropriately be translated, "Free us, free us, Son of David." That is: free us from the yoke of the Roman oppressors. Though the word "hosanna" is usually taken to be a transliteration of a Hebrew word meaning "save us," and is assumed to be a reference to Psalm 118:25—"Please, Yahweh, please save us!"—it can also be taken to be a similar Aramaic word that is the equivalent of "Free us!" in the speech of Jesus' time.[21]

The general acclamation and affirmation of Jesus' Messiahship on the part of many of the Jewish pilgrims gathered for the feast is undeniable. "The eyes of the people are upon their king. Now they will know what to do, because the Lord of Hosts will lead them through his anointed Son of David, as he had led them of old in the days of the Philistines. As the Lord had saved Israel from the Philistines through the consecrated sword of David, so in the days of Antiochus Epiphanes he had saved Israel from the Sons of Greece through the consecrated sword of the Maccabees. Could this be another saviour like the great Judas Maccabaeus?"[22]

Jesus' actions provided real justification for the cries of hosanna from the crowds, and for their acclaiming him King of Israel and Son of David. But it may be, as Dr. W. R. Farmer of Drew University suggests, that the jubilant throngs "read into this act something more of the Maccabean-Zealot meaning than Jesus ever intended, and apparently they took little note of that which is truly distinctive about

Zechariah's king, namely his humility and his concern for peace."[23] For as the week progressed it continued to be evident that Jesus was not willing to be established as king unless God Himself found the Jews worthy and intervened on their behalf to accomplish the redemption of Israel. Luke says that Jesus wept when he got near enough to see the city, and said, "If you in your turn had only understood on this day the message of peace! But, alas, it is hidden from your eyes! Yes, a time is coming when your enemies will raise fortifications all round you, when they will encircle you and hem you in on every side; they will dash you and the children inside your walls to the ground; they will leave not one stone standing on another within you— and all because you did not recognise your opportunity when God offered it!" (Lk. 19:41–44).[24]

This appears, at least in retrospect, to be a prophetic remark about the Fall of Jerusalem in A.D. 70. And yet it seems to have been tied to a clear expectation that the destruction of Jerusalem would be only a prelude to Israel's final liberation. Jesus finished his remarks about the events that would come to pass in those days by saying: "When these things begin to take place, stand erect, hold your heads high, because your liberation is near at hand" (Lk. 21:28).

Jesus' statement may have been only a premonition that even though the people welcomed him as king, they were not yet ready for the Messiah because they failed to comprehend "the message of peace": that is, the kinds of things he had been teaching his disciples and that were taught at Qumran. Without knowledge of those teachings, the people would bring destruction upon themselves. Thus, though Jesus would have been glad for the Davidic promise to be fulfilled in him, as is revealed in the words "if only *on this day* you understood . . . ," nevertheless he could not allow Maccabean history to repeat itself in every regard, causing the People Israel again to be led astray as happened during the Hasmonean rule. He would have to await the blessing of God, which would be in evidence when the angelic forces intervened on Israel's behalf. Or perhaps his words were truly prophetic.

Thus, although Jesus entered the city triumphantly that day and declared himself to be the Davidic Messiah the people had been expecting, no general uprising took place. It could be that only Galileans acknowledged him as king. The Gospels do record that the crowd which acclaimed Jesus joined him in or near Bethany where the Galileans camped. As Dr. Maurice Goguel of the University of Paris wrote, "The people who acclaim Jesus appear to be those who have come up with him from Galilee . . . If this had been an actual triumphal entry this demonstration would not have been without result. Neither the Jewish authorities nor the Roman administration could have regarded it with unconcern. In point of fact, it did not spur them to any kind of action; Jesus was not immediately arrested . . ."[25]

However, Galileans had been known to launch revolts on their own initiative before. Therefore, it seems more likely that Jesus' own refusal to attack the Romans until he had some sign from God prevented the crowd from rising up to establish him as king. Moreover, as we shall see in the later chapters, it is possible that those most prone to violence had found other avenues of expression for their zeal.

After Jesus had gone into the Temple and "looked all round him," he returned with the twelve to Bethany, where they stayed each night during the final week.[26]

THE JERUSALEM TEMPLE

The Temple played a very dominant role in the Jewish world at the time of Jesus in more ways than those to which we have thus far alluded. It was the religious and cultural center of all the Jewish people of the Diaspora; even Jews who were scattered throughout the Empire and who were unable to attend feasts there regularly, looked to Jerusalem's Temple as the center of their faith.[27] It served as the home of the Temple cultus: the one holy site of God's presence on earth where the Jew offered his prayers and sacrifices, sought judgments in religious and civil cases, and gathered for the feast days three times each year. "To the Temple people brought the first-fruits [of the harvest], and here the mother brought the customary offerings for purification after the birth of each child. To the Temple Jews from all over the world sent the Temple tax. To the Temple came each course of priests, Levites and Israelites in turn. To the Temple, three times a year, the whole world of Jewry streamed."[28]

The Temple also served as the economic nerve-center of Palestine and was essential to the economic survival of Jerusalem. Jerusalem's location in the hill country of Judea was an extraordinarily poor site for commercial purposes and the city was lacking in nearly all natural resources, including, most importantly, water. Being in such a poor location made trade necessary in order to maintain a sufficient supply of raw materials. To sustain such trade, capital was essential, and here the Temple with its incredible wealth was crucial to the life of Jerusalem, Israel, and the Mediterranean world.

As Professor Jeremias points out, "What revenues did the city have to promote such trade? . . . the enormous revenues of the Temple, made up of bequests coming in from all over the world, the worldwide levy of a fixed tax, that of the didrachma [a Temple tax levied on every Jew of the world], the sacrifices, the reception of vows, the wood offerings, etc., as well as the produce of the land owned by the Temple."[29] This meant that the "cultus provided the main source of income for the city. It maintained the priestly aristocracy, the priesthood, and the Temple employees. The vast expenditure from the Temple treasury (one need think only of the rebuilding of the Temple) —to say nothing of the many ceremonial activities of the devout such as sacrifices and vows—provided numerous opportunities of money-making for the trade and commerce of the city."[30] The Temple had such wealth in gold that when the city fell and the Temple was sacked by Titus' troops in A.D. 70, the standard price of gold in the province of Syria (of which Judea was a part) depreciated to half of its former value.[31] The Temple provided money changers for the people who flocked to the city. There were shops in the Temple court area, and markets for sacrificial animals located in the Temple's environs which were probably kept up by and to the advantage of the High Priest's family.[32]

In addition to paying the fixed Temple tax of a half shekel per year, each Jew was also required to spend a "second tithe"—one tenth of the profits of his land and livestock—in Jerusalem. Persons entering the market had to pay a special duty to the tax collector, who ruthlessly fulfilled his responsibilities of collection. Money changers in the Temple exchanged all foreign currencies for the Jewish market, handling secular money transactions in addition to religious matters— such as exchanging foreign coins into "acceptable" offerings for the special tax paid to the Temple. The Temple served as a depository for private funds[33] and fulfilled other secular functions as well, contributing as a matter of honor to social welfare. Its resources maintained municipal buildings, paved and cleansed streets, and possibly cared for aqueducts and other water sources for the city.

There was an intricate and mutual relationship between the wealth of the Temple and the privileged position of social status and political power occupied by the pro-Roman priestly aristocracy. The posts of the Temple, such as treasurer and chief of the Temple guard, were filled from among the ranks of the priestly aristocracy, who apparently drew their regular income from its treasury. Dr. Jeremias notes, "We must also remember the trade in sacrificial victims which may have been kept up by the high priestly family of Annas, as well as the plundering of the inferior priests . . . and various acts of violence and cases of bribery. Besides all this we find nepotism rife in the filling of lucrative and influential posts in the Temple, such as those of treasurer or chief priest."[34]

The cultus of the Temple became a focal point of tension and conflict between the chief priests and the lower orders of the priesthood whose livelihood depended on the Temple's funds and who were reduced to a state of poverty. This conflict was so great by the time of the revolt of A.D. 66 that the lower class of priests and even some of the aristocracy were not hesitant to join the revolutionary forces.

JESUS CLEANSES THE TEMPLE

Considering the size, importance, and power of the Temple and the priestly aristocracy, it is easy to understand why the typical Sunday School image of the "cleansing of the Temple," picturing Jesus overturning a card table or two in a fit of "righteous anger," should be considered a serious understatement of what the actual event must have been. In light of the nationalistic fervor of the Jewish People which was even more heightened than usual during the feast days, the Messianic role which Jesus assumed in entering the city, the people's enthusiastic response to him, the profound political implications of his actions,[35] and his subsequent arrest, trial, and execution as an insurrectionist—a charge for which Pilate must surely have felt there was some incriminating evidence—the "cleansing of the Temple" can best be interpreted as an assault on the banking establishment of the Temple and a direct blow at the privileged positions of both the Roman and Jewish hierarchs in Jerusalem.

> So they reached Jerusalem and he went into the Temple and began driving out those who were selling and buying there; he upset the tables of the money changers and the chairs of those who were selling pigeons. Nor would he allow anyone to carry anything through the Temple. (Mk. 11:15–16)

Considering the number of persons who would have been buying and selling in the Temple court, the size of the Gentile court itself (which scholars estimate was at least 750 feet square),[36] the number of money changers who would have been involved, and the number of people coming and going, bringing animals to buy and sell, carrying out business transactions, going to offer sacrifices, etc., it is impossible to imagine that Jesus could have accomplished this "cleansing" single-handedly. To the contrary, he must have been accompanied by a large number of supporters and the attack on the Temple must have been highly organized in order to have succeeded as well as it apparently did.

It is possible that by using whips on the animals, Jesus and his followers caused the larger animals, the sheep and oxen, to stampede, thereby creating pandemonium in which tables were overturned and livestock scattered. In this way, perhaps with the help of other pilgrims in the courtyard who would undoubtedly have welcomed any opportunity to strike back at those who controlled the Temple and contributed to their oppression, Jesus could have "cleansed" the Temple.

In order to have maintained control long enough to be able to teach the people the meaning of his action and to perform healings, while preventing anyone from carrying any merchandise or unclean objects into the area,[37] however, Jesus would have had, in effect, to occupy and control the Temple area. In fact, the Gospels report that after the cleansing he "was teaching daily in the temple."[38] This seems highly unlikely—since the leader of any such disturbance during a feast, then, as today, would have been quickly arrested by the Temple guard (police)—*unless* the crowd with Jesus had been extremely large and they had, in effect, taken control of the Temple. The Gospel accounts indicate that the authorities were afraid to arrest Jesus because of the multitudes which "hung on his words" (Lk. 19:47–48; Mk. 11:18).

The implications of Jesus' "occupation" of the Temple, if that is what it was, for the true nature of his teaching and activity could be even more startling than the implications of his being crucified.[39] As one scholar has expressed it, "Jesus must have had an armed force powerful enough for him to seize this vast edifice and hold it for some time, judging by his reference to the 'day after day' he spent 'teaching' in the Temple . . ."[40] Whether or not Jesus had "an armed force," the original event must have been of a higher magnitude than that which is preserved in the Gospels. It seems likely that Jesus' actions made a deep impression on his followers which they could not entirely ignore, but that in recording the event the Gospel writers sought to soften it in order to dissociate Jesus from those "zealots" who had caused the fall of Jerusalem by their revolt in A.D. 66–70.[41]

SCHOLARLY REFLECTION ON THE CLEANSING

Because any attack on the Temple would inevitably have drawn the attention of both the Jewish hierarchy and the Romans,[42] scholars have debated at great length the purpose of Jesus' cleansing the Temple, and how such an attack could possibly have succeeded. Some have even questioned whether it occurred at all.

There are three main arguments offered by those who contest the historicity of Jesus' cleansing of the Temple. First, it is seen as virtually inconceivable that the Roman garrison, the Temple police, or both, did not intervene. For example, Robert Eisler, the Austrian scholar and author of the work *The Messiah Jesus and John the Baptist,* argues: "If . . . the precaution had already been taken of posting Roman guards at the great festivals on the porticoes surrounding the temple court, ready to nip in the bud any popular disturbances, then it is hardly conceivable that events such as the so-called cleansing of the Temple could have taken place. One would have to regard them, with Origen, as a greater miracle than the changing of water into wine at the marriage of Cana, or else to assume a wholly improbable surprise attack on and intimidation of the Roman garrison."[43]

A second argument rests on the fact that there is no mention of the "cleansing of the Temple" included in the charges laid against Jesus in his trial. For example, Haim Cohn, associate justice of the Supreme Court of Israel, asserts: "Jesus' casting out of the Temple of moneylenders . . . may have amounted to a breach of the peace but was apparently not being held against him."[44]

Third, many consider the Gospel accounts of the event to be an elaboration by the early Church, building on a verbal attack which Jesus made on the buying and selling in the Temple.[45] And Dr. Goguel raises a further question with regard to the dating of the incident: he feels the cleansing of the Temple must have taken place at the Feast of Tabernacles, several months earlier than the Synoptic Gospels indicate.[46] To add to the confusion, the Fourth Gospel places the event at the beginning of Jesus' public activity, and Bishop

John Robinson of Cambridge prefers John's dating because it fits his thesis that Jesus started his public life by acting out the role of Elijah.[47]

On the other hand, the cleansing of the Temple is perhaps the most crucial element in arguments put forth by those scholars who closely identify Jesus with the Zealots. For example, Professor Brandon depicts Jesus' attack on the Temple as designed to gain control of the Temple and to depose the High Priest. He was attempting the same kind of coup as the Zealots managed to pull off in the Revolt of A.D. 66, Dr. Brandon believes.[48] And Joel Carmichael, author of *The Death of Jesus,* relies heavily on the Zealotic nature of the cleansing of the Temple, which is, in his view, "so obviously the springboard for [Jesus'] arrest and trial, that its historicity must be taken for granted." He concludes that Jesus' "seizure of the Temple could have been accomplished by an act of violence, *by armed force.*"[49]

Robert Eisler also believed that Jesus "occupied" the Temple, but he differs from Brandon and Carmichael with regard to the tactics which Jesus employed. Eisler portrayed Jesus' attitude and tactic as one of "radical pacifism" in "his final attack on the sacrificial system and the banking business in the temple which armed the priestly caste against him."[50] Eisler concluded that Jesus sought to abolish the sacrifices as a means of declaring publicly the beginning of a new era of which his self-revelation as Messiah was a part. In Eisler's view, the words attributed to Jesus, "destroy the temple, and in three days I will raise it up," reflect what Jesus actually said on that occasion.[51]

Oscar Cullmann has also explored at length Jesus' relation to the Zealotism in his *The State in the New Testament* and *Jesus and the Revolutionaries.* In this latter work Dr. Cullmann emphasizes the cleansing of the Temple as one of the "characteristics which *closely connect* Jesus with the Zealots."[52] In fact, Dr. Cullmann recognizes the attack on the Temple as perhaps the most convincing justification for closely allying Jesus with the Zealots: "Jesus cleansed the temple. This event seems most clearly to speak in favor of the thesis 'Jesus-Revolutionary,' and it also is always placed in the foreground by the proponents of this thesis."[53] Professor Cullmann goes on to dispute such a thesis: "The cleansing of the temple is an individual act, a prophetic sign performed by Jesus, and not an element of a Zealot program . . . Jesus wishes to abolish the existing customs connected with the temple cult which stand in flagrant contradiction to the essence of all worship and which already *can* be abolished without the violent destruction of the temple cult. The cleansing of the temple concerns directly only a very limited aspect of Jewish worship."[54] Dr. Cullmann does acknowledge, however, that Jesus' action is rooted in the same "eschatological radicalism" which is a fundamental characteristic shared by the Zealots. He believes they differ in that the Zealots' hope is to be realized in a "national-earthly framework."

Professor Paul Winter and Justice Haim Cohn differ even more sharply from those who view Jesus' activity in the Temple as Zealot-like. Dr. Winter reduces the cleansing of the Temple "to the category of what a magistrate today would call a disturbance of the peace. It was neither sacrilege nor sedition, possibly a hubbub, and certainly an attack on vested interests . . . A rude interruption of [the aristoc-racy's] business, possibly involving damage to their property, would out-rage their sense of propriety, and if angry owners reported the incident to their influential kinsmen, the report would have contributed to in-cense the hierarchs against Jesus."[55] Justice Cohn, as we mentioned above, argues essentially the same point: that Jesus' casting out of the Temple money-lenders may have amounted to a breach of the peace, but was apparently not held against him. He specifically rejects Car-michael's argument that Jesus' action must have involved the use of force: "We find no hint of any such—naturally much graver—charge in any of the Gospel accounts . . . Jesus' activities within the Temple may have constituted an offence under Jewish law and enraged the Temple authorities, but was presumably not of much concern to Pilate."[56] Bishop John Robinson basically agrees with this diminution of the significance of the cleansing of the Temple.[57]

Nevertheless, Morton S. Enslin, Professor of Christian Thought and Literature at Dropsie University in Philadelphia, contends that Jesus' cleansing of the Temple was the act "which crystallized the leaders' wrath and led to his speedy arrest and death." While some scholars maintain that Jesus' words predicting the Temple's destruction and "the amazing escape of Jesus, unmolested by the Temple police, after an act so easily construable as one of wanton violence in a sacred shrine" are not based on historical fact and are only later additions to the Gospel accounts of Jesus' life, Enslin argues that "it is impossible to escape the conclusion that prominent among the words actually spoken by Jesus while in Jerusalem were passionate denunciations of what the Temple had become and a prediction of its speedy down-fall."[58] Dr. Enslin concludes that Jesus' condemnation by Pilate "was occasioned by Jesus' passionate avowal that the axe was already laid at the root of the tree and that the end of the present order was at hand, for in the eyes of the authorities this was a direct attack upon both state and Temple."[59]

Professor David Flusser of Hebrew University also pinpoints Jesus' "intervention in the Temple market and his predictions of the future destruction of the Temple" as the two incidents by which he "actively struck a blow against the Temple authorities" and which resulted in his arrest and execution.[60]

THE QUMRAN TRADITION

The historicity of this event need not be doubted, for all that we know about the context in which Jesus lived and about the background of his teachings and his preaching about the Kingdom of God would lead us to believe that his opposition to the Temple cultus and the priesthood, not to mention the financial activities in the courtyard, would have been almost inevitable. Since he stressed the need for repentance and for purity of action as well as obedience to the letter of the Law, it seems fitting that he should have criticized the Temple-centered businesses: "Does not scripture say: 'My house will be called a house of prayer for all the peoples'? But you have turned it into a robbers' den" (Mk. 11:17).[61] And his other challenge: "I tell you solemnly, not a single stone here will be left on another: everything will be destroyed" (Mt. 24:2), is easily understood in light of the Qumranian expectation that when the Messiah came, the Temple would be destroyed and replaced by a perfect one from heaven.[62]

Dr. Bertil Gartner, Assistant Professor of New Testament Theology at Uppsala, Sweden, has put forth an explanation of this incident which is most persuasive in light of the prevalent mood of apocalyptic nationalism in Jesus' day. Dr. Gartner writes, "One aspect of the work of the Messiah in the last days was believed to be the renewal of the temple. In such cases, quite irrespective of whether these hopes were interpreted in imminent or transcendent terms, the coming Messiah was coupled with hopes of a new temple and a new Jerusalem . . . [Jesus'] entry into Jerusalem is clearly Messianic in character . . ." He also notes that although John places the account of Jesus' cleansing

of the temple at the beginning of his Gospel narrative, he still connects
it clearly with the question of the Messiahship.

Dr. Gartner goes on to say:

> Further, the actual events described in the . . . cleansing of the
> temple are an expression of the Messianic consciousness of Jesus.
> They express the idea that Jesus [as the] Messiah now had the au-
> thority to demonstrate, in word and in deed, that the time had come
> for the establishment of the "new" temple and a new and better basis
> of fellowship with God . . . I find it difficult to avoid interpreting the
> [incident] as an expression of Jesus' Messianic attitude to the temple.
> The only one who can behave in this way is the Lord of the temple . . .
> Jesus' cleansing of the temple thus becomes simultaneously a judge-
> ment and an expression of hope in a better fellowship than that
> based on the temple as it then was.[63]

Dr. Gartner also points out that the two Old Testament passages
to which Jesus makes reference as his "motivation" for the cleansing—
"my house will be called a house of prayer for all the peoples"
(Is. 56:7) and making the temple a "robbers' den" (Jer. 7:11)—
both strengthen his interpretation of the event as Messianic in significance.

> Isaiah describes, in contrast to the decline and decay of the temple
> of his time, the future in which the new Zion shall be established
> and "foreigners" be given their rightful place in Israel. The necessary
> condition is that the *Law* be observed and the *covenant* be kept . . .
> [Therefore, Jesus'] demand for righteousness and worship in the same
> context [that is, in the Temple] is fully in accordance with the
> prophetic tradition of criticism of the cultus. The "den of robbers"
> passage in Jeremiah 7 is also connected with a sharp criticism of those
> who fail to observe the Law, notwithstanding their faithful attendance
> at worship in the temple. The blessing of God cannot be secured, save
> as a reward for *complete obedience* to the Law.[64]

Dr. Gartner then makes this pertinent connection:

> We thus see that both texts stress the principle on which the Qumran
> community laid its strongest emphasis: *only when there was perfect
> obedience to the Law could there be blessing in the house of God.*
> And the community had broken away from the temple just because
> the Law was *not* observed . . . It is obvious that behind Jesus' actions
> in the temple lay the thought that the temple and its worship has been

defiled . . . His action in driving the merchants and money-changers out of the temple hit the priests, and those whose responsibility it was to see that the temple functioned properly. They had broken the Law of God under the terms of the covenant, by failing to keep the temple and its worship holy . . . We may observe here how similar [to Jesus' opposition] were the grounds of Qumran's criticism of the temple; the priests had been guilty of profaning the temple, and hence it could no longer function as the true cultic link with God. The altar has become defiled; the temple and its worship *must be replaced.*[65]

And finally, Jesus is accused in the trial narrative of having said, "I have power to destroy the Temple of God and in three days build it up" (Mt. 26:61), and "I am going to destroy this Temple made by human hands, and in three days build another, not made by human hands" (Mk. 14:58).[66] Both statements echo the expectation of the Qumran community that the Temple would be destroyed at the end of days and that a new one—not made by "hands," but made by God—would descend ready-made from heaven.[67] They are also suggestive of the Covenanters' understanding of their own communal life as equivalent to the Temple service and of the early Church's self-conception as a spiritual temple, neither of which was "made with hands" (i.e., idolatrous), but rather by God.[68]

It does not seem improbable, therefore, that Jesus led such a "protest" in the Temple, directed toward calling the People's attention to the need for change (repentance) if they were to merit the Messiah's coming, for his preaching and teaching had been and continued to be very much in the Qumran tradition. The crucial difference between Jesus and Qumran was that Jesus was now openly declaring himself as the Messiah and by his actions in the Temple was announcing that the time for the building of the "new" Temple was upon them.

JESUS AND THE ZEALOTS

While it is apparent that Jesus did not seek to condemn Temple worship or abolish the Temple as such—he sought only to purify it—this was equally true of the Zealots, as is attested to by their actions in the Revolt of A.D. 66 in which they not only attempted to establish what they considered a "legitimate" priesthood but also fought against overwhelming odds to defend the sanctuary. Whether for that reason Jesus should be seen as more closely aligned with the Zealots, however, must remain an open question. There is no historical data bearing directly on the question of Jesus' relationship to the Zealots, and what is known is not conclusive, as the diverse scholarly opinions make evident.

Perhaps the Zealots would have grown impatient with Jesus' strict adherence to nonviolence, a posture which was consistent with his view of the coming of the Kingdom of God. But this split between Jesus and the Zealots was not due to a fundamental disagreement over goals or expectations. Rather, they differed in their sense of timing. While many of the Zealots did not hesitate to confront the Romans violently in the hope of facilitating or hastening the coming of the Kingdom, Jesus stopped short of striking the first blow, apparently because of his belief that the final battle with the forces of darkness was to be initiated by God.

In the sense that Jesus' action in the Temple did not constitute an armed attack on the Romans, it may have disappointed the hopes of the more zealous of his following. But that such a disruption in the Temple court, albeit nonviolent, would have gone unheeded by the Romans during the feast days is entirely inconsistent with what is known about the repressive atmosphere in Jerusalem on the feast days during that period. Gatherings of large numbers of Jewish pilgrims in Jerusalem, especially those from Galilee, were often accompanied by heightened tensions and fervent Messianic expectations. That a serious uprising in the Temple would not have been summarily dealt with by the Roman authorities and immediately suppressed, seems inconceivable.

Dr. Robert Eisler points out that "According to Roman law, one is guilty of a [crime] deserving of death so soon as one openly and without commission assumes powers which are the sole privilege of the government and its officers. The overthrowing of the money-changers' tables in the temple, the expulsion from the sacred precincts of the dealers in cattle for the sacrifices (quite apart from the actual assault with the scourge), the order to carry nothing through the temple—these are so many expressions of an official authority which Jesus assumed unto himself in his own right, and which, according to Roman law, constituted an invasion of the functions of the temple police . . . a crime deserving of death. The tumultuary proclamation of a 'king of the Jews' without licence from Caesar is of course in itself high treason . . ."[69]

If the historicity of the event is accepted, it seems less likely that the Gospels would have exaggerated the event, as Professor Maurice Goguel suggests,[70] than that they would have attempted to minimize its political character and its direct bearing on Jesus' being brought to trial as an insurrectionist. The treatment of the event in the Gospels makes it quite apparent that the Evangelists were not concerned with describing it in great detail. It would seem that either the fact of an actual attack on the Temple led the Gospel writers to include verbal "threats," which they term "teachings" in their accounts, or, as seems more likely, that Jesus did in fact both "cleanse" the Temple and interpret the meaning of his actions to all who would listen.

Whichever is in fact the case, Jesus' words "I am going to destroy this Temple made by human hands, and in three days build another, not made by human hands" are raised in the trial as among the charges made against him (Mk. 14:56–59; Mt. 26:59–63). Though the Gospel accounts indicate that the charge was raised by "false witnesses," the fact that it was included suggests that the incident of the cleansing of the Temple did not go unnoticed, and may in fact have been one of the principal reasons for Jesus' arrest. It seems unlikely that these words would have been attributed to Jesus by the Gospel writers if he had not actually spoken them, since they could so obviously be used as a confirmation of the truth of the charges brought against Jesus.[71]

THE SIGNIFICANCE OF THE TEMPLE EVENT

The least that can be said, then, about the attack made on the Temple by Jesus is that it was large enough and successful enough to prevent his being immediately arrested for it.[72] A possible explanation for the absence of Roman or Jewish intervention will be dealt with in more detail when we consider the Barabbas tradition as it relates to the trial of Jesus. At this point it suffices to say that the occurrence of a violent insurrection in the city simultaneous to Jesus' attack on the Temple may have distracted the authorities. Moreover, the Gospels record that Jesus' broad support among the populace prevented his arrest (Mk. 11:18; Lk. 19:47–48). If in fact the Roman garrison was preoccupied with an uprising in another part of the city, Jesus' large following may have prevented his arrest by the weaker forces of the Temple guard. Therefore, it is possible that the delay in the move to arrest Jesus was a purely strategic one on the part of the Jewish and Roman authorities, as indeed the Gospels themselves suggest.

It seems unlikely, however, that the incident in the Temple area was so minor that it failed to attract the attention of the authorities. The cleansing of the Temple is historically tenable as an act of sufficient provocation to occasion Jesus' arrest for insurrection by the Romans. But if Jesus were in fact the harmless—indeed, ineffective—teacher portrayed by many Christian apologists, it would be impossible to account for his arrest and crucifixion.

The fact of Jesus' crucifixion for sedition as a claimant to the kingship of Israel is not only consistent with, but may actually be partially dependent upon, his attack on the Temple. His actions in the Temple would not have been cause for conviction on strictly religious grounds, but they would certainly have been viewed as an obvious and blatant intrusion into the precincts of the Jewish priestly aristocracy, the duly constituted authorities appointed to run the Temple by the Roman rulers.[73] As such, his cleansing of the Temple would no doubt have been used against him in his trial for sedition.

And finally, with regard to the questions of chronology, we find the Synoptic dating of the triumphal entry and cleansing of the Temple at the beginning of Passion Week fits intelligibly into the progressive development of Jesus' thought and actions, which we have tried to outline, and into the series of events which led to his trial and death.[74] It is difficult to imagine that he would have taken such a bold action before deciding he was willing to die for the sake of the Kingdom and that death might be required of him, and it is equally difficult to imagine that, if he had, the Romans and the High Priest and his cohorts would have let him stay at large.

Jesus attempted to cleanse the Temple, possibly in partial memory of the cleansing and rededication of the Temple at the time of the Maccabean Revolt, in an attempt to arouse the conscience of the People, and, by an intensification of issues, to bring about a situation which would enable God to intervene in history to establish His Kingdom. Apparently neither happened, and instead the event no doubt contributed to his eventual conviction and crucifixion as a Jewish rebel against Rome.

CHAPTER 10

The Apocalyptic Tension of Holy Week

"Abba (Father)! Everything is possible for you. Take this cup away from me. But let it be as you, not I, would have it."   Mark 14:36

In the words of James A. Pike:

"In the end it comes down to this question: 'How complete is your dedication and commitment within your grand hypothesis?' Jesus' commitment was absolute. And therefore there is also a total breakthrough in him from the cosmic side, the divine side, from the One, the All, from God's side. In Jesus we see a total breakthrough of truth, courage and love. Jesus' life is like a still frame from a motion picture about the history of a given time, which comes into focus only within a premise about the way life is which may not be entirely our premise. To me that is not important. What matters is that within that premise there is a totality of giving; therefore, there is a total openness and a total breakthrough.

"Now I am not among those who would say it is the *only* breakthrough, or even the only impressive breakthrough, in history. But it is certainly *a* total breakthrough from God's side, as well as total dedication from Jesus' side. If that's all one could say without claiming 'the one and only' exclusivity, one would still have said a pretty big thing. And therefore, from this historical point of view one can look on Jesus with great awe, particularly when one sees him in the context of this whole movement. Because he carried through to the very end, within his grand hypothesis, with tremendous courage and joy in the midst of pain and tragedy."

———————◆———————

AN APOCALYPTIC VIEW OF THINGS

It could distort the evidence to rush into a discussion of the events which led to Jesus' death without pausing to reconsider the frame of reference within which they all took place. During that final week Jesus spoke with urgency of the events which would accompany the end of days:

> Then he said to them, "Nation will fight against nation, and kingdom against kingdom. There will be great earthquakes and plagues and famines here and there; there will be fearful sights and great signs from heaven.
>
> "But before all this happens, men will seize you and persecute you; they will hand you over to the synagogues and to imprisonment, and bring you before kings and governors because of my name—and that will be your opportunity to bear witness. Keep this carefully in mind: you are not to prepare your defence, because I myself shall give you an eloquence and a wisdom that none of your opponents will be able to resist or contradict. You will be betrayed even by parents and brothers, relations and friends; and some of you will be put to death. You will be hated by all men on account of my name, but not a hair of your head will be lost. Your endurance will win you your lives.
>
> "When you see Jerusalem surrounded by armies, you must realise that she will soon be laid desolate. Then those in Judaea must escape to the mountains, those inside the city must leave it, and those in country districts must not take refuge in it. For this is the time of vengeance when all that scripture says must be fulfilled. Alas for those with child, or with babies at the breast, when those days come!
>
> "For great misery will descend on the land and wrath on this people. They will fall by the edge of the sword and be led captive to every pagan country; and Jerusalem will be trampled down by the pagans until the age of the pagans is completely over.
>
> "There will be signs in the sun and moon and stars; on earth nations in agony, bewildered by the clamour of the ocean and its waves; men dying of fear as they await what menaces the world, for the powers of heaven will be shaken. And then they will see the Son of Man coming in a cloud with power and great glory. When these things begin to take place, stand erect, hold your heads high, because *your liberation is near at hand.*" (Lk. 21:10–28)[1]

These words are clearly apocalyptic, pointing to the end of days when the Son of Man will come and all the promises given to Israel will be fulfilled. "Hold your heads high," Jesus is reported to have said, "because *your liberation* is near at hand." He was confident that they would soon be freed from subservience to the children of darkness and that God's Kingdom would reign on earth.

When did Jesus believe this would all come to pass? He told his disciples a parable:

> "Think of the fig tree and indeed every tree. As soon as you see them bud, you know that summer is now near. So with you when you see these things happening: know that the kingdom of God is near. I tell you solemnly, before this generation has passed away all will have taken place. Heaven and earth will pass away, but my words will never pass away.
>
> "Watch yourselves, or your hearts will be coarsened with debauchery and drunkenness and the cares of life, and that day will be sprung on you suddenly, like a trap. For it will come down on every living man on the face of the earth. Stay awake, praying at all times for the strength to survive all that is going to happen, and to stand with confidence before the Son of Man." (Lk. 21:29–36)[2]

Thus it would appear that Jesus tried to prepare his disciples for the coming of the Son of Man which would climax the trials and tribulations of the end of the era. He did not seem, in the passage quoted above, to identify himself with that figure,[3] for he spoke of the Son of Man in the third person. And he apparently felt that the events of which he spoke would begin to happen very soon—perhaps even in response to his own life and actions.

The teachings which are attributed by the Gospel writers to Jesus during Holy Week focus on two things. In the Synoptic Gospels, the signs of the end and the coming of the Kingdom are stressed,[4] together with references to the People's rejection of God's messengers:

> "Jerusalem, Jerusalem, you that kill the prophets and stone those who are sent to you! How often have I longed to gather your children, as a hen gathers her chicks under her wings, and you refused! So be it! Your house will be left to you desolate, for, I promise, you shall not see me any more until you say: *'Blessings on him who comes in the name of the Lord!'*" (Mt. 23:37–39)[5]

It is apparent that Jesus was more aware with each passing day that not enough of the People were ready for the Kingdom to be established in fullness. If they had been, more of them would have acknowledged him (and other messengers of God, such as John the Baptist[6]) by saying, "Blessings on him who comes in the name of the Lord!" And yet Jesus must have kept hoping right up to the very end that more people *would* repent—that is, change their ways—and that God would be enabled to act at once.

A second reported theme of his teaching during that last week is found in John's Gospel. There Jesus is said to have taught, not the masses or the general public, but his closest disciples, certain "secrets" of the Kingdom.[7] These teachings regarding the strength and insight which would be given to the disciples when they received the baptism of the holy spirit are set in the context of Jesus' last evening with the Twelve. It is as though, sensing that time had run out, he tried to prepare them for going on without him.

> "I tell you most solemnly, whoever believes in me will perform the same works as I do myself, he will perform even greater works, because I am going to the Father. Whatever you ask for in my name I will do, so that the Father may be glorified in the Son . . . If you love me you will keep my commandments. I shall ask the Father, and he will give you another Advocate to be with you for ever, that Spirit of truth whom the world can never receive since it neither sees nor knows him; but you know him, because he is with you, he is in you." (Jn. 14:12, 13, 15–17)

Jesus knew that if God did not intervene, death was inevitable. And yet he had confidence that death had no power over him: "In a short time the world will no longer see me; but you will see me, because I live and you will live. On that day you will understand that I am in my Father and you in me and I in you. Anybody who receives my commandments and keeps them will be one who loves me" (Jn. 14:19–21a).

Again, Jesus seems to be pointing to the time when the Son of Man will come and all will enter the Kingdom together: *"On that day you will understand . . ."* (Jn. 14:20). But he promises them that they will come to deeper understanding before then, when he says: "I have said these things to you while still with you; but the Advocate, the Holy Spirit, whom the Father will send in my name, will teach you everything and remind you of all I have said to you" (Jn. 14:25–26).

He continued to emphasize doing the truth, or living according to the Law: "If you keep my commandments you will remain in my love, just as I have kept my Father's commandments and remain in his love" (Jn. 15:10). "If anyone loves me he will keep my word . . ." (Jn. 14:23). "Anybody who receives my commandments and keeps them will be one who loves me . . ." (Jn. 14:21).

As instruction to the disciples about their life together, Jesus issued an injunction which reflects the goal of the Qumran community: that they be known by their love for one another.[8] "This is my commandment: love one another, as I have loved you. A man can have no greater love than to lay down his life for his friends. You are my friends, if you do what I command you . . . What I command you is to love one another" (Jn. 15:12–14, 17).

APOCALYPTIC TENSION

Tension must have been very high during that last week. Jesus and his disciples knew the fate that awaited them at the hands of the Romans, for many of their compatriots before them had acted in the hope that God would use them as channels for the deliverance of Israel, and they had been executed. The time had not been right for God to intervene. Now Jesus had acted openly, presenting himself as the Messiah in the hope that he would be used. Would this be the time according to God's plan to accomplish the final victory over evil? The only way they could know was to stand fast in the midst of the darkness and await God's power.

The war between the forces of light and the forces of darkness had to be won on many fronts. For Jesus and his disciples it had already been won in their inner lives—decisively, in Jesus' case, for he had received the spirit of holiness in the fullness of its power. Among the People Israel at large, however, the major battle had yet to be fought. It could not even begin until there were sufficient men living in perfect obedience to God's Law to enable God's intervention.

The earthly battle against the forces of darkness was only the most visible aspect of a larger cosmic struggle which involved all the forces of the universe. Since the ultimate confrontation would be between God and the Prince of Darkness (the devil), the children of light on earth could do little more than stand in readiness for that final war—Armageddon—to begin. Only God knew the timing and the precise pattern in the cosmic, or eternal dimension, and only God could see how men's actions fit into that larger scheme.

> "But as for that day or hour, nobody knows it, neither the angels of heaven, nor the Son; no one but the Father. Be on your guard, stay awake, because you never know when the time will come. It is like a man travelling abroad: he has gone from home, and left his servants in charge, each with his own task; and he has told the door-keeper to stay awake. So stay awake, because you do not know when the master of the house is coming, evening, midnight, cockcrow, dawn; if he comes unexpectedly, he must not find you asleep. And what I say to you I say to all: Stay awake!" (Mk. 13:32–37)

This reveals something of the apocalyptic tension in which Jesus stood. He had done what he could. He had called people's attention to the signs of the times manifest in their day. He had urged them to repent. He had taught them how they could live so as to be ready for God's Kingdom. He had trained his disciples for their special roles in the Kingdom. He had himself performed Messianic acts in accordance with prophecy.

More than that he could not do, for he knew that *when the time was right,* God would meet His People in the midst of history with the full power of His angelic forces of light to win the victory. Jesus could not know exactly how or when this would happen. He had done what he could; now he would have to wait and hope and trust.

We have seen a good example of this apocalyptic tension in the Zealots' defense of Jerusalem and Masada during the Great Revolt against Rome.[9] The Zealots had a different attitude from Jesus'. They believed that man had to strike the first blow against the forces of darkness and that God would act in response to man's initiation. They provoked battles and kept hoping God would join them.

When, therefore, the Zealots won an initial victory over the Roman troops of Gallus, they considered the victory to be the first "sign" of deliverance. As a consequence, the whole nation prepared for war. The inevitable retaliation from Rome came in the person of Vespasian, and later in his son Titus, and Jerusalem was sieged by the Romans. The Zealots chose to defend the Temple, the geographical focus of their devout theocratic faith, and they refused any conditions of surrender. For five months the Temple was assaulted by the Romans, and as many as five hundred Jews were crucified a day. But the Zealots persisted in their defense of the Temple: surely God would match their zeal by unloosing His powers to accomplish the redemption of Israel.

Finally, the Temple was burned and pillaged. But the Zealots' faith was undaunted. They were confident that with this final chastisement, God would surely see fit to intervene. They sought to return to the wilderness where the Covenant had been made, but their suicidal effort to breach the Roman circumvallation wall failed and nearly all were killed. A few remaining Zealots were the defenders of Masada. They fought on for three more years, hoping and believing that if they kept up their struggle against the forces of darkness on behalf of the whole nation of Israel, God would at last see fit to save them.

Jesus did not seek to precipitate God's action by striking the first blow, as the Zealots were prone to do. To the contrary, he refused even to *call* for God's angelic troops, even though he felt sure they would be sent if he did. He felt that to strike first would be to succumb to the temptation of testing God, rather than trusting Him utterly: "Put your sword back, for all who draw the sword will die by the sword. Or do you think that I cannot appeal to my Father who would promptly send more than twelve legions of angels to my defence? But then, how would the scriptures be fulfilled that say this is the way it must be?" (Mt. 26:52–54).[10]

THE BLOOD OF THE NEW COVENANT

Jesus' trust in God and in His plan was total. As the week wore on and crucifixion seemed more and more inevitable, Jesus apparently saw that his disciples were not able to suffer all of this with him. He therefore sent the majority of them back to the relative safety of Galilee while there was still time for them to escape arrest.[11] But Jesus was determined to see the tension through to the very end.

Before he dismissed his disciples, Jesus shared a meal with them. He had evidently made arrangements ahead of time for a private room in the home, many scholars have surmised, of the Beloved Disciple, whose name remains unknown. When the disciples asked

where Jesus wanted them to prepare for him to eat the Passover,
Jesus answered: "Go into the city and you will meet a man carrying
a pitcher of water." This was obviously a prearranged sign since only
women commonly carried water jars. "Follow him," Jesus went on,
"and say to the owner of the house which he enters, 'The master
says: Where is my dining room in which I can eat the passover with
my disciples?' He will show you a large upper room furnished with
couches, all prepared. Make the preparations for us there" (Mk. 14:
12–16).[12]

The careful plans indicate Jesus' caution. He knew that when they
left their refuge in Bethany for Jerusalem, there would be real danger
of detection and arrest. He used great discretion in arranging a place
to meet that would be unknown to the authorities and even to his
disciples. There he would be able to have an uninterrupted evening
with the Twelve.

Scholars disagree as to whether the "last supper" was a Passover
seder or an ordinary communal meal. Historically, it is almost impossible to determine what it was because the meal later took on a
profound apocalyptic significance which could not have been fully
anticipated by Jesus and his disciples on the occasion itself. The
"divine" or heavenly meaning of that week was being revealed in
the events themselves and could only be fully understood in retrospect. Perhaps the meal was styled by the Gospel writers, therefore,
to conform to the Passover tradition or to the common meal at Qumran. Or perhaps the Gospel accounts reflect the actual event, but
the authors heightened the Messianic significance of it in the light
of Jesus' death and the resurrection appearances. In any case, the nature of the actual event cannot be clearly determined historically.

Professor Joachim Jeremias, for example, argues that the New Testament accounts of the last supper are in every way suggestive of a
Passover meal conforming to the traditions of Jesus' day.[13] Professor
K. G. Kuhn of the University of Heidelberg, on the other hand,
is convinced that features peculiar to Jesus' last meal, and *un*explainable
by Passover customs, "find their parallels in the Essene cult meal
described in the texts from Qumran."[14] He concludes that the *tradition* regarding the last supper—irrespective of what it actually was,
historically speaking—describes it "not as a Passover meal but as a
communal meal, the forms of which correspond to those of the cult
meal of the Essenes."[15]

We find Kuhn's theory the more illuminating of the two. But whether

Jesus' last supper with his disciples was an expression, to some degree, of the Qumran tradition, or a traditional *seder,* its import for Jesus and his disciples was clearly the same: it was directed toward and focused on the future consummation of the Kingdom of God. According to Dr. Jeremias, the Passover traditions reflect the Messianic hope, just as do the revolts against Rome which repeatedly took place at the Passover, and the prospect of the Messianic future was indissolubly connected with the Passover celebration.[16] We have already seen that the Qumran meal was almost certainly a rehearsal for the Messianic banquet.[17] Therefore, the emphasis Jesus put on the coming of the Kingdom at that last meal would have been an appropriate expression of either tradition.

Jesus used the occasion of this last meal with his disciples to have a kind of "initiation" into the New Covenant.[18] He indicated that he wished his disciples to continue to have such meals together until the Kingdom was established, and in that regard especially he appears to have been acting within the Qumran tradition. That he still expected the imminent breakthrough of the Kingdom is reflected in his words to his disciples that he did not expect to eat such a meal again *until he ate with them in the Kingdom.*[19]

If he spoke to them of his death on that occasion, it surely would have been to reassure them that even if he were killed God's purpose would not be defeated. The forces of darkness were already being overcome: they had seen the signs of that all around them, and as children of light they had experienced the victory in their own lives. Death could not conquer the life which filled Jesus or any child of light. If he died, his death would be in the long line of those prophets who had been persecuted and had suffered and died for the cause of the Kingdom. Hopefully his death would help serve as a ransom for the Many: that is, would save the other members of the desert resistance movement (who called themselves the Many) from further suffering and sacrifice by serving as a sufficient sacrifice to atone for the sins of the whole People.[20] And, like other martyrs in the historical tradition of Judaism, Jesus understood himself to be an agent for the preparation for God's Kingdom. His sacrifice would hasten its coming.[21]

At the last supper, then, Jesus apparently received his disciples into "full membership" of the community of the New Covenant. Just as a two-year novitiate was required of the men who joined the Qumran sect, so Jesus' disciples had been with him at least two years.

During that time he had instructed them in the way of righteousness and had prepared them to keep and pass on the "secrets" of the Kingdom of God. Now they had proved themselves worthy to share in the fullness of the remnant community: "You are the men who have stood by me faithfully in my trials; and now I confer a kingdom on you, just as my Father conferred one on me: you will eat and drink at my table in my kingdom, and you will sit on thrones to judge the twelve tribes of Israel" (Lk. 22:28–30). It was not long after this meal with Jesus that the disciples received the baptism of the spirit—the seal of the New Covenant—and it came, significantly enough, on Pentecost,[22] the same feast day that was the occasion for the renewal of the Covenant at Qumran.

When the meal was over, the disciples headed toward Bethany—the site of their nightly headquarters. On their way, as they climbed the Mount of Olives, Jesus decided to spend some time in prayer. It was then that he took leave of all but three of his disciples, telling them to go on ahead, that he would meet them in Galilee.[23]

Before he left them, however, he is reported to have said, " 'When I sent you out without purse or [bag] or sandals, were you short of anything?' 'No' they said. He said to them, 'But now if you have a purse, take it; if you have a [bag], do the same; if you have no sword, sell your cloak and buy one' . . . 'Lord,' they said, 'there are two swords here now.' He said to them, 'That is enough!' " (Lk. 22:35–38).

Obviously Jesus wanted his disciples to be dependent on no one as they left him. He undoubtedly felt the end was so near, they should be prepared to manage by themselves for the very short interim. He wanted to be sure they had swords (*sicae,* or short daggers) so they would be ready to fight when the final battle began. He hoped they would not fall away from their righteousness and thus in the last moment be found unworthy to inherit the Kingdom: "Pray not to be put to the test" (Lk. 22:40).[24]

Then he went off to a place where he could be alone. He asked Peter, James, and John, the inner three, to stand guard. They were to watch and pray so that the forces of darkness—the Romans and their Jewish collaborators—did not overtake them.[25] Then Jesus prayed, "Father, if you are willing, take this cup away from me" (Lk. 22:42a). He still longed for the intervention of God and he prayed that it might come. But he also reaffirmed his absolute faith and trust in God: "Nevertheless, let your will be done, not mine" (Lk. 22:42b).[26] Jesus would not test God, even in the face of death.

The disciples were so sleepy they could not stay awake either to watch or to pray. According to the Gospel accounts, Jesus woke them twice, urging them to stay alert. The third time that he woke them, he said: "You can sleep on now and take your rest. It is all over. The hour has come . . ." (Mk. 14:41a).[27]

CHAPTER 11

The Arrest of Jesus the Nazarene

"Am I a brigand that you had to set out to capture
me with swords and clubs?"   Mark 14:48

In the words of James A. Pike:

"There is every attempt by the Gospel writers to make Jesus look safe and to create the image of a pacific Christ. Well, Jesus is my kind of pacifist. He is the kind of pacifist I have been involved with in the struggle against the Vietnam War: a nonviolent, up to the edge, activist who identifies across the board with all who are opposed to what is regarded as the evil regime, or evil in general. He used whips on animals to cause a stampede in order to try to knock out the oppressive economic establishment of his day. That's pacifist enough for me. Thoroughgoing pacifists against the Vietnam War have tried all kinds of ways to stop the establishment: by trying to persuade draftees not to go; by having tax strikes; by using napalm on paper, as the Berrigan brothers did, instead of on babies. I don't think that is contrary to pacifism, but it is activism of a nonviolent character.

"We see no sign at all of Jesus' being a violent person. Yet he is not a quietist, either, and he is certainly not a conformist. Nevertheless, the Gospels give the impression—deliberately—that Jesus was not really against the Roman authorities and that he wouldn't really have caused any trouble. They try to make us believe that it was the Jews' fault—even more than the Romans'—that Jesus was executed. But the story is not that easily dismissed or covered up.

"Jesus was a pacifist of sorts, but more actively involved in the resistance to Roman oppression than either the Romans or the Jewish hierarchy would have liked."

———————◆———————

AN APOCALYPTIC REVOLUTIONARY

Historical details regarding what happened in the Garden of Gethsemane before and during the arrest of Jesus are virtually impossible
to ascertain. In fact, the Gospel accounts of everything that happened
during the final days of Jesus' life are both confusing and contradictory. It appears the Gospel writers recorded early traditions which
were themselves inconsistent, and then elaborated upon those traditions
in efforts to elucidate the meaning of the events. It is now difficult to
discern which were the original elements of the tradition (which may
or may not have directly corresponded to the actual events), and
which were the authors' own theological and literary additions.[1]

As a result, any attempt to reconstruct a single coherent story about
the arrest, trial, and crucifixion of Jesus from the Gospels alone is
bound to fail. And all efforts to understand thoroughly the sayings
and actions of Jesus in each situation are at best subjective and
speculative. The most one can do is try to understand these crucial
events in the framework of a larger historical context.

In the course of our study, Jewish apocalyptic nationalism is the
historical tradition which has provided us with the clearest background
against which to understand the words and acts of Jesus. In the
context of Jewish history dating from the revolt of the Maccabees
to the Great Revolt against the Romans, Jesus emerges as one of
many Jewish apocalyptic revolutionaries.[2]

The term "apocalyptic revolutionary" is used in order to distinguish
Jesus from revolutionaries of other periods and from nationalists of
other countries who did not share Jesus' world view—his commitment
to the Covenant, and his expectation of the immediate establishment
of the Kingdom of God on earth. He differed from the Zealots and
the Sicarii in that he did not believe it was a man's prerogative to
strike the first military blow in freeing his people from the yoke
of Roman rule. He differed from the Qumran Covenanters in that
he was actively involved in enlisting the support of the common people
of the land in the cause of Israel's liberation in order to enable the
coming of God's Kingdom. Yet, as an apocalyptic revolutionary, Jesus
shared the goals of, and stood within the bounds of, the historical
tradition of Jewish religious nationalism, as did the Zealots, Sicarii, and

Covenanters. He, and they, expectantly awaited the sign from God inaugurating the final war to redeem the Nation of Israel and establish God's Kingdom on earth.

Robert M. Grant, Professor in the Divinity School of the University of Chicago, has assessed this historical background in the following way: "The context of Jesus' mission . . . lies in the apocalyptic-eschatological movements of the first century . . . It is now evident that the setting of the early Christian movement was not Rabbinic Judaism as later reflected in the Mishnah but the heterodox Judaism which tended to fade away after the failure of apocalyptic hopes and revolutionary activities in [A.D.] 66–70 and 132–135. In the light of these conclusions it is fairly clear that when Jesus proclaimed the imminent coming of the reign of God, to some extent already realized in his life with his disciples, he was announcing the coming of a theocracy which would be substituted for the religious government of Judaea by the Sadducean high priests and the political government by the representatives of Rome."[3]

Professor S. G. F. Brandon closely identifies Jesus with the Zealots. When examining the events in the Garden of Gethsemane he sees Jesus as being "sorely tried in coming to a decision about the future of his movement." Professor Brandon believes Jesus realized he had failed in his original intention to bring about a general uprising against the high priests and the Romans. He was aware that if he stayed in Jerusalem his enemies would eventually seize and punish him. Therefore, he decided to withdraw to Galilee. He sent his disciples on ahead, planning to join them in Galilee later, probably traveling alone so as to avoid detection. Professor Brandon concludes that Jesus clearly had no intention of surrendering himself to his enemies.[4]

We also feel that Jesus was struggling with himself regarding the future, and that on that last night in the Garden he was reassessing things in the light of the most recent events in Jerusalem. It also seems apparent that he sent most of his disciples on to Galilee, for they are not mentioned again until after the crucifixion.[5] He may even have been preparing for flight to Galilee as a "strategic retreat," for he knew he was in grave danger if he stayed in Jerusalem. But we tend not to identify Jesus as closely with the Zealots as Professor Brandon does for the reason stated above.

It does seem that Jesus posted at least three guards during the time he was praying in the Garden. He apparently wanted, and needed, time for prayer in order to determine God's plan for him and did not want to be caught off guard. Therefore, he asked his disciples to watch: "My soul is sorrowful to the point of death. Wait here, and keep awake" (Mk. 14:34).

The instructions to "keep awake" must have had a double meaning. Only a short while before going out into the Garden Jesus had said, "Be on your guard, stay awake, because you never know when the time will come" (Mk. 13:33). He was referring then to the coming of the Son of Man and the Kingdom. Surely in the Garden he must still have hoped for that. But in addition, his "sorrow" indicates that he anticipated the approach of his enemies and that he also wanted his disciples to keep awake to warn him of that.

That these guards were armed seems indisputable. Not only had Jesus checked earlier to be sure the disciples had swords, and determined that they had two, but later Peter is reported to have struck with his. Scholars are in wide disagreement as to the full significance of the "armed guard," however. Professor Brandon asserts, "This precaution can have only one meaning: Jesus intended to resist clandestine arrest."[6] He feels that Mark "found it prudent to conceal the fact that the disciples of Jesus were armed and that his arrest had been violently resisted. Consequently, [Mark] vaguely mentions that 'one of those who stood by drew his sword, and struck the slave of the high priest and cut off his ear.' "[7]

Matthew, however, as Dr. Brandon points out, expands Mark's account of the incident so that it becomes a full reproof by Jesus of his disciples for resorting to armed combat—a reproof which has long since been used by Christians to prove that Jesus was in fact a pacifist: "Then they came forward, seized Jesus and took him in charge. At that, one of the followers of Jesus grasped his sword and drew it; he struck out at the high priest's servant, and cut off his ear. Jesus then said, 'Put your sword back, for all who draw the sword will die by the sword. Or do you think that I cannot appeal to my Father Who would promptly send more than twelve legions of angels to my defence?' " (Mt. 26:50b–53).

Oscar Cullmann takes the latter view. He considers Jesus' words "Put your sword back, for all who draw the sword will die by the sword" as "the saying that condemns all Zealotism."[8] As for Jesus' telling his disciples to arm themselves, Dr. Cullmann writes: "If we regard the saying as genuine (and I hold it is impossible to assail its authenticity), then we must in consequence take this command [to get swords] seriously. Even so I do not believe we may draw the conclusion that Jesus really embraced Zealotism here, even for a moment." Rather, Professor Cullmann reasons, Jesus may have decided that for the sake of proclaiming the Gospel, "defensive sword-bearing may become a necessity for the disciples."[9]

Professor Paul Winter essentially agrees with Dr. Cullmann, in that he believes Jesus intentionally distinguished himself from the Zealot insurgents when he said, "Am I a brigand [Josephus' term for the Zealots] that you had to set out to capture me with swords and clubs? I was among you teaching in the Temple day after day and you never laid hands on me" (Mk. 14:48–49).[10] But Robert Eisler comments, "That Jesus should assume many of his followers to be armed might seem surprising; but it must not be forgotten that even the Essenes, those 'ministers of peace'—by the grace of Josephus— carried nothing with them on their journeys *except arms,* as a protection 'against brigands.' "[11] Dr. Eisler believes Jesus' call to arms is consistent with his command to love one's neighbor, if their use were restricted to a holy war which was intended to bring peace.[12]

In our opinion, Jesus' careful checking to make sure his disciples were armed was consistent with his apocalyptic view of the world. He wanted them to be ready to fight when God's angels arrived to begin the battle. His rebuke of Peter for drawing his sword in the Garden was an indication of his belief that man could not strike on his own initiative without dying by the sword as a result. Had God's angels appeared, however, and Michael the Archangel been there to direct the warfare, the situation would have been entirely different.[13]

In this regard Jesus was different from the Zealots, and his statement "Am I a brigand, that you had to set out to capture me with swords and clubs" stems directly from that difference. Jesus, not being a Zealot, would not resist arrest as long as God did not intervene. The fact that the soldiers *did* come after him with swords and clubs indicates that they did not make the fine distinctions that we are making between the various types of revolutionaries. As far as they were concerned, one insurrectionist was the same as any other.

We do not believe that Jesus intended, as Oscar Cullmann has suggested, that his disciples carry their swords for self-defense. Rather we feel, with Dr. Eisler, that he intended for his disciples to fight only in that war which would bring lasting peace: the final war between the children of light and the children of darkness. And that war, it seems clear, would not be at man's instigation, but at God's; the outcome of it would be entirely under God's direction and supervision.

Thus Jesus did not resist arrest in the Garden of Gethsemane because he trusted God to work things out according to His plan. He rebuked Peter for drawing and using his sword, not on principle, but on the strategic question of timing and initiation. Peter was not to live "by the sword," but in obedience to God's will. When the time was right, Jesus and his disciples would be ready to join in the final battle. Until then, Jesus would undergo whatever was necessary to prepare the way for God's intervention to save His People.

ROMANS OR JEWS?

A question as to who apprehended Jesus arises because of the conflicting traditions given side-by-side in the New Testament. The Synoptic narrative, based on Mark's Gospel, assigns responsibility for Jesus' arrest to the Jewish Temple guard alone, while John's Gospel mentions both Roman soldiers and Temple police. The question is important because it is inextricably bound up with a more fundamental issue: At whose initiative was the arrest made? Who launched the effort to bring Jesus to trial?

There is a general tendency in the Gospels to emphasize the Jewish leaders' responsibility for Jesus' death while minimizing the role of the Roman officials.[14] Therefore Paul Winter believes that it is very unlikely that the author of John's Gospel "whose sympathies lay with the Romans rather than with the Jews would have assigned any part in the arrest of Jesus to the troops of the Emperor if he had not had in his possession a report bearing out such a participation." It seems more likely, Dr. Winter goes on to suggest, that Mark would have *refrained* from mentioning Roman participation in the arrest than that John would have invented it.[15]

The specific mention in John of a Roman "cohort" headed by a "tribune"—both Latin military terms—and the reference to swords which by law only Romans were allowed to use, strengthen the argument that both Jewish and Roman soldiers were involved. Joel Carmichael points out (as have other scholars) that the Greek word *speira* in John 18:3, which is traditionally translated "band," "means a 'cohort,' and refers to the Roman force garrisoned in the Antonia Tower of the Temple: a little later . . . its commander is called *chiliarchos,* translated in Latin and English by the word *tribunus* (tribune) or captain, and making it unmistakable that if the 'band' of people was disorderly it was at any rate 'accompanied' by Roman troops." "In short," Carmichael concludes, "it was a Roman cohort that arrested Jesus . . ."[16]

Dr. Josef Blinzler, who until his recent death was a leading Catholic scholar in New Testament studies, has written one of the major works on the trial of Jesus, and in it he rejects the idea of Roman participation in Jesus' arrest. Blinzler states that it is out of the question that a Roman cohort commanded by a military tribune could have participated in the arrest of Jesus. Such a military unit consisted of six hundred men and it is unreasonable that so large a contingent would have been dispatched to arrest Jesus. Blinzler adds that if the Romans had arrested Jesus he would surely have been taken immediately to the Roman prison.[17]

Gerard Sloyan, chairman of the Department of Religion at Temple University in Philadelphia, suggests, on the other hand, that John's meaning was used in the hyperbolic sense in which one might say "he brought out a whole regiment." Sloyan believes that the priestly aristocracy would have collaborated with the Romans in securing Jesus' arrest because of their vested interest in continuance of the Temple sacrifice and their fear of a Zealot-like uprising.[18] Dr. Sloyan's point strengthens the argument for concluding that Roman forces *were* involved in Jesus' arrest.

Members of the Temple guard or police were drawn from the ranks of the Levites, who formed the lower echelon of clergy in Jerusalem.[19] Their duties included guarding the outer doors and ramparts of the Temple and patrolling the courts of the Gentiles and the women's court. But they were also available for other duties, since they were at the disposal of the Sanhedrin, and often made arrests and punished violators of the Law under the direction of the Temple overseers.[20] The commander of the Temple police was appointed from among the close relatives of the High Priest, and because of his role as overseer of the entire Temple environs and protection of its cultus, and his freedom to arrest offenders, he was second in power only to the High Priest.[21]

Yet, with all his power and influence, the Temple captain and his police force played a subordinate role to the Roman garrison since their very existence as a provincial institution depended upon imperial sanction. That fact, coupled with the fact that Pilate must have known beforehand of Jesus' being brought to him in the morning, suggests that the initiative for the arrest lay with the Roman prefect.[22] "All four Gospels report that Pilate was available in the morning, ready

for Jesus' trial. This indicates that he must have had advance information about what was taking place in the night—a fact which accords
with [John's] statement that the arrest was carried out by Roman
personnel."[23]

On the other hand, Jesus' reproach to the arresting party (Mt. 26:
55: "Am I a brigand, that you had to set out to capture me with
swords and clubs? I sat teaching in the Temple day after day and
you never laid hands on me") is a clear indication that the arrest
was not entirely a Roman effort and that the Temple guard were
also represented,[24] for surely Jesus' remarks would have been addressed to those responsible for order in the Temple. It is even possible
that the Sanhedrin, under threat by Pilate to maintain law and order,[25]
either issued a warrant on their own for Jesus' arrest, or, as is more
likely, directed the Jewish police to assist the Romans in the search
for Jesus. Since Jesus had so large a following that the Jewish authorities had been reluctant to arrest him, it seems probable that the
initiative in the proceedings lay with Pilate.[26]

The Temple guard apparently accompanied the arrest party in order
to transfer Jesus immediately to the custody of the High Priest. Such
an arrangement would have required Pilate's previous consent, for it
certainly did not conform to the normal procedures of either Roman
or Jewish law.[27] However, it does substantiate both the cooperation of
the Temple guard in the arrest and the concern of the High Priest and
his party about it.

BETRAYED BY JUDAS?

One final aspect of the arrest which we should consider is Jesus'
betrayal by Judas—a story which has made Judas an object of scorn
by Christians.[28] In John's Gospel, Judas is not only portrayed as
betraying the whereabouts of Jesus, but he is even credited with
initiating the arrest and *leading* the troops in seizing him. "Judas the
traitor knew the place well, since Jesus had often met his disciples
there, and he brought the cohort to this place together with a detachment of guards sent by the chief priests and the Pharisees, all with
lanterns and torches and weapons" (Jn. 18:3).

While serving as the impetus for much speculative study,[29] the
tradition of Judas' betrayal has quite rightly been questioned on his-

torical grounds.[30] It seems clear that Mark's description of Judas fits more perfectly the schematic pattern of his Gospel than it fits any reasonable explanation one could offer for Judas' behavior. Mark not only burdens the Jewish leaders with the responsibility for Jesus' death, but also denigrates the Jewish people as a whole: the family of Jesus is "convinced he was out of his mind" (Mk. 3:21),[31] the disciples never quite understand him correctly (Mk. 4:13; 9:32; etc.), and a Gentile Roman centurion is the first to acknowledge Jesus' true nature in spite of the crucifixion (Mk. 15:39). In Mark, Judas becomes the epitome of the Jew. As one scholar has expressed it, Judas' act, incomprehensible on the human plane, becomes the personification of a legend that sprang up later and which became the main theme of the Gospels in general. Judas is portrayed as the Jew *par excellence* and the story of his betrayal becomes a legendary way of expressing the Christian tradition embodied in the New Testament: that is, Jesus was undone by the Jews.[32]

This attitude toward the "Jews" on the part of Mark and the compilers of the later Gospels makes it difficult to sort out any of the actual events involving Judas in the arrest of Jesus, and we can only speculate why one of Jesus' apostles would betray him to his enemies. Professor Brandon is right in saying, "Greed seems an inadequate motive for such a crime . . . several more intelligible motives suggest themselves: disillusionment at the failure of Jesus to effect the expected Messianic *coup d'état;* fear of coming retribution for all involved in his attempt; even, perhaps, to force Jesus to use the supernatural power attributed to him by placing him in a desperate position."[33] Professor Maurice Goguel concurs: "If Judas had been essentially a self-centred miser, would he have ever begun to follow Jesus at all?"[34]

If in fact Judas did betray Jesus, it seems likely that he would have acted out of the same motivation as Peter did when he struck out with his sword. Judas, like Peter, tried to take things into his own hands and to force the issue. He must have believed that if Jesus were threatened with arrest, God would intervene to save His Chosen One, and thus the final confrontation between the forces of good and evil would at last be brought about. That in fact Jesus refused to call for the legions of angels to help must have mystified him, for "When he found that Jesus had been condemned, Judas his betrayer was filled with remorse . . . and went and hanged himself" (Mt. 27:3–5).

Had Judas been a callous or calculating person, it is doubtful that he would have chosen, or been chosen by Jesus, to be a desciple. Since he surely would have anticipated Jesus' fate if arrested, Judas as a self-serving person would not have committed suicide even before witnessing the final outcome of his deed. Perhaps it was because Judas' well-intentioned action went so completely wrong that both Luke and John explain that "Satan entered into Judas" (Lk. 22:3. Cf. also Jn. 13:2), thus elevating Judas' betrayal to the level of the cosmic struggle between good and evil and implying that Judas himself had been victimized, or "used."[35]

At the initiative of the Romans, then, and with the aid of the Temple guard, Jesus was taken captive. The few remaining disciples escaped into the darkness amidst the confusion of the arrest (Mk. 14: 50). As W. R. Farmer of Drew University rightly observes: "It was not the crucifixion of Jesus which scattered the disciples, it was his arrest. The cross began to draw the disciples back together again."[36]

THE SCANDAL OF THE CRUCIFIXION

That Jesus was crucified as a revolutionary is the one fact upon which virtually all scholars are in agreement. Amid the many difficulties in sorting out the historical elements in the Gospel accounts of Jesus' trial, the fact that Jesus was sentenced to die on the cross—a punishment assigned by Roman law to those convicted of seditious activity against the empire—emerges as the cornerstone upon which all further historical investigation must be based.[37]

Jesus' death on the cross and Pilate's role in condemning him to such a death were "scandals"[38] which Mark, in writing the first Gospel, was forced to explain.[39] The charge resulting in Jesus' death would have been understood throughout the Empire because of the method of execution. The explanation for his sentence to death by crucifixion could not be omitted from any of the Gospels. Jesus' crucifixion was so singularly important that, while its cause and its meaning were variously interpreted, it could not be ignored.

That nearly all scholars, whether Christian, Jew, unbeliever, orthodox or liberal, acknowledge the crucifixion as the starting point of the historical study of the life of Jesus reveals how crucial it is to our understanding. To move beyond this point and to discern what actually happened at Jesus' trial is much more difficult. The sources on which any conclusions must be based—the New Testament, other Christian literature, Jewish religious writings, and the histories of the early Church fathers and Josephus—are confusing and self-contradictory. It is therefore necessary to begin with the fact of Jesus' crucifixion, and to go on from there.[40]

THE ROLE OF THE SANHEDRIN

According to the Gospel accounts,[41] after his arrest Jesus was led away to the High Priest's house where the Council of all the chief priests, elders, and scribes—that is, the Sanhedrin—was gathered. There a kind of pseudo trial by the Sanhedrin is reported to have occurred. To gain some understanding of the events, it is helpful to look first at the nature of the Council itself.

The Sanhedrin played a difficult role in the political and religious affairs of Israel, acting as the intermediary between the occupying forces of Rome and the subject Jewish people. The Jewish authorities actually had far greater autonomy under the direct rule of the Roman prefect than they had exercised during the stifling reign of Herod the Great—the "client king" who spared the Jewish people the immediate offense of foreign rule for some thirty years.[42] The Romans had need of someone or something to fill the void left by Herod's death, and the Jewish Sanhedrin served that function.[43]

The Sanhedrin inherited from Herod the role of "peacemaker"—acting as a buffer to temper Jewish nationalism and protestations against the Roman rule, and attempting to minimize the impact of imperial dictates on the sensitive religious consciousness of the Jews. Essentially, this amounted to preserving the status quo by forestalling further incursions of the Romans into the daily affairs of Palestine, while dampening the revolutionary fervor of the Jewish people in order to prevent a final, cataclysmic break with the Empire.

Although there were members of the Sanhedrin from the Pharisaic party and from the lower order of the priesthood, the wealthy Jewish aristocracy, which centered around the Temple and its cultus, generally held sway in its decisions. The majority of these aristocrats, whether priests or laymen, were Sadducees.[44] The High Priest himself was usually a Sadducee, and found his main support among the wealthy Sadducees of Jerusalem.[45] While none of the Sadducees' own writings have survived, thereby making it difficult to define precisely the characteristics of their sect, other sources such as Josephus and Philo indicate that they were the conservative party within Judaism. They were ultraconservative in religious matters and tended to collaborate with the Romans in the political realm. They drew their support primarily from the High Priestly aristocracy and the wealthy classes of Jerusalem. Of all the Jews at the time of Jesus, they had the most to lose in a popular revolt against the Romans, as the events in A.D. 66 were to show.[46]

The Pharisees, on the other hand, were the liberals both with regard to the Law and to imperial rule. By and large of the middle class, they were the champions of the common people of Israel and were devout Jews who sought to live their religion faithfully in daily life. Their posture vis-à-vis Roman rule tended toward quietism, as they attempted to make the best of their terrible situation until the Messiah came. But they too longed for the establishment of the Kingdom and waited eagerly for the appearance of the deliverer. The Pharisaic movement centered in the synagogues of rural Israel rather than in the Temple.[47]

At the time of Jesus the Sadducees wielded the greatest authority in the Jewish circles which were most threatened by Jesus and his followers: the Temple authorities and the wealthy. In the Revolt against Rome, however, nearly all the Sadducees were executed by the Sicarii and by the Zealots who, in the first stages of the fighting, turned on the Jews who had collaborated with the foreign rule. As a consequence, the Sadducees ceased to exist as a party after the Fall of Jerusalem. This may account for the fact that the Pharisees, who succeeded the Sadducees as the "ruling party" in Judaism, are assigned primary responsibility for the actions of "the Jews" in the Gospel accounts of the trial, rather than the Sadducees.

Professor David Flusser has pointed out that in spite of the fact that the Pharisees are usually mentioned in the Gospels as the opponents of Jesus, they do not appear in the Synoptic accounts of the trial. They were only added to the accounts by John.[48] Gerard Sloyan of Temple University concurs with Flusser's estimation that the introduction of the Pharisees into the trial narratives is a later addition, dating to "a period of Christian polemic against the predominant Pharisees, when the events of the year 70 had wiped out the priesthood."[49]

Josef Blinzler holds the process by which the term Pharisees was added to the accounts of the trial to be true of the Gospels as a whole. He believes that none of the verses which present the relationship between Jesus and the Pharisees as a radically negative one should be viewed as statements of historical fact. Rather, they should be seen to reflect the prevailing historical situation at the time the Gospels were written. After A.D. 70 Christianity became separated from Judaism and stood over against it as its chief opponent. This later relationship to Judaism and Pharisaism was deliberately interwoven with the earlier traditions about Jesus.[50]

The Gospel writers must, then, have transferred responsibility for Jesus' death from the Sadducean aristocracy of Jesus' day to the Pharisees of their day who had survived the Great Revolt and become the authorities in Judaism and the chief opponents of the Christians. Thus the Pharisees are portrayed as the chief foes of Jesus, even though they had as late as A.D. 62 shown sympathy with leaders of the apostolic community, and Jesus himself in his teaching about the Law stood closer to early Pharisaism than to any other school of thought.[51]

As Professor Paul Winter has expressed it, "If any Jews exercised effective influence in the circumstances which led to the death of Jesus, it would have been prominent members of the priestly aristocracy, persons of the Sadducaean persuasion. Yet there is practically no polemic with, or attack upon, the Sadducees as such in the New Testament. Apologetic and polemic are addressed to the followers of John the Baptist and to the Pharisees. This is no accident. During his life, Jesus had stood in closest relation to these groups, and after his death it was these groups that were most akin to early exponents of the belief in the Messiahship of Jesus. . . . There would have been no point in arguing with the Sadducees; they were too far removed from the Christian position and could not have been converted either by pleading or by abuse. Yet, apostolic preachers felt, Baptists or Pharisees could perhaps be won over to their side."[52]

Thus we can see two principal reasons why the chief blame for Jesus' death is attributed to the Pharisees: the Sadducees ceased to exist as a separate party after the Fall of Jerusalem; and the early Christians may have directed their appeal to the followers of John the Baptist, the Pharisees, and the Essenes (or Covenanters), feeling that because of their affinity of belief they would be the easiest to convince that Jesus was in fact the Chosen One of God. And finally, there *were* certain Pharisees with whom Jesus had disagreed on matters of interpretation of the Law. It is possible that they had in fact viewed him as a false Messiah.

A dynamic tension between Pharisees and Sadducees on religious and social questions was reflected in the Council itself. However, during the period of Jesus' life, and up to the Revolt of A.D. 66, the Sadducean aristocracy maintained the upper hand. Quite obviously, their conservative posture had the effect of guaranteeing the continuity of their privileged status in the Judean province.

In spite of the influence and power of the Sanhedrin in the life of the Jewish people, however, it was definitely subject to the direction of the Roman administration. By the third decade A.D., possession of the High Priest's robes—the symbol of his office—had been transferred from the Sanhedrin to the Roman governor, thereby publicly acknowledging the subservience of the Jewish leaders to the occupying power.[53] Such subservience would have been apparent to the People who would have viewed the Sanhedrin, to the extent that it was controlled by the Sadducean party, as collaborating with the pagan oppressors.[54]

THE "JEWISH TRIAL"

The most widely accepted view of the Sanhedrin's role in the events of Passion Week is the *Jewish Trial Theory,* according to which the High Priest convened the Sanhedrin at night in his home to try under Jewish Law a capital case involving Jesus, who was finally convicted of blasphemy on the basis of his own confession, and condemned to die. This theory is hardly plausible, however, for it contradicts all that we know from reliable sources regarding the law and procedure obtaining at that time. Justice Haim Cohn has delineated six elements of the "Jewish Trial Theory," demonstrating its incongruities and improbabilities in light of the law of the time, in such a succinct manner that we include them verbatim:

> (1) The Sanhedrin could not, and never did, exercise jurisdiction in the house of the High Priest or anywhere outside the court house in the Temple precincts. [The Sanhedrin met in the "Chamber of Hewn Stone," one of the southwestern chambers in the Court of Priests.[55]]
> (2) Criminal trials had to be conducted and finished during daytime; no session of a criminal court was permissible at night.
> (3) A criminal trial was not allowed to take place on the eve of a feast day (nor on the feast day itself).

(4) No man could be found guilty on his own confession.

(5) A conviction must rest on the testimony of at least two truthful and independent witnesses, both as to the commission of the offence in their presence and as to the knowledge of the accused that the act was punishable.

(6) The offence of blasphemy is not committed unless the witnesses testify that the accused had in their presence pronounced the name of God (which may only be pronounced once a year, on the Day of Atonement, by the High Priest in the innermost Sanctuary of the Temple).[56]

The New Testament sources represent both part and all of the Jewish Court meeting as taking place at different times (during the night or the next day, or both), at different places (the High Priest's residence or the Sanhedrin's own council hall), and for different reasons (to interrogate Jesus, to prepare the case for Pilate, or to try the case itself). Such an impressive case as that presented by Justice Cohn above would seem to make doubtful the authenticity of the Gospels' confusing description of the meeting of the Sanhedrin. Some Christians, however, have regarded the contradictions as evidence of the blatant illegality of Jesus' trial. This evidence, as far as they are concerned, confirms their conviction that the Jews were responsible for Jesus' death.[57]

However, in the light of the evidence cited by Justice Cohn, it seems clear that no official meeting of the Sanhedrin could have taken place under the circumstances described in the Gospels. In fact, Professor Flusser has noted that "In the whole of Luke, not only just in his description of the Passion, a verdict of the supreme court is not even mentioned. In addition, John makes no reference at all to a session of the Sanhedrin in which Jesus was condemned to death. It would be safe to assume that the Sanhedrin was not mentioned in the Gospel sources. In them only the chief priests and the elders and scribes had been named and this unholy trio was identified by the Synoptic authors with the Sanhedrin."[58]

Moreover, nothing Jesus is reported to have said in the trial would have justified his conviction for blasphemy. As Justice Cohn points out, "In times of distress, the appearance of self-appointed saviours, purporting to be sent and inspired by God himself, was nothing unusual; and in a religion (like the Jewish) in which the link and dialogue with God was never monopolized by the professionals, such ecstatics were left in peace, so long as they did not preach idolatry ('false prophets') or disturb public tranquility. The messianic presumptions maintained by Jesus in no way exceeded these limits of legitimacy."[59] The only basis on which a person could be convicted of blasphemy was if he pronounced the name of God, which is never spoken aloud by Jews,[60] and nowhere is Jesus accused of that offense.

That Jesus was persecuted for espousing "heretical" beliefs is even less likely than his conviction for blasphemy. He was, as we have shown, very much within the bounds of Pharisaic thought in his teachings. In any case, there were no clear lines of "orthodoxy" during that period of Judaism. The whole notion of "heresy" seems to be something foreign to Judaism. Only in Hellenistic Christendom did religious authorities begin to persecute persons for professing "unorthodox" views. "There were many divisions among the Jewish people in the time of Jesus, but no religious party denied another party the right to propagate their teachings. Concepts such as 'orthodoxy' or 'heresy' did not exist. Heresy in its modern sense is an achievement of Christian history . . . The idea that a belief was wrong in the sense of its protagonists were to be considered as being outside the pale—an entailment of 'orthodoxy'—is un-Jewish; it derives from Hellenistic Christianity."[61]

It would seem, then, that the Gospel writers tried, apologetically and polemically, to shift responsibility for Jesus' death from the Romans to the Jews by implying that Jesus was found guilty of blasphemy by the religious authorities.[62] Such a shift would have become important after the Fall of Jerusalem when Christians began to function as a separate sect, no longer in the mainstream of Judaism. The followers of Jesus seem to have made every effort to gloss over the real nature of his execution and to make him appear a politically inoffensive pacifist.[63] However, his conviction and sentencing to death on the ground of blasphemy seem historically untenable.[64]

In presenting himself as the Messiah, Jesus would have been a folk hero of the Jews. Even if he turned out to be a false Messiah, no harm was done by giving him a chance to show the fruits of his efforts. The only real difficulty a Messianic pretender presented to the authorities, whether Jewish or Roman, was as a threat to public order, to the stability of imperial rule. "The grounds for his arrest had nothing to do with personal or religious differences between Jesus and any other Jews. Rather than the content of his teaching, it was the effect which his teaching had on certain sections of the populace that induced the authorities to take action against him."[65] He posed a *political* threat to the Romans and their Jewish collaborators because of his *religious views* regarding the coming of the Kingdom of God. He was an apocalyptic revolutionary, and as such, in Roman eyes, was deserving of crucifixion.

THE SANHEDRIN AS PEACEKEEPER

The Sanhedrin's intention appears to have been to act as mediator, rather than prosecutor. Any popular movement such as that headed by Jesus, with its tremendous religious momentum and highly volatile political effect, would inevitably have aroused the interest and concern of the Jewish aristocracy, if only out of their own self-interest. The Gospel according to John records a meeting of the Sanhedrin which is illuminating in just that regard:

> Then the chief priests and Pharisees called a meeting. "Here is this man working all these signs" they said "and what action are we taking? If we let him go on this way everybody will believe in him, and the Romans will come and destroy the Holy Place and our nation."[66] One of them, Caiaphas, the high priest that year, said, "You don't seem to have grasped the situation at all; you fail to see that it is better for one man to die for the people, than for the whole nation to be destroyed" (Jn. 11:47–50).

Historically, this incident seems authentic because it is at least a sensible attitude on the part of the Temple hierarchy. In fact, although the author of John's Gospel obviously intends for it to contribute evidence of the Jews' responsibility for Jesus' death, the incident need not even imply real hostility to Jesus. Caiaphas' plea urges the choosing of a lesser evil. It is a shrewd man's attempt to save his nation from the consequence of its own hotheadedness.[67]

As S. G. F. Brandon has put it, "According to John, the Sanhedrin had eventually become profoundly alarmed about the seriousness of the political danger that Jesus constituted. The high priest Caiaphas ended their perplexity by counseling them to take action to destroy Jesus. He argued that drastic action was necessary to save the nation from the disasters that Jesus would inevitably bring upon it, if allowed to continue his subversive activity . . . As Caiaphas saw it, the precarious balance of Jewish relations with the Roman occupying power was imperilled by Jesus. Consequently, although he was one of their own nation, his suppression in the interests of preserving that balance was imperative."[68]

If Jesus' Messianic movement had continued unbridled, the inevitable result would have been direct Roman intervention, and possibly a further lessening of Jewish autonomy. If the Sanhedrin proved ineffective in keeping the peace, they no longer would serve any useful and necessary purpose as far as the emperor was concerned. Its very future was in question.[69]

With that in mind, it seems quite likely that the Sanhedrin—or at least prominent members thereof, including the High Priest—met to consider the best way to prevent a popular uprising, led by Jesus, during the upcoming feast days.[70] Pilate, knowing full well the potential for trouble in the city, might even have warned the Sanhedrin of possible repercussions were any rebellions to occur.[71]

At the beginning of the week Jesus had led a Messianic demonstration which undoubtedly heightened the tensions in the city and encouraged the people's anxious anticipation of a much larger drama to come. Jesus' attack on the Temple may have appeared to be the event the people were waiting for. At the order of the High Priest, the Temple police had attempted to apprehend Jesus, but the number of his followers was too great and the people's enthusiastic support for Jesus prevented his arrest.[72] The Romans, meanwhile, had evidently rounded up suspected leaders of an insurrection which had occurred elsewhere in the city, as we shall see below. The High Priest may well have learned that an attempt was to be made to seize Jesus— both for his part in the tumult and to keep him from causing further trouble. An arrest would mean a trial, and a trial could mean crucifixion. The death of a popular leader would only further inflame the situation.

It is probable then that the priestly aristocracy secured permission from Pilate to take Jesus into their custody to see if they could prevent a disaster. As Professor Brandon puts it, "It must be remembered that the Jewish leaders were a priestly aristocracy, whom the Romans entrusted with the management of Jewish domestic affairs. They had to justify their position by preserving peace among their people and by effective cooperation in maintaining Roman rule. Jesus, a Messianic figure, backed by considerable popular support, had seriously challenged their control of the Temple, the very source of their wealth and national leadership . . . he continued to be powerfully supported, and could only be arrested in a clandestine operation . . . Jesus had not only challenged the position of the high priest and his party, he also constituted a menace to orderly government, for which Pilate would hold them responsible . . . It was, therefore, the obvious duty of the Jewish leaders to discover the exact nature of Jesus' intentions, which appeared to be subversive of the established order, and, with that evidence, to hand him over to Pilate for judgment and sentence."[73]

While it is conceivable that part of the priestly aristocracy assisted Pilate in the preparation of charges against Jesus for the coming morning's trial, it is impossible that such a nightly gathering could have been an official meeting of the Jewish court. As a result, scholars question the historical authenticity of the reported night session.[74]

Justice Cohn has offered a plausible explanation for Jesus' extraordinary nightly appearance before the Sanhedrin. He feels that the Jewish leaders knew Jesus was to be tried by Pilate at any early hour the very next morning.[75] If anything was to be done to avert the trial, it had to be done immediately—during the night. If the Jewish leaders could prevent Jesus' execution by bringing about his acquittal or at least winning a suspended sentence pending good behavior, they might still forestall serious repercussions among the people who had supported him. In order to secure his acquittal, Jesus would have to be persuaded to defend himself against the charges by a plea of innocence, and witnesses would have to be found to support his plea. Jesus would also have to foreswear any further involvement in treasonable activities. To assume responsibility before the Roman governor for the future behavior of Jesus, the High Priest would have to examine him and win Jesus' assent to his plan.[76]

Had the High Priest and the others succeeded during the night in persuading Jesus to deny his claims of Messiahship, Justice Cohn believes, they would then have marshaled their forces to testify in his behalf, offering "false witnesses" who would testify that Jesus was not claiming to be king but had only created a disturbance because of supposed violations of religious law. Pilate might then have agreed to drop the charges, or to acquit Jesus, or to suspend his sentence on the recommendation of the priestly aristocracy. This would be a more effective means of neutralizing the troublemaker than his execution, for it would tend to discredit Jesus' Messianic claims in the eyes of the people gathered around him instead of making him another martyr for the cause of Israel's freedom.

The plan could only work if Jesus would deny his Messianic pretension and agree to cooperate with the Sanhedrin. Such cooperation would imply Jesus' approval of the ecclesiastical authorities and affirm the legitimacy of their collaboration with the Romans. But this Jesus refused to do. The High Priest rent his clothes—a customary Jewish expression of grief—not because of any "blasphemy" uttered by Jesus, for the assertion by Jesus that he was the true Messiah did not constitute any criminal offense under Jewish religious law. Rather, according to Justice Cohn, it was Jesus' rejection of the offer made to him that caused the grief.[77]

Professor Brandon agrees with Justice Cohn that the night session could not have been a formal trial. But he differs from the interpretation offered above in that he believes the original intent of the High Priest was to interrogate Jesus in order to prepare the case against him.[78] Dr. Brandon concludes, therefore, that "after their interrogation of Jesus, the Jewish leaders formulated their charge of sedition and delivered him to Pilate, for the confirmation and execution of the prescribed penalty. In taking this action, the Jewish leaders . . . were performing their constitutional duty."[79]

Cohn, on the other hand, believes it was only on the next day that the Sanhedrin called a formal session to prepare charges. Since Pilate expected them to do this, they had no other choice. Once their plan to seek Jesus' acquittal had failed, the only alternative open to them was to expedite the proceedings and finish the matter as quickly and surreptitiously as possible. They did decide, in effect, that it was better to have one man die than to jeopardize their own position and the future of their nation. But they did this only when all other alternatives seemed closed to them.[80]

We find Cohn's the most convincing explanation for the extranormal night meeting of certain members of the priestly aristocracy and the following morning's session of the Sanhedrin.

CAPITAL PUNISHMENT BY JEWS?

If in fact no formal trial by the Sanhedrin took place and no charges of blasphemy were brought, as our examination would suggest, the question as to whether or not the Jewish court at the time of Jesus was empowered to try and execute capital cases is really superfluous.[81] However, for the sake of more accurately representing the situation in Jesus' day, we believe it warrants some clarification.

It appears that at the time of Jesus the Sanhedrin still exercised authority both to try and execute capital cases,[82] possibly pending approval by the Roman authorities.[83] If such confirmation by the Romans was necessary, Pilate would have had to be convinced of the merits of the case against Jesus. The death sentence would have required Pilate's judgment and the ultimate responsibility would have been his. It is, however, the scholarly consensus that the Sanhedrin was perfectly competent to inflict death sentences. Aside from this, it is clear that the author of Mark's Gospel knew of no impediment to the Sanhedrin's power. If he had, he would have mentioned it, for it would have given him a very plausible explanation for why the Jews did not kill Jesus in spite of their desire to.[84]

Further, the death sentence under Jewish Law was carried out by stoning, hanging, or burning, and not by crucifixion. Therefore, "It is the mode of execution that is the most convincing demonstration of the Romans' decisive role in the execution of Jesus. For if Pilate had merely *confirmed* a decision made by a Jewish tribunal, the punishment would have had to be Jewish too—stoning, the stake, strangling, or decapitation."[85]

The whole discussion of Jewish Law and its jurisdictional prescriptions fades in significance next to the one fact which served as the starting point for our investigation: Jesus was tried by the Romans' official representative, was sentenced according to Roman law in the Judean province to die a death by Roman punishment on a cross.[86]

CHAPTER 12

The Crucifixion of a Rebel: King of the Jews

"Anyone who makes himself king is defying Caesar."
John 19:12

In the words of James A. Pike:

"There were at least four persons arrested during that Passion Week—two *lēstēs,* or guerrillas, who later got hung on crosses with Jesus; Barabbas, a rebel who was responsible for at least one death in *the* insurrection; and Jesus.

"The Gospels report that it was customary during the Passover for a prisoner to be released to the Jews. It seems very odd, with things as tense in Israel as they were during this whole period, that Pilate would offer to the people an assassin, or Zealot, who had committed murder in the insurrection. But the Gospels say he offered the people a choice. He said, 'Do you want Barabbas, or do you want Jesus the Nazarene? I will release one of them.' They said, 'We want Barabbas; and as for Jesus the Nazarene, crucify him.'

"We should remember what the crowd was like. Just a few days before, when Jesus had come into the city offering them the possibility of freedom, they had all shouted 'Hosanna,' which means 'free us,' and had waved palms, the symbol of a liberated Israel. They were eager for deliverance from their oppressors. If Pilate did offer them a choice between the Jesus pictured by Mark as saying, 'Pay tribute money to Caesar' (which is the impression Mark seems to want to give the reader)—a man who would say 'don't cause any trouble,' 'turn the other cheek,' and so on—and Barabbas, the freedom fighter and national hero, how else could the crowd have been expected to answer? Of course they asked for Barabbas.

"So Jesus was crucified. They hung him on a cross, probably tying him with ropes at the wrists and at the ankles. The crown of thorns they put on him was not really a part of the torture. They put it on him, not in cruelty, but in mockery. It was not as Christian art shows it, digging into the flesh and causing blood to flow. And they really didn't need the nails—though they may have used them in addition to ropes—because after the scourging there would have been a loss of blood anyway. The cross was a painful enough death without the nails. But the principal reason the Romans hung people on crosses was to say very plainly to the public: 'Don't try to get away with opposing our Roman authority or our Pax Romana. This is what will happen to you.'

"At first Jesus seemed to be taking his death calmly. He spoke of forgiving those who had crucified him, and talked to John about taking care of his mother. But then he said, 'I thirst.' It was as though the physical pain had begun to get to him.

"Then he said something which made such an impression that the Gospel writers recorded it in the original Aramaic, rather than in Greek, and our English translations still do the same: 'Eli, Eli, lama sabbachthani?' [Mt. 27:46]. 'My God, my God, where are the angels?' In other words, he was agonizing over the realization that God was not going to intervene to save him and his people.

"Many of us have thought that Jesus was referring to Psalm 22 which starts out with those words. But Jesus knew Hebrew, the language of the Bible, and if he had been referring to the Psalm, he would have used Hebrew. This is Aramaic, his native language, and is, therefore, an expression of very real despair.

"Then he said, 'It is finished.' I have had it. This is it. None of it had turned out the way he had hoped and planned. It was all over for him. He had done all he could.

"But the last words are very significant. On Masada the Zealots in their last stand kept up their hope right until the very end— and even when they committed suicide, it was in the spirit revealed by a fragment of scroll found there: 'Oh Son of Man. These bones will stand for the whole people of Israel.' So too the last words of Jesus on the cross are, 'O.K. I have done my best. Father, into Thy hands I commit my spirit.' Just like the Zealots of Masada, he believed right down to the very end that God would still work things out according to His plan, and Jesus was willing to trust even his own life and death to that."

———◆———

PONTIUS PILATE, PREFECT OF JUDEA

"The whole assembly then rose, and they brought him before Pilate. They began their accusation by saying, 'We found this man inciting our people to revolt, opposing payment of the tribute to Caesar, and claiming to be Christ [the Messiah], a king . . . He is inflaming the people with his teaching all over Judaea; it has come all the way from Galilee, where he started, down to here.' " (Lk. 23:1, 2, 5)

It was because Jesus' activities and teachings constituted—or were construed to constitute—a threat to public order that he was brought before Pontius Pilate, the *prefect of Judea*. This office supplemented the provincial administrative structure of the Roman senatorial legates and proconsuls, and Romans of nonsenatorial rank, usually commanders of regiments in the army, were generally appointed to it.[1] Prefects governed small areas or provinces which required special attention, generally serving as heads of military governments in rebellious or newly acquired regions.[2] Though a lower officer, the prefect exercised essentially the same jurisdiction as proconsuls or legates. He even possessed the *imperium*—the right to exercise his own discretion —a power which was vested in Roman administrators and amounted to an unbridled authority against which the common provincial subject had little recourse.[3]

The primary concern of the Roman prefect (or governor) was maintenance of public order. Administrators of the Greek and Seleucid powers attempted to strengthen their rule by a concerted effort to universalize the cultures of their occupied territories through the process of Hellenization. The Romans, on the other hand, tolerated much of the indigenous culture and many of the local customs in the provinces, permitting local and municipal courts to handle cases of lower jurisdiction and allowing minor matters to be handled according to native law. The Roman governor dealt primarily with matters affecting public order, and included among those were major statutory offenses against the government such as the capital crimes of adultery, forgery, bribery, murder, and treason.[4]

Jurisdiction in capital cases rested entirely on the prefect's *imperium*. He was free to follow local custom for minor offenses, but all major decisions depended on the free exercise of the prefect's judgment, and his judgment alone.[5] He had either to try the accused person himself, or to transfer his trial to Rome, and he did not have any right of pardon or of staying proceedings. The right of pardon was the prerogative of the emperor, and to usurp that right would have been to exercise a treasonable excess of powers. Furthermore, the prefect had no right to delegate his powers or functions in capital cases to anybody else, or to local courts. To do so was also treasonable.[6]

As the prefect, then, upon whom fell the responsibility for maintenance of order and the preservation of Roman rule, Pontius Pilate could not have avoided ruling in Jesus' case. Gerard Sloyan writes that "considerable Gospel evidence points toward the fact that the execution was a normal, imperial, precautionary measure."[7] All three of the charges laid against Jesus in the Lukan narrative concern political subversion: misleading the Jewish people, forbidding the paying of the tribute to the Romans, and pretension to Messiahship, that is, a self-proclamation as the King of Israel. He was reported to have headed a subversive movement from Galilee to Jerusalem.[8] Such charges made Pilate's participation in the trial of Jesus not only understandable, but unavoidable. Accusations that he was guilty of blasphemy would not only have been insufficient to force Pilate's intervention; they could not possibly have justified Pilate's condemnation of Jesus under Roman law.[9]

The Roman historian Tacitus attests to the responsibility of Pontius Pilate for the judgment in the capital trial of Jesus in his account of the persecution of Christians during the reign of Nero: "Christus, the founder of the name, had undergone the death penalty in the reign of Tiberius, by sentence of the procurator Pontius Pilate [at the time of Tacitus' writing, the term procurator had succeeded the title prefect], and the pernicious superstition [that is, Christianity] was checked for a moment, only to break out once more, not merely in Judea, the home of the disease, but in the capital itself, where all things horrible or shameful in the world collect and find a vogue."[10]

According to Mark's Gospel, the Sanhedrin convened the morning after the arrest in order to deliver Jesus to Pilate: "First thing in the morning, the chief priests together with the elders and scribes, in short the whole Sanhedrin, had their plan ready. They had Jesus bound and took him away and handed him over to Pilate" (Mk. 15:1). Whether the Jewish authorities were the first to inform Pilate of the subversive nature of Jesus' activities, only helped to prepare the charges against him, or actually appeared in court to make accusations against him on behalf of the prosecution cannot be clearly determined.[11] Matthew says, "he was accused by the chief priests and the elders" before Pilate (27:12); Mark reports that the "chief priests brought many accusations against him" (15:3); and Luke tells us that "the whole assembly" of chief priests and scribes went before Pilate to accuse him (23:1, 2). What is clear is that Pilate, as the representative of the Roman emperor, tried, condemned, and executed Jesus for insurrectionary activity: claiming to be "King of the Jews" was a treasonable offense.[12]

THE CHARACTER OF PILATE

Pontius Pilate was evidently very well suited for the office of prefect for he served an extraordinarily long term of ten years. Yet in the Gospels he is pictured as a weak man, seeking to placate the Jewish leaders, easily swayed by the whims of the Jewish crowd, and giving the Jews their choice between prisoners in order to be able to release Jesus, whom he believed innocent. Even Pilate's wife is pictured as recognizing Jesus' innocence. After speculating as to what truth is, Pilate is said to have washed his hands of the whole affair and turned Jesus over to be crucified.[13]

This description of Pilate by the Gospel writers is quite the opposite from his portrayal in other historical sources such as Josephus and Philo. "All the evidence in our hands goes to show that Pilate was irascible, cruel, merciless and despotic, and that he was responsible 'for countless atrocities and numerous executions without any previous trial.' This kind of picture is hardly reconcilable with that of the reticent judge who has to be persuaded and implored not to let a criminal go free but to try him and pass sentence upon him. True to his real nature, he would rather have ordered Jesus to be hanged without much ado, even without bothering about a trial and a confession, than have made any effort to save him."[14]

Josephus relates in detail Pilate's rule in Judea, and the "tumultuous" series of events which occurred during his decade of rule,[15] and Pilate is represented throughout as highly contemptuous of those over whom he had jurisdiction.[16] A less suspect assessment of Pilate is probably to be found in the writings of Philo, an Alexandrian Jew who was a contemporary of Pilate. Philo seems totally unaware of

Jesus in his writings, and is therefore unlikely to have been influenced by any apologetic considerations concerning Pilate's condemnation of Jesus. He wrote that Pilate feared that Jewish notables would send a deputation to Tiberius and expose his arbitrary government in Judea, "denouncing his insolence, his rapacity, his high-handed treatment of his subjects, and his disposition to cruelty which led him in numerous cases to order the execution of people without previous trial. Philo's report of Pilate's activities during his procuratorship combines the reproach of arbitrariness with that of responsibility for countless atrocities."[17]

Pilate as described in the Gospels cannot be reconciled with the Pilate revealed in the writings of Philo and Josephus.[18] The only hint that they are the same man is that provided by Luke 13:1, which reports that "It was just about this time that some people arrived and told [Jesus] about the Galileans whose blood Pilate had mingled with that of their sacrifices."

How then do we account for this discrepancy? Professor Paul Winter has discussed at length the circumstances in which the authors of the Gospels compiled their works and the effect which their particular apologetic concerns and theological considerations had on their portrayals of Pilate. Dr. Winter compares the descriptions of Pilate's final decision about Jesus, and points out the reticence of all four Gospel writers to state that the Roman governor pronounced the sentence of death. In all four Gospels any explicit statement is avoided and Pilate is reported only to have "handed over" Jesus to be crucified. The implication is that he might *not* have pronounced sentence himself, even though Jesus' death by crucifixion makes such a sentence absolutely essential.[19]

Professor Winter finds a correlation between the development of a benevolent picture of Pilate and the degree of persecution of Christians by Rome. "There is a definite connection between two facts: the more Christians are persecuted by the Roman State, the more generous becomes the depiction of Pontius Pilate as a witness to Jesus' innocence."[20] By the time the Apostles' Creed is adopted (c. A.D. 400) his name is mentioned only noncommitally ("suffered under Pontius Pilate"). Tertullian (third century) has Pilate attesting to Christian truth and even records that Tiberius had recommended to the Roman Senate that Jesus be included in the Pantheon, at Pilate's suggestion.[21]

While the development of the increasingly favorable and sympathetic Christian attitude toward Pilate abruptly ends in the reign of Emperor

Constantine (c. A.D. 308–337) when persecution ceases and Christianity is adopted as the official religion of the Empire,[22] certain traditions continued to emphasize Pilate's witness to Jesus. For example, "Pilate is commemorated as a martyr in the Coptic Church on 25 June . . . As a holy figure, Pilate grew in popularity among the Copts in the sixth and seventh centuries; in middle Egypt his name was frequently used as a baptismal name. The Ethiopian Christians adopted his cult from the Copts; a Coptic history of Pilate, dating from the fourth century, was translated in Ethiopic from an Arabic translation. The 'apotheosis' of Pilate reaches its fullest development in an Ethiopic *Martyrium Pilati,* which describes his crucifixion by the Jews as a disciple of Jesus. Pilate is saved from death by divine intervention. Although he subsequently restores the dead son of Tiberius to life by laying him in the tomb of Jesus, Pilate is eventually beheaded, after crucifixion, on the orders of Tiberius. In this extraordinary writing Herod (Antipas) is held as chiefly responsible for crucifixion of Jesus. Pilate is also a witness of Christ's resurrection."[23]

The Gospel writers' description of Pilate, then, seems to have been influenced by their concern in the face of heightened persecution to convince the imperial authorities of the nonsubversive character of the Christian movement. In their effort to explain how it happened that Jesus was crucified as a Zealot at Pilate's order, they shifted the grounds for execution from the political to the religious domain, and responsibility for it from the Romans to the Jews. Pilate was portrayed as an unwilling or resisting accomplice to a conspiracy against Jesus on the part of Jewish leaders.

As Professor Morton S. Enslin points out, however, "to see Pilate as racked by pangs of conscience, knowing that he was being forced to do a colossal wrong" is to view his decision in the light of subsequent history and "not through the eyes of a contemptuous Roman officer who saw it as but one more chore which was his as the governor of those utterly incomprehensible Jews."[24]

THE ROLE OF HEROD

Luke (23:6–12) records that Pilate sent Jesus to Herod for questioning. This account is of doubtful historicity. The incident purportedly occurred because responsibility for trying the Galilean Jesus rightfully fell upon

Herod, the ruler of the area of Jesus' residence. However, no such understanding of jurisdiction according to residence prevailed at the time of Jesus' trial. Other recorded cases reveal that it did not matter where one resided. What mattered was where the offense was committed, and Jesus' activities in Jerusalem obviously warranted Pilate's action. As Dr. A. N. Sherwin-White, Reader in Ancient History at Oxford University, points out, "Neither Pilate nor Felix nor Gallio in Achaea hesitated to deal with a defendant whose place of origin was *outside* their own province when the man was charged with a crime *inside* their province."[25]

It has been noted that according to Josephus, Herod the Great had the right to extradite for trial criminals who had fled his kingdom to other parts of the Empire.[26] Recollection of this tradition may have provided the core of the Lukan tradition of Jesus' transfer to Herod, since many of Jesus' activities were in Galilee. While Pilate could not have avoided judgment in Jesus' case, Oxford's Sherwin-White states that the dispatch of Jesus to Herod *could* have been part of proper trial procedure.[27]

BARABBAS AND JESUS' TRIAL

The apparent attempt on the part of the Gospel writers in their trial narratives to place all responsibility for Jesus' execution on the Jews rather than the Romans is perhaps most evident in the Barabbas episode.[28] A close reading of the stories of Barabbas' introjection into Jesus' trial reveals that none is consistent within itself, and that the only thing upon which all four Gospels agree is that the Jewish people had the choice of a prisoner to free during the Passover feast.[29] Moreover, the Gospels say very little about Barabbas himself, but make much of the fact that the "Jews" played an active role in securing Jesus' condemnation and execution:

> The chief priests, however, had incited the crowd to demand that he should release Barabbas for them instead. Then Pilate spoke again. "But in that case," he said to them "what am I to do with the man you call king of the Jews?" They shouted back, "Crucify him!" "Why?" Pilate asked them "What harm has he done?" But they shouted all

the louder, "Crucify him!" So Pilate, anxious to placate the crowd, released Barabbas for them and, having ordered Jesus to be scourged, handed him over to be crucified." (Mk. 15:11–15)

The "Jews," according to Mark's account (15:1–15), interrupted in mass the trial proceedings and demanded of Pilate that they be allowed, according to the custom, to elect which prisoner would be released. Pilate "used to," Mark says, release a prisoner for them, "anyone they asked for." But in this case Pilate "realised it was out of jealousy that the chief priests had handed Jesus over," so he suggested that Jesus be released.

Had Pilate found the charges against Jesus without basis, he could have released Jesus at any point during the proceedings. It was entirely within his right, indeed it was his duty, if he was convinced Jesus was not guilty as charged. But according to Mark, at the urging of the chief priests the crowd frustrated Pilate's intention by demanding instead the release of Barabbas, to whom Mark specifically refers as one of *"the rioters"* [RSV: "rebels"] who had been imprisoned for committing murder in *"the* uprising" [RSV: "insurrection"].

Before releasing Barabbas, Pilate first asked the Jewish mob's opinion as to what course of action ought to be followed with Jesus. The "Jews" pronounced sentence on Jesus, calling for his crucifixion. Pilate, still convinced of Jesus' innocence, tried once more to dissuade the crowd from causing Jesus' death: "Why, what harm has he done?" But to no avail: the crowd continued to shout for his crucifixion. Wishing to please the crowd, Mark says, and following their lead, Pilate then released Barabbas and, after scourging Jesus, "handed him over to be crucified."

The whole thrust of this narrative in Mark, even the last line which implies that Jesus was handed over to the Jewish crowd for crucifixion, is clearly designed to explain how Jesus came to be executed by the Romans for insurrectionist activities: Jesus was innocent (even Pontius Pilate testified repeatedly to his innocence), but the Roman prefect was compelled by a Jewish mob to crucify him.[30]

The Gospel of Matthew differs in that Barabbas is described only as "a notorious prisoner" (Mt. 27:16) and in that Pilate freely offered the crowd a choice between Jesus and Barabbas (v. 17). Matthew also adds the report of Pilate's wife having sent word of a dream which led her to instruct Pilate, "Have nothing to do with that man . . ." (v. 19). Again the chief priests and, in Matthew, "the elders" intervened and "persuaded the crowd to demand the release of Barabbas and the execution of Jesus" (v. 20). This even though Pilate need not have sentenced Jesus—regardless of the request to free Barabbas.

Once again, Pilate asked what to do with Jesus if he freed Barabbas (v. 22). We presumably are to believe that it was also a custom for the Jewish mob to pass sentence, even if the sentence contradicted the prefect's opinion! Then Pilate went so far as to wash his hands with water, declaring his own innocence and placing full responsibility for Jesus' death on the "Jews" (v. 24).[31] He instructed them: "It is your concern." The Jews' response, "His blood be on us and on our children!" (v. 25), has for two thousand years been the cornerstone for Christian anti-Semitism and active persecution of Jews on the pretext of their ancestors' having willfully accepted the responsibility for "deicide"—the murder of the Son of God.

So, oddly enough, Matthew, the most Jewish of all the Gospels, unwittingly provided justification for centuries of anti-Semitism. Matthew's original intent was more than likely twofold. First, to save the Jewish Christians from persecution by convincing the Romans that Jesus had *not* been guilty of political insurrection and that his death was in fact the result of religious differences among the Jews themselves. And, second, to prod the conscience of his people, the Jews, and awaken them to the fact that Jesus *had* been the Messiah. By their blindness in looking for a political leader of Barabbas' type they had, in effect, condemned Jesus to death. If they would repent, however, God was still prepared to send His holy army to redeem Israel under Jesus' leadership.

Matthew concludes his account by vaguely stating that Pilate "handed [him] over to be crucified" (Mt. 27:26), again skirting the issue of Pilate's having ordered Jesus' death, as the mode of execution attests.

In Luke 23:13–25, the Jews are reported to have taken the initiative in demanding the release of Barabbas after Pilate told them that both he and Herod found that Jesus was not guilty of any of the charges brought against him "as a political agitator" (v. 13) and had done nothing deserving of the death penalty. Pilate entreated them three times to let him release Jesus, but the shouting crowd prevailed upon him and, "He released the man they asked for, who had been imprisoned for rioting [RSV: 'insurrection'] and murder, and handed Jesus over to them to deal with as they pleased." Hence it was their, that is, "the Jews'" will, that Jesus be crucified, and, in the Lukan passage as in Mark and Matthew, it is written that "they" led him away, implying that "the Jews" took him even though the Gospels make clear the Romans carried out the actual execution.

John 18:38b–40 records that Pilate took the initiative in leaving the trial to go "out again to the Jews" to remind them of *their* custom —in other accounts it was Pilate's custom—to have him release for them a prisoner at Passover. The Jews are said to have cried out against Jesus (though Jesus was still inside the hall while Pilate addressed the crowd) and to have demanded the release of Barabbas, "a brigand" [RSV: "robber"]. Pilate then prepared Jesus for execution, scourging him and dressing him in mockery as the "King of the Jews," and took Jesus (already prepared for the cross) out before the people, saying, "Look, I am going to bring him out to you to let you see that I find no case"! When Jesus emerged, dressed in the crown of thorns and the purple robe, the chief priests and "the guards" cried out for Pilate to crucify him. Pilate replied, "Take him yourselves and crucify him: I can find no case against him." But the Jews insisted that Jesus had violated *their* Law by declaring himself Son of God, and that *Pilate* must crucify him. But had Jesus violated Jewish religious Law, he would have been executed according to Jewish Law, by stoning.

Pilate re-entered the praetorium, where Jesus was waiting for him (the logistics of the series of events in the trial narratives are nearly impossible). There he stated what was, and is, perfectly obvious, though not consistent with the theme of the Gospel: "Surely you know I have power to release you and I have power to crucify you?" Again Pilate tried to release Jesus but was prevented from doing so by the Jews (though he had just stated that he was vested with the power to release Jesus if he chose to). It was at that point, John reports, that the Jews questioned Pilate's loyalty to Caesar: "If you set him free you are no friend of Caesar's; *anyone who makes himself king is defying Caesar.*"[32]

Finally, the "Jews" cried out for Pilate to crucify Jesus, whom Pilate himself called "your king" and, when the chief priests answered, "We have no king except Caesar," Pilate "handed him over to them [the Jews?] to be crucified." Had the chief priests declared that they had no king but Caesar, they would have lost all credibility with their people—and would probably have been stoned to death by the crowd for denying the all-inclusive claim of Yahweh, the one God.

In the following verses (Jn. 19:17–25a) it is made clear that it was Pilate who posted the charge for Jesus' execution and Roman sol-

diers who placed him on the cross. Yet the definite impression given is
that the Jews themselves were responsible for Jesus' death, and the
Roman Pontius Pilate was no more than an unwilling accomplice.[33]

INCONGRUITIES IN THE GOSPELS

Professor Brandon has pointed out that not only is the Barabbas
story as told in the Gospels "an incredible situation" in itself, but it
interrupts the sequence of events in Jesus' trial.[34] In John's Gospel,
for example, Pilate passes from inside to outside the praetorium in a
series of unintelligible moves in order to negotiate Jesus' fate with
the Jews. The Gospels present "a most extraordinary and illogical
transaction," for they represent the senior Roman official bargaining
with a Jewish mob over the fate of a man about whose innocence he
has already been sufficiently convinced to declare it several times.
Such a scene is inconsistent with what is known from other sources
about the type of man Pilate was, about the duties and limits of the
office he held, and about the customs and practices of the Roman
legal system during that period. Hence Gerard Sloyan concludes that
Pilate's "exchange with the crowds, ending with his earnest desire
to please them (Mark 15:9–15), can scarcely be historical, as it
stands."[35]

Secondly, the priests are able to sway the opinion of the Jewish
crowd at will. One day the masses' support for Jesus prevented his
arrest by the Jewish hierarchy. The very next day the crowds were
convinced without any difficulty by the same Jewish officials to demonstrate against Jesus and force his crucifixion by Pilate. This seems
highly unlikely, if not patently absurd, in light of all we know of
the "mobs" which attended the Passover feast and of their feelings
toward the collaborationist Jewish hierarchy.

Third, the active role which the Jewish crowd is reported to have
played in the trial of Jesus is historically untenable. From everything
else that is known of the personality of Pilate and his attitude toward
the Jewish people gathered in Jerusalem for feast days, it is incredible
that he would have been as putty in their hands. The week of the
Passover celebration was traditionally the most active period for anti-
Roman agitation. That Jews would have been demonstrating before
Pilate requesting that he *crucify* one of their leaders seems absurd,

and that Pilate would have allowed such a demonstration in the midst of trial proceedings—especially during that particular feast—is almost impossible to believe.[36]

The most reasonable conclusion to draw is that the crowd scenes are literary creations of the authors of the Gospels, which, while serving very well for the purpose of interpretation regarding the responsibility for Jesus' death, are less than accurate records of historical events. As Justice Haim Cohn of the Israeli Supreme Court has written, "Neither the persuaders nor the persuaded were suited for the role ascribed to them . . . any active participation of the Jews in the trial before Pilate is legally untenable and logically and psychologically improbable. The Gospel stories can reasonably be explained only by the tendency to shift the blame from the Roman Procurator, where it belonged, to the Jews."[37]

The traditional response to the question as to why the people would have changed overnight from one extreme to the other is that they had been disappointed by Jesus. The argument says that Jesus fell short of his followers' expectation that he would establish the Kingdom of God by his triumphal entry into the city and his occupation of the Temple.[38] While this argument has merit, it would apply with equal force to Barabbas, whose "insurrection" had also proved unsuccessful, and whose pretensions to leadership (perhaps even Messiahship), had been similarly disproved by his arrest by the Romans. Why would the crowd have remained any more faithful to Barabbas than to Jesus?

The story may have been introduced in order to offer a clear contrast between a Zealot leader like Barabbas and the passive, unjustly charged and condemned Jesus. In this way the Gospel writers could further stress the *a*political nature of Jesus' life and activities. Yet such a contrasting portrayal is not convincing. If the Jewish crowd had been given a choice between a pacifist Jesus and Barabbas, a Zealot leader, Pilate would have been foolish to expect any other outcome. Naturally, the resistance-oriented Jews would have chosen to have Pilate free Barabbas, who had fought for the freedom of Israel, and to execute in his stead Jesus.[39] That Pilate would have placed himself in such an untenable position—having to release a murderer and insurrectionist for an innocent man—is in no way credible, especially in light of Pilate's dealings with other revolutionary leaders.

Finally, there remains the question of whether or not the alleged Passover custom existed at all. This is the one fact on which the four Gospels are unanimous, and on which the whole episode depends: the customary special release at Passover of a Roman prisoner by the prefect at the request of the Jews.

There has been general agreement among a variety of scholars who have approached the matter from all but strictly apologetic vantage points that there was no such custom.[40] Such scholars argue that had Pilate observed such a custom, or had he released Barabbas in this particular instance under the circumstances described without first securing the emperor's approval, he would have been guilty of an intolerable usurpation of the powers of the emperor. It did not fall within the duties or privileges of Pilate's office to pardon prisoners, and to do so would have been treasonous in the eyes of his superiors, resulting in Pilate's removal from office at the very least, and quite possibly costing him his life.[41]

Though there is no evidence of the *privilegum paschale* as a *Roman* custom, there is a Talmudic source which indicates that *the Jews* had such a custom, perhaps dating back to the Seleucid rule. In *Pilgrimage at the Time of the Second Temple* by the Israeli scholar Shemuel Safrai, reference is made to a passage in the Talmud which mentions the custom of releasing a prisoner at Passover in order that he might make the customary offering of a sacrificial Passover lamb.[42] The Talmudic source makes clear (1) that the custom dated back to pre-Roman times, and perhaps began as early as the Maccabean period (c. 165 B.C.); (2) that prisoners were not automatically released, since there was no amnesty, and therefore the Jews often had to go and request that the ruler "observe" the custom; (3) that the custom held that "at least one" prisoner be released; (4) that often the prisoner was not set free until too late for him to make the sacrificial offering; therefore, the Jews sought to obtain his release as early as possible.

It may be, therefore, that the Barabbas incident is based on history: that a crowd of Jews had in fact petitioned Pilate to release a prisoner *according to their custom*. The urgency of their demand that Barabbas be released could have been because the time for the Passover feast was fast approaching and they wanted Barabbas to be able to offer a sacrifice. If the Gospel accounts are accurate, by the time Barabbas' release was secured, it was already too late for him to make his offering according to the sacrificial Law of the Book of Exodus.[43] That Pilate happened to be dealing with the trial of Jesus when the crowd arrived could have been purely coincidental.

It should be recalled, however, that even if such a custom did exist, and even if Barabbas was in fact released for the Passover feast, neither of these factors need have affected Jesus' trial. Pilate's decision as to Jesus' guilt or innocence was another question altogether. If Pilate was persuaded of Jesus' innocence, he could have released him. Or, if he had some doubt, he could have continued the case so further evidence could be gathered, or he could even have removed the court to Caesarea where the trial could be conducted in more favorable circumstances. The point is that the two cases need not have been in any way dependent one on the other, since, in the words of Gerard Sloyan, "Rome did not execute by default or accident."[44] Even if Pilate had pardoned Barabbas, he could still have freed Jesus by his own order—regardless of what fate Barabbas faced.

Thus the Barabbas incident as described in the Gospels could have been based on historical fact. If so, it would seem that the connection between Barabbas' release and Jesus' trial was added for the apologetic purposes of the Gospel writers.[45]

BARABBAS, THE ZEALOT

What, then, could have been the basis for the association of the figure of Barabbas with the trial of Jesus if, as it would appear, there was such a tradition?[46] Perhaps the clue lies in the rebel's name, Barabbas. "Bar" is the Aramaic word meaning "son"; "abba" in both Aramaic and Hebrew means "father," and is also used as a proper name, even today. Therefore, "Barabbas" means "Son of Abba," if Abba is used as a proper name, or "Son of the Father." It is also possible that the name was "Bar Rabba," since "Rabba" is also a proper name in Hebrew, in which case the meaning would be "Son of Rabba." "Rabba" is so close in spelling to "rabbi," meaning teacher, that other scholars have speculated that the name may have meant "son of a rabbi."

Knowing that the name "Barabbas" lends itself to several interpretations, and taking into account the added fact that variant texts of Matthew 27:16, 17 record that the rebel's first name was "Jesus,"[47] it is not difficult to understand why the incident regarding Barabbas' release lent itself to incorporation into the Gospel narratives of Jesus' trial.

Professor Paul Winter feels that it is impossible to discern definitely whether Mark intended to include Barabbas among the rioters or revolutionaries who had committed the act of murder. He does feel, however, that it can be stated that Barabbas was implicated in the insurrection by virtue of his arrest and trial. Still, according to Winter, this does not explain the Gospel accounts: "The nearest we can get to the facts . . . is that Barabbas was suspected of participation in a revolutionary act in which murder had been committed . . . If Barabbas was under suspicion of having committed a crime for which he had not yet been sentenced, the procurator had no right to stop the proceedings. If he had been sentenced for a crime, his release without reference to the Emperor in Rome would have been even more incredible."[48]

Winter's tentative explanation of the case: two men, with the name of Jesus in common, were arrested after the insurrection and there was some confusion as to which was the Jesus the Romans sought to prosecute. Winter believes that after a determination of identity, Jesus Barabbas was released.[49] What in fact was Pilate's inquiry to determine "which" Jesus was the one they hoped to try for sedition, was inflated by the compilers of the Gospels to appear the example *par excellence* of the Jewish people's rejection of Jesus, and their responsibility for his death.

Dr. Robert Eisler suggests a similar explanation for the source of the Barabbas tradition. He believes that there was a popular demonstration for the release of another "Jesus" who had been arrested by accident during the insurrection. This second Jesus, the son of a rabbi, was in Eisler's view related to the priestly aristocracy and therefore, when his identity was established, he was released. Only in the Gospels was Barabbas associated with the "insurrection"—and by such association of Barabbas with the insurrection and the attempt to contrast Jesus of Nazareth with Jesus Barabbas, the Gospel writers succeeded in obscuring the original and historical association of the "insurrection" with the triumphal entry and cleansing of the Temple by Jesus. Hence, from Mark's account, which refers to "the insurrection" as though the event were well enough known to require no further explanation, the occurrence is obscured in Luke to "a certain riot that happened in the city" (cf. Lk. 23:19).[50]

The general tide of opinion goes against explanations such as those proposed by Winter and Eisler.[51] Most scholars seem to accept the appraisal given by Oscar Cullmann when referring to Mark 15:7: "Here no doubt is possible: we have to do with a Zealot uprising, and Barabbas was a Zealot. When he is set alongside Jesus it is quite clear that for the Romans both cases involved the same crime and the same verdict. Jesus like Barabbas was condemned by the Romans and not by the Jews, and in fact *as a Zealot.*"[52]

The original tradition associating the name of Barabbas with the arrest and trial of Jesus must also have included the reference to an insurrection or the Gospel writers would surely not have mentioned it, since they were trying to dissociate Jesus from treasonous activities. All details of this insurrection are omitted from the Gospels, however, except that Luke does specifically locate it in Jerusalem (Lk. 23:19). The simultaneous imprisonment of Jesus and Barabbas suggests that "the insurrection" happened during the same week and in the same city as did Jesus' triumphal entry and cleansing of the Temple. That the two men appeared before Pilate together suggests further that Jesus' Messianic entry and his attack on the Temple, and the insurrection of which Barabbas was a part, resulting in the commission of murder and in his own arrest, were somehow related in the eyes of the Roman authorities.[53]

Professor Brandon suggests that the relationship between the Zealot uprising of Barabbas and Jesus' Passion Week activities may have been much closer than is traditionally suspected. Surely the two activities shared a common religious zeal. Might they not, Dr. Brandon queries, have had similar principles and purpose?[54]

"We are not told where in Jerusalem the action against the Romans, in which Barabbas was involved, had occurred. If it had been directed against one or both of the chief Roman centres in the city, the two obvious locations would be the Antonia fortress on the northwestern side of the Temple, and the Herodian palace in the upper city.[55] An attack on the Romans in the Antonia, coincident with Jesus' attack in the Temple, would have constituted an intelligible pattern of insurrectionary action, designed to involve at one time the forces both of the procurator and the high priest. That both operations, though seriously challenging these authorities, had failed, is significant, and further supports the likelihood that they were concerted."[56]

To the Jewish and Roman authorities, according to Professor Brandon's theory, Jesus and Barabbas would have appeared to be "co-conspirators." Dr. Brandon suggests that the Jewish leaders represented Jesus as the real leader of the insurrection by seeking Barabbas' release. He, after all, was the self-proclaimed leader. The fact that Pilate listed Jesus' crime as being that of claiming to be "King of the Jews" tends to substantiate Brandon's theory. According to Brandon,

Pilate had Jesus executed "to make him the example of the fate that awaited any who aspired to kingship against Caesar."[57]

However, as we have seen in earlier cases, such as during the revolt in 4 B.C. when two thousand rebels were crucified, crucifixion was more than just an exemplary punishment. Pilate need not have chosen just one to execute. Pilate's principal concern was the social and political stability of Palestine, and while the crucifixion of an individual, particularly a leader, served as an example to dissuade others from revolutionary activity, there was nothing to prevent him from crucifying many. In fact, Jesus *was* crucified with two other Zealots. So Pilate was not faced with a choice between Jesus and Barabbas; both could have been executed.

JESUS, "SON OF THE FATHER"

The following seems to be the most plausible reconstruction of the events which led to the Gospel accounts of the Barabbas incident. It seems likely that the insurrection in which Barabbas was arrested did occur simultaneously with Jesus' attack on the Temple, for this would explain why Jesus was able to remain in the Temple and teach, and later to retreat unscathed from the Temple precincts without having drawn an immediate response from the Roman garrison.[58]

Whether such an insurrection was planned as part of a coordinated attack we cannot, of course, determine. But it does seem clear that the uprising which Barabbas led culminated in violence and death, whereas there is no suggestion anywhere that Jesus' cleansing of the Temple had any such results. It would have been logical for the Romans first to pursue and suppress the rebels involved in the violent attack on their forces (probably in the fortress or some other part of the city), and only later, as part of a clean-up operation designed to prevent further uprisings during the festival week, to have sought Jesus the Nazarene who had led a nonviolent attack on the Temple. This would also explain why Jesus alone was arrested and not his followers. If there had as yet been no violence on their part, the Romans may only have wanted to remove the leader as a preventive measure, hoping to forestall a Messianic uprising before it gathered momentum.

Jesus and Barabbas, together with other insurrectionists arrested that week, would then have come to trial at the same time and for the same charges: treason. It is not surprising that Pilate would have viewed them as alike. Even if Jesus had *not* been responsible for violence, he *had* declared himself King of the Jews and Pilate would have considered such a claim treasonous. Pilate would undoubtedly have condemned them both to death on the cross.[59]

It seems the Gospel writers used the very fertile material provided by an actual historical event to interpret the significance of Jesus' death. A man named Jesus Barabbas, Jesus son of the Father, was being tried alongside of Jesus the Nazarene, whom they believed to be the son of the Father (God) chosen to redeem their people, the Jews. Since the principal mode for determining whether a man was in fact the Messiah was to judge by his fruits—that is, did he or did he not succeed in freeing his people from the yoke of foreign bondage— the Gospel writers may have tried to use the Barabbas episode to illustrate how things had gone wrong for Jesus the Nazarene.

Their message may well have been this: Jesus had tried to show by the cleansing of the Temple, that his people Israel had to be purified in every aspect of their life if their "worship" was to be acceptable to God. In this he stood in the tradition of the prophets who warned that the Temple tended to become idolatrous and its worship a substitute for obedience to God's will. It was the prophet Jeremiah who first proclaimed that the Temple had become a "robbers' den" (Jer. 7:11) and that the sacrifices offered there were not pleasing in God's eyes because the People did not do God's will (Jer. 7). It was also Jeremiah who first prophesied the new covenant in which the Law would be written on the hearts of the people of Israel, and proper worship and sacrifice of righteous obedience would be restored (Jer. 31:31–34).

Jesus launched his attack on the Temple by recalling the words of Jeremiah, saying, "Does not scripture say: *'My house will be called a house of prayer for all the peoples?* But you have turned it into *a robbers' den"* (Mk. 11:17). He also said the Temple had become idolatrous (the phrase "made with hands" means idolatrous)[60] and that it would have to be destroyed and restored by one made "in heaven," that is, according to the will of God. He apparently then took advantage of the situation to teach and explain his actions.

If at the same time another group led by Barabbas was attacking the Romans, it is possible that many of the People, disposed to violence and impatient for their immediate deliverance from the pagan rule, joined Barabbas. They tried, in effect, to take a short cut to "redemption" by getting rid of their foreign oppressors immediately, instead of first purifying their own lives and their false religious practices. Rather than living in obedience to God's Law and trusting in His power to free them from all that oppressed them (as Jesus urged and did), the Jews had, according to the Gospel writers, preferred or "chosen" a violent revolution (Barabbas). Expanding on the thought Jesus expressed upon entering the city, the Evangelists imply that had enough Jews heeded Jesus' teaching and manifested righteousness in their lives, the Kingdom would indeed have come in all its power. But in their choice of Barabbas, as it were, the Jews proved lacking in righteousness, and therefore Jesus was crucified.

We would view the Barabbas event, then, as the Gospel writers' allegorical interpretation of the significance of Jesus' death, using the fruitful material of actual history to build the story. In this way the Gospel writers could have made clear to their Roman readers that Jesus, though crucified, had not been an insurrectionist. And also, hopefully it would have prompted their Jewish readers to reconsider Jesus' approach to the establishment of the Kingdom and to see that he was in fact the Messiah.

Surely it would not have been the Gospel writers' intent, however, to give Gentiles justification for *excluding* the Jews from the Kingdom on grounds of deicide. To the contrary. Such prophetic interpretations of past history, pointing out the failure of other Jews to be obedient to their God, were always intended to bring a response of repentance so that Israel's redemption could be hastened.

HUNG ALIVE ON A TREE

Jesus was led away to be crucified. The practice of crucifixion was many years old at the time. It was adopted by the Romans as a means of execution because it was considered the most degrading and excessively painful way of death. It was considered so inhumane a treatment that its use was eventually limited to slaves and imperial subjects who were convicted of sedition against the Empire.[61] The Roman rulers of Palestine used crucifixion as an exemplary punishment intended to discourage revolution and nationalistic aspirations, but they also crucified groups of rebels if the situation seemed to merit it.[62]

Death on the cross was anathema to the Jewish people. They found crucifixion especially loathsome because of the Deuteronomic statement "one who has been hanged is accursed of God" (Deut. 21:23). This abhorrence of crucifixion by pious Jews is revealed in the Commentary on Nahum, discovered among the fragments of Qumran's Cave IV. The text from the Book of Nahum and the commentary by the Covenanters read as follows:

"The lion tears sufficient for his cubs, and strangles for his lionesses prey." . . . Its interpretation concerns the Lion of Wrath [God] who will smite by his nobles and the men of his counsel [the Covenanters] . . . "And he filled with prey his cave and his den with torn flesh" . . . *vengeance* on the Seekers-after-Smooth-Things [Jewish collaborators] *when he hangs men up alive* . . . in Israel before-time, *for of the man hanged alive upon a tree it reads: "Behold I am against thee says Yahweh of hosts,* and I will burn in smoke thine abundance, and thy young lions the sword shall devour. And I will cut off from the land his prey."[63]

So despised was crucifixion as a form of execution that even in their most desperate moments and during their most bitter reprisals in the Revolt of A.D. 66—when the Romans were totally at their mercy—the Jews never resorted to it.[64] The cross was to the early Jewish Christian equally disgraceful and a source of constant derision by pagans who shared their contempt for a crucified man.[65] It was only reflection on such Old Testament passages as Isaiah 53 which gave Christianity the means to transform the cross from a sign of disgrace into one of victory.[66]

The Romans were no doubt aware that the Jews found crucifixion a doubly offensive mode of execution and probably used it with the hope that it would serve as a shocking deterrent to any Messianist or nationalist movements against their rule. In fact the opposite result obtained, for mass executions by this most abhorrent method caused the Jews to oppose their Roman rulers even more vehemently. As a consequence of the Roman policy of crucifixion, however, the possibility of such a death was something which every Jew who chose to join the liberation struggle against Rome had to face.[67] Even Jesus, when explaining to his disciples the "cost" of following him, instructed them, "If anyone wants to be a follower of mine, let him renounce himself and take up his cross and follow me" (Mk. 8:34). He obviously anticipated the fate which he and his followers would inevitably face if the Romans identified them with the Messianic movements of their people.[68]

The People of Israel had witnessed during the Roman rule and quite possibly under Persian and Greek rule as well, the crucifixion of many of their national resistance leaders and thousands of their followers. Josephus records that as early as the rule of the Seleucid Antiochus Epiphanes (175–163 B.C.) Jews were crucified for refusing to abandon their religion.[69] He also reports that even the Jew Alexander Janneus (103–76 B.C.) was guilty of crucifying fellow Jews who rebelled against his rule.[70] We have already recounted that under Varus some two thousand rebels were crucified at one time. Jewish prisoners of war were crucified by the Roman legions during the Great Revolt. Josephus also says that Florus practiced crucifixion as procurator and that during the final stages of the Revolt the threatened crucifixion of a Jewish rebel commander was so abhorred by the Jews who defended the fortress Machaerus that they surrendered in order to spare him that fate.[71]

THE MANNER OF CRUCIFIXION

Thus we have ample evidence of the practice of crucifixion. And yet contemporary descriptions of the manner in which such executions were carried out are greatly lacking. While the procedure varied according to circumstances (time and place, the availability of materials for the crosses, and the number of men to be crucified), it would appear that the normal crucifixion made use of a vertical post permanently situated in a site of public executions. The prisoner, fixed to a crossbar, was hoisted up so that the crossbar rested on top of the stand post (in a T position) and so that the victim was suspended with his feet off the ground.

There is much controversy as to whether or not nails were used. While Josephus reports the nailing of Jewish rebels on crosses during the Great Revolt in *War* V. 451, the Gospel accounts do not state that Jesus was nailed to the cross.[72] If nails were used, however, they were probably driven into the forearm or the wrist of the condemned man—and not into his palm, for it has been shown that anatomically the flesh and bone structure of the hand is too weak to support the weight of a man's body.[73] Christian representations dating centuries after the fact and showing Jesus nailed to the cross are apparently based on reflection on such Old Testament prophecies as Zechariah 12:10, "They will look on the one whom they have pierced."

Winter explains that the prisoner's arms were tied with ropes to the crossbar which he then was forced to carry to the place of execution. There the condemned man was lifted onto the vertical post. Winter writes, "though sometimes nails may have been driven into the prisoner's palms. No nails were used for affixing the feet. They were either left dangling a short distance above the ground, or were fastened to the post by ropes. Stripped of his clothes, the condemned was left on his cross till death intervened."[74]

Nevertheless, the skeleton of a man, dating from the period of the Second Temple prior to A.D. 70, was recently discovered in Jerusalem and has given the first archaeological evidence of a crucifixion from the period in which Jesus lived. According to a report by Dr. N. Haas of the Department of Anatomy of the Hebrew University-Hadassah Medical School in Jerusalem, the cross was made of olive wood. The victim was supported on the crossbar by nails driven *through his forearms near the wrist,* as revealed by the marks on the bones scored by the victim's movement while nailed to the cross. The plaque ("titulus") which declared the charge of his crime had been posted on the olive wood cross by a nail driven *through the victim's heels.* Fragments of the plaque still attached to the nail found in the skeleton's feet indicate that it was made of ash wood. The body had been twisted at the waist, so that the feet were side-by-side, with one ankle flat against the cross, rather than overlapping so that the soles of the feet were next to the wood as in traditional portrayals. The legs were drawn up under the victim nearly to his buttocks, providing a certain amount of support for his torso.[75]

It would appear, then, that the most reliable and efficient—and therefore, the most likely—method of crucifixion was to lash the victim to the crossbar, with the man's arm draped over the bar to support his weight. If nails were used in addition to ropes, they would have served to hasten the death (through loss of blood) and possibly to increase the pain. A peg may sometimes have been driven between the victim's legs or a wooden block placed under his buttocks for added support. Or, as in the case mentioned above, the victim's own feet may have been pulled up beneath him for that purpose.

The recent find suggests the method of crucifying men may have been quite diverse.

Physically, crucifixion caused a slow and painful death which usually required three days before the victim finally expired from sheer exhaustion.[76] The preliminary scourging was designed to expedite the death by weakening the prisoner.[77] While no fewer than five instances of physical abuse of Jesus are recorded in the Gospels, such beating fits intelligibly into the sequence of events in his trial *only after* his conviction and sentencing to death.[78]

The Gospels report abuse of Jesus while appearing before the Jewish leaders. We read that the members of the Sanhedrin spat in Jesus' face and hit him with their fists (Mt. 26:67–68); that the attendants "rained blows on him" while "some of them" spat at him, blindfolded him, and hit at him with their fists (Mk. 14:65); and that Jesus was mocked, assaulted, blindfolded, and beaten by those who "guarded" him—presumably the police, prior to the meeting of the Sanhedrin (Lk. 22:63–64). Justice Haim Cohn believes that if one must accept that any of the Jewish leaders struck Jesus, the story in the Gospel of John is the most probable: "one of the guards standing by gave Jesus a slap in the face, saying, 'Is that the way to answer the high priest?' Jesus replied, 'If there is something wrong in what I said, point it out; but if there is no offence in it, why do you strike me?'" (Jn. 18:23). This account, in Cohn's opinion, has "some authentic flavour . . ."[79]

Although the Romans were accustomed to flogging prisoners in order to weaken them before hanging them on a cross, and thus to hasten death, the possibility of abuse by the Sanhedrin during a formal trial is extremely unlikely. Justice Cohn explains that it would have been quite improper, and well-nigh inconceivable, for a member of the court to raise his hand against a prisoner under sentence of death because "The Biblical command, Love thy neighbour as thyself (Leviticus 19:18), was invoked to exhort judges to make the end of a prisoner sentenced to death as light and fair as humanly possible." Even raising a hand to strike another was considered sinful.[80] If, however, as we have concluded, the meeting of the Jewish leaders was not a formal meeting of the Sanhedrin, but an unofficial gathering for purposes other than trying Jesus, then such physical abuse of Jesus is not impossible.[81]

As for the celebrated incident in which Jesus was given a "crown of thorns" and robed in purple garb, this does not appear to have been part of the preparation for crucifixion, either. It would seem that the Roman soldiers mocked Jesus "in their belief that he had claimed to be a political, or nationalist, Messiah, and thus to demonstrate the absurdity of his claim, as they regarded it."[82]

Christian art over the centuries has portrayed the crown of thorns as a bloodletting instrument of torture. In fact, however, Gospel narratives provide no basis for such an interpretation, and Clement of Alexandria (second century) was apparently the first writer to describe it so. The Gospel accounts suggest that the crown, together with the purple robe, was used not as a punishment but as part of the mockery of Jesus as a "king" who had no kingdom:

> The governor's soldiers took Jesus with them into the Praetorium and collected the whole cohort round him. Then they stripped him and made him wear a scarlet cloak, and having twisted some thorns into a crown they put this on his head and placed a reed in his right hand. To make fun of him they knelt to him saying, "Hail, king of the Jews!" And they spat on him and took the reed and struck him on the head with it. And when they had finished making fun of him, they took off the cloak and dressed him in his own clothes . . . (Mt. 27:27–31).

The crown of thorns was probably used as an imitation of the radiate crown of a divinized king or emperor.[83] Coins of the period give examples of the radiate crown which combines rays with the diadem indicating that the wearer is pictured as a divine ruler. The rays, as would be natural, thrust *out* from the head, not into it.

Among the coins which have been preserved as specimens of the thirty pieces of silver for which Jesus was betrayed are ones which show on the facing the radiate head of Helius. The radiate crown of the divine ruler had been systematically publicized on coins in the east for some centuries before the incident reported in the Gospels.[84] Thus it is likely that this was the symbolic crown utilized by the Roman soldiers to accompany the improvised royal robe and scepter with which they decked out a prisoner who had been convicted and ordered executed as an insurrectionist. The attire was relevant because of Jesus' aspiration to be the God-chosen king of a subjugated people yearning for their independence.

The material used to make this caricature of a crown was probably the date palm. When wrapped around someone's head as a crown, the thorns or spines of the palm would thrust outward and upward. They probably would not have pierced Jesus' head, but would have thrust upward as in the radiate crown.[85]

So there is no basis for the common assumption among Christians that the crown of thorns was an instrument of torture—other than psychological: the humiliating caricature of the mock radiate crown of the divine ruler made out of the very thing which symbolized the freedom movement of the now captive nation of Israel. Here the palm branch, the symbol of freedom used annually in the feast of Hanukkah to keep alive the hope of the restoration of freedom and only a few days before used to welcome Jesus to Jerusalem as one who "came in the name of the Lord," becomes the means of caricaturing the failure of Jesus' cause. As Bishop Pike put it, "Bitterly ironic—and in that way cruel enough. But not an instrument of physical torture: no streams of blood."[86]

Because crucifixion was very slow and painful, it was the practice of the Jews to take special measures to ease the suffering of the victim. One such measure was the offering of a concoction to kill the pain.[87] According to Talmudic sources, the women of Jerusalem voluntarily prepared and administered a drink of wine and incense intended to bring on unconsciousness to all men condemned to death on a cross. It must have been these women who were present at Jesus' execution, offering him a drink of wine and myrrh, which he refused.[88]

It was apparently also these women Jesus addressed en route to execution: "Daughters of Jerusalem, do not weep for me; weep rather for yourselves and for your children . . . For if men use the green wood like this, what will happen when it is dry?" (Lk. 23:28 ff.). Dr. Cullmann believes that Jesus was referring in this statement to the Romans, who were about to put him to death: "if the Romans put him to death as a Zealot, who is no Zealot and who has always warned against essential characteristics of the Zealots—if they put him to death, who therefore is 'green wood,' what will they one day do with the true Zealots ('dry wood')?" The Jewish Revolt some forty years later brought the answer to Jesus' question. According to Professor Cullmann, in this exchange with the "daughters of Jerusalem" we find confirmed that "Jesus was condemned as a Zealot, but at the same time that he *was no Zealot,* although he took an interest in this parallel and yet so different movement during his entire ministry."[89]

CRUCIFIED AS A ZEALOT

To sum up what seems to have been the historical sequence of events, then: having heard the charges against Jesus, having interrogated him and having been convinced of his guilt, Pilate followed the only course open to him: exercising his *imperium,* he ordered Jesus crucified as dictated by Roman law.[90] The Roman soldiers, using the opportunity for their own enjoyment, first put a crown and robe on the "King of the Jews" to make a mockery of him; then, according to custom, they flogged him to weaken him, and led him away for execution.[91]

The Gospels of Mark and Matthew state that Jesus was crucified between two "robbers," and the Gospel of Luke reports an exchange of words between Jesus and those crucified with him, whom Luke calls "criminals."[92] When one looks again at this scene, through the "spectacles" that a deeper understanding of the historical context of Jesus' life and death provide, it becomes clear that it has a significance quite different from that traditionally ascribed to it.

The most obvious conclusion which can be drawn is that the men executed with Jesus were tried and sentenced at the same time he was. The Barabbas incident already discussed indicates that the fate of other men involved in insurrectionist activities was closely tied with Jesus'. While Jesus' trial in the New Testament is reported as if it were an individual and private session before both the Sanhedrin and Pilate, the mode of execution of the two "robbers," and the fact that all three crucifixions were carried out at the same time, makes it reasonable to assume that all three men (and possibly others, like Barabbas) were tried and sentenced at the same time, for the same crime.[93]

The word for "robbers" used by Mark is *lēstēs*—the word which was used by Josephus as a derogatory name for the Zealots. Because this word was translated into English to read "robbers" or "thieves," the meaning of the whole scene has been obscured. Crucifixion was not a means of execution for those convicted of robbery unless, of course, such a crime accompanied insurrectionist activities. Thus surely the *lēstēs* or "robbers" crucified with Jesus had, like him, been convicted of treasonous acts.

Luke makes it clear that those sharing Jesus' fate were under the same sentence of death and implies that they were among those whose expectations Jesus had heightened earlier in the week. One of those crucified with Jesus asks, "Are you not the Christ [the Messiah]? Save yourself and us as well" (Lk. 23:39). As Dr. Robert Eisler has suggested, these are "very natural words if he had taken part in the undertaking of Jesus which had ended so disastrously, but hardly explainable if, according to the usual view, the speaker was a highwayman without the remotest connexion with Jesus and whom the Messiah had not the least reason to save."[94] The second Zealot rebuked him, saying, "Have you no fear of God at all? You got the same sentence as he did" (Lk. 23:40).

The account of Luke goes on to "clear" Jesus of any guilt in his execution as a Zealot: "but in our case we deserved it: we are paying for what we did. But this man has done nothing wrong" (Lk. 23:40b–41). We have already seen that Pilate must have found cause in Jesus' case to justify his death on the cross as a Zealot, but it is possible that the men crucified with Jesus recognized that his motives were pure and that he was not guilty before God for any deed of his. Or perhaps the other two had engaged in violence and Jesus had not. Or, as is most likely, the comment may be an editorial addition by Luke to dissociate Jesus from those with whom he was crucified.

Nevertheless, that the other men crucified would have addressed themselves to Jesus in such a manner as reported in the New Testament suggests the elevated esteem, and great Messianic expectation, with which his activities earlier in the week (the triumphal entry and cleansing of the Temple), had been met. This is reflected in the Zealot's next statement, "Jesus, remember me *when you come into your kingdom*" (Lk. 23:42).[95]

The *titulus,*[96] or inscription on the cross, was designed to give public notice of the crime for which the condemned man was sentenced to death. "The inscription giving the charge against [Jesus] read: 'The King of the Jews'" (Mk. 15:26). This makes abundantly clear that the charge against Jesus was insurrection against the Roman Empire. Dr. Oscar Cullmann explains the meaning of the inscription: "Translated into the legal parlance of the Roman State, this means: Jesus was condemned to death by hanging as a rebel against the Roman State in one of its subject provinces. In other words, he was nailed to the cross as a Zealot."[97]

The public proclamation of the charge against Jesus at his crucifixion proves the Romans' responsibility for Jesus' death. Dr. Cullmann writes, "The inscription over the cross is further confirmation that Jesus was not condemned by the Jews for blasphemy, but by the Romans as a Zealot, a pretender to the royal throne of Israel . . . What we have here is standard procedure, obligatory among the Romans in the case of the passing of a death sentence: the grounds of the verdict had to be posted on the cross . . . This titulus states a purely political crime: King of the Jews."[98] "Thus Jesus suffered the *Roman* death penalty, crucifixion, and the inscription, the 'titulus,' above the cross, named as his crime the Zealotist attempt of having strived for kingly rule in Israel, a country still administered by the Romans."[99]

Dr. Paul Winter has also written that the titulus was included in Mark (15:26) as a legal detail of the execution, clearly stating the grounds for Jesus' death. In John's Gospel this plain statement of the offense is elaborated, giving it an ironic prophetic significance according to which Pilate was an unwitting witness to Jesus' final coming into power, for he ordered the inscription despite the opposition of the Jewish leaders. The exchange which John reports between Pilate and the Jews is largely theological in character, and therefore probably not historical. Moreover, Pilate's action in placing on the cross the titulus listing Jesus' offense was actually a customary part of Roman penal procedure.[100]

The Roman soldiers are reported to have cast lots for Jesus' garments, dividing them among themselves. Sherwin-White asserts that this was customary for executions at that time, a remnant of the right of soldiers to collect booty after a battle.[101]

TOTAL COMMITMENT AND TRUST

The last glimpses we are given of Jesus on the cross confirm his deep longing for the redemption of his people, his profound disappointment that he had not been able to accomplish what he had set out to do, and his unfailing trust in God in spite of all.

He is reported to have said on the cross, "Father, forgive them; they do not know what they are doing" (Lk. 23:34), thereby demonstrating his own obedience to the commandment he gave his disciples: to love even their enemies.

He cried out in his native tongue, Aramaic, "Eloi, Eloi, lama sabachthani?" which means, *"My God, My God, why have you deserted me?"* (Mk. 15:34; cf. also Mt. 27:46). Had Jesus intended to quote scripture or cite a psalm, as has so often been suggested, he would have used Hebrew, the language of the Bible. The fact that the words have been preserved in the Gospels in Aramaic is evidence that they made a deep impression on those who heard them. Jesus was reflecting his very human despair at the apparent failure of the cause he had undertaken in what he believed to be obedience to God.

A moment of resignation seems to be reflected in the words, "It is finished" (Jn. 19:30c, RSV). Or perhaps he was frankly stating the fact that the coming of the Kingdom, as he had conceived of it, had failed to occur. Nevertheless, his complete trust in God and in His plan overcomes even this human despair and Jesus is able to reaffirm the commitment made in the Garden of Gethsemane to do God's will rather than his own: "Father, *into your hands I commit my spirit.*" Having said those words, the Gospel reports, he breathed his last breath (Lk. 23:46).[102]

We are told that "All of [Jesus'] friends stood at a distance; so also did the women who had accompanied him from Galilee, and they saw all this happen" (Lk. 23:49).[103] Their despair and disappointment must have been complete: like so many others who had stood for the redemption of Israel, the man whom they had believed to be the Messiah had been crucified by Pilate, and had died on a cross.[104]

CHAPTER 13

Not the Messiah, Yet Raised from the Dead

*"Our own hope had been that he would be the one
to set Israel free."*   Luke 24:21

In the words of James A. Pike:

"I am not known as being terribly credulous about doctrine, but I do believe in what is called the resurrection.

"I was very put off at first, when I began my study of the history of the resurrection appearances, by the garbled set of stories we are provided with. There are conflicts in the mode of the resurrection appearances—some claim to be physical, Jesus being able to eat fish and to let Thomas feel the wounds; others claim to be spiritual, in the sense of Jesus' being able to walk through closed doors, appear and disappear at will—and in the location of them—some stories say the appearances were in Galilee and others in Jerusalem.

"But after some experiences of psychic phenomena myself, I began to realize how easy it is to get a story garbled. If I hadn't made notes of my own experiences,[1] the story would have gotten all distorted. A lot of things get bigger and bigger, and many important things get forgotten. You tell the story to a few people and they question you. So to convince them, you build it up a little, or fill out the explanation. Then the next time you remember what you last said, not what actually happened. So I began to appreciate that there could very well have been appearances by Jesus to his disciples even though the stories are fairly mixed up. That does not discount the reality to which they point.

"Second, there is enough of this kind of thing happening all over the world even today—that is, people who see and communicate with persons after their death—that Jesus' resurrection fits into my category of the natural, not the supernatural. If it is true that man survives death and that man can make himself seen and can communicate even without a physical body, then it is natural to men to do so, and not some supernatural event mysteriously pulled off in one isolated case. If it is not true that man survives death, then it is not of the nature of man and it was not possible for Jesus. We are talking about Jesus as man here. No one is worried about God surviving death; only man and the continuity of his life are in question.

"Paul wrote about this same point. In I Corinthians 15 Paul says, 'If there is no resurrection of the dead, Christ himself cannot have been raised, and if Christ has not been raised then our preaching is useless and your believing it is useless, because we swore in evidence before God that he had raised Christ to life. For if the dead are not raised, Christ has not been raised' (I Cor. 15:14–18). Then he goes on to say, 'How are dead people raised, and what sort of body do they have when they come back?' (v. 35). This is a generic question. In other words, it is for everybody, or for nobody. If it is not of the nature of man, then to call it supernatural doesn't bail it out.

"Third, looking at all of the pieces of this enormous jigsaw puzzle we have been putting together—a jigsaw puzzle which seems very nearly complete—the reality of that to which the resurrection narratives point is quite essential. Without it, the picture falls apart. There were other significant Messiah figures, Messiah pretenders if you wish, and they are very interesting. Take Bar Kochba, for example. He thought he was the Messiah and he certainly showed more evidence of it than Jesus because he was able to gain freedom for the whole country from the Romans for three whole years and to run an independent government. That is no mean achievement. And yet after he was defeated by the Romans in A.D. 135, he was no longer believed to be the Messiah. To be the Messiah you have to win. Over and over again, a man was believed to be the Messiah up to the time he was defeated or killed. Then that was it.

"There is a basis for believing that Jesus was not regarded by many people as the Messiah until *after* he was defeated. Bishop John Robinson wrote an essay as a New Testament scholar, when he was Dean of Clare College and Lecturer in Divinity at Cambridge University, in which he analyzed the earliest Christian preaching. I think he established it very well. It is not in the Pentecostal sermon of Peter in Acts 2, though that is pretty primitive. Bishop Robinson finds a more primitive layer in Acts 3, and he establishes it with the proof of a lawyer.

"What were they saying when preaching about Jesus? 'The Messiah is coming; the Son of Man is coming. And when he comes, who will he be? He will be this Jesus whom we have known.' That is an interesting way of putting it. Not that Jesus *was* Messiah; not that Jesus *is* Messiah: no ontology about this. But *he who is to come,* when he comes, *will be the one we have known.* They had not labeled Jesus. They hadn't started talking about the logos and pre-existence and a divine human with two natures and all that. Just that one is coming from the divine realm, and when he comes, he will be this one whom we knew. That was the earliest preaching of the Christian Jews.

"The Messiah, in a sense, is always the one who is to come.

"To return to Paul, then. In answering the question about how the dead are raised up, Paul says, 'flesh and blood cannot inherit the kingdom of God.' It cannot be a physical body. It will have to be a spiritual body. There is a mode in which the personality will go on, but it is not this physical mode.

"It would seem that the portrayal of Jesus as having a physical body is a late elaboration of the narrative which seems less plausible than the incidents in which he appears through closed doors. But we can't make judgments about *how* it was experienced by the disciples. In terms of how we would assess the nature of the phenomenon, to me Paul's explanation of a spiritual, but real, body, or means of communication—that's all the body is, a means of relating—is more acceptable than the physical resurrection. But in terms of how it is experienced, that could be in very diversified forms, including the eating of the fish episode.

"My favorite resurrection story, and the one that rings more true to me in light of other experiences I have had and have read about in the *psi* field, is found in Luke (24:13 f.). Two disciples are going home along the road to Emmaus and are talking about how dreadful everything is. Someone joins them and asks what the trouble is. They ask him if he hasn't seen the papers or heard what's going on. Then they tell him about Jesus, and they finish by saying, 'But we had hoped that he was the one to redeem Israel' (RSV). Now the coins issued during the Bar Kochba period, as well as those issued by the Jews during the Great Revolt of A.D. 66 to 70 when the resistance had captured Jerusalem, were stamped 'For the redemption of Israel.' That's what it was all about. To redeem doesn't mean to save the souls of everyone in the country. It means to save the country—to free it from Roman oppression. 'We had hoped that he was the one to redeem Israel.'

"They talked some more about it, and they learned a lot about the Bible and understood the prophecies a lot better. When it started to get dark, they arrived home. So they said to the one who had joined them on the road, 'It's late. Come on in and have supper with us.' Then they took the wine and the bread, and the story says that they 'knew him' in the breaking of the bread.

"This is a very restrained, very delicate narrative, and very meaningful to me as the kind of thing this communication must have been after Jesus' death. Something like this—a reality—must have happened. It couldn't have been just a memory of him. It had to be a reality to explain why Jesus' Messiahship grew after he failed and was killed, whereas in every other case the Messianic movement was over as soon as the leader had failed to redeem Israel.

"We are persuaded that phenomena like those recorded in the Gospels are real, and that the reality behind the development of a strong Messianic movement which centered around Jesus after his death was his communication with his disciples. There was a kind of breakthrough of meaning and love and truth and courage—all within the presuppositions we have been talking about—which had a quality to it which seemed to abide. It was something that men could center on and thus rejoice in. They could believe that he who will come will be this one whom we have known.

"We know already the quality of that which shall be in the coming Kingdom, and we have confidence in that and rejoice in it. It will be like this Jesus, whom we have known."

———◆———

A MESSIANIC FAILURE

If there shall be a king of the house of David, a scholar of the Torah performing the Lord's commandments according to the written and the oral Law, and if he shall constrain all Israel to walk in their light, to establish them and to defend them—he shall do all these things by virtue of his being the potential Messiah. If he succeeds and conquers all the peoples about him, and builds the Temple in its place, and gathers in all the remnants of Israel, then he will indeed be the Messiah. But if he fails to do these things, or is killed, then he is not the Messiah promised in the Torah, but as any of the ordinary—albeit perfect and righteous—kings of the house of David who have died.[2]

With these words the great Jewish philosopher and rabbi Maimonides (A.D. 1135–1204) explained the process of redemption by which the Jewish people could faithfully determine whether a man was indeed the expected Messiah. The criteria he applied were not different from those by which Messiahs were measured in Jesus' day, even though Maimonides wrote nearly twelve centuries later in the face of Christian persecution of the Jews for their failure to accept Jesus as the Messiah.[3]

By Jewish standards Jesus failed the Messianic test. He was not able to constrain "all Israel" to walk in the light of the Law; he did not succeed in overthrowing Israel's Roman oppressors; he did not have an opportunity to rebuild the Temple according to the Law and to gather the remnants of Israel to him. He was killed. As Maimonides suggests, in all these regards, he was no different from other "potential" Messiahs, many of whom we have mentioned in the course of our book. He may have been perfect in his righteousness and therefore highly respected and much loved. But he could not be considered the Messiah, for he was killed.

The fact of Jesus' death on the cross was more than a stumbling block to Jesus' disciples; it was evidence that God had *not* chosen to use Jesus as His deliverer of Israel. It marked the end of his followers' hopes and expectations that Jesus was the Messiah. "Accursed of God" was anyone who had been hanged.[4] As one British scholar, Dr. James McLeman, puts it: "To the populace, to Pilate, to the Sanhedrin, the crucifixion of Jesus was the answer, final and irrevocable . . . That Jesus could be crucified was sufficient to convince the Jewish leaders that He had been an imposter. Whatever estimate Pilate made of Him, it was not high enough to forbid His being treated as a criminal. In the eyes of the people the Cross was the end, whether they regretted it or not. For all these the incident was closed."[5]

The Book of Acts records an incident which reflects this attitude on the part of the Jews:

> One member of the Sanhedrin, however, a Pharisee called Gamaliel, who was a doctor of the Law and respected by the whole people, stood up and asked to have the men [followers of Jesus] taken outside for a time. Then he addressed the Sanhedrin, "Men of Israel, be careful how you deal with these people. There was Theudas who

became notorious not so long ago. He claimed to be someone important, and he even collected about four hundred followers; but when he was killed, all his followers scattered and that was the end of them. And then there was Judas the Galilean, at the time of the census, who attracted crowds of supporters; but he got killed too, and all his followers dispersed. What I suggest, therefore, is that you leave these men alone and let them go. If this enterprise, this movement of theirs, is of human origin it will break up of its own accord; but if it does in fact come from God you will not only be unable to destroy them, but you might find yourselves fighting against God." (Acts 5:34–39).

Rabbi Gamaliel (with whom it is believed Paul studied) included Jesus as a Messianic pretender and revolutionary leader along with Theudas (who had offered to lead the people through the Jordan River, thus presenting himself as the potential new Moses) and Judas of Galilee (who had led the resistance to the census of A.D. 6 and the revolt against the paying of tribute money to Caesar which followed), and was obviously applying the criterion listed by Maimonides as the final test of Messiahship: since Jesus had been killed, his followers would soon disperse if the movement he had started was not of God.

What, then, were Jesus' disciples to do in the face of this tragic end to the life of the man they had hoped would be the Messiah? The Gospel accounts suggest that they returned to Galilee—probably even before his death—and that they were discouraged and depressed.[6]

The remarkable thing is not that Jesus thought he had been chosen by God to be the Messiah; not that he had been a righteous teacher and a prophetic voice; not that he was crucified as a rebel; not that his disciples scattered and returned to their homes after the failure of their Messianic thrust. The remarkable thing is that the story does not end there.

Jesus is the only example we have of a "Messianic pretender" or "potential Messiah" whose following grew after his death.[7] In all other cases a man's cause died with him, because death was evidence of God's failure to intervene to save His People through the medium of this man. To be sure, those who had followed a man such as Bar Kochba[8] would have continued to revere his memory, but he was no longer believed to be the Messiah after his revolt was suppressed and he was killed.

In the case of Jesus, however, the story is radically different. We cannot be certain what his disciples believed about him before his death and even less can we know what Jesus believed about himself, for the Gospels clearly are written in the light of the resurrection faith.[9] Yet even from the Gospel accounts, we get the impression that Jesus did not have a clear, and certainly not a fixed, image of himself as a Messianic figure, nor of his role in the sequence of events in the unfolding of Messianic history.

Jesus appears to have been a man totally obedient to God's will and open to have that will revealed anew to him in the midst of whatever circumstances presented themselves. He seems to have acted out some aspect of nearly all the major Messianic images of his day at some point in his public life. Though it is certain that the Gospel writers read their own understanding of Jesus' role back into the events of his life as they narrated them, nevertheless we consider it unlikely that they *invented* the situations in which they picture him. More likely is that the disciples, in looking back, saw profound meaning in the occasions they recalled and talked about, as well as in the words Jesus spoke in those situations. They may have elaborated the incidents in order to heighten the impact of the meaning, but it seems unlikely they would have made them up. That the disciples were able to see in Jesus' life the elements of so many Messianic roles is in itself helpful to us in getting a feeling for the complex and deeply committed man Jesus must have been.

MORE THAN A PROPHET?

Jesus is portrayed as having acted out the image of Elijah returned, preaching the prophetic word which would lead to repentance. He appears as the "prophet like Moses" in situations such as the Temptation in the Wilderness, the Feeding of the Five Thousand, and the Sermon on the Mount. For his entrance into Jerusalem, he is shown in the style of the Davidic Messiah, the conquering king. When cleansing the Temple he again manifests the characteristics of the prophetic Messiah figure, seeking to cleanse the heart of the ritual life of the nation. The prophetic image seems to dominate in the Gospels—so much so that many scholars believe that Jesus never saw himself as more than a prophet; that he never in fact presented himself as the Messiah.[10] There is also strong evidence to suggest that Jesus' disciples did not believe him to be more than a prophet before his death, and perhaps not even *after* his death.

Professor David Flusser, in commenting on an Arabic manuscript discovered and studied by Professor Shlomo Pines, also of Hebrew University in Jerusalem[11]—a document which sheds considerable light on the nature of Jewish Christianity before the Fall of Jerusalem—says: "Thanks to Pines' discovery it has become clear that both the Ebionites and the Nazarenes [both Jewish Christian groups] agreed on one central point: for both Jesus' main function was to be a prophet and not the Messiah."[12] The concept of Jesus as a prophet —or even the "true prophet"—had its origin in the first generation of Jesus' disciples, as can be seen in the Gospels and even in the words of Jesus himself (Lk. 13:33). From the beginning, then, we can be certain that at least some of Jesus' disciples "saw in their master a prophet, and perhaps not the Messiah at all," for the Ebionites and Nazarenes originated from this faction of Jesus' movement.[13] Whether others saw Jesus as the Messiah in the beginning, and whether he saw himself in that role, is far more difficult to ascertain.

It is impossible within the scope of this book to deal adequately with the question of Jesus' Messianic consciousness, and with the way he used the terms "Son of Man," "Son of God," etc.[14] What we can affirm is that everything Jesus did and said would have been understood by him, and by his disciples and the Jewish masses, in the context of apocalyptic Messianism. Ambiguities in Jesus' self-understanding, or the seeming slowness to grasp the meaning of things on the part of his disciples, can be attributed largely to the fact that they were living in an apocalyptic age where everything was in flux and change. In such an age, meaning is in the process of being revealed as lives are lived and events experienced. There are no abstract or fixed concepts to be focused on because everything is emerging and taking new shape.

There were no clearly defined systems of belief or "doctrines" in Judaism at that time. Apocalyptic expectations were often vague and imprecise and were seen as part of an extremely comprehensive "program of events" for the end of days. Man could not fully know that "program" until it had come to pass. However, what Jesus taught about the coming Kingdom falls within the scope of the general expectations of the Messianists of his time. As the eminent French scholar Charles Guignebert has pointed out, all the Messianists of Jesus' day had "the liveliness of their hope and the eagerness with which they awaited its fulfillment" in common.[15]

Neither Jesus nor his disciples could be certain about his Messianic role until they had lived it out and God had revealed His will in the events of their lives. It seems likely that Jesus felt he had been chosen by God to play a special role in Messianic history and that he had been vested with special authority;[16] that he offered himself to be used by God as God saw fit; and that he did not call himself Messiah because he felt that was a title which only God Himself could confer. Yet his actions, such as the entry into Jerusalem, make it clear that he offered himself as a channel through which the Messiahship could be realized if God so chose.

There has been a rather common understanding among Christians that Jesus avoided the title "Messiah" because it carried with it the idea of worldly leadership, a warrior-king who would help the Jews to throw off the humiliating yoke of Roman occupation.[17] However, as our study has shown, Jesus shared the expectation of his people that God's Kingdom would be established *on earth*. Therefore, his avoidance of the title "Messiah" can hardly be attributed to his opposition to such a "worldly" role.

Rather, it would seem Jesus preferred to use the term "Son of Man" because that title had an enigmatic character. It actually could mean only "man" in a most casual sense, and used by the person speaking it could mean "I" or "me." But it could also refer to that angelic figure spoken of by the prophet Daniel, who would come at the end of the age to bring fulfillment of God's promise to Israel.[18] Perhaps, therefore, Jesus chose it as a suitably ambiguous term to be used in the stage of anticipation when it could not yet be known with certainty whether or not *he* was God's Chosen One.

Likewise, Jesus' disciples undoubtedly considered him a great prophet—perhaps even *the* prophet of Deuteronomy. But they must also have hoped he would be shown to be more than that: that God would choose him as His Messiah. The two disciples on the way to the village of Emmaus after the crucifixion are reported to have said: "Jesus of Nazareth [or, the Nazarene] . . . proved he was a great prophet by the things he said and did in the sight of God and of the whole people . . . Our own hope had been that he would be the one to set Israel free" (Lk. 24:19, 21). This surely reflects what the disciples must have felt about Jesus.

HIS FOLLOWING GROWS

Fifty days after Jesus' death, the disciples were back in Jerusalem preaching the gospel of the imminent coming of the Kingdom with renewed fervor and with the added power of the holy spirit with which they had been baptized at Pentecost (Acts 2). The message they were preaching went like this: "Now you must repent and turn to God, so that your sins may be wiped out, and so that the Lord may send the time of comfort. *Then he will send you the Christ [Messiah] he has predestined, that is Jesus*" (Acts 3:19–20. Italics ours). In other words, they were announcing the imminent establishment of the Kingdom, but with a new note. Now they *knew* who the Messiah *would be:* Jesus, whom they had known and followed as a prophet before his death; and whom they now expected to return *in power* as the Messiah.[19]

Now, the disciples were convinced, there was no need to look further for a Messiah nor to wait in suspended animation for his appearance. They knew who the Messiah was—or rather, who he would be when he came in power. God had chosen Jesus, whom they knew and loved, and he would come again very soon to establish the Kingdom. Their task was to prepare for his coming by urging as many people as possible to repent and believe the good news.

The followers of Jesus became even *more* fervent in their Messianic zeal *after* Jesus' death than they had been before. The power and authority of their teaching and preaching were such that their movement grew by leaps and bounds.[20] Their expectation of the imminent establishment of the Kingdom was higher than ever, and they concentrated their activities in Jerusalem where they knew the final events would take place.

Many scholars accept the tradition cited by the church historian Eusebius that the early Christians fled to Pella, in Transjordan, before the Fall of Jerusalem in A.D. 70.[21] Some of them may have fled—not because they were primarily interested in an "other-wordly" Kingdom, but rather because Jesus had warned them: "When you see Jerusalem surrounded by armies, you must realise that she will soon be laid desolate. Then those in Judaea must escape to the mountains, those inside the city must leave it, and those in the country districts must not take refuge in it" (Lk. 21:20–21).

It is possible that others may have been involved in the Great Revolt against Rome in A.D. 66. They may have fled to Masada and held out there against the Romans for three years after the Fall of Jersualem, daily waiting and praying for the Son of Man to appear.[22] For Jesus had said, "And then they will see the Son of Man coming in a cloud with power and great glory. When these things begin to take place, stand erect, hold your heads high, because your liberation is near at hand" (Lk. 21:27–28).

Still others may have stayed in Jerusalem, and the more zealous would undoubtedly have fought alongside their countrymen.

All must have seen the events of those days as the fulfillment of Jesus' prophecies. For he is reported to have told his disciples, during his last week with them, all that would happen before the Kingdom could be ushered in by God. Jerusalem, he said, would fall to the enemy, the people of Judea would be taken captive and dispersed among the nations, and Jerusalem would become a Gentile city "until the age of the pagans is completely over" (Lk. 21:20–24).[23] He predicted that his people would suffer *"such distress as, until now, has not been equalled* since the beginning when God created the world, nor ever will be again" (Mk. 13:19). He spoke at length of the other signs of the end for which his disciples were to watch, and said, "When these things begin to take place, stand erect, hold your head high, because your liberation is near at hand" (Lk. 21:28). He assured them that "before this generation has passed away all will have taken place" (Lk. 21:32).[24]

Most of the conditions he had described were fulfilled by A.D. 70. His disciples cannot help but have watched attentively during those years (from A.D. 66 to 73) in eager anticipation that the Son of Man would soon appear.

It is possible, of course, that these words were not in fact prophecies of Jesus', but rather were attributed to him by his followers after Jerusalem had fallen. Even if that were the case, however, they would still give us insight into the mind-set and expectations of the early Christians. They remembered Jesus as one who had spoken to them of the coming liberation of Israel. They expected the events of the end of days to happen in their lifetime. They were fervent in their announcing of the Kingdom's imminent establishment.

It is no wonder, then, that the Romans were still persecuting

Christians as political insurrectionists long after the majority of Jews had made a conscious decision to dampen their Messianic fervor. As each new element of the prophecies of Jesus (or what they believed to have been his prophecies) was fulfilled, their conviction that the end of the age was indeed upon them would have grown stronger. They kept up the apocalyptic tension and the Messianic expectation which had been fermentation leading to revolt for over two hundred years. The Romans could not tolerate such treasonous teachings, and sought to eliminate the Christian movement.

It was only after the crushing defeat of the Jews in the Bar Kochba revolt of A.D. 132–135 that all Jews were expelled from Jerusalem and forbidden to return. Jerusalem was converted into a completely Gentile city, and even its name was changed—to Aelia Capitolina. The last of Jesus' prophecies was finally fulfilled. Yet Jesus had not returned "in power." The early Christians were forced to come to terms with the fact that—in spite of the fulfillment of prophecy—Jesus had *not* returned with power and the Kingdom of God had still *not* been established on earth.

THE DISCIPLES SEE JESUS

What was it, then, that happened to the disciples to cause them to move out of the dejection and discouragement brought on by Jesus' arrest and crucifixion and into a conviction that Jesus *was* in fact the one chosen by God to be His Messiah? The answer is to be found in a series of confused, confusing, and contradictory accounts given in the New Testament of what the disciples called "appearances" of the "risen" Jesus.

The Gospels do not provide us with a consistent account of Jesus' resurrection appearances. Scholars have acknowledged this for years.[25] All we can do is to try to reconstruct what happened, using all that we have so far learned about the disciples, the times in which they lived, and their beliefs and expectations, as background.

The Reverend Neville Clark, Minister of Amersham Free Church in Buckinghamshire, England, has stated very well the task that confronts the historian who seeks to understand this aspect of the historical Jesus:

The true historian probes the deposits of the past with the delicate tools of his techniques, and endeavours to set these facts against a background and interrelate them within a context that provides appropriateness and coherence. In this process he does not operate as a detached and neutral observer. He is more than a chronicler. He has a standpoint and a perspective; he works with presuppositions. Only as he interprets the evidence before him does he produce history . . . What emerges is a construct of interpreted fact, which is of living present significance. What is attained, in terms of correspondence with the reality of the events, is never certainty, only probability.[26]

It is obvious that the Resurrection itself is not a "historical" event in any ordinary sense of that term. The New Testament views it as the eschatological deed of God which shatters history. The historian has to conclude that he has no framework which will contain it, no corresponding happening with which he might compare it, no language which will capture it. In terms of historical investigation, the last and indisputable facts which lie on either side of the Resurrection are the death and burial of Jesus and the belief of the early Church that he has risen. Between these two facts lies some reality which seems to defy definition but demands explanation.[27]

From the Gospel accounts, and with the help of scholars who have examined them carefully in an effort to sort out the material, it appears that what happened was something like this:

After that final meal with Jesus in Jerusalem, the majority of the disciples went back to Galilee as Jesus had told them to do. After Jesus' arrest, James, Peter, and John, having escaped in the darkness of the Garden, joined the others there. Apparently they did not expect anything like a resurrection or they would not have fled, nor would they have been so discouraged.[28]

The women among Jesus' followers apparently stayed on in Jerusalem. They were present at the crucifixion[29] and they hoped that, when the Passover feast had ended, they would be allowed to give Jesus' body an appropriate burial. When, on the morning after the feast had ended,[30] they went to the tomb where they believed him buried, the tomb was empty. They were unable to find his body anywhere, and they were distraught and frightened by the turn of events.[31]

In Galilee, meanwhile, the disciples were having experiences which profoundly changed their understanding of Jesus' death on the cross. Evidently Peter was the first to "see" the risen Jesus,[32] but the other disciples saw him too and became convinced that he had been raised from the dead by God.[33] They returned to Jerusalem feeling "commissioned" by Jesus himself to continue with his work of preaching the coming of the Kingdom of God, baptizing those who repented, and teaching them to keep the Law in perfect righteousness.[34]

When the disciples returned from Galilee to Jerusalem, the women told them of the empty tomb and the disciples believed it to be evidence of the conviction they had come to as a result of their experiences: that Jesus had been raised from the dead.[35]

Finally, James, the brother of Jesus, and Paul "saw" the risen Jesus, as did a large number of disciples in Jerusalem.[36]

The disciples' immediate response to the resurrection experiences seems to have been to renew the preaching of the coming Kingdom —that is, to continue Jesus' own message and teachings. The fact of Jesus' resurrection was affirmed by the disciples only as proof that he was the one chosen by God to come as Messiah. It was only after Jesus' return as the Messiah was delayed, and the Church began to expand into the Gentile world, that the resurrection itself began to be preached. Then narratives about the appearances were developed, and the empty tomb began to be cited as proof of a *bodily* resurrection. These later embellishments of the story were intended to add weight to the conviction held so firmly by the first disciples: that the experiences they had had in which they saw Jesus after his death were evidence that Jesus had been raised from the dead by God.[37]

RAISED FROM THE DEAD?

What, then, can we say happened? All we can really know historically is that the disciples *said* they had seen Jesus after his death and that they *believed* that he had been raised from the dead. We cannot say as an historical fact that Jesus *was* resurrected. "Is Jesus risen?—we can only reply: That cannot be established. *In historical terms it can only be established* (though quite reliably) that witnesses, after the death of Jesus, claimed that something had happened to them which they described as seeing Jesus, and reflection on the experience led them to the *interpretation* that Jesus had been raised from the dead."[38]

The fact that the disciples had the experiences which they describe as "resurrection appearances" we must accept on their own testimony, though their own change of attitude and vigorous preaching after

Jesus' death lend credibility to their statements. As Bishop Pike has written concerning the conviction of the disciples that they had apprehended Jesus' continuing life after death:

> The experience was corporate and multiple. (And, it must be granted, inconsistent. This evident fact can be used as an answer to the position that the accounts were corporately contrived.) Hence quite implausible is the assumption of individual hallucination. The public testimony of the disciples to the experience was at a cost and, in the temper of the time to personal *dis*advantage as far as reputation and safety goes. Hence fairly implausible is the assumption of group fraud.[39]

Something must have happened. There is no reason to doubt that it was what the disciples say it was. But their interpretation of those events we need not accept as proof of the *fact* Jesus was resurrected. Their interpretation reflects the period in which the disciples lived and the beliefs in which they were emersed, but it cannot prove that, historically speaking, Jesus was raised from the dead.

Neither does the fact that it was their *interpretation* necessarily *dis*prove Jesus' resurrection, however. It really does not affect the question "was Jesus raised from the dead?" one way or another. The disciples *believed* that he was; historically, we cannot know.

In writing about this historical problem, Bishop Pike said the following:

> Several decades elapsed before the writing of the accounts as we now have them; and the form of testimony, in some cases, suggests prior challenges to the oral narration. Therefore, it is not surprising that there are some contradictions among the reports: as to time, place, and percipients; as to the nature of the experience (there is a difference between an apparition in which a person is perceived as eating a fish and one in which he is perceived as walking through a closed door); and in the form of the messages reported as coming through. Nevertheless, if on a broader empirical base it should be concludable that the phenomena which these narratives point to are in the category of reality *and* that the deceased persons can be the source of them, one would not rule out, a priori, belief as to the ongoing life of Jesus and his being in contact with his disciples because of these variations in reporting and in interpretation. When it comes to various doctrines which the percipients and others believing in the reality of their experiences have regarded as being established by the phenomena, one must make a logical separation here with which we are already familiar. The modern critic's or believer's view regarding

one or another of the meanings affirmed as part of the account neither proves nor disproves the truth of the report of events; nor would the reality of the events establish the truth or relevance of any one of the reporters' meaning-affirmations.[40]

The disciples interpreted their experiences in light of the resources of their own tradition.[41] As we have already shown, the belief in the resurrection of the dead on the judgment day had come to be generally accepted by the time of Jesus. The breakthrough to a resurrection belief came in two directions—first by way of national hope, and second by way of individual hope. These beliefs, some scholars hold, came as a result of the frustrations which the Jewish people had experienced during and after the Babylonian exile, and because of their invincible hope in God. They were not content to accept frustration as the meaning of life.[42]

Therefore, a belief had developed in a coming Kingdom on the earth in which Israel would be justified before the world and enjoy abundant prosperity. Secondly, there emerged a belief in immortality for the individual man whose whole trust was in God. The meeting of these two expectations generated belief in resurrection. Individual saints (believers) would be raised to enjoy the blessings of the Kingdom on earth with those alive at the time. The Jews anticipated a bodily resurrection on this earth to an earthly Kingdom which would last forever.[43]

When the disciples, after Jesus' death, "saw" him, their first conclusion would not have been that Jesus alone had been raised from the dead, but rather that the general resurrection at the end of times had begun. Otherwise, how could Jesus have been resurrected? "The belief in the general resurrection is the prior conviction; it is not itself dependent upon belief in the resurrection of Jesus. What is totally unexpected is the fact that the general resurrection has moved from the End to take present shape in the one case of Jesus the Messiah."[44]

The urgency of the disciples' proclamation of the Kingdom after these events is due to their belief that the series of events "scheduled" for the end of times had been set in motion. Jesus' resurrection was the "first-fruits" (I Cor. 15:20) of the general resurrection; the rest of the "program" could not be long in following.[45] James McLeman observes, "the genius of the New Testament literature lies in the belief that in Jesus who rose from the dead the New Age has been inaugurated and the future is now estimated in reference to Him.

'That' which the prophets foretold is now 'This' which is happening and will happen."[46]

It was only because the remainder of the expected events did not follow Jesus' resurrection, that the disciples began to reflect further on the meaning of their experiences.[47] Because of their experiences, they knew the resurrection to be a fact. Later they sought to reinterpret that fact.

Their first conclusion was that it had been necessary for Jesus to die in order that the prophecy in Isaiah 53 could be fulfilled. Jesus had suffered in order to atone for the sins of the whole People Israel.[48]

> We had all gone astray like sheep, each taking his own way, and Yahweh burdened him with the sins of all of us. Harshly dealt with, he bore it humbly, he never opened his mouth . . . Yes, he was torn away from the land of the living; for our faults struck down in death . . . By his sufferings shall my servant justify many, taking their faults on himself (Is. 53:6, 7a, 8b, 11b).

Still later, Christological doctrines of a much higher order—most borrowed from the apocalyptic literature of Judaism—were applied to Jesus to explain why he had been raised from the dead when the remainder of the "end of times" had not yet been brought to fulfillment.[49] He was called "the only Son of God," who had come to pay the ransom for the sins of the whole world *by his death* on the cross. He was seen to have already established the Kingdom of God for those who would believe in him. He was identified with the logos, or "the word," and said to have been pre-existent, born of a virgin, fully God and without sin. He was represented as the Second Adam whose expiatory death had freed man from the sin of the First Adam. As Bishop Pike used to express it, larger and more elaborate frames were put around the picture of Jesus, as time wore on, to pay due respect to it.[50]

WHAT DOES THE RESURRECTION MEAN?

Certainly a clear distinction must be made between the disciples' interpretations of their resurrection experiences and the event itself. As Professor Willi Marxsen of the University of Münster, Germany, points out, that which supplied the real basis for the growth of the Christian movement after Jesus' death was *"the fact,* not of the resurrection itself, but of Jesus' *appearances"* and to speak of the raising from the dead as a fact is *"to turn into history what was the result of an interpretation."*[51]

But all too often today, even the *possibility* that Jesus' resurrection could have been a fact is rejected because the *interpretation* seems unacceptable. To deny the historical validity of the disciples' experiences, and to dismiss out of hand any possibility that Jesus could in some way have lived on after death solely because the world view of the early Christians is not our own, is equally dogmatic, unscientific, and ahistorical.

The power of Jesus' life, death, and resurrection for the disciples was that they saw in him the embodiment—the living out—of all the major themes of their beliefs and expectations. He became for them a confirmation of the truth of the prophecies and of the teachings which he himself had passed on and in which the disciples had placed their trust. Thus Jesus became for them a special "sign" from God that all would work out just as had been foretold by the prophets.

Because Jesus fulfilled the prophecies, as they understood them and as they interpreted his life, death, and resurrection, the disciples concluded he must be the Messiah. If he was the Messiah and he had been raised from the dead, the end of times and the final resurrection had already begun and would surely be culminated soon. They expected his return within their lifetime.

Over nineteen centuries have passed since then. Apocalyptic predictions of the second coming of Jesus have been calculated and recalculated endlessly. But he has not returned to complete the schedule of events for the end of days. That is an historical fact. By Maimonides' test, stated at the opening of this chapter, we have to say that Jesus is still not the Messiah anticipated by the Jews—*including* the Jewish disciples of Jesus during the first century A.D. It is perfectly understandable, therefore, why so few people—even "believing" Christians —any longer expect Jesus to return, and why so many of us find the world view of the disciples (and of Jesus) inadequate to meet our needs for a meaning structure today.[52]

Jesus' description of the coming of the Kingdom and the Son of Man was very explicit: "But in those days, after that time of distress, the sun will be darkened, the moon will lose its brightness, the stars will come falling from heaven and the powers in the heavens will be shaken. And then they will see the Son of Man coming in the clouds with great power and glory; then too he will send the angels to gather his chosen from the four winds, from the ends of the world to the ends of heaven" (Mk. 13:24–27).

If, in contrast to Jesus' description, the Kingdom of God was established as subtly as Christian theologians would have us believe, how can the Jews—or anyone else—be blamed for failing to recognize Jesus as the Messiah?

After nearly two thousand years, it would not be precipitous, it seems, to conclude that the disciples were in error in their interpretation of the meaning of the resurrection experiences. It seems apparent that Jesus was not the Messiah which he and his people expected: Israel has still not been redeemed; she does not yet live in peace and harmony; the eschatological program has still not been accomplished.

Bishop Pike used to tell the story of a conversation he had with the late Martin Buber, the great Jewish philosopher and mystic. Together with the now Cardinal Jean Daniélou, they were discussing Jesus in a Paris hotel. "You Christians," Dr. Buber said, "say that in Jesus the world has been redeemed. But, my dear Jim, I look around me [he made a sweeping gesture with his arm toward the window and the city below] and I see that, sadly, the world is not redeemed." Surely this is the assessment any objective man must make, historically speaking.

But if the disciples were in error in their interpretation, does that invalidate their experiences? We think not. The meaning they saw in Jesus' life and teachings can still have profound meaning for us today if properly understood. And, it may be that we are only now beginning to develop the ability to examine such experiences as facts, leaving aside the interpretations. The new scientific research into and experimentation with the *psi* factor of the human personality[53]—that dimension of our nature which is able to transcend time and space— may soon enable us to talk about the disciples' experiences and Jesus' resurrection as natural phenomena rather than as supernatural, miraculous, or unique occurrences.[54] Perhaps we will discover that what constituted a breakthrough in human history was not the fact of Jesus' resurrection from the dead, but the fact that he was able to *appear* to his disciples after his death, that they were able to *see* him, and that they *recognized* him as Jesus raised from the dead.

Parapsychological investigation is as new today as space research was twenty-five years ago. But the fact that we are now able to travel in space should be sufficient cause for at least the suspension of judgment on whether it could have been possible for Jesus to live in another kind of body after his physical body died.[55] Perhaps in twenty-five years (or less) we will have adequate data to be able to answer the question satisfactorily.

Until then, as historians we can say that the disciples' experiences in which they saw what they believed to be Jesus resurrected from the dead, changed the whole course of history. Such an historical event is worth examining again and again, for the power inherent in it has obviously still not been fully tapped nor adequately understood.

The quest for the historical Jesus must not, it seems to us, end with the crucifixion. The cross is perhaps evidence that Jesus was not the Messiah. But then came the resurrection. If not the King of the Jews, and if not the Messiah as understood by the Apostles, then what?

NOTES

PREFACE

1. The terms "Jewish" and "Jews" are used throughout to denote the people who find their primary identity in being a part of the Mosaic Covenant with Yahweh (the One God). Their ancestors, during the Patriarchal period prior to Moses, are generally referred to as the "Hebrews." After Moses led the Hebrews out of Egypt and the Covenant was entered into with Yahweh, they came to be called "Israelites." The term "Israel" was used to identify the whole covenanted people, but also designated the northern tribe (and later kingdom) of Israel, as contrasted with the other tribes and the southern kingdom of Judea. During the time of Jesus, "Israel" was the term used for the whole Chosen People, who were divided into two principal groups: the "Galileans" from the north and the "Jews" from Judea in the south. Nevertheless, except where we make clear in the text that we are following New Testament usage, we use the terms "Jews" and "Jewish" to describe all those who make up the People Israel, as we believe this will communicate more clearly to our readers for whom this is the accustomed usage in our day.

2. For the full story of these events, read *The Bishop Pike Affair*, by William Stringfellow and Anthony Towne, New York: Harper & Row, 1967.

3. Cf. James A. Pike, *If This Be Heresy*, New York: Delta Publishing Co., 1969, pp. 69 ff., where Bishop Pike analyzes the works of Professor Charles Y. Glock and Dr. Rodney Stark, undertaken by the Survey Research Center of the University of California at Berkeley. Percentages of positive affirmation to the statement "I know God really exists and I have no doubts about it" ran: Congregationalists, 41%; Methodists, 60%; Episcopalians, 63%; Disciples of Christ, 76%; United Presbyterians, 75%; Lutherans, 73%; American (Northern) Baptists, 78%; Lutherans, Missouri Synod, 81%; Southern Baptists, 99%; Roman Catholics, 81%. On the question of the Virgin Birth of Jesus, the percentages of those who could affirm such a belief were much lower: Congregationalists, 21%; Methodists, 34%; Episcopalians, 39%; Disciples of Christ, 62%; United Presbyterians, 57%; Lutherans, 66%; American Baptists, 69%; Lutherans, Missouri Synod, 92%; Southern Baptists, 99%; Roman Catholics, 81%. To the

question of whether Jesus will actually return some day, the affirmative responses were: Congregationalists, 13%; Methodists, 21%; Episcopalians, 24%; Disciples, 36%; United Presbyterians, 43%; Lutherans, 54%; American Baptists, 57%; Lutherans, Missouri Synod, 75%; Southern Baptists, 94%; Roman Catholics, 47%. Bishop Pike observes, "Complete logical consistency in theological belief is not displayed by this survey or by others. A rather comprehensive Gallup Poll made in England in 1965 showed that just fewer than one half of the members of the Church of England believed in a personal God; but that two thirds believed that Jesus is the Son of God—reminding one of what is said to be the conviction of many Latin Americans: there is no God, but Mary is His Mother! . . .

"For example, in my own Church, it would appear from the survey drawn from above (and its conclusions are in general validated not only by the reliable methodology adhered to by the staff, but also—though less precisely of course—by many candid statements of laymen by correspondence and in person) that 61 per cent of Episcopal laymen cannot affirm as historical the Virgin Birth and 53 per cent will not affirm the doctrine of sole salvation through Jesus—just to take as samples two Prayer Book doctrines for nonaffirmation of which I am at present the defendant in pending heresy proceedings" (pp. 72–73).

4. For Bishop Pike's own exposition of this concern, read *If This Be Heresy.*

5. "Christianity in Retreat," *Look,* Vol. 24, No. 26, December 20, 1960.

6. One month's speaking engagements, for example, included Pacific University (Forest Grove, Oregon); Arizona State University; Temple Beth Israel in Phoenix; Gettysburg College in Pennsylvania; the Valley Jewish Community of North Hollywood; the University of California at Santa Cruz; the Unitarian Church of Los Angeles; The National Council of Churches Convention in Dallas; a Bill of Rights dinner in Houston; the Fort Worth Knife and Fork Club; Texas Technical College of Lubbock; the University of Wisconsin; the Newman Center of Berkeley; Claremont College, California; Ventura College in California; a Pomona College (California) Seminar; and the California Elementary Administrators Convention in Santa Paula, California. His audiences ranged in size from several hundreds to more than ten thousand at the Kansas State College at Manhattan.

7. The story of that wilderness journey and its meaning for one of your present authors is told in *Search,* by Diane Kennedy Pike, Garden City, N.Y.: Doubleday, 1970; New York: Pocket Books, 1971.

INTRODUCTION:

In Quest of the Historical Jesus

1. Jacob Jervell, *The Continuing Search for the Historical Jesus*, Minneapolis: Augsburg Publishing House, 1965, p. 9; and James M. Robinson, *A New Quest of the Historical Jesus*, London: SCM Press Ltd., 1966, p. 27.
2. *Op. cit.*, p. 35. [Italics his.]
3. Jervell, *op. cit.*, p. 21.
4. *Ibid.*, p. 13.
5. Albert Schweitzer, *The Quest of the Historical Jesus*, first published in German, *Von Reimarus zu Wrede*, 1906. The references are to the 1968 paperback edition, New York: The Macmillan Company, 1968, with a new introduction by James M. Robinson. Even Vincent Taylor, C. J. Cadoux, and T. W. Manson, who as participants in a symposium entitled "Is It Possible to Write a Life of Christ?" concluded that any "biography" of Jesus was impossible, have each published a life of Jesus. Cf. James M. Robinson, *op. cit.*, p. 9 (2).
6. *Op. cit.*, p. 4.
7. *Ibid.*, "Introduction" by James M. Robinson, p. xxi.
8. *Ibid.*, p. 6.
9. *Ibid.*, p. 401.
10. *Ibid.*, p. 316, quoting Albert Kalthoff.
11. *Ibid.*, p. 399.
12. *Ibid.*, p. viii in Preface by F. C. Burkitt (1910).
13. *Ibid.*, pp. xxiv–xxv, "Introduction."
14. Jervell, *op. cit.*, p. 83; James M. Robinson, *op. cit.*, p. 12; and Joachim Jeremias, *The Problem of the Historical Jesus*, Philadelphia: Fortress Press, 1964.
15. Jeremias, *op. cit.*, "Introduction" by John Reumann, pp. xi ff.
16. *Op. cit.*, pp. 29, 30.
17. *Ibid.*, p. 39.
18. James A. Pike, *If This Be Heresy*, pp. 75 ff.
19. Jeremias, *op. cit.*, p. 17, differs on this point. He states that the Dead Sea Scrolls give a greater example of the preoccupation of late Judaism with efforts "to establish God's holy community. We can now assess more clearly than heretofore the significance of the emphatic denial

with which Jesus met all these attempts." Hence, in Jeremias' view, studies in the period of the time of Jesus have served only to emphasize "the sharpness of Jesus' opposition to the religiosity of his time."

20. See James A. Pike, *If This Be Heresy*, Chapter III, "The Authority Crisis"; and Albert Schweitzer, *Pilgrimage to Humanity*, New York: Philosophical Library, 1961, who has written: "Today there is not only a neglect of thought but an actual distrust or depreciation of it. The organized political, social and religious groups of our time are bent on inducing the individual to take up uncritically ready-made beliefs rather than inviting him to work out for himself by thought his own convictions. A man who thinks for himself and therefore is free is a troublesome and strange being. There is no assurance that he will fit comfortably into their organizations. All organized groups today find their strength, not so much in the spiritual values of their ideas or of the people who are their members, but in achieving the highest possible degree of unity and exclusiveness. In this they find their strongest power and surest defense" (p. 93). And also, "I am persuaded that the abiding spiritual significance which the religious thought of the past has for us finds its greatest worth and vigor when we enter into that piety as it really was, not as we interpret it for ourselves. A Christianity which does not dare place historical truth in the service of spiritual truth is not internally sound, even if it appears outwardly strong. The reverence for truth as such, which must be a part of our faith if it is not to be impoverished, includes a respect for historical truth" (p. 82).

21. New York: Harper & Row, 1964.

22. Pike, *If This Be Heresy*, p. 7.

23. *The Bishop Pike Affair*, pp. 47–48.

24. *If This Be Heresy*, p. 8.

CHAPTER 1

The Freedom Struggle of the Jewish People

1. Alexander the Great's conquests, reaching as far east as India before his death in 323 B.C., had proven a tremendous boon to the dissemination of Hellenistic culture throughout the Middle East. The competition for control of the Empire which followed the death of Alexander centered around two of his generals, Ptolemy and Seleucus; and the period preceding the full coming to power of Rome in the area was marked by a tug-of-war between the Egyptian Ptolemaic dynasty with its capital in Alexandria and the northern Seleucid king with Antioch in Syria and Seleucia in Babylonia as capitals.

Ptolemy won the first series of battles and gained control of Israel. It was at the time of Ptolemy's initial conquest of Jerusalem that large numbers of Jews were forcibly transported to Alexandria—thus forming the nucleus of what was to become the greatest Jewish colony in the Diaspora, and the site where the Hebrew scriptures were to be translated into Greek. Ptolemaic rule was generally benevolent and the Jews enjoyed a great measure of autonomy, merely paying annual tribute to the Ptolemaic rulers.

In 198 B.C., "Jerusalem, having lived for more than a century under the 'Greeks of Egypt,' the Ptolemies, now came under the 'Greeks of Syria,' the Seleucids" (Teddy Kollek and Moshe Pearlman, *Jerusalem, Sacred City of Mankind,* Jerusalem: Steimatzky's Agency Limited, 1968, p. 85). With the coming of the Seleucid dynasty a perceptible change in the affairs of Israel took place: the process of Hellenization which had occurred gradually and at a natural pace under the Ptolemies, was accelerated by intentional efforts to assimilate the Jews. This forced cultural conformity reached its most extreme expression during the reign of Antiochus Epiphanes. "It became the object of his life to 'civilize' his dominions, as he considered it, by the introduction of Greek standards of life. The shallow, unbalanced nature which caused him to assume the name of Epiphanes (the illustrious), converted this ambition into something little less than a mania" (Cecil Roth, *A History of the Jews,* New York: Schocken Books, 1961, p. 71). "With cultural unity as his aim, and idolising Greek ways, he sought to impose a standard pattern of life upon his heterogeneous vassals and to advance the worship of Greek gods" (Kollek and Pearlman, *op. cit.*, p. 85).

In the words of James A. Pike, the Seleucid practice was a "forced Hellenization by the destruction of local customs; the melting pot concept, except on *our* (i.e., the Seleucids') terms." The Jews refused to accept the "terms," and Seleucid persecution was met by Jewish resistance, which in turn brought more repression and increased rebellion. "The crusading zeal of Hellenism left no room for neutralism in the new Jewish state, and attempts to impose religious and political norms by the Seleucids and Ptolemies produced predictable reactions among Jews" (W. F. Albright and C. S. Mann, "Qumran and the Essenes," *The Scrolls and Christianity*, Matthew Black, ed., London: S.P.C.K., 1969, p. 18). This process of persecution and resistance finally resulted in the Maccabees' revolt, as "the Jews struck back at their oppressors in a national war of resistance . . . The Liberation and 'cleansing' of Jerusalem and freedom of worship—which now meant freedom from Seleucid rule—was the aim of the campaign . . ." (Kollek and Pearlman, *op. cit.*, p. 86).

The Jewish resistance to the process of Hellenization took on a religious importance, for, as Bishop Pike once said, they were "zealous for the law and for its distinctive cultural forms codified in the Torah which therefore had religious significance." The reaction against Hellenism was "rooted in Jewish piety . . . its motivation was theological" (W. R. Farmer, *Maccabees, Zealots and Josephus*, New York: Columbia University Press, 1958, p. 48).

While the Maccabean Revolt was successful in momentarily stemming the influx of Hellenistic customs and ideas, "this victory was mainly an internal victory over the radical Hellenizing tendency within Judaism. The triumph over the heathen, though it was truly marvelous, was only temporary. The Maccabean victory accomplished no perceptible change in the Hellenistic character of the outer environment in which Israel still had to live and breathe" (*Ibid.*, p. 51).

During the long reign of Herod the Great, the conflict between Judaism and Hellenism continued. While Herod was protective of certain of the Jewish religious customs, he continued the Hellenization of the country: "Nothing earned Herod so much domestic unpopularity as his devotion which he showed to the fashionable Hellenic culture, to the complete neglect of everything Jewish. In all his building operations (excepting possibly the Temple) the classical style of architecture was employed. The urban centers throughout Palestine, and especially the new cities which he developed, came entirely under Greek and Roman influence. In Jerusalem, itself, he constructed a Hippodrome, where the games which had so scandalized a former generation were carried on. The Hellenization against which the Hasmonaeans had fought thus became deeply implanted in a period of profound peace" (Roth, *op. cit.*, p. 98).

The Romans exhibited a greater tolerance toward the indigenous Jewish culture than the Seleucids. But the more tolerant attitude toward native customs and ideas by the Romans was largely unappreciated by the Jews. As far as they were concerned, the Roman Empire played essentially the same role in the conflict between Judaism and Hellenism as the Seleucid kingdom before it: one heathen was as bad as the next. "It does not matter that to some of us moderns the policy of the Romans toward the Jews seems quite moderate and reasonable. The important historical question to ask if we are to understand Jewish nationalism is, 'How did the Jews regard the Romans?' . . . From the point of view of the pious Jew, both the Romans and the Seleucids threatened the supremacy of the Torah and the inviolate sanctity of the national temple" (Farmer, *op. cit.*, p. 92).

Such Roman concessions as suspending the payment of tribute directly to the emperor (until A.D. 6), restricting the use of the decorative standards of their legions, and overlooking the people's failure to sacrifice to the emperor (accepting instead a token sacrifice in the Temple), were not sufficient to the pious Jews.

The Romans normally assumed a tolerant attitude toward the religious and cultural customs and beliefs of local areas, relying on the more gradual processes of assimilation and infiltration rather than overt persecution. According to W. R. Farmer, the aristocratic priestly class within Judaism favored this gradual Hellenization, but the Torah provided conservative religious factions with a rallying point to resist Hellenization. It was the Law which was the focal point of Jewish resistance (I Macc. 2:27). Furthermore, the Hellenistic religious toleration "was based on the presupposition that different peoples really worshipped the same god under different names, which supposition also provided the basis for Hellenistic syncretism— the practice of uniting names and cults. In so far as the Jew held to the belief that Yahweh was the jealous, covenant God of Israel who absolutely forbade the making of any graven image, he stood diametrically opposed to the practical application of this principle to the cult life of Israel" (Farmer, *op. cit.*, p. 55).

It is important to recognize this conflict between Judaism and Hellenism, for it not only resulted in continual religiously motivated nationalistic rebellion by the Jews, but it also was a direct cause of the emergence of the pious apocalyptic desert sects, such as the Qumran sect made famous by the discovery of the Dead Sea Scrolls, which we will later discuss. The appearance of the *Hasidim* or "pious ones," who later became the Pharisees, the Zealots, and the wilderness sects such as Qumran, coincided with the Maccabean Revolt against the Seleucids. The removal to the wilderness by certain of the *Hasidim* reflected their disappointment in the Hasmonean rule which, to their mind, was excessively concerned with civil independence and power, and which continued to be Hellenized, a friction seen in I Macc. 7:9–16. Archaeological evidence suggests that Qumran was founded during this period, about 140 B.C.

The conflict between Judaism and Hellenism was primarily responsible for Jewish sectarianism as it existed at the time of Jesus: "As the Sadducees had their spiritual roots in the extreme Hellenizing influences of the early Maccabean period, so the Pharisees, Essenes, and Zealots had their spiritual roots in the conservative reaction against those same influences in the same period" (Farmer, *op. cit.*, p. 189).

2. Farmer, *op. cit.*, pp. 49 and 84.

3. The Books of I and II Maccabees are included in Roman Catholic and most Episcopal Bibles as Apocryphal Old Testament books. They are also available in translations. For example cf. R. H. Charles, *The Apocrypha and Pseudepigrapha of the Old Testament* (2 vols.), London: Oxford University Press, 1963; M. R. James, *The Apocryphal New Testament,* Oxford: The Clarendon Press, 1963; Edgar Hennecke, *New Testament Apocrypha* (2 vols.), W. Schneemelcher, ed., Philadelphia: Westminster Press, 1963.

4. Cf. also *Ant.* XII. 268 ff.

5. S. G. F. Brandon, *The Trial of Jesus of Nazareth,* New York: Stein & Day, 1968, p. 175 (10), and *Jesus and the Zealots,* New York: Scribner's, 1967, pp. 32, 37, 48–50 and "The Trial of Jesus," *Judaism,* Vol. 20, No. 1, Winter 1971. Cf. W. O. E. Oesterley, *A History of Israel,* Vol. II, Oxford: The Clarendon Press, 1945, pp. 383 f. Oscar Cullmann, *The State in the New Testament,* New York: Charles Scribner's Sons, 1956, writes of the Zealots, "Here the theocratic ideal finds its sharpest expression" (p. 10).

6. Abba Hillel Silver, *A History of Messianic Speculation in Israel,* Boston: Beacon Press, 1959, p. ix.

7. Otto Ploger notes a shift in the concept of a theocracy at the time of the Maccabean Revolt (*Theocracy and Eschatology,* Oxford: Basil Blackwell, 1968). Because of the Seleucid persecution, the *Hasidim* joined the Maccabees in the revolt and distinguished themselves as courageous men loyal to the Law (I Macc. 2:42). Yet they had a mixed attitude toward the revolt and the subsequent founding of a Jewish state by the Hasmoneans. After the initial unity (cf. II Macc. 14:6, which virtually equates the Maccabees and the *Hasidim*), a basic disagreement over the interpretation of events produced a "cleavage" within the ranks of the anti-Hellenistic Jews (pp. 7, 8). This split is reflected in the literature of the period: the first Book of Maccabees (I Macc. 2:49–68; 7:12, 13), with its pro-Hasmonean sympathies, deals very cautiously with the role of the *Hasidim* in the opposition (p. 8); the Book of Daniel (11:34) writes only reservedly of the Maccabees, displaying a passive but loyal attitude toward them which is shared by the *Hasidim* (p. 17. Cf. I Macc. 2).

According to Ploger this division was deeper than a split over tactics. Essentially, the Maccabees did not view the events involving the Seleucids as associated with the establishment of the Kingdom on earth (pp. 17–18), while the *Hasidim* did: "The original reluctance of the *Hasidim,* however, to take part in armed resistance, and their swift reversal to a policy of waiting passivity . . . can, in view of the religious courage displayed by the 'Pious,' only be explained in terms of a fundamental renunciation of every political tie. In some ways this attitude is reminiscent of that once demanded by Isaiah—to trust in Yahweh and wait with faith" (p. 9).

The interpretation of historical events as related to the final establishment of God's Kingdom on earth by the *Hasidim* was a basis for membership in separatist sects understanding themselves to be the "true Israel" of the prophets (p. 19). The eventual corruption of the Hasmonean state and its seduction by Hellenistic influences further strengthened the view of such eschatologically minded sects that "the true Israel was more fully embodied in their own ranks" (p. 45). The conception of the world held by the apocalyptic sects combined an eschatological view of history—the fervent expectation of the imminent transformation of the world on a cosmic scale, resulting in their institution as the true Israel—with an emphasis on the present righteousness of their members. "Apocalyptic eschatology . . . expressed the future hope of a community which was conscious of being a religious body absolutely separate from the national and religious life of the rest of mankind and which, being unique, could only express a future hope in terms of the manifestation of its own distinctive existence, while living at the same time in the belief that 'the manner of this world is passing away' " (p. 50).

Such a world view had several constitutive elements: "a religious, deterministic point of view, stemming from the plan of Yahweh proclaimed by the older prophets; the unity of the world as the enemy of God, embodied in the great homogeneous empire which is in subjection to the power of evil; the limitation of human influence in favour of the unilateral activity of God in a supernatural, miraculous form, and . . . a strong emphasis on angels and demons; a pessimistic-dualistic view of the world, which resulted in a marked other-worldliness combined with expectation of judgement and individual resurrection" (pp. 27 f.).

Those Jews who accepted the status quo theocracy of the Hasmoneans came into conflict with the eschatological sects whose disillusionment by the Hasmoneans led them to believe that they themselves had to constitute the true Israel—according to the terms of the understanding of the Law and history revealed to them—an Israel which would come to its rightful position with the coming of the end of times: "the theocratic community began to regard itself as a constituent of Yahweh's heavenly kingdom, to emerge in the eschatological [final] revolution as part of the new aeon, when the substance of this world passes away" (p. 112).

The expectation of the eschaton (the end of the present world order) and the coming judgment of all people was so strong that the apocalyptic sects believed the date of the judgment could be calculated (p. 28). Silver (*op. cit.*) attributes the intense Messianic agitation of the first century A.D., particularly of the generation immediately preceding the revolt, to *"the pop-*

ular chronology of that day that the age was on the threshold of the Millennium . . . When Jesus came into Galilee, 'spreading the gospel of the Kingdom of God and saying the *time is fulfilled* and the Kingdom of God is at hand' [Mk. 1:14–15], he was voicing the opinion universally held that the year 5000 in the Creation calendar, which is to usher in the sixth millennium—the age of the Kingdom of God—was at hand. It was this chronologic fact which inflamed the Messianic hope of the people rather than Roman persecutions" (pp. 5–6. Cf. also pp. 12, 13, 16). The Book of Daniel gave at least six specific dates which inspired such Messianic calculations (p. 243).

8. The authors use the term "zealot" in a broad sense, "to refer to those who actively resisted Rome, and more especially to the party of Judas of Galilee," as does W. R. Farmer (*op. cit.*, p. 24 [3]). Josephus uses the term to designate one of the parties involved in the Great Revolt against Rome, and assigns the beginning and leadership of the Zealot movement to the steps taken in A.D. 6 by Judas of Galilee. The authors use the term "Sicarii" to designate the extremist wing of the Zealots—those who did not hesitate to use violence whenever it seemed expedient. Josephus is inconsistent in his use of both these terms. In *War* VII. 254–56 he names the followers of Judas of Galilee (A.D. 6) the "sicarii"; while in *War* II. 254–57 he says the sicarii began during the procuratorship of Felis (A.D. 52–60) with the murder of Jonathan. In the parallel account of Jonathan's assassination found in *Ant.* XX. 163–65, Josephus calls the assassins "brigands" (his customary name for the Zealots) and not sicarii. Elsewhere Josephus uses the terms brigand and Zealot interchangeably. The terms are also used variously in Acts 21:38 and in Rabbinic sources (e.g., Makshirin I. 6). Cf. Brandon, *Jesus and the Zealots,* pp. 30–32, 41–43, 46–47, 109, 113; Joseph Klausner, *Jesus of Nazareth,* Boston: Beacon Press, 1964, pp. 162 and 204 ff.; and Oscar Cullmann, *Jesus and the Revolutionaries,* New York: Harper & Row, 1970, Appendix, pp. 73 ff.

Our principal source of information about the Zealots, a Jewish historian of the period named Flavius Josephus, seems to have had a definite bias against them (Brandon, *op. cit.,* pp. 30–42; Cecil Roth, *The Dead Sea Scrolls: A New Historical Approach,* New York: W. W. Norton & Co., Inc., 1965, p. 24 ff.; Klausner, *op cit.,* pp. 204–6; and H. St. J. Thackeray, "Introduction," *Josephus: The Jewish War,* Cambridge: Harvard University Press, The Loeb Classical Library Edition, 1961, pp. viii f.). In the light of the overall history of the Jews, and more specifically in light of the Maccabean Revolt and how it was regarded by Jews during the period of the Second Temple, one comes to the conclusion almost of necessity that Josephus' portrayal of the Zealots was purposely distorted.

Josephus, born Joseph bar Mattathia Kahana of Jerusalem in the year A.D. 37–38, was of an aristocratic family of priests. On his mother's side, Josephus claimed direct descendancy from the Hasmoneans.

In his youth Josephus successively joined and studied with the three major Jewish sects of that period, the Pharisees, Sadducees, and Essenes. Disillusioned with the aforementioned groups, Josephus then joined Bannus, a hermit who lived in the wilderness. The term Bannus connotes "baptist" or "hermabaptist," and as a disciple of Bannus, Josephus apparently familiarized himself with the wilderness movements of which John "the Baptist" and Jesus were a part. Still unsatisfied, Josephus returned to mainstream Pharisaic Judaism.

In A.D. 63–64 he visited Rome and witnessed the grandeur and power of the Empire, an occasion which was to influence profoundly his reaction to future events. Two short years after Josephus' return from Rome, the Jewish people rose in revolt in an attempt to throw off the yoke of Roman rule and again to establish the ideal of their theocratic state on the historical plane. Josephus was forced to decide whether to side with the revolutionaries or with the Romans and their Jewish collaborators.

Of Josephus' role in the Jewish Revolt of A.D. 66, we have a very unclear picture. In his earliest work, *The Jewish War*, Josephus portrays himself as a commander of the revolutionary forces in Galilee. In *Jewish Antiquities*, "Josephus was commissioned to go to Galilee not to organize the defense against the Romans, but . . . on a pacific mission to disarm the rebels and to endeavor to keep the peace" (Solomon Zeitlin, *Josephus on Jesus*, Philadelphia: The Dropsie College for Hebrew and Cognate Learning, 1931, p. 6). Robert Eisler says of Josephus that "his position was somewhere between that of an army chaplain and an army clerk" (*The Messiah Jesus and John the Baptist*, New York: Lincoln Macveagh, The Dial Press, 1931, p. 25). *Jewish Antiquities* was published in A.D. 93 during the reign of Domitian when the situation in Rome had changed and Josephus had fallen out of favor with the imperial family—hence his account of his part in the revolution was quite different.

That Josephus served as a representative of the revolutionary government in Galilee at the beginning of the Revolt in A.D. 66 seems certain. During that struggle he defected to the Romans when it seemed apparent to him that the Jews could not win, and after the Fall of Jerusalem in A.D. 70, the Emperor Vespasian granted him an annual pension sufficient to support him in comfort, in order that he might write a history of the war of the Jewish people against Rome. He was well qualified to write the account since he was an eyewitness and active participant in many of the events described. In addition, Josephus availed himself of other histories of the period and of the official archives of the Empire—which unfortunately have not otherwise survived.

However, Josephus' freedom of expression was severely compromised by the fact of his imperial patronage: he had been personally befriended by both Emperor Vespasian and his son, Emperor Titus. He had been allowed to go to Rome when other Jews had been executed for their sedition. He had been granted the privileges of Roman citizenship and he had even been given the emperor's family name "Flavius" as a special tribute. It was difficult, therefore, for Josephus to write *The Jewish War* (published between A.D. 75 and 79) without including a great deal of praise for the Flavian dynasty. In fact, at one point in his histories, Josephus argues that Vespasian was the Messiah, the ruler of all the world, whom the prophets had foretold (*War* VI. 312–315). Needless to say, his argument was unconvincing to most Jews.

It is also true, however, that Josephus was the only Jew who was in a position after the Fall of Jerusalem to defend the Jewish people in the eyes of Rome. By claiming that the rebel forces who were responsible for the Jewish war were not "true" Jews—that they acted against their religion and in disobedience to the will of God—he helped to salvage the image of "faithful" Jews for his Gentile readers, especially the Roman officials. Hence Josephus served as an apologist for the Jews as well as a laudit for the Romans.

Third, it should be recognized that religious Jews were accustomed to read military defeat as "judgment"—as in the case of the Babylonian captivity. Therefore it was not out of character for Josephus to conclude, after the disastrous effect of the Revolt, that the rebels had not been pleasing in the eyes of God. After all, the Temple had been destroyed, Jerusalem had fallen, and tens of thousands of Jews had been killed or exiled. Was that not sufficient evidence that the war had not been fought with God's favor?

Finally, the intended purpose for his history of the Revolt, and the reason for his imperial support, was to provide an account of the unsuccessful Jewish Revolt which would be a lesson to Jews throughout the Empire—and any other potential revolutionaries as well—that revolt against the Empire was futile. In his introduction, Josephus makes abundantly clear his aim to discourage any further revolts against the Empire. (Cf. *War* III. 108; II. 345 ff.; and Thackeray, *op. cit.*, p. xi.) Zeitlin, *op. cit.*, pp. 15 f., writes, "he was working in the propaganda department of the government, for the purpose of discouraging revolt and of extolling the Flavian family."

The complexities of Josephus' motives, his being a Jew concerned for the preservation of his own people while writing for the Roman emperor and describing the catastrophic defeat of the Jewish people by the imperial legions, makes it very difficult to differentiate historical fact from fancy. Undoubtedly Josephus is guilty of some conscious fabrication and other historical inaccuracies in his works. (Cf. W. R. Farmer's introduction to *The Great Jewish War*, New York: Harper & Brothers, 1960.) Josephus was not above changing the text or essence of a speech or his description of an event if the situation at the time of its writing indicated the necessity for doing so. The translator of the Penguin Classics edition (Baltimore: 1967) of *The Jewish War*, G. A. Williamson, writes of a speech attributed to Herod: "Josephus, dissatisfied with this effort of composition, in *Antiquities* provides Herod with a different speech" (Baltimore: Penguin Books, 1967, p. 72 [1]).

In light of the cross purposes of his histories, therefore, it is not surprising that Josephus described the Zealots as sinners who were infected by a mad seditiousness and that he blamed them for the disastrous fate of the Jews. Even so, there is a thread of respect for the heroism of these freedom fighters throughout Josephus' account in *The Jewish War,* and in his later major work, *Jewish Antiquities.* In the latter he was apparently freer to express pro-Jewish sentiment, and he described the Zealots as one of four "philosophic sects" of Judaism, mentioning that they held all things in common with the Pharisees, except that they had an inviolable attachment to liberty, and taught that God was to be their only ruler and Lord (*Ant.* XVIII. 23). This distinguishing characteristic attributed to the Zealots is precisely that which served as the motivation for the Maccabees' victorious revolt against the Seleucids.

In spite of Josephus' contradictory portrayal of them, the Zealots clearly considered themselves to be, and were undoubtedly regarded by their contemporaries as in direct continuity with the tradition of Jewish nationalism founded by the Maccabees, and therefore within the line of the most pious and righteous of Jews. We would agree with W. R. Farmer, author of a most interesting book about the close relationship between the Maccabees and the Zealots, that Josephus had three basic reasons for obscuring the fact of the continuity between the Maccabees and Zealots: ". . . *politically,* as a pro-Roman Jewish apologist, while he could praise the Maccabees who had been allies of Rome, he had to blame those Jews [the Zealots] who in his day were the enemies of Rome; *theologically,* he could glorify the Maccabees as the saviours of Israel, but the victory of Rome over the Jews proved in his view that the Jewish leaders [or Zealots] were rebels against the will of God; *personally,* Josephus was linked by descent to the royal house of the Hasmoneans; naturally proud of the great achievements of his famous ancestors, he could hardly admit that his most bitter enemies [the Zealots] were their true spiritual heirs" (*op. cit.,* p. 126).

9. The Jews were resentful of Herod from the outset of his reign. He was looked upon as a foreigner, for he was a product of the forced circumcision of the Idumaeans ordered by John Hyrcanus, the last Maccabean ruler before the establishment of the Hasmonean dynasty. Moreover, it was widely known that while serving as governor of Galilee during Hyrcanus II's rule, Herod had suppressed the revolt of a "brigand chief" from Galilee named Hezekiah. After executing Hezekiah Herod had been forced to appear before the Sanhedrin, the Jewish high court of Law, to answer for his action because the victim was held in such high repute.

Silver, *op. cit.,* p. 14 (39), says: "Geiger suggests that the Hezekiah here mentioned is identical with Hezekiah the Galilean, who was killed by Herod and whose son Judah [or Judas] was the founder of the party of the Zealots. Judah's son Menahem played an important role in the revolt of [A.D.] 66. This family may have claimed Davidic descent and entertained

Messianic ambitions." Rabbinic sources attribute a Messianic significance to Hezekiah, e.g. *Sanhedrin* 99a, 94a.

The Jews' fears that Herod would undermine their traditions were not unfounded. In order to bring stability to his kingdom and to guarantee peace, Herod increased the foreign population of Israel by hiring foreign mercenaries for his security force and by founding large Greek cities—in particular, Sebaste and Caesarea. Herod's court resembled the courts of the Hellenistic kings of the east in every regard and many of his principal officers were of Greek origin. Moreover, visitors from various parts of the Greco-Roman world played important roles in the internal relations of the royal house from time to time, and Herod submitted to the ideology of the Roman Empire, worshiping Caesar and building temples in his honor outside of the centers of Jewish population. Josephus writes, "In short, one can mention no suitable spot within his realm, which he left destitute of some mark of homage to Caesar. And then, after filling his own territory with temples, he let the memorials of his esteem overflow into the province and erected in numerous cities monuments to Caesar" (*War* I. 407).

In spite of all his offenses, however, Herod managed to keep peace throughout Israel by ruling with an iron glove and by making carefully timed concessions upon occasion (*The Jews in Their Land,* ed. by David Ben-Gurion, London: Aldus Books, 1966, p. 146). Herod feared for his throne for several reasons. Not only did his Jewish subjects reject his rule and pose the threat of revolt, but Cleopatra continued to entice Marc Antony to depose Herod and return Palestine to Ptolemaic, or Egyptian, control. Herod sought to preserve internal security, therefore, by a massive military presence and an elaborate system of spies which kept him well informed of any attempts to foment rebellion in his court or among the populace. He also sought to quell the religious fervor of his Jewish subjects and to win their favor by such grandiose projects as constructing an aqueduct to bring water to Jerusalem and rebuilding and refurnishing the Jerusalem Temple on an unprecedented scale. The grandeur and beauty of the Second—or Herodian, as it came to be known throughout the Empire —Temple were essentially the result of his improvements.

Herod transformed Jerusalem into one of the most splendid capitals of the east by erecting a royal palace, by building a theater, a hippodrome, and an amphitheater, and by adding three great towers to the Upper City. He built a fortress overlooking the Temple to house the Roman garrison and named it Antonia after his Roman patron. As protection against any external attempts to remove him from the throne, Herod undertook the construction of tremendous new forts and strengthened the fortification of the cities throughout his kingdom. He built Caesarea and Sebaste on the ancient sites of Strato's tower and Samaria, and the fortresses of Herodium where he was to be buried, Alexandrium on the plains of Jericho, and Machaerus where John the Baptist was later executed.

In case either internal or external threats materialized, Herod constructed a refuge for his royal court and personal guard at Masada, a desert fortress on the southwest shore of the Dead Sea. Masada was so huge and impregnable that Herod, with his entire entourage of servants and personal guards, expected to be able to withstand a fifteen-year siege of the desert fortress without needing to leave its walls!

And finally, despite the hatred with which the Jews regarded him, Herod softened the impact of Roman domination for nearly four decades, serving as a buffer between the seething Jewish population and direct imperial rule. For example, during Herodian rule the Jews paid taxes to what was nominally a Jewish king and much of the tax revenue went to projects of which the Jews approved, such as remodeling the Temple. S. G. F. Brandon writes that the Jews "had much reason to hate Herod; but at least he had professed the Jewish faith, had generally respected their religious scruples, and had rebuilt their Temple on a most magnificent scale: moreover, his long reign had given them an unusual period of peace and economic prosperity . . . the hated Idumaean had long shielded the Jews from the brute reality of Roman power" (*Jesus and the Zealots,* p. 27).

10. Though the Gospel of Matthew records the slaughter of all male children under two years of age in 4 B.C. at the time of Jesus' birth, there is no historical evidence to corroborate that report. It would appear that the Gospel writer, in his meticulous effort to show that every prophecy about the Messiah had been fulfilled in Jesus' birth and life and death, included this story to fulfill a passage of scripture which was not even prophetic in nature. (Cf. Mt. 2:16–18.) The birth narrative of Matthew also suggests that Jesus was a second Moses by employing the literary motif of the flight to Egypt (cf. W. D. Davies, *The Setting of the Sermon on the Mount,* Cambridge: Cambridge University Press, 1964, pp. 78 ff.), thus strengthening the argument (see Chapters 8, 9, and 13 below) that Jesus fulfilled the Messianic expectation of Deuteronomy 18:15–18. It appears that the threatened slaughter of babies served as an excuse for Matthew to have Joseph and Mary take Jesus into Egypt. As S. G. F. Brandon points out, if Matthew was writing his Gospel in Alexandria, such a journey would have provided his readers with a special point of identity with this Messianic figure, who, like Moses, had begun his life in Egypt (*op. cit.,* pp. 296–300).

Had such a wanton slaughter of innocent children actually occurred it would surely have been included by Josephus in his histories which chronicle all the atrocities and offenses committed by the various rulers of the Jewish peoples, but we find no such mention in Josephus or in any other histories of the period. Cf. *The Interpreter's Bible,* Vol. VII, p. 260.

11. *Ant.* XVII. 149 ff. and *War* I. 648–55.

12. Judas, according to Josephus, aspired to royalty (*Ant.* XVII. 272). Two of Judas' sons were executed by Tiberius Alexander (A.D. 46–48) and a third named Menahem was to play a predominant role in the Great Revolt some sixty years later (cf. *War* II. 433). Eleazar, of whom we will hear more when we discuss the Zealots' suicidal defense of the Herodian fortress

Masada at the end of the Revolt, was also a direct descendant of Judas. The position of influence in the movement held by Judas and his sons indicates a dynastic succession of Zealot leadership and a continuity of the movement through the time of Jesus' life. Scholars have suggested that the succession of James, brother of Jesus, to control of the primitive Christian Jewish movement, and the succession of thirteen relatives of Jesus to the head of the Christian community in Jerusalem until A.D. 135, may have been patterned after the "family caliphate" of the Zealots.

In fact, one of the most striking similarities between the organization of the early Christian movement and that of the Zealots is the dynastic succession of their leadership. This principle of dynastic succession has been described as a "family caliphate" of the order seen later in Islam. Cf. H.-J. Schoeps, *Jewish Christianity,* Philadelphia: Fortress Press, 1969, p. 32, who also remarks that the family of Jesus continued to occupy a prominent position in the Ebionite [Jewish Christian] community because of their close relationship to "the Lord." That the family of Jesus was considered closest to the Messianic throne is attested by Hegesippus in Eusebius' *The History of the Church* (tr. by G. A. Williamson, Baltimore: Penguin Classics edition, 1965), III. 32. 5–6. Cf. also Jean Daniélou, "Christianity as a Jewish Sect," in *The Crucible of Christianity,* Arnold Toynbee, ed., London: Thames & Hudson, 1969, p. 276: "It would seem to be very much in line with Semitic customs that Jesus' family should have assumed this position in the Judaeo-Christian community. Stauffer calls it 'the Caliphate.' This dynasticism is likewise to be found in the Zealot movement, and later in Islam."

13. See note 8 above.

14. *Ant.* XVII. 295; *War* II. 75.

15. The census in A.D. 6 marked the time when the provinces of Judea and Samaria were first brought under the rule of the Roman procurator. Herod's son Archelaus was nominally ruler of the areas as "ethnarch" from the death of Herod until the full imposition of Roman control in A.D. 6. The Romans eventually removed Archelaus after a decade of instability and continuing Jewish insurrection.

16. In the Lukan birth narrative, the date of Jesus' birth is associated with this census. The two reference points for situating the time of Jesus' birth in the history of the period are that he was born during the reign of Herod (37 to 4 B.C.), and that he was born at the time of census of Quirinius (A.D. 6). The majority of commentators resolve the discrepancy of ten years by opting for the earlier point of reference and place Jesus' birth sometime during the reign of Herod. Most commonly the birth of Jesus is dated four years *Before Christ,* a circumstance created by an error in calculation made by Dionysius Exiquus in the sixth century when the present calendar was fixed. Cf. "The Life and Ministry of Jesus," *The Interpreter's Bible,* Vol. VII, p. 115, where Vincent Taylor suggests it may have been as early as 8 B.C.

17. Brandon, *op. cit.*, p. 53 says: "In protesting against Israel's subjection in A.D. 6, Judas was in the true line of succession to the prophets of old and to the Maccabees"; Farmer, *op. cit.*, p. 14, agrees: "The distinctive features of the sect [the Zealots], said to have originated with Judas of Galilee, are precisely those for which the Maccabees were remembered, as the Maccabean literature, and even Josephus himself, indicates." Cf. also *op. cit.*, pp. 24–33, 67 (52).

18. The High Priest Joazar's siding with the Romans raised another issue in the struggle—that of the appointment of the High Priest. One of the greatest sources of humiliation and offense for the Jews was the fact that following Herod's death, the Romans had assumed the prerogative of appointing the High Priest. The High Priest represented the People of Israel before God on their most solemn and sacred occasions. It was only the High Priest who was permitted to enter the Holy of Holies, the innermost part of the sanctuary of the Temple, and he entered it only one day a year to offer prayers on behalf of the People and to speak the name of God (in a whisper), an act which also was unique on the Day of Atonement (Yom Kippur). For the Chosen People to be represented on such holy days by a priest appointed by pagan rulers, was a great and unending offense to the Jews.

As though to add to the insult, the Romans later took possession of the ceremonial robes of the High Priest so that he could only appear in the appropriate garb on the holy days by appealing to the Romans for permission to use the garments which were rightfully his by virtue of his office, further emphasizing the Jews' subservience to Rome (Brandon, *op. cit.*, pp. 67, 101). Joazar's sanctioning the tribute called attention to this new policy, for it seemed that the High Priest had become a lackey for the Romans. Later the appointment of the High Priest was returned to Agrippa, but the appointment still went to men who "toed the Roman line" (*op. cit.*, pp. 113–14).

19. Cf. Mt. 22:15–22; Mk. 12:13–17; Lk. 20:20–26.

20. Cf. I Macc. 2:23–27.

21. Brandon, *The Trial of Jesus of Nazareth*, p. 34: "Zealotism, true to the prophetic tradition, had both a social and political aspect, and hence was regarded by the Roman authorities and the Jewish aristocracy as doubly subversive of the established order."

22. Brandon, *Jesus and the Zealots*, pp. 39–41, 109–11.

23. Jewish nationalism was not a passive waiting for divine deliverance, even though their actions were inspired by the expectation of supernatural aid. Even in the "holy war" the *human agent* was not forgotten. To the contrary, human involvement was critical. ". . . the Jewish nationalists in the Roman period would have derived comfort and hope . . . from the story of the miraculous defeat of Sennacherib [by the direct intervention of God]. However, in contrast to the story of Sennacherib's defeat, the stories from the Seleucid period probably carried a very activistic moral;

for in the Maccabean victories God had assisted the Jews who were *zealously active in defense* of his interests" (Farmer, *op. cit.,* p. 109. Italics ours). The holy war was a two part drama to be climaxed by the arrival of legions of angels from heaven. But the first action depended on man: ". . . the wonderful victories of the Maccabees over the armies of the Seleucid empire provided an unambiguous historical affirmation and validation of the theological tenet that if those Jews who were zealous for the Torah and the temple would take up the sword and strike a blow for Yahweh, he would give them the victory—no matter what the odds against them" (*op. cit.,* pp. 104 f.).

24. An inscription discovered at Caesarea Maritime in 1961 is the first archaeological evidence of Pilate's term of office in Judea. The inscription indicates Pilate held the office and title of "prefect" (*praefectus*) rather than "procurator." Cf. Chapter 12 below, and David Flusser's *Jesus,* New York: Herder and Herder, 1969, p. 6.

25. Cf. Mt. 27:2, 11–26; Mk. 15:1–15; Lk. 23:1–7, 13–25; and Jn. 18:28–40; 19:1–16.

26. Cf. Chapter 12, pp. 215 ff., below, on the character of Pilate.

27. *Ant.* XVIII. 55–59; *War* II. 169–71.

28. Brandon, *op. cit.,* pp. 68–75.

29. *Ibid.,* pp. 75 f.

30. Cf. accounts of atrocities committed against other Messianic pretenders during the Roman period which follow in this chapter.

31. John Hyrcanus of the Hasmonean rule had destroyed the first Samaritan temple. The Taheb-Restorer "is just as dim and vague as the whole eschatology of the Samaritans, with the exception of one thing. The Samaritans rest their expectation of the advent of the Restorer on the promise given in their tenth commandment [the Samaritans counted the Jews' commandments as nine and added one more] and on Deut. XVIII. 15 and 18: 'The Lord thy God will raise up unto thee a prophet from the midst of thee, of thy brethren, like unto me; unto him ye shall hearken,' and 'I will raise them up a prophet from among their brethren, like unto thee; and I will put my words in his mouth, and he shall speak unto them all that I shall command him' [KJV]. They therefore interpret this promise to mean that out of the tribe of Levi, i.e. Moses' brethren, a prophet will arise like unto Moses; and as no one can be like unto Moses in all his perfection, they hold that perhaps Moses himself will come to life again and bring them the promised happiness. He will carry the rod of Moses in his hand, and perform all those signs aforementioned, and as further proof that he is the true Restorer, he will discover the hidden vessels of the Temple" (Moses Gaster, *The Samaritans,* London: Oxford University Press, 1925, pp. 90–91). Cf. also J. Bowman, "Early Samaritan Eschatology," *Journal of Jewish Studies,* Vol. 6, No. 2, 1956, pp. 63, 67.

32. *Ant.* XVIII. 85–89. See also Brandon, *op. cit.,* p. 80.

33. Farmer, *op. cit.*, pp. 41, 42, 125–58.

34. *Ant.* XX. 97–99; Acts 5:36.

35. *Ant.* XX. 169–72; *War* II. 261–63. Cf. also Acts 21:38.

36. Cf. *Ant.* XX. 160, 168, 188; *War* II. 259–60, etc.; Brandon, *op. cit.*, pp. 108 ff.

37. Brandon, *op. cit.*, p. 112.

38. Brandon, *ibid.*, p. 141.

39. *War* II. 426–27.

40. Brandon, *op. cit.*, p. 132. See also *ibid.*, pp. 56, 199, 338; Brandon, *The Fall of Jerusalem and the Christian Church,* London: S.P.C.K., 1957, pp. 155–56; *The Jews in Their Land*, pp. 157–58: "The revolt against Rome was also a social revolution in many ways. The debt-ridden and landless lower classes together with refugees from the border areas provided the backbone of the rebel forces. There were also some extremist groups, ardent revolutionaries whose leaders (posing as kings or Messiahs) regarded the revolt as a war not only against the Romans but also against those members of the upper classes who had collaborated with the authorities. The extremists pursued these definite ends from the beginning of the revolt, setting fire to the archives of Jerusalem in order to destroy loan contracts, and using terrorist tactics against the leading representatives of the upper classes." Cf. also Eisler, *op. cit.*, p. 489; Joachim Jeremias, *Jerusalem in the Time of Jesus,* Philadelphia: Fortress Press, 1969, pp. 54–59; and F. C. Grant, *The Economic Background of the Gospels,* London: Oxford University Press, 1926, pp. 92–110.

41. *War* II. 538–55.

42. Kollek and Pearlman, *op. cit.*, pp. 128–30, 132.

43. *Op. cit.*, p. 111.

44. *War* II. 433. For the full story of the history of Masada and its excavation, see Yigael Yadin, *Masada,* New York: Random House, 1966.

45. (a) While the speech attributed to Eleazar is obviously Josephus' creation, it embodies many of the sentiments of the Zealots and witnesses to their devotion to God and their essentially religious motivation. The fact of Josephus' putting a long speech in the mouth of Eleazar should not be surprising or necessarily make the views it contains entirely suspect. Such a practice of supplying speeches for historical characters at appropriate times was common among historians of that period, and the speeches often reflect the actual situation: "These speeches [of Josephus], in accordance with the conventions of Hellenistic historiography, reflect, as accurately as is consonant with the clear expression of the true intent of the speaker, exactly what was said—or, if not what was actually said, then what appropriately could have been spoken under the circumstances. The literary purpose of the speeches is to bring out the true import of the events being described, and as such they can be expected to reflect not only the thoughts of the speaker but, if he is attempting to confute the views of others, to some degree the thoughts of his opponents as well. This

is exactly the kind of speeches we have at certain crucial points in the histories of Josephus. Like the great Thucydides, who had given classical expression to this form of historiography, Josephus was an eyewitness of many of the events he describes. Therefore, in dealing with those speeches which he places in the mouths of personages active in the great war with Rome we are handling sources of the greatest historical significance. Their importance—if not their reliability and literary merit—is quite comparable to the famous speeches of Thucydides preserved in his celebrated history of the Peloponnesian War" (Farmer, *op. cit.*, p. 100; also pp. 69–70). Cf. Brandon, *Jesus and the Zealots,* pp. 57–58, 143–44.

(b) For other examples of suicide during the Zealot activism against Rome, see *Ant.* XIV. 429–30; *War* II. 49; III. 331; 355 ff.; VI. 280. Of religious self-destruction during the Maccabean Revolt against the Seleucids, see II Macc. 14:37–46. Cf. Farmer, *op. cit.*, pp. 69–70.

CHAPTER 2

Apocalyptic Nationalism

1. Farmer, *op. cit.*, p. 49.
2. I Macc. 1:41–63; II Macc. 6:18; Philo *In Flaccum; War* II. 150–53.
3. *Legatio ad Gaium* 31.
4. *Against Apion* II. 271–72. Cf. also I Macc. 2:23–25, 44, 48; 3:5–6, 8, 20, 21; II Macc. 2:22; 8:21.
5. *Ant.* XIV. 429–30; *War* II. 49; III. 331; VI. 280.
6. Farmer, *op. cit.*, p. 70; *The Jews in Their Land*, pp. 157 ff.
7. *Ant.* XIII. 257–58, 318–19; *Life* 112–13.
8. I Macc. 2:45–46.
9. *Ant.* XIV. 58–63; *War* I. 145–47; II. 623–34; IV. 97–105; *Life* 155–64; I Macc. 1:39; 2:29–38.
10. Farmer, *op. cit.*, pp. 76–77; *The Jews in Their Land*, pp. 132 f.
11. Farmer, *op. cit.*, p. 77.
12. *Ibid.*, p. 85.
13. *Ibid.*, p. 107.
14. *Ibid.*, pp. 114, 181; *The Jews in Their Land*, p. 157. I Macc. 7:41–42; II Macc. 15:22–24; Man. of Disc. 2:5a–10.
15. Farmer, *op. cit.*, p. 120: "Israel could still exist as a covenant community by interpreting the fall of the temple as the judgment of God upon the sins of his people. This judgment was not to be understood as a repudiation of his people by Yahweh. The covenant God had not chosen Israel for the sake of the temple, but the temple for the sake of Israel. God allows calamity to fall upon the nation not that it may be destroyed but that it may be chastened. The mercy of God is never completely withdrawn from his people. God may punish, but he never abandons Israel. That which has been destroyed will be rebuilt in God's due time. The temple which has been forsaken by God in his wrath will be restored in all its glory when He becomes reconciled . . . perhaps we ought [also] to consider the possibility that they were inspired by some kind of Messianic hope in which Messianic deliverance was associated with the wilderness."
16. See note 14 above. Cf. Is. 10:20–23; 11:11, 16; Mic. 2:12.
17. I Macc. 2:29–30; Ps. of Sol. 17:19.

18. Farmer, *op. cit.*, p. 118. Cf. *Ant.* XX. 97–99; 168; and *War* II. 258–60.

19. *Ant.* XVIII. 116–19; John 6:14–15. Cf. also Farmer, *op cit.*, pp. 117–18, and Hugh Montefiore, "Revolt in the Desert? (Mk. 6:30 ff.)," *New Testament Studies*, 8, 1961–62, pp. 135–41.

20. D. S. Russell, *The Method and Message of Jewish Apocalyptic*, Philadelphia: Westminster Press, 1964, p. 36.

21. See Farmer, *op. cit.*, pp. 97 ff., 109, 115, 180, 181 ff., 194.

22. *Ibid.*, pp. 191–94.

23. Russell, *op. cit.*, pp. 17 f.

24. *Ibid.*, p. 263.

25. Cf. Dan. 12:1 and Jub. 23:13 ff.

26. Russell, *op. cit.*, pp. 273 ff.

27. *Ibid.*, p. 276.

28. Cf. II Bar. 4:2–6.

29. *Ibid.*, pp. 205 ff.

30. *Ibid.*, pp. 254 ff.

31. *Ibid.*, pp. 240 ff.

32. *Ibid.*, pp. 285 ff.

33. Jub. 31:13–15; Test. of Levi 8:11–14.

34. Ps. of Sol. 17:23–51; II Sam. 7; Is. 9:6 f.; 11:1 ff.; Jer. 23:5 ff.; Zech. 9:9; Mic. 5:2. Cf. Russell, *op. cit.*, pp. 306 f.

35. Cf. Man. of Disc. 9:11; Dam. Doc. 12:23; 13:10; 14:19.

36. Cf. Dan. 7:13.

37. Russell, *op. cit.*, p. 327.

38. *Ibid.*, p. 331.

39. There are some relationships between the Saving (Suffering) Servant idea of Deutero-Isaiah, which is also a corporate image, and the Messianic figures, however. Apparently, both the Qumran Covenanters and Jesus sought to interpret their Messianic roles by a kind of unified concept from Deutero-Isaiah and Daniel. Cf. Russell, *op. cit.*, p. 338.

40. *Ibid.*, p. 359.

41. I Enoch 27:1.

42. *Ibid.*, p. 365. Kollek and Pearlman, *op. cit.*, p. 67.

43. Ploger, *op. cit.*, pp. 18–19, explains the development of the notion of two resurrections as arising out of the conflict of Judaism and Hellenism. Since the Jews believed all of God's Chosen People would be raised from the dead, according to the prophets, the idea developed of two resurrections—one to eternal life and one to eternal shame. The first resurrection was for those loyal to the Torah, and the second for the Hellenizers.

44. Russell, *op. cit.*, p. 372.

45. *Ibid.*, pp. 16, 48 ff.; Ploger, *op. cit.*, p. 10. See also W. H. C. Frend, *Martyrdom and Persecution in the Early Church*, New York: New York University Press, 1967, p. 38, who writes of the Book of Daniel: "In this vision, one finds for the first time militant apocalypticism accompanying

the struggle of adherents of a revolutionary creed opposed to a world empire . . . It was an appeal too, directed to the common people to whom the overthrow of the mighty, especially if they appeared to be traitors as well, was welcome indeed."

46. Cf. Rev. 21:27 where the same act is referred to again, if only indirectly. The Book of Revelation is a Christian apocalyptic writing of the second century A.D.

47. Russell, *op. cit.*, p. 16.

48. Farmer, *op. cit.*, pp. 191–92.

CHAPTER 3

The Dead Sea Scrolls Community

1. Frank Moore Cross, Jr., *The Ancient Library of Qumran*, Garden City, N.Y.: Doubleday & Company, Inc., 1961, pp. 12 ff. Cf. n. 2 below *re* Rengstorf who holds the books belonged to the Temple Library and were hid near Qumran during the Great Revolt in order to preserve them.

2. Cf., for example, Matthew Black, *The Scrolls and Christian Origins*, New York: Thomas Nelson and Sons Ltd., 1961, pp. 7 ff.; Millar Burrows, *The Dead Sea Scrolls*, New York: The Viking Press, 1955, p. 298; Theodor H. Gaster, *The Dead Sea Scriptures in English*, Garden City, N.Y.: Doubleday & Company, Inc., Anchor Books, 1964, p. 3; A. Dupont-Sommer, *The Essene Writings from Qumran*, Oxford: Basil Blackwell, 1961, pp. 39 ff.; F. M. Cross, *op. cit.*, p. 51; and H. H. Rowley, "The History of the Qumran Sect" in the *Bulletin of the John Rylands Library*, Vol. 49, No. 1, Autumn 1966, pp. 207 f. One Dead Sea Scrolls scholar, K. H. Rengstorf, *Hirbet Qumran and the Problem of the Library of the Dead Sea Caves*, Leiden: E. J. Brill, 1963, maintains that the Dead Sea Scrolls were part of the Temple Library and thus can tell us nothing about the people who lived at Qumran.

3. Cecil Roth, *The Dead Sea Scrolls: A New Historical Approach*, pp. 63 ff., esp. p. 69; G. R. Driver, *The Judaean Scrolls*, Oxford: Basil Blackwell, 1965, pp. 237–51.

4. Cf. F. F. Bruce, *Second Thoughts on the Dead Sea Scrolls*, London: The Paternoster Press, 1966, p. 135, who expresses the same conviction in this regard.

5. See Driver, *op. cit.*, pp. 100 ff.

6. See, for example, F. M. Cross, *op. cit.*, p. 53; Rowley, *op. cit.*, p. 232; Driver, *op. cit.*, pp. 6 f.; etc.

7. Cf. F. M. Cross, *op. cit.*, pp. 78 and 203; Black, *op. cit.*, p. 18; Farmer, *op. cit.*, p. 194.

8. F. M. Cross, *op. cit.*, pp. 163 ff. See also John M. Allegro, *The Dead Sea Scrolls*, Baltimore: Penguin Books, 1966, pp. 59 and 134; and Bruce, *op. cit.*, pp. 41 ff.

9. Allegro, *op. cit.*, p. 59; Driver, *op. cit.*, p. 442.

10. F. M. Cross, *op. cit.*, p. 165.

11. See Chapter 2, p. 29 above.

12. F. M. Cross, *op. cit.*, p. 169.

13. *Loc. cit.* Cf. also Allegro, *op. cit.*, pp. 41 f.

14. F. M. Cross, *loc. cit.* Cf. also Chaim Rabin, "The Dead Sea Scrolls and the History of the O. T. Text," *Journal of Theological Studies,* N.S., Vol. VI. Pt. 2, October 1955, pp. 174–82.

15. *Op. cit.*, p. 203. Cf. Russell, *op. cit.*, Ch. I, pp. 15 ff.

16. Cf. F. M. Cross, *op. cit.*, p. 61 (16); Black, *op cit.*, p. 18; Farmer, *op. cit.*, p. 194; Russell, *op. cit.*, p. 17.

17. F. M. Cross, *op cit.*, p. 200, and postscript, pp. 239 ff.; Russell, *op. cit.*, p. 34.

18. See F. M. Cross, *op. cit.*, pp. 58, 59, and Ch. III, pp. 109 ff.; Gaster, *op. cit.*, p. 3; Driver, *op. cit.*, pp. 581, 584 ff. believes that the Scrolls were approximately contemporary with the New Testament, that is, the first century A.D.; Roth, *The Dead Sea Scrolls,* pp. 1–4, dates them between 200 B.C. and A.D. 75.

19. Cf. their apparent vacillation during the reign of Alcimus as High Priest: I Macc. 7:8–18. Cf. F. M. Cross, *op. cit.*, pp. 131 f.

20. *Ibid.*, pp. 132 ff.; Driver, *op. cit.*, pp. 80 ff.; Edmund F. Sutcliffe, S.J., *The Monks of Qumran,* London: Burns & Oates, 1960, p. 41; etc.

21. Cf. Man. of Disc. 8:1 to 9:26; Dam. Doc. 1, 2.

22. See Sutcliffe, *op. cit.*, p. 25, and n. 18 above.

23. *War* I. 370–72; *Ant.* XV. 121 ff.

24. F. M. Cross, *op. cit.*, pp. 58–61.

25. *Ibid.*, p. 26 and 64 (20).

26. John M. Allegro, *Qumran Cave 4: I* (*4Q158–4Q186*), London: Oxford University Press, 1968.

27. During the early years of discussion about the Dead Sea Scrolls a great deal of controversy centered around the Teacher of Righteousness because some scholars saw him as a kind of prototype for Jesus. Because of certain similarities between the two—both were great teachers on whose interpretation of the Law new communities were formed which claimed to represent the faithful remnant of Israel; both were highly venerated by their followers; both were prophets; both were persecuted by the religious leaders of their day—at least one scholar, Dr. J. L. Teicher, went so far as to identify them as one and the same person. See Dupont-Sommer, *op. cit.*, pp. 396 f. Others suggested that the similarities between the two are so striking that perhaps the Teacher of Righteousness served as a model either for Jesus himself or for his disciples as they wrote up the story of Jesus' life. Cf. A. Dupont-Sommer, *The Dead Sea Scrolls,* Oxford: Basil Blackwell, 1956, pp. 99 f. We tend to feel, with Millar Burrows, *op. cit.*, p. 185, that as little is known about the Teacher of Righteousness as about Jesus. In fact, less. We know nothing, for example, about the Teacher's life or death, whereas we know enough about Jesus to establish without question the period in which he lived, where he came from,

who his disciples were, and the cause and mode of his execution. In the Teacher's case, our information is not only less specific, but, as Jean Carmignac, *Christ and the Teacher of Righteousness*, Baltimore: Helicon Press, 1962, pp. 69 f., says, even what we have is extremely tenuous information. Gaster has suggested, *op. cit.*, pp. 6, 30 f., that the references in the Scrolls may not even be to a specific person, but rather to an office in the community. For scholarly reflections and opinions on who the Teacher of Righteousness was and what similarities and differences there are between him and Jesus, see, for example, Dupont-Sommer, *op. cit.*, pp. 99 f.; F. F. Bruce, *The Teacher of Righteousness in the Qumran Texts*, London: The Tyndale Press, 1957; Carmignac, *op. cit.*, esp. Chs. II and III; Sutcliffe, *op. cit.*, pp. 58 ff.; and F. M. Cross, *op. cit.*, pp. 156 ff.

28. F. M. Cross, *op. cit.*, p. 112; Burrows, *op. cit.*, p. 268; Roth, *op. cit.*, p. 64.

29. Cf., for example, Is. 50 ff.

30. F. M. Cross, *op. cit.*, p. 114; Bruce, *op cit.*, pp. 39 ff.; Burrows, *op. cit.*, p. 223.

31. See especially A. R. C. Leaney, *The Rule of Qumran and Its Meaning*, London: SCM Press Ltd., 1966, pp. 37 ff.

32. See, e.g., Leaney, *op. cit.*, p. 41.

33. See, e.g., Dupont-Sommer, *The Essene Writings from Qumran*, pp. 164 ff.

34. Man. of Disc. 4:2–8.

35. Man. of Disc. 4:15–26.

36. *Loc. cit.* See also Leaney, *op. cit.*, p. 43.

37. Man. of Disc. 4:6–8. Cf. F. M. Cross, *op. cit.*, p. 210 and Leaney, *op. cit.*, p. 152.

38. Man. of Disc. 2:25b to 3:12.

39. Cf. Leaney, *op. cit.*, pp. 154–61; Driver, *op. cit.*, pp. 461, 581 ff. Cf. also Jesus in this regard, Chapter 8 below.

40. See Leaney, *op. cit.*, pp. 56–75, esp. pp. 63–75.

41. Man. of Disc. 11:1–8.

42. I En. 6–11.

43. I En. 8:3, 4.

44. I En. 10:4–7.

45. I En. 6–16. Cf. Mt. 8:29; 12:24–28, 43–45; 25:41; Lk. 11:14–26. The conviction that Jesus had "descended into hell (sheol)" to free the spirits in bondage there is based on this story from I Enoch. One of the acts of the Messiah in the last days was to set the fallen angels free so they could be restored to their former "heavenly" state. Because Jesus was believed to be the Messiah, it was natural that he also should have been believed to have "descended into hell" as I Peter 3:19, II Peter 2:4 ff., and Eph. 4:9 indicate. That belief, which was written into the creeds of the Church, puzzled Christians for years who did not have access to the Enochian

literature and who believed it meant Jesus had descended into the hell of torment and fire. I Enoch makes it clear it was Sheol Jesus would have entered, and for a specific purpose.

46. *War* II. 138–42 says that Essenes will not reveal their secrets to outsiders even on pain of death. Cf. Man. of Disc. 8:11a–12; 10:24b–26. Cf. also Mt. 7:6; and II Cor. 6:14–18.

47. It seems likely to us, however, that we have the "secrets" in the apocalyptic writings. What is lacking is for them to be "revealed," or interpreted. This happens, according to the Qumran sect, only when the Spirit of Truth descends on one. Cf. Man. of Disc. 11:2b–9. Undoubtedly, interpretations were not written down, but passed on by word of mouth, since they could only be confirmed by personal revelation. Cf. Chapter 5, pp. 70–72 below.

CHAPTER 4

The Style of Life at Qumran

1. Man. of Disc. 8:13. Cf. also 5:13–20; 9:3–21, esp. 19–20; etc.
2. Cf. Man. of Disc. 1:16–20, and Testimonies.
3. Cf. Is. 10:20–27.
4. Man. of Disc. 8:5–10; 9:3–6; Rule of Cong. 1:1–3. Cf. also Man. of Disc. 2:8; 3:6, 8; 5:6; 11:14.
5. Man. of Disc. 8:1–10. Cf. the War Scroll.
6. Man. of Disc. 5:2; 9:14; Dam. Doc. 4:1; Blessings 3:22; etc.
7. Cf. Man. of Disc. 1:21; 2:2; 5; 11; 20.
8. Cf. War Scroll 4–5.
9. Jub. 6:34 ff. Cf. Dan. 7:25. See Leaney, *op. cit.,* pp. 80 ff. for a thorough discussion of the problem of the calendar. Also, Roth, *The Dead Sea Scrolls,* p. 58; Sutcliffe, *op. cit.,* p. 112.
10. Leaney, *op. cit.,* pp. 92 ff. and pp. 237 ff. Cf. also Bertil Gartner, *The Temple and the Community in Qumran and the New Testament,* Cambridge: Cambridge University Press, 1965, pp. 4 ff.
11. Yigael Yadin, "The Temple Scroll," *The Biblical Archaeologist,* Vol. XXX, No. 4, December 1967, p. 138.
12. Cf. Mt. 26:61; 27:40; Mk. 14:58; 15:29–30.
13. I En. 90:28 f.; Jub. 1:28 f. Cf. Yadin, *loc. cit.*
14. Gartner, *op. cit.,* p. 17. Gartner's book provides a very thorough discussion of the subject of the Temple and the attitudes toward it on the part of both the Qumran community and the early Church.
15. *Ibid.,* p. 20; F. M. Cross, *op. cit.,* p. 101. Cf. *Ant.* XVIII. 18–19 where Josephus describes the Essenes as sending offerings to the Temple, but "employing a different ritual of purification" and for that reason debarred from the common precinct, performing sacrifices by themselves.
16. F. M. Cross, *op. cit.,* pp. 69 f.; Gartner, *op. cit.,* p. 13. Cf. Man. of Disc. 9:3–6 where the system of sacrifice in the Temple is contrasted with the worship of praise offered by the Covenanters. See Leaney, *op. cit.,* pp. 224 f. Cf. also Sutcliffe, *op. cit.,* p. 110, who believes the bones are not evidence of sacrifice at Qumran.
17. *Ant.* XVIII. 18–19; Allegro, *The Dead Sea Scrolls,* p. 164.
18. *Op. cit.,* p. 95.

19. *Ibid.*, pp. 46 f. Cf. also p. 39: "This attitude is preserved in the prayer habit of the Jew, who associates morning-prayer not with sunrise but with the appearance of light, with the time 'from the rise of dawn to sunrise.' . . ."

20. *War* II. 128.

21. War Scroll 14:12–14; Hymns 12:4–11; Man. of Disc. 10. See also Leaney, *op. cit.*, pp. 179 and 239.

22. Leaney, *op. cit.*, p. 185.

23. F. M. Cross, *op. cit.*, p. 69.

24. Man. of Disc. 6:6b–8a; Leaney, *op. cit.*, pp. 184 f.

25. Leaney, *op. cit.*, pp. 239 ff.

26. *War* II. 124 f.; Dam. Doc. 7:6; 14:3, 8–9; Driver, *op. cit.*, p. 101; Leaney, *op. cit.*, p. 173.

27. Driver, *loc. cit.;* Marcel Simon, *Jewish Sects at the Time of Jesus,* Philadelphia: Fortress Press, 1967, p. 15. Cf. Brandon, *Jesus and the Zealots,* p. 111, who calls attention to Acts 21:38, which makes reference to four thousand Sicarii.

28. See n. 26 above.

29. F. M. Cross, *op. cit.*, p. 72 (33).

30. G. Vermes, *The Dead Sea Scrolls in English,* Baltimore: Penguin Books, 1966, pp. 16 f.

31. Man. of Disc. 5:7b–20a.

32. Dam. Doc. 6:11b to 7:9a; 10:11 to 11:18; 13:14–16.

33. Sutcliffe, *op. cit.*, pp. 31 f.

34. E.g., Dam. Doc. 7:6 f.; 11:11; 12:1; 14:14–16; 15:5 f.; 16:10.

35. For descriptions of the ruins of the Qumran community's head-quarters, see, for example, F. M. Cross, *op. cit.*, pp. 57, 65–69, and Sutcliffe, *op. cit.*, pp. 26 ff.

36. Man. of Disc. 1:11b–13; 5:1–7a; 6:17b–23; Dam. Doc. 9:10b–22; 13:15b–18; 14:8b–13; 15:14.

37. Cf. *War* II. 137.

38. If is interesting to note that I Macc. 3:58 gives Judas Maccabeus' venture the character of a holy war (Deut. 20:5–8), implying that all who wanted to follow him had to abandon all personal ties with normal life—including both wives and possessions. Cf. also to Jesus, Chapter 8 below. See Leaney, *op. cit.*, p. 164, who comments: "Jesus, with an urgency greater than that of Judas Maccabaeus, demanded in his time the same renunciation (Mark 10:21 pars.). In Qumran we see but one example of a well-established tradition."

39. Cf. Dam. Doc. 14:12b–17. It is interesting that though Jesus and his disciples had no possessions either, they are reported to have given money to the poor, as Mk. 14:5 and Jn. 13:29 suggest.

40. *War* II. 127.

41. *War* II. 124 ff. Cf. Driver, *op. cit.*, pp. 185 ff., who points out that Josephus describes the *sica* as the characteristic weapon adopted by the

extremist groups of the Jewish rebels c. A.D. 55–60 in their struggle against Rome, and that the author of the War Scroll, a Qumran document, describes the same weapon as that to be used in the final war. Driver suggests that it may be more than coincidence that the Qumran Covenanters carried the *sica* for protection and expected to use it in the final battle against the forces of evil. He believes that both the Zealots and the Covenanters were oriented toward and preparing for the same chain of events.

42. Man. of Disc. 5:24b to 6:3; cf. Mt. 5:22, 18:15 ff.; see Kurt Schubert, "The Sermon on the Mount and the Qumran Texts," *The Scrolls and the New Testament,* ed. by Krister Stendahl, New York: Harper & Bros., 1957, pp. 125–26.

43. Man. of Disc. 1:7a–11a; 5:20b to 6:8a.

44. Man. of Disc. 1:16 to 3:12.

45. Man. of Disc. 6:13b–23.

46. See Matthew Black, *op. cit.,* pp. 102–15, where he suggests that this banquet may well have served as a prototype for the Christian Eucharist. Cf. F. M. Cross, *op. cit.,* pp. 90 f.; Sutcliffe, *op. cit.,* pp. 110 f. Driver, *op. cit.,* pp. 506 ff. and p. 516, thinks the Qumran meal had no connection at all with the last supper Jesus had with his disciples; and Leaney, *op. cit.,* pp. 182 ff., believes the meal was not Messianic, but just an ordinary meal of the community.

47. Man. of Disc. 6:4b–6a.

48. Rule of Cong. 2:11–22.

49. Man. of Disc. 3:1–12; 4:18b–23a; 5:13a–15; Dam. Doc. 10:10–13. See Leaney, *op. cit.,* pp. 139 f., who states (referring to comments by David Flusser in "The Baptism of John and the Dead Sea Sect"): "Ritual acts cleanse from ritual defilement, repentance from moral defects. The sect is the first group within Judaism of whom we know who believed that moral failure (sin in our modern sense) incurred ritual defilement. They taught that to be cleansed from sin demanded *both* repentance *and* ritual purification." See also *ibid.,* pp. 131 f., 141 ff., and 158 f.; Black, *op. cit.,* p. 168, who also points out that the Covenanters were unique in their baptism of repentance into the New Israel, and pp. 97 f.; and H. H. Rowley, *The Dead Sea Scrolls and the New Testament,* London: S.P.C.K., 1964, pp. 14 ff. Driver, *op. cit.,* pp. 496 ff., disputes the assertion that Qumran was a baptizing sect.

50. Leaney, *op. cit.,* p. 223: "The spirit's work is seen with regard to the Scriptures in two complementary ways: the prophets have been divinely led to write mysteries or secrets; and the Teacher of Righteousness and his sect have been given the equally divine ability to reveal the true interpretation of them." Cf. also p. 35: "God will grant his Messiah the power to make the spirit of his holiness known to the 'remnant,'" p. 36; etc.

51. Man. of Disc. 3:6–8; 8:16; 9:3; Hymns 7:6, 7; 9:31, 32; 12:11, 12; 13:19; 14:15; 16:2, 11, 12; 17:17; Dam. Doc. 2:12.

52. Man. of Disc. 5:20b–25; 6:24 to 7:25. See Leaney, *op. cit.*, pp. 104 ff.

53. Man. of Disc. 1:16 to 2:18; 2:19 to 3:12; F. M. Cross, *op. cit.*, p. 95 (96a).

54. Leaney, *op. cit.*: "In the New Testament Pentecost clearly bears the character of a covenant renewal, recalling the great event on Sinai. The feast is mentioned three times, receiving a full exposition in story form in Acts 2, an exposition implying the final, eschatological fulfillment of the festival. The passage is clearly typological, v. 1–4 describing a new Sinai when the Holy Spirit speaks again to all the nations of the world" (p. 98). "The giving of the Law in the convenant from Sinai inaugurated a great era, and its giving was annually commemorated in the Feast of Weeks, or Pentecost. This feast was used by the sect [Qumran] as a time of solemn renewal of the covenant, and the form which this ceremony took was determined by a long tradition of such ceremonies recorded in the Scriptures" (p. 104). See *op. cit.*, pp. 95 ff.

55. *Op. cit.*, p. 233.

56. Russell, *op. cit.*, pp. 308 ff.

57. Deut. 18:15–18. Cf. Man. of Disc. 9:11 and Testimonies.

58. See Black, *op. cit.*, p. 163. See also Chapter 9 below.

59. Mal. 3:1; 4:5; Is. 40:3. Cf. J. A. T. Robinson, "Elijah, John and Jesus," *Twelve New Testament Studies*, London: SCM Press, 1965, pp. 28 ff., esp. pp. 35 f., who argues convincingly that it was "Jesus and the Church who between them fixed the notion that 'Elijah' meant 'the forerunner of the Christ.'" (p. 35) The prophecy in Malachi says that Elijah is to come "not before Christ, but before 'the great and terrible' day of the Lord." (p. 36) And "The first clear reference to Elijah as the precursor, and indeed anointer, of the Messiah occurs in Justin Martyr's *Dialogue with Trypho* (8.4; 49.1)." (p. 36)

60. Is. 9:6 f., 11:1 ff.; Jer. 23:5 ff. Cf. Com. on Is. 2:1–5; Blessings 5:20–29; War Scroll 5:1; 12:10–15; Rule of Cong. 2:11–12; Patr. Blessings; Messianic Collection; Dam. Doc. 6:6 ff.; and 7:16 ff.; etc.

61. See Gartner, *op. cit.*, pp. 35 ff.; Russell, *op. cit.*, pp. 316 ff.

62. Jub. 31:13–15; Test. of Levi 8:14; Test. of Reub. 6:5–12; etc.

63. See F. M. Cross, *op. cit.*, p. 220 (and n. 44 on that page); and Russell, *op. cit.*, pp. 310 ff.

64. Russell, *op. cit.*, pp. 324 ff.

65. Burrows, *op. cit.*, p. 265; Gartner, *op. cit.*, pp. 36 ff.; Matthew Black, *The Dead Sea Scrolls and Christian Doctrine*, London: The Athlone Press, 1966, p. 4 ff.; Bruce, *Second Thoughts on the Dead Sea Scrolls*, pp. 80 ff. Cf. also John Allegro, "Further Messianic References in Qumran Literature," *Journal of Biblical Literature*, Vol. LXXV (1956), pp. 174 ff.

66. See F. M. Cross, *op. cit.*, pp. 223 ff.

67. F. M. Cross, *op. cit.*, pp. 225 ff.; Leaney, *op. cit.*, pp. 227 f.

68. Man. of Disc. 9:11; Dam. Doc. 14:19; etc.

69. See Driver, *op. cit.*, pp. 237–51, esp. pp. 249 ff., and pp. 439 ff.,

where he gives the psychological explanation for such devoutly religious men engaging in violence: "The most pious are often the most savage" (p. 439); Roth, *op. cit.*, pp. 63 ff., esp. p. 69; also pp. 85 ff.

70. It seems evident from Josephus' description of the Revolt that the struggle for power and control, and the failure of a strong leader to emerge and unite the rebels were the major contributing factors in the defeat of the Jews in the Great Revolt. This infighting was strategy and power oriented, however; it was not rooted in differences of Messianic interpretation or apocalyptic expectation as far as we can determine.

71. Black, *The Dead Sea Scrolls and Christian Doctrine*, pp. 18 and 4. W. H. C. Frend, *op. cit.*, pp. 115 f., writes that to the Covenanters the Day of the Lord was to see the literal overthrow of idolatry and lists the Qumran sect among those who believed "that the first necessity for the coming of God's kingdom was the cleansing of Israel and the expulsion of the Roman idolators. The Dead Sea community, to whom Christianity may owe something of its organization and liturgy at this period, continued to believe in a Warrior Messiah of the House of David who would do this work . . . they abominated the Romans. To such men abatement of the Law in favour of idolators, such as Roman centurions, would be abhorrent. They shared the views of the Zealots on the inevitability of war with Rome . . ."

72. Fragment of the Book of Ezekiel (37:11) found at Masada.

CHAPTER 5

Jesus and the Early Christians: A Continuity
of the Qumran Tradition

1. For a book addressed specifically to this subject, see *The Scrolls and the New Testament,* ed. by Krister Stendahl. Cf. also Millar Burrows, *More Light on the Dead Sea Scrolls,* London: Secker & Warburg, 1958, pp. 87 ff. and pp. 95 ff.; Driver, *op. cit.,* pp. 517 ff. and p. 571; Sutcliffe, *op. cit.,* pp. 114 ff.; Gaster, *op. cit.,* pp. 14 ff.; etc.

2. "The Dead Sea Scrolls and Early Christianity," *Bulletin of the John Rylands Library,* Vol. 49, No. 1, Autumn 1966, p. 90. See also H. H. Rowley's "The Qumran Sect and Christian Origins," *Bulletin of the John Rylands Library,* Vol. 44, No. 1, September 1961.

3. *Op. cit.,* p. 200.

4. *Ibid.,* pp. 199 ff.

5. The phrase is Rudolph Bultmann's (*Theology of the New Testament,* Vol. I, New York: Charles Scribner's Sons, 1951, p. 42). See F. M. Cross, *op. cit.,* p. 203 and n. 8 on that page.

6. *Op. cit.,* p. 258. Cf. Rom. 8:28 f.; 11:3–5; Gal. 4:28; Phil. 3:3; Lk. 2:34; Mt. 21:42; I Peter 2:8 ff. See also Burrows, *The Dead Sea Scrolls,* p. 268, and F. M. Cross. *op. cit.,* p. 112.

7. F. M. Cross, *op. cit.,* pp. 217, 239 ff.; Stendahl, *op. cit.,* pp. 11–17; F. F. Bruce, "The Dead Sea Scrolls and Early Christianity," pp. 74 f.; James McLeman, *Resurrection Then and Now,* London: Hodder & Stoughton, 1965, pp. 79 and 81. Cf. also Leaney, *op. cit.,* pp. 103 f.

8. Man. of Disc. 8:10.

9. *Op. cit.,* pp. 242 f.

10. Cf. Man. of Disc. 3:13 to 4:26; and Jn. 8:42–47; I Jn. 5:19; II Cor. 6:14 to 7:4; etc.

11. Cf. Jn. 9:5, 12:46; I Jn. 2:1, 4:13; Rev. 12:7–12; and War Scroll 13:9b–13; 17:5b–9; Man. of Disc. 3:24, 25. See F. M. Cross, *op. cit.,* p. 213; Leaney, *op. cit.,* p. 43; and Gartner, *op. cit.,* p. 4.

12. Mt. 21:1–11; Mk. 11:1–11; Lk. 19:29–44; Jn. 12:12–19.

13. See also Jn. 1:21, 25; 6:14.

14. Cf. Bruce, *Second Thoughts on the Dead Sea Scrolls,* p. 152, who

points out the parallel which existed even with regard to the fulfillment of the suffering servant ideal of Isaiah 42:1–4; 49:1–6; 50:4–9; 52:13 to 53:12.

15. A distinction has to be made between the Jerusalem Church, which was led by James the brother of Jesus, Paul's movement among the Jews of the Diaspora and among the Gentiles, and the Galilean branch of the movement, which was under Peter's direction. These divisions persisted until after the fall of Jerusalem in A.D. 70. See L. E. Elliott-Binns, *Galilean Christianity*, Chicago: Alec R. Allenson, Inc., 1956, esp. Chs. IV–VII.

16. Acts 2:44 ff.; 4:34–37; 5:1–11; Man. of Disc. 1:12; 6:16–20, 24–25; Dam. Doc. 9:11 f.; 14:20 f. Cf. *War* II. 122–27. The punishment for lying about one's property at Qumran was exile from the community (or at least from their communal meal and ritual baths) for a year and being deprived of a quarter of one's rations (Man. of Disc. 6:24–25). A much more severe punishment is recorded in Acts 5:1–11 where Ananias and his wife Sapphira drop dead on being confronted with their sin. Leaney (*op. cit.*, p. 200) says their sin's "gravity did not derive from its being a lie about property, for Peter expressly draws attention to the fact that the lie to the Holy Spirit was inexcusable partly because before the sale the property and after it the proceeds were both at Ananias' disposal (Acts 5:4a). He was evidently under no compulsion to give the proceeds to the Church." Even more to the point, it seems to us, is the fact that *even in matters regarding property*, the members of the early Church were thought to be directly accountable to God ("You have not lied to men but to God," Acts 5:4b, RSV), evidence that they, like the Many at Qumran, were in a Covenant relationship with God and that their communal life was merely an expression of that. The story of Ananias and Sapphira underlines that point. Whether all who lied about property would have dropped dead upon confrontation we of course have no way of knowing, but that relationships and responsibilites in and to the Church were taken very seriously because they were considered bonds with God is clearly revealed.

17. Acts 15:12; 6:2, 5; 15:30. Cf., e.g., Man. of Disc. 6:1, 8b, 11 f., 16–23; etc. See F. M. Cross, *op. cit.*, p. 231.

18. Lk. 22:30; Man. of Disc. 8:5–8. Cf. also Eph. 2:20; Heb. 11:10. F. M. Cross, *op. cit.*, p. 232. Cf. Leaney, *op. cit.*, p. 212.

19. Dam. Doc. 13:7–13; Man. of Disc. 6:12–15; I Peter 2:25; I Tim. 3:1–7. F. M. Cross, *op. cit.*, pp. 232–33 (81).

20. Man. of Disc. 2:25 to 3:12; 4:20–22; 5:8–23; etc.; Mt. 28:19; Mk. 14:22–25; Lk. 22:14–20; I Cor. 11:17–34; Didache 9:2; 10:6; Acts 2:46. F. M. Cross, *op. cit.*, pp. 234 f.; Black, *The Scrolls and Christian Origins*, pp. 91 ff.

21. Stendahl, *op. cit.*, p. 130 f.; Leaney, *op. cit.*, pp. 139, 141 ff. and 158; Black, *The Scrolls and Christian Origins*, pp. 97 f. and 168. Cf. Rowley, *The Dead Sea Scrolls and the New Testament*, pp. 15 f.

22. Stendahl, *op. cit.*, pp. 130 f.; Leaney, *op. cit.*, pp. 35 ff.

23. See Leaney, *op. cit.*, pp. 141 f.; Robinson, "The Baptism of John and the Qumran Community," *op. cit.*, pp. 19 f.

24. See Black, *op. cit.*, p. 115.

25. War Scroll, 7:3b–4a; Lk. 20:34–36; I Cor. 7:29–31; etc. Cf. Deut. 23:9–11.

26. F. M. Cross, *op. cit.*, pp. 98 f. and 237 f.

27. I Cor. 11:25.

28. Man. of Disc. 8:8b–14.

29. Cf. Vincent Taylor, *The Life and Ministry of Jesus*, New York: Abingdon Press, 1955, pp. 28 f. and 51 ff.; James A. Pike, *What Is This Treasure*, New York: Harper & Row, 1966, pp. 47 f.

30. Mt. 1:2–17; Lk. 3:23–38. It is interesting to note that John does not include any data regarding Jesus' birth, even though he indicates that questions were raised about it: "Several people who had been listening said, 'Surely he must be the prophet,' and some said, 'He is the Christ,' but others said, 'Would the Christ be from Galilee? Does not scripture say that the Christ must be descended from David and come from the town of Bethlehem?' So the people could not agree about him" (Jn. 7:40–43). The obvious implication of this passage is that Jesus was *not* born in Bethlehem, but in Galilee. Yet the author of the Fourth Gospel makes no attempt to correct this impression. He apparently did not feel it was important to comment on the question one way or another.

31. Mt. 1:16 and Lk. 3:23.

32. Paul Winter, "Magnificat and Benedictus—Maccabean Psalms?" *The Bulletin of the John Rylands Library*, Vol. 37, No. 1, September 1954. Cf. J. A. T. Robinson's discussion of this theory in "Elijah, John and Jesus," *op. cit.*, pp. 48 ff. Robinson thinks that the Church wrote the canticle spoken by Zechariah in honor not of John, but of Jesus.

33. Winter, *op. cit.*

34. Many scholars believe the Gospel writer intended Elizabeth to speak the words of the Magnificat, not Mary, as most modern translations indicate. See Winter. *op. cit.*

35. Lk. 2:4, 39. Cf. Mt. 2:22. For a succinct description of Galilee in the time of Jesus, see Elliott-Binns, *op. cit.*, pp. 15 ff. Eusebius, *The History of the Church*, IV. 22, mentions Galileans as a separate sect of Jews.

36. "In the eyes of Judaean Pharisees, a minor offence of Jesus was that he was a Galilaean; for, in Judaean Jewish eyes, Galilaean Jews were suspect. 'Galilee of the Gentiles' had been converted to Judaism only a century before the probable date of Jesus' birth. We do not know whether the Galilaeans had been voluntary converts or had been converted forcibly, like the Idumaeans and the Ituraeans. In any case, the Galilaeans tended to run to two opposite extremes, both of which were obnoxious to Judaean Jews. If a Galilaean Jew became a Pharisee, he tended also to become a Zealot, i.e., a militant political nationalist and, as such, an embarrassment to Pharisees of the majoritarian school whose policy was to be politically obedient to

any government, Jewish or gentile, that left them free to practise their religion according to their own lights. At the opposite extreme, Galilaeans were suspected of being prone to relapse into paganism, as the high priest Caiaphas evidently assumed that Jesus was relapsing when Jesus declared: 'Hereafter shall ye see the Son of Man sitting on the right hand of power and coming in the clouds of heaven'—appearing, in fact, in the guise of the Canaanite storm-god Baal-Hadad." Arnold Toynbee, *The Crucible of Christianity*, p. 14.

37. Farmer, *Maccabees, Zealots and Josephus*, pp. 28 f.

38. W. R. Farmer, "The Palm Branches in John 12, 13," *Journal of Theological Studies*, N.S., Vol. III, Pt. 1, April 1952, pp. 63 f.

39. Mt. 13:55; Mk. 6:3.

40. Farmer, "The Palm Branches in John 12, 13," p. 64.

41. Especially since historians record no such slaughter of babies. See Chapter 1, n. 10 above.

42. Mt. 2:23; Lk. 2:39. Cf. also Mk. 1:9; Lk. 4:16; etc.

43. Cf. *The Interpreter's Bible*, Vol. VII, p. 262: "The village of Nazareth is not mentioned in any ancient records." However, Professor David Flusser pointed out to the authors that Nazareth was mentioned in an old Talmudic passage (only an abbreviated form of which was finally included in the Talmud) which listed the towns in which priests had found refuge after the destruction of the Temple in A.D. 70. Professor Flusser feels that this is clear evidence that such a village did exist at the time of Jesus.

44. The allusion may be to Judges 13:5 ("the boy shall be God's nazirite"), but the word used there comes from a different Hebrew verb root and is not "Nazarene."

45. Cf. W. F. Albright, "The Names 'Nazareth' and 'Nazoraean,'" *Journal of Biblical Literature*, LXV, 1946, pp. 397–401.

46. Eisler, *op. cit.*, pp. 232 ff. Cf. also Hans-Joachim Schoeps, *op. cit.*, p. 11: "This name [*nozrim*] . . . was probably not derived from the place Nazareth, but should be considered as a substantive formed from the root *nṣr*, meaning 'to keep,' 'observe,' so that those who bear the name are to be thought of as 'observers of secret traditions.'"

47. Eisler, *op. cit.*, p. 233.

48. Eisler, *loc. cit.*

49. *Ibid.*, p. 234.

50. *Ibid.*, p. 235. The wilderness resistance movements sought in their manner of living to emulate the nomadic way of life of the Rechabites. Marcel Simon, the dean of the Faculty of Letters at the University of Strasburg, in *St. Stephen and the Hellenists in the Primitive Church* (London: Longmans, Green & Co., 1958, p. 82) writes that the Prophet Nathan's protest recorded in Jer. 35, "is of the same nature as the protest of the Rechabites, who dwell in tents and not in houses, against every form of sedentary civilization." Further evidence of adherence to the nomadic

ideal of the Rechabites is seen in the community organization of the Qumran Covenanters and in the life and teaching of Jesus. See the discussion of the nomadic elements of the Qumran communal life in Chapter 4, pp. 50 ff. above, and in the life and teachings of Jesus and his followers in Chapter 8, pp. 128 ff. below.

51. Marcel Simon, *op. cit.,* pp. 91–94, has traced the use of the terms *nasaraioi* and *noṣᵉrim* in the transition from the mother religion Judaism to the daughter faith of Christianity. He writes that the Greek term *nasaraioi* was used by Epiphanius to describe a pre-Christian Jewish sect located along the Jordan River. While members of this sect were circumcised and observed the sabbath and the Jewish feasts, they made a distinction between the Pentateuch used by the Jews of their day and what they considered to be the true Law given to Moses. Holding to this belief in two Mosaic Laws, the sect followed all of the observances of the Jews except the offering of sacrifices and the eating of the flesh of animals. This Jewish sect maintained that animal sacrifice and flesh-eating were later interpolations added to the true Law followed by the Patriarchs.

Professor Simon believes that *nasaraioi* may be a different form of the Greek transliteration of the Hebrew *noṣᵉrim,* a term which means "observant" and which apparently was used to describe various Jewish sects in Israel before the birth of Christianity. He observes that St. Stephen, the first Christian martyr, professed the same beliefs as the Jewish sect of *nasaraioi/noṣᵉrim* which was critical of the Jerusalem Temple and its sacrifice, and that "it can at least be taken for granted that [Stephen] represented a sort of Judaism very close to that of the [*nasaraioi/noṣᵉrim*] group." (p. 94) A continuity of the beliefs of this Jewish sect is seen later in the Christian Jewish sect known as the Ebionites. Simon concludes that St. Stephen and the "Hellenists" of Acts 6:1, etc., represent a link between the pre-Christian Jewish sect of *nasaraioi/noṣᵉrim* and the later group of Ebionites. Noting their common rejection of the Jerusalem Temple and its sacrifical cult, Simon also concludes that the sect at Qumran was probably very close to the Hellenists and that the priests brought into the church at Stephen's bidding in Acts 6:7 may very well have been "not official priests of the Temple but members of some priestly sect like that of the Essenes." (p. 91)

52. As was the Teacher of Righteousness. See Chapter 3, pp. 36 ff. above.

CHAPTER 6

John the Baptist: A Voice in the Wilderness

1. Mt. 3:4–12; Mk. 1:5–8; Lk. 3:7–18.
2. Mt. 3:4; Mk. 1:6. Cf. also II Macc. 5:27.
3. See Charles H. H. Scobie, "John the Baptist," *The Scrolls and Christianity,* ed. by Matthew Black, London: S.P.C.K., 1969, p. 66.
4. Lk. 7:33.
5. Man. of Disc. 6:4–6.
6. *Ibid.,* p. 67. For a discussion of an alternative theory regarding John's food and clothing, see Eisler, *op. cit.,* pp. 235 ff., who believes they are deemed appropriate for "Enosh" (Adam, or "the Man").
7. See W. H. Brownlee, "John the Baptist in the Light of Ancient Scrolls," *The Scrolls and the New Testament,* p. 35; Scobie, *op. cit.,* p. 69; J. A. T. Robinson, "The Baptism of John and the Qumran Community," *op. cit.,* p. 12; Jean Daniélou, *The Dead Sea Scrolls and Primitive Christianity,* New York: The New American Library, 1962, pp. 16 ff., and *The Work of John the Baptist,* Baltimore: Helicon Press, 1966, pp. 37 ff. Cf. also Sutcliffe, *op. cit.,* pp. 123 f.; and Driver, *op. cit.,* pp. 491 ff., who do not think John was a member of, or closely related to, Qumran.
8. *Loc. cit.*
9. See Scobie, *ibid.,* pp. 62 ff. Cf. J. A. T. Robinson, *op. cit.,* pp. 19 f.; Man. of Disc. 1:24 to 2:1; 3:3–9; and Chapter 4, n. 49 above.
10. Cf. Lk. 3:7 and Hymns 5:27 f.
11. Cf. Lk. 3:8; Man. of Disc. 3:6b–9; 4:20–23; Scobie, *op. cit.,* p. 65. Eisler, *op. cit.,* pp. 251 f., 269 f., suggests that John may have been referring here to the Deuteronomic "royalty law" (Deut. 17:14 ff.) which declares to the Israelites, "You are not to give yourself a foreign king who is no brother of yours" (17:15b). Under this law, anyone who had submitted to the Roman rule would have automatically excluded himself from the house of Abraham and only by being cleansed and restored to purity could he once again receive his rightful inheritance.
12. Cf. Lk. 3:9; Mt. 3:12; Lk. 3:17; Man. of Disc. 2:8, 4:13; Hymns 6:18; Dam. Doc. 2:5, 6; J. A. T. Robinson, *op. cit.,* p. 17.
13. Cf. the oath of the Essenes in *War* II. 139: "First that he will

practise piety towards the Deity, next that he will observe justice towards men." See also Chapter 4 above.

14. Eisler, *op. cit.*, pp. 251 f.

15. Scobie, *op. cit.*, p. 68; Brownlee, *op. cit.*, p. 39.

16. See Chapter 4 above. Cf. also Hymns 3:28 ff.; 7:6 f.; Man. of Disc. 4:20–21; Dam. Doc. 2:12 f. Brownlee, *op. cit.*, discusses the question of the three baptisms on pp. 41 ff. See also J. A. T. Robinson, *op. cit.*, p. 19; Scobie, *op. cit.*, pp. 59 ff.

17. Scobie, *op. cit.*, p. 65; Black, *The Scrolls and Christian Origins*, p. 98.

18. *Op. cit.*, p. 18.

19. *Op. cit.*, p. 267.

20. *Ibid.*, p. 270.

21. But cf. J. A. T. Robinson, *op. cit.*, p. 45, who suggests that it is John the Baptist and the men who would enter the Kingdom who suffer the violence, not they who engage in it. This is perhaps not altogether inconsistent with Eisler's theory, since John may well have, like Jesus and the Qumran sect, advocated abstention from violence until the final war began. Cf. Chapter 11, n. 13 below.

22. Cf. Joseph Klausner, *op. cit.*, p. 206.

23. Eisler, *op. cit.*, p. 264.

24. *Loc. cit.*

25. *Ibid.*, p. 265.

26. *Loc. cit.*

27. Eisler, *op. cit.*, pp. 265 f., quoting from the Halosis document. Italics indicate words which are lacking in the Greek translation of the *Jewish War*, which has the corresponding section in indirect address and somewhat condensed.

28. Eisler, *op. cit.*, p. 266 (2) calls attention to a midrash composed by the Zealots around the revolutionary High Priest Phineas and Prince Kenedaios of Adiabene between A.D. 66 and 70: "God said to them: 'If you go up with a pure heart, fight! but if your heart is defiled, go not!' "

29. *Op. cit.*, p. 43.

30. Eisler, *op. cit.*, p. 266.

31. Eisler, *op. cit.*, pp. 266 f.

32. This passage is found in the Slavonic version of Josephus. Cf. Thackeray, Appendix to *War*, pp. 644–45. [Italics ours.]

33. Mt. 14:3–5; Mk. 6:17–20.

34. Thackeray, Appendix to *War*, pp. 648 f.

35. *Ibid.*, pp. 646–47.

36. Cf. Mk. 1:2–4; Lk. 1:17, 76; Mal. 3:23.

37. Cf. also Mk. 9:13; Lk. 7:26–27.

38. *Op. cit.*, p. 101.

39. Brownlee, *op. cit.*, p. 46.

40. *Ibid.*, pp. 46 f.; Scobie, *op. cit.*, p. 69; C. H. Dodd, *Historical Tradition in the Fourth Gospel*, Cambridge: Cambridge University Press, 1965, p. 253. In addition to the substantive material garnered from the Scrolls to help validate John's as an early Gospel, archaeological excavations have contributed significantly to the legitimization of the Fourth Gospel as an important historical source. See J. A. T. Robinson, *op. cit.*, pp. 100–1. The author of the Fourth Gospel seems to have been far better acquainted with the geography of Judea, Samaria, and Galilee than the authors of the Synoptic Gospels. Therefore, the routes he traces for people make more geographical sense and his location of events seems accurate. For example, John the Baptist is said in Jn. 3:23 to have preached at "Aenon near Salim," an area mentioned only in the Fourth Gospel. This site has now been discovered by W. F. Albright in the semi-arid region southeast of Shechem, at springs near the headwaters of Wadi Farah. Brownlee, *ibid.*, p. 36; cf. also C. H. Kraeling, *John the Baptist,* New York: Charles Scribner's Sons, 1951, p. 4. In dealing with John's relationship to Jesus, as well as in writing of Jesus' travels and activities, we treat the Fourth Gospel as of equal historical value with the Synoptics.

41. Brownlee, *op. cit.*, p. 52; J. A. T. Robinson, *op. cit.*, pp. 11 ff.

42. Brownlee, *loc. cit.*

43. Brownlee, *op. cit.*, p. 46.

44. *Op. cit.*, pp. 37 f.

45. *Op. cit.*, p. 62.

46. *Op. cit.*, pp. 41–52.

47. See J. A. T. Robinson, "Elijah, John and Jesus," *op. cit.*, pp. 28 ff., esp. pp. 37 ff.

48. Cf. Mt. 3:5–6; Mk. 1:5.

49. See, for example, Jn. 1:35–39; 3:22–26; Mt. 11:2–15; 14:12; Lk. 7:18–30.

50. Jn. 1:35–39.

51. Adherents of the Mandaean faith, a surviving branch of the Semitic stock, may be found living either as larger communities or as distinct family groups in cities and small market towns on the lower Euphrates, the lower Tigris, and the rivers which water the eastern Iraq al-Arabi, and the adjacent Persian province of Khuzistan (Arabistan). They live on rivers because they are believers in adult baptism by immersion in living (running) water. They earn their livings as tradesmen—carpenters, smiths, locksmiths, goldsmiths (suggestive of the ancient *Noṣᵉrim* mentioned in Chapter 5 above)—or as shopkeepers, and have at the heart of their religion carefully guarded "secrets" which only an inner circle of priests have revealed to them. The major studies of the Mandaeans have been done by Lady E. S. Drower: *The Mandaeans of Iraq and Iran,* Leiden: E. J. Brill, 1962; *The Secret Adam,* London: Oxford University Press. 1960; etc.

52. J. A. T. Robinson (see n. 47 above) thinks John believed Jesus to be

Elijah and was disappointed when Jesus' self-understanding changed. We will deal with this change in Chapter 8 below.

53. Cf. J. A. T. Robinson, "Elijah, John and Jesus," *op. cit.,* p. 47.

54. For examples of Messianic pretenders during the time of Jesus, see Chapter 1 above.

55. Mt. 12:31–35; 16:1–4; Lk. 11:29–32.

56. Cf. also Jn. 2:11, 23; 3:2; 4:54; 6:2, 14, 26, 30; 9:16; 11:47.

57. Mt. 11:2–15; Lk. 7:18–30.

58. Is. 29:18 ff.; 35:5 f.; 61:1.

59. *Op. cit.,* p. 38.

60. Jn. 3:22–36. Cf. also Jn. 4:1–3.

61. J. A. T. Robinson, *op. cit.,* pp. 40 ff.

62. David Flusser, "Jesus in the Context of History," *The Crucible of Christianity,* p. 227, writes that "Essenism" (as found in the Qumran Scrolls) is "the second source of Jesus' teachings," the first being Pharisaism. Flusser believes that Jesus was influenced by the fringes of "Essenism," and that such influence was probably mediated to Jesus through John the Baptist.

63. Cf., for example, Jn. 10:40.

64. Mt. 21:23–27; Mk. 11:27–33; Lk. 20:1–8.

65. Robert Eisler, *op. cit.,* pp. 291, 319, xiii, disputes Luke's chronology, pointing out that Luke confuses the dating of the births of the two (saying they were born while Herod the Great was still ruling, which could not have been later than 4 B.C., the year of Herod's death) and the census of Quirinius (which Luke places in the year of Jesus' birth, but which actually took place in A.D. 6 according to Josephus and other historians). Cf. Lk. 1:5 and 2:1 f. Eisler suggests that Josephus' dating is more reliable since he had the Roman documents and records at his disposal, and using Josephus' data he reconstructs the dating of the lives of the two.

Eisler is convinced that John was much older than Jesus; that John had been preaching and administering the rite of baptism for a whole generation before Jesus came to receive it for himself (which would agree with the Mandaean tradition); that Jesus was baptized in A.D. 19; that soon after his baptism Jesus separated from John and his followers; that Jesus was crucified in A.D. 21; and that John was not executed until A.D. 35.

Eisler's chronology would make more plausible and probable a significant influence by John on Jesus and his disciples, for his influence among the general populace would have been well established and would have continued throughout Jesus' public work.

66. Mt. 4:12–17; Mk. 1:14–15. But cf. Jn. 1:35; 4:2.

67. Mt. 14:1–12; Mk. 6:14–29. Cf. also Lk. 9:7–9.

CHAPTER 7

Jesus: A Teacher of the Law

1. E.g., Lk. 4:31–32, 44; 6:6.

2. Jn. 5:1; 7:14, 15, 28; 8:20; etc.

3. See also Mt. 7:28–29; Mk. 1:22.

4. J. A. T. Robinson, *op. cit.*, pp. 24 f.

5. Mt. 3:13–17; Mk. 1:9–11; Lk. 3:21, 22. Cf. also Jn. 1:32–34.

6. Scientists are already examining such data. See, for example, Maurice Bucke, M.D., *Cosmic Consciousness*, New York: E. P. Dutton & Co., 1964; Robert Crookall, D.Sc., Ph.D., *The Interpretation of Cosmic and Mystical Experiences*, London: James Clarke & Co., 1969; *Altered States of Consciousness*, ed. by Charles T. Tart, Ph.D., New York: John Wiley & Sons, Inc., 1969; Raynor C. Johnson, Ph.D., D.Sc., *Nurslings of Immortality*, New York: Harper & Brothers, 1957; etc.

7. Man. of Disc. 4:2–8; 8:12b–16a.

8. I Cor. 12:4–31, esp. 8–10. Cf. Man. of Disc. 4:2–8; 11:2b–9a; and *War* II. 159.

9. Cf. Mt. 12:31–32; Mk. 3:28–30.

10. Cf. Mt. 12:43–45 and Lk. 11:24–26.

11. Mt. 4:1–11; Mk. 1:12, 13; Lk. 4:1–13.

12. *The Work of John the Baptist*, p. 43.

13. Robinson, "The Temptations," *op. cit.*, p. 60.

14. *Ibid.*, pp. 54–57.

15. *Loc. cit.*

16. *Ibid.*, pp. 59 f.

17. Leaney, *op. cit.*, p. 221.

18. Ulrich Mauser, *Christ in the Wilderness*, London: SCM Press Ltd., 1963, p. 34.

19. J. A. T. Robinson, *op. cit.*, p. 38.

20. Cf. F. F. Bruce, "Jesus and the Gospels in the Light of the Scrolls," *The Scrolls and Christianity*, pp. 70 ff., who compares Jesus' early preaching as recorded in Mk. 1:15 and that of Qumran (Dam. Doc. 1:12 and Com. on Hab. 7:4 f.): "Thus he served notice that the time appointed for the accomplishment of God's promises to Israel had arrived; that the everlasting kingdom of the God of heaven, foreseen in

the visions of Daniel, was about to be set up—indeed, that it was in a sense already present in his own words and deeds. This eschatological emphasis is perhaps the most outstanding feature common to the Gospels and the Qumran literature." (p. 71)

21. The attitude on the part of the Romans is reflected in the tradition of Mt. 2:1–18. Though no such mass murder of male babies is recorded in any histories of the period, the tradition reflects the awareness the Jews had that if the Romans or their collaborators learned of a Messianic figure who was beginning to be recognized by the people as their "king," they would go to great lengths to see that the person was executed. Thus the story, which might otherwise seem excessive and exaggerated, would not have appeared preposterous to first- and second-century Jews who had witnessed many mass murders of their rebel leaders by the Romans. Cf. *The Interpreter's Bible*, Vol. VII, pp. 260 f.

22. We mentioned in Chapter 1, for example, Josephus' account of Pilate's dismissal from office for his massacre of Samaritans (p. 14, above). See also *Ant.* XX. 197–203 where Josephus tells of the newly appointed High Priest Ananus who illegally killed James, the brother of Jesus, who was known as an especially devout Jew and was so highly respected among the lower Temple priesthood that his unlawful execution caused a great protest among leading Jews of Jerusalem. For this offense Ananus was deposed after only four months in office. Cf. also Williams, *Eusebius: The History of the Church*, 2.23, and Brandon, *Jesus and the Zealots*, pp. 115 ff.

23. See other examples in Mt. 8:4; 17:9; esp. 16:13–20; Mk. 1:44; 3:11–12; 4:10–12; 5:42–43; 7:35–37; 9:9–10; esp. 8:27–30 and 9:30–32; Lk. 5:14; 8:9–10, 55–56; 9:36. But cf. Mk. 5:19–20 in which Jesus admonishes the Gerasene whom he healed of "legions" of devils to go home and tell his friends what had happened. Perhaps the fact that his home was in the Decapolis and therefore somewhat removed from Jesus' customary sphere of activity, made the difference.

24. Cf., for example, Jn. 8:45 ff., in which the "Jews" corner Jesus in the Temple in Jerusalem and ask him, "Are we not right in saying that *you are a Samaritan* [italics ours] and possessed by a devil?" Jesus answers that he is not possessed, apparently not finding it important to deny that he is a Samaritan. Similarly, in Jn. 7:52 the "Jews" taunt Nicodemus, who has suggested Jesus be given a fair hearing, by saying, "Are you a Galilean, too? Go into the matter, and see for yourself: prophets do not come out of Galilee." Both incidents reflect a clear *regional bias* on the part of the writer of the Fourth Gospel, who may well have been a sectarian (perhaps a Galilean or a Samaritan, and almost surely a follower of the Baptist) who had become a follower of Jesus and who felt, in the wilderness tradition, that the Temple authorities and all who lived peaceably with them had turned from the will of God. He apparently felt closer to the Samaritans than he did to the Judeans whom he called "Jews." In keeping

with this regional focus, the Fourth Gospel indicates that John the Baptist carried out a special preaching "mission" in Samaria, where he baptized many people (Jn. 3:23). The author portrays Jesus as fleeing Judea for fear of the Pharisees and going to Galilee for safety (Jn. 4:1–3). He relates a very meaningful encounter between Jesus and a Samaritan woman with whom Jesus does not hesitate to associate and with whom he engages in a theological discussion (Jn. 4:4–26). He portrays the Samaritans as responsive to Jesus, for many believed in him (Jn. 4:39–42).

The bitterness of the writer of the Fourth Gospel is apparently directed toward the urban Jews of the southern province of Judea, whose capital was Jerusalem, and not against "Jews" in general. Many Christians have mistaken the tone of John's Gospel for anti-Semitism instead of seeing it for what it is: a reflection of a regional conflict between anti-Temple, wilderness-oriented sectarians and Temple-centered Judeans who had worked out a not too uncomfortable compromise with Roman rule.

Bishop Pike had this insight while studying the Samaritans and their relationship to the Qumran sect, Setphen's Hellenistic sect, and the early Christians. Having already discovered that the Scrolls and archaeology enable us to reinstate John's Gospel as historically valid and as representing perhaps one of the earliest strands of tradition (as is pointed out in Chapter 6, n. 40 above), Bishop Pike was excited to discover at least one of the roots of Christian anti-Semitism which has been nourished by the Gospels. A study of the dislike of "the Jews" in the Fourth Gospel shows that it was *not* racial or ethnic, *but regional and philosophical*. See also Robinson, "The Destination and Purpose of St. John's Gospel," *op. cit.*, p. 118.

25. Marcel Simon, in *Jewish Sects at the Time of Jesus*, p. 86, says: "The Herodians and the 'scribes' mentioned by Epiphanius (*Panarion* 1.20; 1.14) *undoubtedly never existed as sects*. Both are mentioned in the New Testament (Mt. 22:16; Mk. 3:6), and this is where the author has come across them. But the Herodians were probably nothing more than partisans of Herod or men in his pay." [Italics ours.] Cf. also Brandon, *Jesus and the Zealots*, p. 200 (4).

26. See also Jn. 7:32–52; 11:45–53.

27. Man. of Disc. 8:5–8.

28. Cf. Mk. 5:35–43; 9:2–13; 14:32–42; Mt. 17:1–13; 26:36–46; Lk. 9:28–36.

29. F. M. Cross, *op. cit.*, pp. 231 f.

30. Cf. also Mt. 13:11 and Mk. 4:11, 12.

31. W. D. Davies, *The Setting of the Sermon on the Mount*, pp. 235 ff. believes that the Sermon on the Mount is a polemic against the Essene sect which was only later edited to make the critical references to the Essenes read "Pharisees." Cf. also F. F. Bruce, "Jesus and the Gospels in the Light of the Scrolls," p. 74. Kurt Schubert, "The Sermon on the Mount and the Qumran Texts," *The Scrolls and the New Testament*,

p. 120, also sees in Mt. 5:43 ff. the key to an historical and religious understanding of the Sermon on the Mount. Jesus' saying, "You have learnt how it was said: 'You must love your neighbour and hate your enemy.' But I say this to you: love your enemies . . ." is in Schubert's opinion directed at the Qumran sectarians, whose writings include among the duties of the members "to love all that He (God) has chosen and to hate all that He has rejected" (Man. of Disc. 1:14) and to "hate all the sons of darkness, each according to his guilt in God's vengeance" (1:10); "And the Levites shall curse all the men of the lot of Satan, saying: 'Be cursed . . . !'" (2:4). Such instructions to hate one's enemies are found nowhere else in Jewish tradition or in the Old Testament, Schubert asserts. Such a view presupposes that both Jesus and those who listened to him were well-acquainted with the teachings of the sect, if indeed Jesus' intent were as definitely anti-Qumran as Bruce, Davies, and Schubert assume.

In light of Jesus' admonition to his disciples that anyone who came after him had to "hate" father, mother, wife, children, sisters, and brothers (Lk. 14:26; cf. also Mt. 10:35–38), we do not think the above need necessarily be seen as anti-sectarian. Rather, it could be that in the Sermon on the Mount Jesus is talking about personal relationships, not the matter of idolatry and of decision to follow the one God as in the Lukan and Matthean passages on hate. See our discussion of this matter below, pp. 113 ff.

32. Cf. W. D. Davies, *Paul and Rabbinic Judaism,* New York: Harper & Row, 1967, for a full discussion of the parallels and similarities between Paul and Pharisaic, or so-called "legalistic," Judaism.

33. "Jesus in the Context of History," p. 225. Such criticism between teachers within the same Pharisaic school of thought should not surprise us when we take note of the internal reformation—with the abundant criticism of "Christians" by other Christians—now going on within the Christian Church in nearly all of its sectors.

34. Professor Flusser has written about the meaning and use of the term "Pharisee," but unfortunately his article is only available in Hebrew.

35. "Jesus in the Context of History," p. 225. Italics ours.

36. Cf., e.g., A. Powell Davies, *The Meaning of the Dead Sea Scrolls,* New York: The New American Library, 1956, p. 128.

37. Flusser, *loc. cit.*

38. Cf. Schubert, *op. cit.,* p. 128.

39. *Mishnah Yoma* 8, 6 (83a).

40. Flusser, *loc. cit.*

41. Dam. Doc. 11:16 f.

42. Dam. Doc. 11:13 f.

43. *Loc. cit.*

44. *Loc. cit.*

45. *Loc. cit.*

46. See Chapter 4, pp. 49 and 52 ff. above. Cf. also F. M. Cross, *op. cit.*, p. 85.

47. Kurt Schubert, *op. cit.*, p. 119, has argued that in weighing the seemingly contradictory statements of Jesus (Mt. 11:30: "my yoke is easy, and my burden light"; and Mt. 5:17–18: "Do not imagine that I have come to abolish the Law and the Prophets. I have come not to abolish but to complete them. I tell you solemnly, till heaven and earth disappear, not a dot, not one little stroke, shall disappear from the Law until its purpose is achieved"), "The view that Jesus demanded fulfillment of the Mosaic Law is a peculiarity of the Jewish Christians." Such a view is reflected in a Jewish Christian polemic of the Pseudo-Clementine apocryphal literature which reads: "What he abolished did not belong to the Law" (Hom. 3:51). The Jewish Christians, in this view, believed that Jesus affirmed rather than abrogated the Mosaic Law. Our discussion of Flusser's works has indicated that such a view as that held by the Jewish Christians is substantiated by a careful reading of the Synoptic accounts of Jesus' disputes with the Pharisees.

48. Dam. Doc. 13:10 ff.

49. Cf. Schubert, *op. cit.*, p. 126.

50. Cf. also Mk. 10:2–12.

51. Dam. Doc. 4:20 to 5:2a.

52. For this insight, we are indebted to Professor David Flusser of Hebrew University who, in personal conversations with the authors, helped us to understand the religious Jew's attitude toward keeping the Law as the manner of expressing his Covenanted relationship with God, and why it is difficult for a Gentile to adopt that attitude.

53. Man. of Disc. 1:6; 4:10; Com. on Hab. 5:7; Dam. Doc. 3:3. Schubert, *op. cit.*, p. 126.

54. Cf. Mt. 5:33–37 and Dam. Doc. 15:1–5. Cf. also 4, 13, 35a; *War* II. 135; *Ant.* XV. 370–71.

55. Flusser, "Jesus in the Context of History," p. 226.

56. Krister Stendahl, "Hate, Non-Retaliation, and Love" in the *Harvard Theological Review*, Vol. 55, 1962, p. 344.

57. *Loc. cit.* Stendahl concludes "The non-retaliation is undoubtedly based and motivated by the deference to God's impending vengeance. It is not deduced from a principle of love or from within the Wisdom tradition [as with the Testaments of the Twelve Patriarchs]. Neither Qumran, nor Paul speak about love for the enemies. The issue is rather how to act when all attempts to avoid conflict with the enemies of God and of his Church have failed." (p. 354)

Stendahl has offered a plausible explanation for the discrepancy between the description of the Essenes as pacifists by Josephus and other historians, and the very nonpacifistic attitudes expressed in their literature. "The 'eternal hatred' ["everlasting hatred"] is thus practiced in a hidden way [by the Covenanter], in that he does not interfere with the affairs of the world. He does not raise any just claims on behalf of God regarding such matters. The world is allowed to run its course, toward the Day of Vengeance. He conceals his hatred by appearing obedient and subdued and peaceful and willing to be deprived of property and produce." (p. 349) Thus, the hidden way in which the Covenanters secreted their hatred and anticipated revenge toward the men of darkness may explain the categorization of the Essenes as pacifists by Josephus and others.

58. Lk. 9:51–56; 10:1–16.

59. "The Qumran Scrolls and the Johannine Gospel and Epistles," *The Scrolls and the New Testament*, p. 198. Brown also quotes Grossouw's opinion: "One gets a strong impression that in these [Qumran] writings man's mind is preparing for the Christian precept of love."

60. See A. P. Davies, *op. cit.*, pp. 127 f.

61. Man. of Disc. 10:17 f.

62. Schubert, *op. cit.*, p. 127.

63. Flusser, *op. cit.*, pp. 226 f. See also Stendahl, "Hate, Non-Retaliation, and Love," p. 350: "In the Testaments of the Twelve Patriarchs we find, however, a different spirit in regard to love, non-retaliation and hatred. The most striking examples are Test. Benj. 4–5 and Test. Gad 6–7. Here the possibility of winning the enemy over by showing mercy is clearly stated. Furthermore, the righteous takes a posture of prayer, and in Test. Jos. 18:2 this is definitely a prayer for the one who seeks to harm him. In Test. Gad 6:7 the ultimate recourse is to the vengeance of God, but this is not done in a spirit of concealed eternal hatred, but with 'forgiveness from the heart.'"

64. *Op. cit.*, p. 226.

65. Man. of Disc. 1:5; 5:3.

66. Man. of Disc. 4:24.

67. Man. of Disc. 8:6.

68. On p. 196, *op. cit.*, Raymond Brown points out other parallels in Johannine literature. E.g., I Jn. 1:6: "If we say that we have fellowship with him, and walk in darkness, we lie, and are not practicing the truth." And on p. 287 (65) he mentions that the Man. of Disc. 4:6 and 15 "speaks of walking in the ways of the two spirits, as compared to walking in truth." Cf. 2 Jn. 4: "I rejoiced greatly that I found some of thy children walking in truth . . ."; and 3 Jn. 3: "I rejoiced greatly when some brethren came and bore witness to thy truth, even as thou walkest in the truth. I have no greater joy than to hear that my children are walking in the truth."

69. Bruce, *op. cit.*, pp. 70 ff.; Stendahl, *The Scrolls and the New Testament*, p. 7.

70. See our Introduction: "In Quest of the Historical Jesus," pp. xxvii ff. above.

71. Stendahl, *loc. cit.*

72. Blessings 1a.

73. Hymns 18:14–15. [Translation Flusser's. See n. 74 below.]

74. *Israel Exploration Journal,* Vol. 10, No. 1, Jerusalem: Central Press, 1960, p. 4 (of reprint).

75. Flusser, *op. cit.,* p. 5. Dr. Flusser also points out: "Besides 'contrite of spirit' and 'poor of spirit' the Sons of Light called themselves 'paupers of grace' (Hymns 5:22), 'paupers of Thy redemption' (War Scroll 11:9), 'desperate of justification' (Hymns 5:22). These appellations are characterized by a paradoxical combination of a term depicting the abject state of the Sect in the present, with a second one, which proclaims triumphantly the plenty of God's grace bestowed on His elect. This paradoxical contrast between the present plight and persecution of the blessed and their future glory in the kingdom of heaven is also the main burden of the Beatitudes." (pp. 5 f.) "This is also one of the most important opinions of the Sect. Hymns 11:19–27 is, for example, a fine poetical elaboration of the theme 'Blessed are they that mourn, for they shall be comforted' (Mt. 5:4)" (p. 6 [13]).

76. *Op. cit.,* p. 9. Schubert, *op. cit.,* p. 122, also notes the use by the sect of the term "poor ones," or *ebionim* to identify themselves, and Jesus' use of the term, suggesting that the audience was familiar with this group and their teachings.

77. Cf. Flusser, *op. cit.,* p. 7, who says, "the sectarians explained, in the same way as Jesus, the meek of Ps. 37:11 as paupers, but, at least in the sectarian commentary known to us today, they understood the words 'they shall inherit the earth' of the biblical verse in a material-political sense," implying that Jesus did not. We see no reason to assume that Jesus would have given it a less practical and more ethereal interpretation. The "earth of eschatology" to which Jesus is referring, according to Flusser, is surely the same earth of the sectarians, transformed after the coming of the Kingdom. It seems probable that Jesus meant precisely what the Covenanters meant by the phrase.

78. Cf. also Mt. 13:1–9, 24–30, 31–32, 33, 45–46, 47–50, 52; 18:23–35; 20:1–16; 21:33–43; 22:1–14; 25:1–13, 14–30; and parallel passages.

79. See Flusser, "The Dead Sea Sect and Pre-Pauline Christianity." Reprint from "Aspects of the Dead Sea Scrolls," *Scripta Hierosolymitana,* Vol. IV, Publications of the Hebrew University of Jerusalem, 1958, pp. 256 (144).

80. Man of Disc. 11:16–17; 4:22 f.

81. Man. of Disc. 4:2–8; 11:2–8. See also *War* II. 135, where Josephus calls the Essenes "very ministers of peace."

82. Schubert, *op. cit.,* p. 125, observes: "It also becomes probable in the light of the Qumran literature, that the tradition of Manasseh's persecution of Isaiah and of his martyrdom was originally peculiar to the Essenes. From the allusion in Mt. 5:12 it is, in my opinion, evident that Jesus was dealing with people conversant with this special tradition. Consequently, it does not seem improbable that the words, 'the prophets who are/were be-

fore you' are in general to be interpreted as referring to Jesus' listeners at the Sermon on the Mount, also having reference to the Essene tradition of the persecution of important prophets." Cf. also F. F. Bruce, *Second Thoughts on the Dead Sea Scrolls*, p. 152, who believes the Covenanters sought to fulfill the role of Isaiah's suffering servant just as Jesus himself did.

83. "Blessed are the Poor in Spirit," p. 12.

84. Man. of Disc. 2. Cf. also War Scroll 13; etc.

85. Cf. Matthew Black, "The Dead Sea Scrolls and Christian Origins," *The Scrolls and Christianity*, pp. 105 f.

86. Mt. 22:23–33, esp. verse 29; Mk. 12:18–27; Lk. 20:27–38.

87. Flusser, "Jesus in the Context of History," pp. 229–30.

88. *Op. cit.*, p. 384.

89. Eusebius, Book IV.5, writes that a succession of fifteen bishops, all circumcised Jews, headed the Jerusalem Church until the Bar Kochba Revolt (A.D. 132–135). With the Roman suppression of the second Jewish Revolt the city was destroyed and renamed Aelia Capitolina. A Gentile was then appointed bishop of Jerusalem.

90. See Farmer, *Maccabees, Zealots and Josephus*, p. 190, who writes: "If there were such a thing as 'normative Judaism' in the first century A.D., we would have to define it in terms of this national resistance movement, which as we have seen placed so very great importance upon the Land, the Law, and the Temple." Cf. Cullmann, *Jesus and the Revolutionaries*, pp. 4 and 31 ff. who also highlights the fact that anti-Roman agitation by the Jews was *the* predominant mood of Jesus' day—in both the political and religious spheres.

CHAPTER 8

Jesus: A Preacher of the Kingdom

1. Cf. Jn. 3:22; 4:1–3; Mt. 19:1–2; Mk. 10:1.

2. Mk. 1:16–20 and Mt. 4:18–22. Cf. also Lk. 5:1–11.

3. Lk. 4:16–30. Cf. also Mt. 13:53–58 and Mk. 6:1–6a.

4. Mt. 9:9; Mk. 2:14; Lk. 5:27–28.

5. Mt. 10:1–4; Mk. 3:13–19a; Lk. 6:12–16. Cf. also Acts 1:12 f.

6. On Simon's being called "the Cananaean" in Mark 3:18 and Matthew 10:4 (KJV and RSV), see Brandon, *Jesus and the Zealots,* p. 244 (5), and Cullmann, *The State in the New Testament,* pp. 14 f., who suggests that ὁ καναυῖος, used by both Gospel writers, is a Greek transliteration of an Aramaic word meaning "Zealot."

7. Cf. Brandon, *op. cit.,* p. 203 (6). It is not insignificant that these "sons of thunder" were two of the inner circle of three and that Peter, the third, carried a sword in the Garden the night of the arrest and attacked a centurion's guard with it.

8. Brandon, *op. cit.,* p. 204, points out that "Barjona" could reasonably be taken to mean "outlaw." See also Eisler, *op. cit.,* pp. 253 ff., who says that the Zealots were called "Barjonim." It is interesting—and perhaps significant—that Jesus called Peter "Barjona" just after he had declared Jesus to be the Messiah, for the declaration obviously had revolutionary implications. Cf. Mt. 16:13–20. Note also that Peter had a sword (dagger) with him the night of Jesus' arrest, and used it.

9. Though the meaning of "Iscariot" has never been explained to everyone's satisfaction, Oscar Cullmann suggests in *The State in the New Testament,* pp. 15 f., that a corruption of the Greek word for "Sicarii" accounted for its translation as "Iscariot." Since there is no place of "Carioth," the standard Christian explanation that Iscariot means "man from Carioth" is no longer accepted by serious scholars. See also Brandon, *op. cit.,* p. 204 (1). It is interesting to note that John 6:71 refers to Judas as the son of Simon Iscariot, since Simon is also a Maccabean name. This would seem to establish further Judas' ties and sympathies with the revolutionary movement.

10. Farmer, *Maccabees, Zealots and Josephus,* pp. 28 f.

11. Cf. Jesus' words, "I have come to bring fire to the earth; and how I

wish it were blazing already!" (Lk. 12:49; cf. also verses 50–53). John Robinson, "Elijah, John and Jesus," *op. cit.,* pp. 42 ff., believes these passages belong to the period of Jesus' public work when he believed himself to be Elijah, as John had proclaimed. If so, the suggestion James and John made was not inappropriate, just ill-timed, since, according to Robinson, by the time James and John suggested the idea, Jesus had given up the role of Elijah.

12. Jn. 18:10; Mt. 26:51; Mk. 14:47; Lk. 22:49–50.

13. Cf. also Mt. 10:35–39 and Lk. 12:51–53.

14. Mt. 10:34–39; 19:27–30; Mk. 10:28–31; Lk. 14:25–33; 18:28–30.

15. Mt. 19:29; Mk. 10:29–30; Lk. 18:29–30.

16. Mt. 8:19–20; Lk. 9:57–58.

17. Mt. 19:10–12.

18. Italics ours. Cf. Mt. 16:24–28; Mk. 8:34 f.; Lk. 14:25–27.

19. F. M. Cross, *op. cit.,* p. 238.

20. Mt. 19:16–24; Mk. 10:17–25; Lk. 18:18–25. Cf. also Mt. 6:19–34.

21. Mt. 4:24–25; Mk. 3:7–8; Lk. 6:17; etc.

22. Mt. 8:28–34; 9:32–33; 15:21–28; 17:14–21; Mk. 1:23–28; 5:1–20; 7:24–30; 9:14–29; Lk. 4:33–37; 8:26–39; 9:37–43a; 11:14.

23. Mt. 8:1–4, 5–17; 9:20–22, 27–30; 20:29–34; Mk. 1:29–34, 40–45; 5:25–34; 7:31–37; 8:22–26; 10:46–52; Lk. 4:38–41; 5:12–16; 7:1–10; 8: 43–48; 13:10–13; 17:11–19; 18:35–43; Jn. 4:46–54; 5:2–9; 9:1–7.

24. Mt. 9:1–8; Mk. 2:1–12; Lk. 5:17–26; 7:36–50.

25. Mt. 9:18; Mk. 5:21–43; Lk. 7:11–17; 8:40–56; Jn. 11:1–44.

26. Mt. 8:18, 23–27; 14:13–21, 22–33; 15:32–39; Mk. 4:35–41; 6:30–44, 45–52; 8:1–10; Lk. 8:22–25; 9:10–17; Jn. 2:1–11; 6:1–14, 16–21.

27. Mt. 4:23–25; 9:26; 14:34–36; Mk. 1:28, 45; 3:7–12; 6:53–56; Lk. 4:37; 5:15; 7:17.

28. Cf. Mt. 13:58 and Mk. 6:5–6a.

29. Mt. 9:8; 15:29–31; Mk. 2:12; 5:19; Lk. 5:25–26; 7:16; 8:39a; 9:43a; 17:15–19; 18:43. Cf. Jn. 9:24–34.

30. Lk. 4:42–44; 5:15–16; Mk. 1:35–39. Cf. Jn. 6:25–27.

31. Cf. Lk. 4:13.

32. Cf. Mk. 1:34.

33. Mt. 10:1, 7; Mk. 6:7, 12, 13; Lk. 9:1–2, 6. For the following comments about the disciples' preaching missions, see Mt. 10:1–16; Mk. 6:7–13; Lk. 9:1–6; 10:1–12.

34. Cf. Man. of Disc. 4:2–8.

35. In these passages, when Jesus refers to "the Son of Man," he must surely be referring to the corporate figure representing the People Israel fulfilled through the establishment of the Kingdom of God on earth. Cf. Russell, *op. cit.,* pp. 338 ff. He could not have meant himself, for he (Jesus) had obviously *already come,* and to tell his disciples that they would have gone through all the towns of Israel *before* the Son of Man came (Mt. 10:23b) would have been nonsensical if he was referring to

himself. It seems clear, then, that in this passage Jesus means to say,
"Before your mission is completed, the Messiah will come to establish
the Kingdom and the *whole people* (the Son of Man) will be redeemed—
that is, set free from slavery to the forces of darkness."

36. Montefiore, *op. cit.*, pp. 140 f. Joel Carmichael, *The Death of Jesus,*
New York: Macmillan, 1962, pp. 128 ff., perceives a clear turning point in
Jesus' career in the abrupt break in the Gospel narratives which occurs
after his having dispatched his disciples to declare the Kingdom and their
return. Having been disappointed at his reception in Galilee, Jesus then
decides on a change of plan—"he brings his whole career to a sharp focus
by a decision to go to Jerusalem. The entry into the Holy City is obviously
heavy with meaning." (p. 129) Carmichael attributes this decision by
Jesus to his "failure in Galilee," and sees the disciples "filled with enthusiasm and anticipation of the longed-for event as they drew near Jerusalem." (p. 131. Cf. Mt. 19:28.) Eisler, *op. cit.,* had earlier spotlighted
the sending out of the disciples as a crucial point in Jesus' public ministry:
"The mission could not be other than a complete failure, could not but
end with a shattering of the trustful confidence even of those first converts
of the hidden Messiah. God had not intervened, and the coming of the
'Son of Man' announced by Jesus did not take place before the return of
his delegates. His call died away unheard." (p. 363) Schweitzer, *The Quest
of the Historical Jesus,* pp. 359 ff., had surmised as early as 1906 that
Jesus expected the coming of the Kingdom at the harvest time, and that it
was obvious from his charge to the disciples in Matthew 10:23, that Jesus
did not expect to see the disciples again in "the present age." The coming
of the Son of Man, "which is logically and temporally identical with the
dawn of the Kingdom, will take place before they shall have completed a
hasty journey through the cities of Israel to announce it" (p. 359). After
the non-arrival of the Son of Man and the Kingdom, in Schweitzer's
view, Jesus adopted a change of plans: "the new conviction that had
dawned upon Him [was that] He must suffer for others . . . that the
Kingdom might come. This change was due to the non-fulfillment of
the promises made in the discourse at the sending forth of the Twelve.
He had thought then to let loose the final tribulation and so compel the
coming of the kingdom." (p. 389)

37. "Elijah, John and Jesus," *op. cit.,* p. 38.

38. It is in part for that reason that Bishop John Robinson prefers
the Fourth Gospel's dating of the cleansing of the Temple: that is, at the
beginning of Jesus' public activities rather than at the end (Jn. 2:13–25). The
first act of God's "messenger" (Elijah), according to Malachi, will be to
cleanse the temple: "I am going to send my messenger to prepare a way
before me. And the Lord you are seeking will suddenly enter his Temple
. . . he will purify the sons of Levi [i.e., the priests] and refine them like
gold and silver, and then they will make the offering to Yahweh as it
should be made" (Mal. 3:1a and 3b). Therefore, Robinson believes that

Jesus would have tried to cleanse the Temple first in his eagerness to fulfill John the Baptist's conviction that he, Jesus, was Elijah (*op. cit.*, p. 40).

Dr. Robinson goes on to propose that Jesus' temptation in the wilderness may have come *after* this initial period of Jesus' work when he was trying out the role of Elijah, since John's Gospel infers that Jesus went to Galilee to preach and teach because of a kind of rivalry with John the Baptist: "When Jesus heard that the Pharisees had found out that he was making and baptising more disciples than John . . . he left Judaea and went back to Galilee" (Jn. 4:1, 3). Robinson feels that Jesus might have gone into the wilderness to struggle with the temptation which popularity and notoriety of success represented to him (*op. cit.*, p. 43), and that having overcome that temptation he *then* went to Galilee to carry on his work so as not to compete with John the Baptist. There, Robinson believes, Jesus began to model himself on the servant-son image of the baptismal voice (Mk. 1:11; Jn. 1:33 f.; cf. Is. 42:1) rather than the mighty one of John's proclamation (*loc. cit.*). In Galilee Jesus would have begun to act out a role other than that of Elijah the messenger who was to prepare the way for the Kingdom's establishment.

If one accepts Bishop Robinson's thesis, it is difficult to explain the record of Jesus' teaching and preaching provided by the other three Gospels, which clearly indicate that Jesus went up to Galilee to preach repentance and the coming Kingdom—the very role which Dr. Robinson suggests he rejected *before* going to Galilee. The theory needs to be mentioned, however, as it is one way to account for John's dating of the cleansing of the Temple at the beginning of Jesus' ministry.

39. Jean Daniélou (*op. cit.*, p. 43) believes that the wilderness temptation story repeats themes from the Exodus of the Israelites from Egypt, as we saw in Chapter 7, page 98, above. According to Daniélou's interpretation of the temptation story, from the beginning Jesus could be seen as emerging as "the prophet" of Deuteronomy—the new Moses. Cf. Eisler, *op. cit.*, p. 367: "In the early period of his messianic career, the period of the sermon on the mount, Jesus was a thorough quietist. Exactly how he departed from this attitude we do not know. It may be that the Zealots among his disciples, whom he had already won over in spite of his pacifistic doctrines, gradually drove him forward on the fatal road. It may also be that in the face of the impenetrable silence of heaven he decided on his own account to give up waiting, and, in the role of the 'prophet like Moses' promised in Deuteronomy, to lead the people out of the land of bondage to freedom." Cf. also Simon, *St. Stephen and the Hellenists*, p. 58: In St. Stephens' speech in Acts 6 and 7, "Stephen aims at demonstrating that Jesus is, in the fullest meaning of the phrase 'a prophet like unto Moses.' He continues, restores, fulfills, the work initiated by Moses."

40. Cf. also Mt. 15:32–39 and Mk. 8:1–10.

41. Cf. also Mk. 6:44; Lk. 9:14a; Jn. 6:10b; Mt. 15:38.

42. Cf. War Scroll 4:1–5; and Montefiore, *op. cit.*, pp. 137 f.

43. Montefiore, *op. cit.*, p. 135.

44. *Ibid.*, p. 136.

45. *Loc. cit.* Italics ours. Cf. also Numbers 27:16 ff. "According to Numbers, Moses prayed that the Lord would appoint a man over the congregation 'who shall go out before them and come in before them, who shall lead them out and bring them in; that the congregation of the Lord may not be as sheep which have no shepherd.' It may be noted that according to Numbers this incident took place in the wilderness, and that there is a reference to the coming and going of the people, and that the name of the man appointed was Joshua (Jesus)" (Montefiore, *op. cit.*, p. 136 [3]). Cf. also Manson, *The Servant-Messiah*, London: Cambridge University Press, 1966, p. 70.

46. Montefiore, *op. cit.*, p. 136.

47. Manson, *op. cit.*, p. 71. Cf. also Maurice Goguel, *Jesus and the Origins of Christianity*, Vol. II, New York: Harper & Brothers, 1960, p. 377, and Montefiore, *op. cit.*, p. 138.

48. Montefiore, *loc. cit.*

49. Jn. 6:25–71; Mt. 16:5–12; Mk. 8:14–21.

50. Cf. also Mk. 8:14–21.

51. See, for example, Mk. 6:14–15; Mt. 14:2, 5; Lk. 9:7–9; Jn. 6:14b; 7:40–41.

52. See also, Mt. 16:13–16; Lk. 9:18–20.

53. Bishop John Robinson believes that Mark's account of the Caesarea Philippi event (Mk. 8:27–30) is the most primitive and therefore the most reliable. He says, therefore, that in the succeeding verses Jesus "rebuked" Peter (Mk. 8:31–33), indicating that he rejected Peter's use of the title "Messiah" (or "Christ"). Jesus, Robinson believes, had decided that "Son of Man" was a more appropriate title for himself. It seems clear, however, that Jesus' rebuke of Peter stemmed from the fact that Peter rejected his teaching regarding the Son of Man, about whom he spoke in the third person. His rebuke, "The way you think is not God's way but man's." (Mk. 8:33), is related to Peter's refusal to admit the possibility that the corporate Son of Man figure, which represented the People Israel redeemed and restored to perfection, would have to suffer, be rejected by the elders and chief priests and scribes, be killed and rise again (Mk. 8:31). Since Jesus had earlier told his disciples they would have to believe his teachings if they were to inherit the Kingdom, his rebuke of Peter for his disbelief seems quite in character. It was not necessarily related in any way to Peter's "confession" which preceded it. Moreover, the fact that Matthew later expanded Mark's account of Peter's "confession" by relating Jesus' *praise* of Peter for saying he was the Christ (Mt. 16:17–20), suggests that the disciples recalled it as an experience

which confirmed Jesus' role, rather than contradicted it, and which met with Jesus' approval.

54. Mt. 17:1–13; Mk. 9:2–13; Lk. 9:28–36.

55. Cf. also Mt. 17:5 and Mk. 9:7.

56. Cf. Mt. 17:9; Mk. 9:9 f.; Lk. 9:36.

57. Cf. James McLeman, *Resurrection Then and Now*, p. 187.

58. See, for example, Maurice Bucke's description of such experiences in *Cosmic Consciousness*. Cf. also Raynor Johnson's *The Imprisoned Splendour*, New York: Harper & Row, 1953, and Evelyn Underhill's *Mysticism*, London: Methuen & Co., Ltd., 1967.

59. See note 36 above. Also, cf. Albert Schweitzer's *The Kingdom of God and Primitive Christianity*, London: Adam & Charles Black, 1968, pp. 3 ff. He contends that "Christianity is essentially a religion of belief in the coming of the Kingdom of God." He shows how the delay of that event —the Parousia—influenced the development of the Jewish conception of the Kingdom of God according to the Prophets, the apocalyptic conception of the Kingdom dating from Daniel to the Fall of Jerusalem (and including the Enochian literature and Psalms of Solomon which foresee at the beginning of the final events a great rebellion, miracles, great tribulation, the resurrection, Son of Man, and judgment), and the beliefs of the early Christians.

60. Brownlee, "John the Baptist in the Light of Ancient Scrolls," pp. 49 f., elucidates the transfiguration experience with these words: "Rev. 11, a passage whose presence in a Christian document can only be explained as appropriated and adapted from an older Jewish work, presents us with the picture of two martyred prophets, namely, Moses and Elijah *redivivus* [reincarnate], and for a period before their martyrdom 'fire pours from their mouth and consumes their foes.' In the old Jewish source, these prophets were two Messiahs, for they are explained as 'the two olive trees and the two lampstands' of Zech. 4, and therefore as the 'two anointed ones' of Zech. 4:14. By means of this passage two contending explanations of the Prophet of Deut. 18:15 were joined, by allowing for both Moses (Rev. 11:5, 6b; cf. Num. 16:35; Ex. 7:17, 19) and Elijah (Rev. 11:5, 6a; cf. 2 Kings 1:10; 1 Kings 17:1) who are presented as persons essentially alike. This expectation of the return of Moses and Elijah lies back of the transfiguration experience of Jesus, but when they appear they bear witness rather to *his* suffering and resurrection, thus correcting the notion that it is they who must become martyrs. When it comes to Elijah's suffering, we have a reference in Mk. 9:13, which is highly significant: 'But I tell you that Elijah has come, and they did to him whatever they pleased, as it is written of him.' The only natural interpretation of this passage is that John the Baptist's martyrdom is in fulfillment of prophecy regarding a suffering Elijah."

The Teacher of Righteousness was also seen to have suffered persecution— thus fitting in with Brownlee's analysis above—and to have been regarded by some as the new Moses—that is, the one who gave a new Law and a New Covenant to the people in the wilderness. See, for example, Carmignac, *op. cit.,* pp. 48 ff. and Brownlee, *The Meaning of the Qumran Scrolls for the Bible,* New York: Oxford University Press, 1964, pp. 71 and 72 (19).

61. John Robinson believes that Jesus had determined to model himself on the "servant-Son of the Baptismal voice" (*op. cit.,* p. 43), and that after the transfiguration experience he began to prepare his disciples for the fact that he would have to suffer in order to fulfill his chosen role. Professor David Flusser, on the other hand, does not believe that Jesus thought of himself as the Messiah and as also having to suffer, since there is no precedent in Judaism for the concept of a martyred Messiah. The concept of martyrdom as a vicarious suffering for Israel was widespread, however, Flusser asserts ("Jesus in the Context of History," p. 233. Cf. also Joseph Klausner, *Jesus of Nazareth,* p. 301). It is our feeling that Jesus thought suffering was likely—even probable—as a consequence of his confrontation with the forces of darkness in Jerusalem, and that if his suffering was necessary, he anticipated that it would have expiatory significance. We are not convinced, however, that he thought his death was predetermined—nor that he thought it essential—for the fulfillment of his Messianic role. To the contrary, it seems he hoped until th. very end that God would choose to use him as the one who would redeem, or liberate, Israel. Cf. Goguel, *op. cit.,* p. 421.

62. See, for example, Mt. 16:21–23 and parallels; Mt. 17:11–12; Mk. 9:12, 30–31 and parallels; Mk. 10:32–34 and parallels.

63. Cf. Matthew Black, "The Dead Sea Scrolls and Christian Origins," pp. 101 ff.; R. K. Harrison, "The Rites and Customs of the Qumran Sect," *The Scrolls and Christianity,* pp. 30 f.; John Pryke, "Eschatology in the Dead Sea Scrolls," *The Scrolls and Christianity,* p. 51; Flusser, *op. cit.,* p. 233; F. F. Bruce, "Jesus and the Gospels in the Light of the Scrolls," pp. 80 f.; Brownlee, *op. cit.,* pp. 50 f.

64. Flusser, *op. cit.,* pp. 233 f.; Klausner, *op. cit.,* pp. 301 f.

65. The word for "many" is *rabbim,* the same one used in the name of the sect: "The Many." It is possible that Jesus was thinking of himself as a ransom for those who belonged to the movement, that is, that he was literally giving himself for the cause. Cf. Joachim Jeremias, *The Eucharistic Words of Jesus,* London: SCM Press Ltd., 1966, p. 227, who points out that "rabbim," "the Many," as used in the Targum on the prophets when paraphrasing Isaiah 52:13 to 53:12, means "the house of Israel." Of course Qumran understood itself to be the righteous remnant of that house, and Jesus may thus have hoped to serve as a ransom for the whole "House of Israel."

66. Mk. 8:34 to 9:1 and parallels.

67. This passage clearly reveals that *not all* Pharisees were "out to get" Jesus.

68. See e.g., Jn. 8:12–59; 9:1–41; 10:1–21.

69. Mt. 22:15–22; Mk. 12:13–17; Lk. 20:20–26.

70. Cullmann, *The State in the New Testament*, p. 35.

71. Brandon, *The Trial of Jesus of Nazareth*, p. 67.

72. *Loc. cit.*

73. *Loc. cit.* See also Brandon, *Jesus and the Zealots*, pp. 45–49.

74. Cullmann, *op. cit.*, p. 34.

75. *Ibid.*, pp. 35 f.

76. Cullmann, *Jesus and the Revolutionaries*, p. 45.

77. *Maccabees, Zealots and Josephus*, p. 200.

78. *Jesus*, p. 84.

79. Winter, *On the Trial of Jesus*, Berlin: Walter de Gruyter and Co., 1961, p. 130. Winter refers to the early Jewish Christians, but we believe the question is equally applicable to Jesus and his attitude toward the Roman state.

80. A. N. Sherwin-White, *Roman Society and Roman Law in the New Testament*, London: Oxford University Press, 1963, pp. 126 f., indicates that other than Roman coins were in circulation at the time of Jesus (witness Mt. 22:19 where Jesus asks for "the money you pay the tax with"—implying the Roman *denarius* was the coin paid as tax)—as evidenced in the diverse coins mentioned in the Gospels. According to the Gospel reports of money changers who accepted Jewish coins, the disciples' purse need not have contained any of the "idolatrous," that is, Roman, coins.

81. Cf. Mt. 9:9–13; Mk. 2:13–17; Lk. 5:27–32; 15:1–7.

82. See, for example, Mt. 26:8, 9; Mk. 14:4, 5; Jn. 12:4, 5.

83. Mt. 21:23–27; Mk. 11:27–33; Lk. 20:1–8.

84. "Jesus in the Context of History," pp. 228 and 230.

85. Jn. 10:39–42; 11:54; Mt. 19:1–2; Mk. 10:1.

86. *The Quest of the Historical Jesus*, p. 371.

87. *Ibid.*, pp. 370 f.

CHAPTER 9

Jesus: A Prophet of the End of Days

1. *On the Trial of Jesus*, p. 142.
2. Mt. 21:1; Mk. 11:1; Lk. 19:29.
3. Cf. Jn. 12:12–18.
4. *Jerusalem in the Time of Jesus*, p. 62.
5. *Ibid.*, p. 73.
6. *Ibid.*, p. 76.
7. *Ibid.*, p. 84.
8. *War* II. 43, 223–24; etc. See Montefiore, *op. cit.*, p. 136.
9. Josephus, *loc. cit.* W. R. Farmer, *Maccabees, Zealots and Josephus*, p. 200.
10. Winter, *op. cit.*, p. 141.
11. Cf. Mk. 11:8–10; Mt. 21:8–9; Lk. 19:37–38.
12. Cf. Zech. 9:1–10.
13. Farmer, *op. cit.*, p. 198.
14. Mt. 21:1–7; Mk. 11:1–8; Lk. 19:28–35.
15. Farmer, *op. cit.*, p. 199.
16. J. C. McRuer, *The Trial of Jesus*, London: Blandford Press, 1965, p. 39.
17. Cf. W. R. Farmer, "The Palm Branches in John 12:13," pp. 64 ff., and *Maccabees, Zealots and Josephus*, pp. vii f.
18. Farmer, "The Palm Branches in John 12, 13," pp. 65 f.
19. Winter, *op. cit.*, p. 142. Cf. Jeremias, *op. cit.*, p. 43: "According to John 12:13, the people took branches of palm trees in Jerusalem. According to the parallel passage in the Synoptic Gospels, however, it was not the crowd going out from Jerusalem to meet Jesus which paid homage, but the festal pilgrims in whose train he approached the city, and it was not palm branches plucked in Jerusalem with which they decked his way, but bunches of leaves from the trees between Bethany or Bethphage and Jerusalem (Mk. 11:1, 8; Mt. 21:1, 8). Yet if we recall that there are a few palm trees in Jerusalem even today and that Pseudo-Aristeas 112 enumerates dates among the products of Jerusalem (pp. 41 f.), John's account appears to be within the bounds of possibility."
Eisler, *op. cit.*, p. 480, believes the mention of the palm branches to be

inauthentic: "It now becomes clear that it was only through the artificial alteration of *'osha'na*, 'Free us,' into *hoshi'ana* of the Psalmist that the palm-branches found their way into John's narrative. The festal bouquets of the Feast of Tabernacles, of which the principal item was a palm-branch, were expressly known as 'Hoshannas.' At the Passover feast, of course, none of the pilgrims carried 'the palm-branches' in their hands . . . that they bore 'the palm-branches' in their hands is clearly an invention of later Greek ignorance on Jewish matters." However, had Eisler been familiar with the symbolic significance of the palm branches which Farmer makes clear in his above quoted article, we suspect he would have adjusted his opinion on the historicity of John 12:13. The fact that the pilgrims would not have been carrying the palm branches for their festal offerings is evidence that they would have been previously prepared and handed out to the crowds as part of a planned Messianic demonstration.

20. Winter, *op. cit.*, p. 142: "If used in the welcome of Jesus, palm branches would have had to be imported specially for that particular purpose." And Farmer, "The Palm Branches in John 12:13," p. 65: "It is quite clear from St. John's account that the palm branches are not casually gathered from alongside the road nor cut down from trees just outside the city on the spur of the moment."

21. Carmichael, *op. cit.*, p. 184. Eisler's comments (*op. cit.*), p. 478, are particularly enlightening in this regard: "The most instructive and noteworthy passage, in the otherwise insignificant and absurd so-called *Acta Pilati* of the fourth century, is the curious, inconclusive dispute between the Jewish plaintiffs and the lackey or 'runner' (*cursor*) of Pilate, concerning the true meaning of the people's cry, 'Hosanna'" [the passage reads: "Pilate saith unto them (the Jews): 'And the *Hosanna* and the rest, how is it interpreted?' The Jews say unto him: 'Save now, thou that art blessed in the highest, blessed is he that cometh in the name of the Lord.'"] (p. 476). Eisler goes on, "This gallant runner entirely suppresses the words of political significance which stand out prominently in Mark, Luke and John, 'Blessed be the kingship of David,' 'Blessed be he that cometh, the king,' 'Blessed be the king of Israel'—words which, moreover, have already disappeared in Matthew. Here we have, then, an obvious attempt to brazenly deny that Jesus was really acclaimed king by the people, and in this the Jews were at one with the Christians in disclaiming before the Romans all responsibility for the treasonable cry . . . in the current Aramaic vernacular this simply means 'Free us'" (p. 478).

22. Farmer, *Maccabees, Zealots and Josephus*, pp. 198–99. Cf. Goguel, *op. cit.*, Vol. II, p. 425: "Thus in his own eyes, as in those of his disciples, this entry into the Holy City was the act of a future Messiah."

23. *Ibid.*, p. 200.

24. See also Lk. 21:20–28.

25. *Op. cit.*, p. 411.

26. Cf. Mk. 11:11.

27. The rival temple built by Onias III at Leontopolis in Egypt (c. 170 B.C. to A.D. 73) was insignificant in comparison with the Jerusalem Temple. Cf. Jeremias, *op. cit.,* p. 29.

28. *Ibid.,* p. 75; cf. also Carmichael, *op. cit.,* p. 136.

29. *Op. cit.,* pp. 27 f.

30. *Ibid.,* p. 138.

31. *War* VI. 317.

32. Jeremias, *op. cit.,* pp. 48 f.: "Jesus came into the temple court and overturned the 'tables of the money-changers,' and the 'seats of those who sold doves.' According to John this meant those 'who sold oxen, sheep and doves.' The authenticity of this evidence has been questioned, but with no good reason. Zechariah 14:21 already speaks of traders in the sanctuary [fourth to third century B.C.]. [Talmudic and Mishnaic sources] give evidence of money-changers in the Temple court. The shops on the aqueduct were probably in the Temple court . . . there is a rabbinic tradition which indicates the sale of cattle in the Temple area. According to [one source], R. Baba b. Buta (a contemporary of Herod the Great) had three thousand head of small livestock brought to the Temple hill to be sold for whole burnt offerings and peace-offerings . . . there were shops [which] apparently belonged to the high-priestly family . . . So we are forced to conclude that in the Court of the Gentiles, in spite of the sanctity of the Temple area, there could have been a flourishing trade in animals for sacrifice, perhaps supported by the powerful high-priestly family of Annas."

33. IV Macc. 4:3; II Macc. 3:4–6; *War* VI. 282. Jeremias, *op. cit.,* p. 56.

34. *Op. cit.,* p. 99. Ananus, son of the High Priest Ananias, appears in A.D. 52 as captain of the Temple, a rank second only to that of the High Priest (*Ant.* XX. 131; *War* II. 243). Another son of Ananias, Eleazar, held the same office in A.D. 66 (*War* II. 409; *Ant.* XX. 208).

35. Winter, *op. cit.,* p. 172 (9): "The word [Messiah] denotes a worldly ruler, a man among men, not a leader of celestial beings. The Gospels leave no doubt as to the fact that a claim to 'kingship' was made on Jesus' behalf by his disciples, and that Jesus was tried and executed on such a charge." While Winter attributes the claim of "kingship" to Jesus' disciples, we believe that Jesus himself played a more active role in his designation as "Messiah" than Winter implies. Throughout his work *On the Trial of Jesus,* Winter depreciates the part of Jesus in the events of Passion Week, attributing little or no responsibility to Jesus himself for the events leading to his death. The result of such an approach is to strip Jesus of any character or personality—and to remove him from any active role in the events which concern us. We believe the whole story hangs together more coherently if one ascribes to Jesus an active, conscious role in the developments of which he was the major focus and motivator. It is difficult to believe the disciples would have wanted to proclaim a "spineless" and "characterless" man their king.

S. G. F. Brandon, in reviewing C. H. Dodd's *The Founder of Christianity,* New York: The Macmillan Co., 1970 ("The Messiah," The Manchester *Guardian,* Feb. 25, 1971) makes a similar point, saying that C. H. Dodd creates a paradoxical portrait of Jesus. It is, he suggests, difficult to reconcile Jesus' Messianic entry into Jerusalem with his withdrawal from any attempts to make himself a king. Dodd's work contains no mention of the tribute issue (paying taxes to Caesar) or of Jesus' disciples bearing arms. Brandon rightly observes that according to Dodd, Jesus is "done in" by a misunderstanding *which he himself caused.* Brandon assesses Dodd's work as "an orthodox defense" which, oddly enough, does not provide a very good image: Jesus is a well-meaning character, but his words and actions are all misunderstood; he is an innocent playing with fire.

36. Alfred Edersheim, *The Temple: Its Ministry and Services,* Grand Rapids, Michigan: Wm. B. Eerdmans Publishing Company, 1965, p. 45.

37. Cf. Mk. 11:16, 17; Mt. 21:13, 14; Lk. 19:46.

38. Cf., for example, Lk. 19:47.

39. Carmichael, *op. cit.,* pp. 134 ff.

40. *Ibid.,* p. 140. Cf. Mk. 14:49.

41. Cf. Carmichael, *op cit.,* p. 139.

42. Cf. Eisler, *op. cit.,* p. 469, as quoted on p. 174 below.

43. P. 486.

44. Haim Cohn, *Reflections on the Trial and Death of Jesus,* [Reprint of (1967) 2 Israel Law Review, pp. 332–79], Jerusalem Post Press, p. 29 (130). See also "Reflections on the Trial of Jesus" in *Judaism,* Vol. 20, No. 1, Winter 1971, pp. 10–23, and the recently published expanded English version, *The Trial and Death of Jesus,* New York: Harper & Row, 1971.

45. Cullmann, *Jesus and the Revolutionaries,* pp. 16 ff., discusses these three points.

46. Maurice Goguel, *op. cit.,* pp. 396 ff.

47. *Op. cit.,* p. 40. Cf. Jn. 2:13–22. See also, Chapter 8, n. 38 above. Robinson believes the cleansing was a type of public demonstration and a nuisance, but not an event of any magnitude.

48. *The Trial of Jesus of Nazareth,* p. 84.

49. *Op. cit.,* p. 138. Italics his.

50. *Op. cit.,* p. 342.

51. *Op. cit.,* pp. 495 ff.

52. *Jesus and the Revolutionaries,* pp. 8 ff. Italics his.

53. *Op. cit.,* p. 16.

54. *Ibid.,* p. 20.

55. *Op. cit.,* p. 143.

56. *Op. cit.,* p. 10 (17).

57. See note 47 above.

58. "The Temple and the Cross," *Judaism,* Vol. 20, No. 1, Winter 1971, p. 27.

59. *Op. cit.*, p. 29.

60. "A Literary Approach to the Trial of Jesus," *Judaism*, Vol. 20, No. 1, Winter 1971, p. 34.

61. Cf. Mt. 21:13; Lk. 19:46. Bishop John Robinson feels that this reference to the Temple as a "den of robbers" reflects Jesus' opposition to the Zealots, since "robbers" is the term used by the historian Josephus to describe the Zealots. There are two difficulties with such an interpretation. First, Jesus is quoting a passage of Old Testament scripture (Jer. 7:11) which was written long before Josephus, and we have no indication Jeremiah was referring to anything like the Zealot movement in his statement about the Temple as a den of robbers. Second, at the time Jesus cleansed the Temple, the Zealots were *not* in charge of it; the High Priest and his collaborators with the Romans were. Thus, if Jesus was expressing his opposition to the Zealots, he chose a most inappropriate method of doing so: he attacked the *enemies* of the Zealots, rather than the Zealots themselves.

62. See Chapter 4, pp. 46 ff. above.

H. J. Schoeps (*op. cit.*, pp. 83, 86, 118–21) discusses the historical continuity of anti-cultic elements in Judaism from the Rechabites to the Essenes and to the Ebionites. He speaks of the "ancient wilderness-ideal of the prophets" which may have been the determining factor in inspiring the exodus to the wilderness of the Rechabites and later of the Essenes. This prophetic ideal held that the wilderness was a place of grace (Jer. 31:2), and that God himself called men to flee to the wilderness (Hos. 2:14) where He would build a road (Is. 43:19). The complementary attitude of this wilderness-ideal shared by the prophets and nomadic peoples within Judaism, was a hostility toward the sacrificial cult of Jerusalem. Such antisacrificial groups as the Ebionites viewed the laws of the sacrificial cult as late and false additions to the Mosaic Law. They rejected the monarchies of David and Solomon because they were responsible for construction of the Temple. Such groups based their rejection of the Temple on the prophetic proclamations of Nathan (II Sam. 7) and Ezekiel (20:25 f.). The belief that construction of a stone temple was a perversion of the Mosaic religion survived for many centuries in the apocryphal thought of nomadic circles and the Rechabites, Essenes and Ebionites. While Jesus' cleansing of the Temple seems to have been geared toward purifying rather than abolishing the sacrifice, Schoeps believes that the continuity of the anti-cultic movement in Christian Judaism, or Ebionitism, must have found justification for its rejection of sacrifice in Jesus' own teachings. For further comment on prophetic criticism of the Temple cultus, see Gartner, *op. cit.*, pp. 45 f.

W. H. C. Frend, *op. cit.*, p. 144, reports that at the time of the Fall of Jerusalem many Jews shared the view that the Temple's destruction was due to the Jews' own idolatry and godlessness: "These Jews spoke instead of a 'sacrifice of prayers,' of the restoration of spiritual worship without buildings made with hands, inaugurated by the prophets." We have seen that the Qumran Covenanters saw their holy way of life as a surrogate for Temple worship, and believed that their community was a spiritual temple which would serve until a new, and cleansed temple could be established by God. Paul and the early Church seem to have believed in much the same concept.

The *Naṣaraioi,* in which tradition Jesus the Nazarene stood, were against the Temple and believed that the Pentateuch passages referring to sacrifice were interpolations. The Pharisees were also opposed to the Temple cultus. Only the Sadducees failed to criticize the Temple, and they were the party which constituted the majority of the collaborationist Jewish hierarchy. Any opposition to the Temple was an implicit threat to the hierarchy, and therefore had revolutionary implications, and quite naturally the Sadducees were not a part of such movements.

Professor David Flusser, in conversation with the authors, suggested that in view of the inscription on the cross: "Jesus the Nazarene, King of the Jews," recorded in John 19:19, it may be that being a "Nazarene" was the first or second crime of which Jesus was convicted. The charge might have read: "Jesus the Iconoclast; King of the Jews." Professor Flusser believes that the fact that the Ebionites (as a Jewish Christian sect) believed that Jesus abolished Temple worship contributes to the impression that Jesus was anti-Temple. It would seem that Jesus stood in the line of prophets who taught that Temple worship bordered on pagan idolatry.

That criticism of the Temple was considered an extremely serious matter—and even one deserving of death—is corroborated by the story of the death of Stephen told in Acts 6:8–15, 7:1–60. Stephen was arrested on charges of having said that "Jesus the Nazarene is going to destroy this Place [the Temple] and alter the traditions that Moses handed down to us." (Acts 6:14) Stephen answered their charges with a long speech, ending with the words, "Even so the Most High does not live in a house that human hands have built: for as the prophet says: 'With heaven my throne and earth my footstool, what house could you build me, what place could you make for my rest? Was not all this made by my hand?'" (Acts 7:48–50). When the Sanhedrin heard this, "they all rushed at him, sent him out of the city and stoned him" (7:57). Such open criticism of the Temple was apparently considered a crime worthy of punishment with death, even though Stephen had not taken direct action against those who operated the Temple. How much more, then, must Jesus' attack on the Temple have offended and threatened them.

63. Gartner, *op. cit.,* pp. 105–8 passim.
64. *Ibid.,* pp. 108 f. passim. Italics ours.
65. *Ibid.,* p. 109 passim. Italics ours.
66. Cf. Stephen's speech in Acts 7:2–53.
67. See Chapter 4, p. 47 above. Cf. also Gartner, *op. cit.,* pp. 111 f. Gartner, p. 113, thinks that by the expression "in three days" Jesus was

making reference to the establishment of a "spiritual" temple (as in the sentence which follows in our text) by his own resurrection and return. We will deal with the question of Jesus' resurrection in Chapter 13.

68. Gartner, *op. cit.,* pp. 113 ff. Cf. also Oscar Cullmann, "The Significance of the Qumran Texts for Research into the Beginnings of Christianity," *The Scrolls and the New Testament,* p. 22; F. F. Bruce, "Jesus and the Gospels in the Light of the Scrolls," p. 76; and Flusser, "The Dead Sea Sect and Pre-Pauline Christianity," pp. 229 ff., who writes: "To sum up: As the Qumran covenanters thought that the Jerusalem Temple was polluted, they could not take part in the Temple service of their time. This inability to offer real sacrifices engendered an ambivalent attitude to the sacrificial rites: On the one hand the sect hoped to offer sacrifices according to its own rites and by its own priests in a purified future Temple; on the other they believed that their non-sacrificial rites (lustrations, prayers, strict observance of the Law) could serve as a full substitute for Temple service. This belief led them to speculation about the equality of the two services, to the use of symbols taken from the Temple ritual when describing Sectarian rites, and, finally, to the view that the sect itself was a kind of spiritual Temple. We have shown that one of the New Testament passages which express this concept is directly dependent on a Sectarian prototype: we have reason to believe that the concept itself came from Sectarian circles. This view, that the Church is a spiritual Temple, did not only mean for the Christians that the Church was a united body which contained holiness, but also that, being a spiritual Temple, it was superior to the material Temple of the Jews. The concept thus helped in the separation of Christianity from Judaism, in a way analogous (though not equal) to its influence on the estrangement between the [Qumran] sect and the rest of Judaism, for whom the actual sanctuary of Jerusalem was a symbol of religious unity." (pp. 235 f.) Note also Flusser's suggested parallel between this passage from the Rule of the Community (8:4–10):

> When these come to pass in Israel, the council of the community will be truly established for an eternal planting, a holy house for Israel and a foundation of holy of holies for Aaron, true witnesses for justice and the elect of God's will, to make atonement for the land and to render to the wicked their recompense. This is the tested wall, a precious cornerstone; its foundations will not tremble or move from their place; a dwelling of holy of holies for Aaron in the knowledge of all for a covenant of justice and to offer a pleasant savour, and house of perfection and truth in Israel to establish a covenant for eternal statutes. And they shall be acceptable to atone for the land . . . (p. 233)

with this from the First Epistle of Peter (2:5–6):

... and like living stones be yourselves ... sacrifices acceptable to God through Jesus Christ. For it stands in scripture: "Behold, I am laying in Zion a stone, a cornerstone chosen and precious, and he who believes in him will not be put to shame." (RSV)

First Peter, Flusser concludes, depends in its form and content on a Sectarian prototype (pp. 233 f.).

For further reflections on the question of the term "made with hands" meaning idolatry, cf. Simon, *St. Stephen and the Hellenists*, pp. 87–89.

69. *Op. cit.*, p. 469.

70. *Op. cit.*, p. 415: "At the outset the record must have been a great deal simpler than it is now. Originally it would have said that Jesus protested against the presence of the sellers of merchandise and money-changers in the Temple. Quite naturally the saying of Jesus was transformed into an incident, and, at a third stage of development, the saying and the story to which it had given rise were combined."

71. S. G. F. Brandon, *The Trial of Jesus of Nazareth*, p. 187 (47), comments that "Jesus' attack on the Temple establishment doubtless inspired the belief that he had threatened the Temple and its cultus. Josephus similarly charged the Zealots with destroying the Temple (*Ant.* XX. 166; *War* II. 391–94; 397–401), despite the fact that they were profoundly attached to it."

72. Brandon, *op. cit.*, p. 85.

73. Brandon, *op. cit.*, p. 145 and Eisler, *op. cit.*, p. 469, quoted above on p. 174.

74. Brandon, *op. cit.*, p. 185 (13): "John's dating of the 'Cleansing' not only contradicts the other three Gospels, but it raises insuperable difficulties for understanding the course of Jesus' ministry."

CHAPTER 10

The Apocalyptic Tension of Holy Week

1. Cf. also Mt. 23:37–39; 24:1–31; Mk. 13:3–27. Italics ours.
2. Cf. also Mt. 24:32–36; Mk. 13:28–31.
3. There are scholars who believe he did identify himself with the Son of Man. See Oscar Cullmann, *The Christology of the New Testament*, Philadelphia: The Westminster Press, 1963, pp. 152 ff., esp. pp. 159 ff.; J. A. T. Robinson, *Jesus and His Coming*, London: SCM Press Ltd., 1967, pp. 36 ff., esp. p. 82. But see Reginald H. Fuller, *The Foundations of New Testament Christology*, New York: Charles Scribner's Sons, 1965, pp. 119 ff.
4. See Mt. 22 to 25; Mk. 13; Lk. 21.
5. Cf. also Mt. 21:28–46; 22:1–14; Mk. 11:12–25; 12:1–11; Lk. 20:9–18; Jn. 12:23–50.
6. Cf. Mt. 21:23–27; Mk. 11:27–33; Lk. 20:1–8.
7. Cf. Jn. 14–17.
8. Cf. Man. of Disc. 1:7–11a; 5:20b to 6:8a.
9. See Chapter 1 above.
10. Cullmann, *Jesus and the Revolutionaries*, pp. 40 f.: "This is the 'opportune time' for which the Devil according to Luke 4:13 waited: the final temptation. Jesus is tempted to shrink back from death. According to Luke (22:49) certain of his disciples are armed. The Roman cohort approaches. Would it not be possible to kindle a popular revolt? Has the moment not come when the Zealot ideal, the holy war, is to become a reality? And would not God assist him with 'more than twelve legions' (Matt. 26:53)? Jesus resists this decisive temptation. 'Put your sword back into its place' (Matt. 26:52)."
11. See n. 23 below.
12. Cf. also Mt. 26:17–19; Lk. 22:7–13.
13. *The Eucharistic Words of Jesus*, esp. pp. 41 ff.
14. "The Lord's Supper and the Communal Meal at Qumran," *The Scrolls and the New Testament*, p. 84 and passim. Cf. also F. M. Cross, *op. cit.*, pp. 234 f.; and Black, *The Scrolls and Christian Origins*, p. 115.
15. Kuhn, *op. cit.*, p. 85. Another strong argument for viewing Jesus' last meal as belonging to the Qumran tradition rather than the Temple-

oriented tradition in Judaism, is put forth by Annie Jaubert in her book *The Date of the Last Supper,* Staten Island: Alba House, 1965. Jaubert believes that Jesus and his disciples were celebrating a Passover feast, but according to the solar calendar which was followed by the Covenanters. The Temple operated on the lunar calendar. This would have meant that they would have had their meal on Tuesday evening rather than the Thursday evening of the regular Passover feast (pp. 52, 61, 63, 65).

We have already spoken of the calendar dispute which arose between the Qumran sect and the Temple priesthood when the latter adopted the pagan lunar calendar and began to fix feast days by it. The Qumran calendar, outlined in the Book of Jubilees, begins each year on Wednesday since, according to the creation story, "the stars were created on the fourth day" of the week. Jaubert observes that "it was logical to make [Wednesday] the point of departure for their planetary revolutions" (pp. 24, 40). According to the solar calendrical system, Wednesday, Friday, and Sunday emerge as the most important days of the liturgical calendar, with a special emphasis on Wednesday. These same days, Jaubert points out, were the liturgical days of the primitive Christian community, thus apparently representing some form of liturgical continuity with the Qumran sect (p. 54). According to the official lunar calendar, Passover fell on Friday that year. But according to the solar calendar the feast always fell on the same day of the week—Wednesday (pp. 21, 52). Thus Tuesday would have been the eve of the Passover for those using the Jubilees calendar.

This thesis gains credibility in that such a dating—a Tuesday night "Last Supper"—was preserved in the earliest Christian traditions as found in its liturgical formulations. Speaking of I Cor. 11:23–24, *The Apostolic Tradition of Hippolytus, The Testament of Our Lord Jesus Christ,* and the *Apostolic Constitutions,* Jaubert writes: "These are the early formulas of the liturgy. The formula, 'on the eve of his death,' does not occur, to my knowledge, in any early liturgy, though it would have been the normal formula if the liturgy had followed the Thursday tradition" (p. 84).

A Tuesday evening date for the last supper would make the whole week's sequence of events more intelligible. If Jesus entered the city on a Sunday, cleansed the Temple on Monday, and was arrested on Tuesday night, then only a day would have passed from the time of his Messianic demonstration in which he occupied the Temple, until his apprehension by the Romans. The larger three-day interval is more difficult to explain. Moreover, a Tuesday night arrest would give three full days for the trial and crucifixion, and in light of the number of different maneuvers which reportedly occurred, a longer period of time seems more plausible. We deal with these questions in Chapters 11 and 12 below.

16. Jeremias, *op. cit.,* pp. 207 and 61.
17. See Chapter 4, pp. 52–53 above.
18. I Cor. 11:23–26. Cf. Mk. 14:24.
19. Mt. 26:29; Mk. 14:25; Lk. 22:14–20. Cf. Jeremias, *op. cit.,* pp.

217 f.: "The next meal of Jesus with his disciples will be the Messianic meal on a transformed earth," etc.

20. Mk. 14:24. The "Many" (*rabbim*) in Mk. 14:24 is the same word used by the Covenanters as a name for their congregation. Perhaps Jesus hoped that if he had to die, his death could save some of his brethren in the community of those who eagerly awaited the coming of the Kingdom, the necessity of similar suffering and death. This image of atonement for others would be in keeping with the tradition of Qumran, which sought to atone for the sins of the People Israel in order that God might redeem her. See F. F. Bruce, *Second Thoughts on the Dead Sea Scrolls*, p. 152; R. K. Harrison, "The Rites and Customs of the Qumran Sect," pp. 30 f.; Leaney, *op. cit.*, pp. 258 f. Cf. also Jeremias, *op. cit.*, pp. 227 ff.: "*his death is the vicarious death of the suffering servant, which atones for the sins of the 'many,' the peoples of the world, which ushers in the beginning of the final salvation and which effects the new covenant with God*" (p. 231. Italics his).

Neville Clark, *Interpreting the Resurrection*, London: SCM Press, 1967, p. 42, writes: "There is no need to doubt that Jesus saw his death as possessed of vicarious significance. That the suffering and death of the righteous might atone for the sins of others was a widespread belief in the Judaism of his time (II Macc. 7:37 f.; IV Macc. 1:11; 6:28 f.; 17:20 ff.). This conviction seems to have come to full flower amid the agony of the Maccabean age . . ."

Flusser disagrees. In *Jesus*, p. 98, he writes: "The Jews of those days were, it is true, acquainted with the image of martyrdom as an atoning sacrifice; but . . . Jesus did not intend to die in order to expiate the sins of others by his own brief passion. Nor did he see himself as the suffering, atoning servant of God of the Prophet Isaiah. This idea arose retrospectively in the early Church—not until after the crucifixion. Jesus had neither subtly nor mythically worked out the idea of his own death from the ancient writings, and then carried out the idea. He was no 'Christ of the festival,' for he wrestled with death to the very end." The concept of Jesus' having foreseen his death in the terms of the suffering servant of Isaiah, in Flusser's view, leads to such "abstruse concepts" as those found in Hugh J. Schonfield's *The Passover Plot* (New York: Bantam Books, 1967). See Chapter 11, n. 29 below.

21. W. H. C. Frend, in his book *Martyrdom and Persecution in the Early Church*, discusses the way in which Christian martyrdom was styled consciously after Jewish martyrdom, especially that exhibited during the Maccabean period. In discussing what the martyrs—both Jewish and Christian—expected their act of suffering to accomplish, he lists several conclusions to be drawn from the prototypical martyrs of II Maccabees 6. The conclusions which the Jews (and later the Christians—by inheritance) drew from the Maccabean martyrs were: (1) "no deviations from the prescription of Torah were permissible, particularly if these could be interpreted as giving even a tacit assent to idolatry" (p. 35); (2) "the martyr was regarded

as representative of the people of Israel . . . The victim was personally innocent, but died as a vicarious sacrifice on behalf of his people . . ." (p. 35); (3) "A third and most important point concerns eschatology. The martyr was the agent for the preparation of the Age to come. Reconciliation between God and His people through the 'hastening of God's mercy' would be speeded by his sacrifice" (p. 36); (4) "Finally, the sacrifice was willing and unresisting" (p. 36). It would seem that it was in this spirit that Jesus prepared himself and his disciples for his possible death.

22. Acts 2.
23. Mt. 26:30–32; Mk. 14:26–28; Lk. 22:39; Jn. 18:1.
24. Cf. also Mt. 26:36, 41; Mk. 14:32, 38; Lk. 22:46.
25. Mt. 26:37, 38; Mk. 14:33, 34.
26. Cf. Mk. 14:36; Mt. 26:39.
27. Cf. Mk. 14:37–42; Mt. 26:40–46; Lk. 22:45.

CHAPTER 11

The Arrest of Jesus the Nazarene

1. Cf. Winter, *op. cit.*, p. 48.

2. Cf. W. R. Farmer, *Maccabees, Zealots and Josephus*, p. 196, who uses the term "apocalyptic Zealotism" to refer to this same tradition. Farmer's point of view, among scholars, most nearly parallels our own.

3. Robert M. Grant, "The Trial of Jesus in the Light of History," *Judaism*, Vol. 20, No. 1, Winter 1971, p. 38.

4. *The Trial of Jesus of Nazareth*, p. 148.

5. It should be noted, however, that in Matthew 26:36 and Mark 14:32 Jesus does not send the disciples to Galilee, but rather tells them to "stay here while I pray." Later the Gospels report, "And they all deserted him and ran away" (Mk. 14:49b and Mt. 26:56). They do not say where the disciples ran. They may well have gone to Galilee.

6. *Loc. cit.*

7. *Ibid.*, p. 77.

8. *The State in the New Testament*, p. 32.

9. *Ibid.*, pp. 32 f.

10. *Op. cit.*, p. 49.

11. *Op. cit.*, p. 369.

12. *Ibid.*, pp. 364–65.

13. Cf. Leaney, *op. cit.*, p. 249, who, in commenting on Man. of Disc. 10:18b–20a (part of the closing hymn of the Qumran Manual of Discipline), says: "The author preserved his understanding of zealot ideals, but his reading of the will of God for the times made him believe that this included *abstention from violence until the final war* which he identifies with the day of vengeance" [italics ours].

14. This point will become more clear in the discussion in Chapter 12 of Pontius Pilate's role in the trial and of his portrayal in the Gospels.

15. *Op. cit.*, pp. 45–46.

16. P. 22. Cf. Cohn, *op. cit.*, p. 15: "At least once, we find some express reference to a Roman captain, a tribune, commanding the cohort which arrested Jesus. Both this reference and the mention of swords —which were weapons reserved for the use of Roman soldiers—have led modern scholars to the conclusion that both Roman soldiers and Temple

police were reported to have taken part in the arrest of Jesus, so that there must have been some collaboration between the Jews and the Romans, however unlikely any such collaboration would at first sight appear"; Brandon, *op. cit.*, p. 196 (155); and Winter, *op. cit.*, pp. 44–49.

17. "The Trial of Jesus in the Light of History," *Judaism,* Vol. 20, No. 1, Winter 1971, p. 52.

18. "The Last Days of Jesus," *Judaism,* Vol. 20, No. 1, Winter 1971, p. 64. For a similar use of the term, see Mt. 27:27: "The governor's soldiers took Jesus with them into the Praetorium and collected the whole cohort round him."

19. Jeremias, *Jerusalem in the Time of Jesus,* pp. 207 f.: "The Levites, descendants of the priests of the high places deposed by the Deuteronomic code, formed an inferior clergy . . . the Levites stood lower in rank to the priests, as a *clericus minor,* and as such took no part in the offering of sacrifice; they were entrusted solely with performing the Temple music and carrying out inferior duties."

20. *Ibid.,* pp. 209–10.

21. *Ibid.,* p. 163: "It was the captain of the Temple, for example, who arrested the apostles in the outer court of the Temple (Acts 5:24–26; cf. 4:1). The extent of this official's power can be gauged from this example: Eleazar, the *sāgān* [or captain] of A.D. 66, made the decision to discontinue the sacrifice for Caesar, which was equivalent to a declaration of war against Rome, and was the immediate occasion of it (*War* II. 409). Towards the end of the same year this same man was appointed by the leaders of the uprising as commander of Idumea (*War* II. 566). Nothing could more clearly illustrate the power of the captain of the Temple which he exercised there, and the reputation he enjoyed."

22. Brandon, *op. cit.,* p. 132, writes, "if [John] is right in representing the arrest as being made by the Romans, then Pilate could not have been ignorant of Jesus when the Jewish authorities delivered him at the *praetorium.* Conversely, if Jesus' case was indeed unknown to Pilate, then John cannot be right about the Roman arrest."

23. Winter, *op. cit.,* p. 47. Cf. also Cohn, *op. cit.,* p. 15.

24. Jeremias, *op. cit.,* p. 210, bases his argument that it was a Jewish force which arrested Jesus on that saying of Jesus: "Jesus' words of reproach uttered at his arrest, that day after day he was in the Temple teaching and was not taken, become most clearly understood if it was the Temple police who came to arrest him."

25. Winter, *op. cit.,* p. 145.

26. Cf., for example, Mt. 26:3–5; Mk. 14:1–2; Lk. 22:1–2, 6. Cf. also Winter, *op. cit.,* p. 147, and Cohn, *op. cit.,* p. 15.

27. Blinzler, *op. cit.,* p. 52. Winter, *op. cit.,* p. 49, believes that Jesus, as a prisoner, "was conducted to the residence of the high-priest, apparently with the order to prepare an indictment for the procuratorial trial." To Cohn, *op. cit.,* pp. 21–22, the reason for the participation of the Jewish

guard is less clear, since "no Jewish trial was (or was intended to be) conducted." He differs from Winter, saying, "the purpose of the Jewish police in arresting Jesus can have had nothing to do with preparations for any such trial. The fact that he was brought not into a Roman [jail], but into the house of the High Priest, may perhaps provide us with the solution to the question. It would appear that the Jewish police obtained from the Roman troops permission to take Jesus into custody until his trial before Pilate the next morning and, in the circumstances, such permission must have been requested so as to be granted. On their part, the Jewish police must have had instructions to ask for Jesus to be given into their custody for the night, and there can be little doubt that those who issued such instructions (presumably the High Priest himself) desired Jesus to be brought into the High Priest's house."

28. See, for example, McRuer, *op. cit.*, p. 46: "In the plot to take Jesus by stealth and kill him a ready accomplice was found in none other than one of the twelve disciples. Judas, the only disciple that was not of Galilean origin, offered his services, but at a price. For thirty pieces of silver his name was made a timeless symbol of treachery."

29. Cf., for example, Hugh Schonfield, *The Passover Plot*, p. 128, in which the author depicts Jesus as inducing Judas unconsciously to betray him. The incident of Mary's washing Jesus' feet with oil is a means by which the plot is worked out. According to Schonfield, Jesus did not know in advance that Judas would betray him, "though he may quickly have formed a strong suspicion that it might be Judas." Jesus tricked Judas into helping him fulfill his plan: "By harping on his betrayal and the circumstances of his death he was not only insisting upon what it was vital for his disciples to apprehend, he was cleverly prompting reactions which would confirm what he must know. His stratagem now was designed to pile on the pressure at the crucial moment and induce the traitor to act . . . the value of the perfume was intended to play on the weakness of Judas. The episode had the desired effect, as Jesus could observe."

30. As Cohn, *op. cit.*, p. 22 and 22 (86), has pointed out, Judas' betrayal of Jesus is "an incongruous story in itself, of theological rather than historical import . . . notwithstanding this unanimity among the Gospels, the historicity of Judas' betrayal has been doubted by many scholars." But Goguel, *op. cit.*, pp. 497 f., differs from Cohn's assessment: "It was only included in the story because there were solid reasons for believing that it actually happened."

31. David Flusser, in conversation with the authors, has expressed the belief that a comparison of the Greek texts reveals that this is a fabrication by Mark. While it is clear that Mark intended to say that Jesus was crazy, the usage is not based on the Hebrew and is clearly a Greek mode of expression. Only in Mark is Jesus said to have a

demon (Mk. 3:22–30) and, as it is not found in Luke, Flusser believes the Markan passage is a dramatization.

32. Carmichael, *op. cit.*, p. 19. Robert M. Grant (*op. cit.*, p. 42) has dealt candidly with the difficult question of the Jews' responsibility for the death of Jesus. He concludes, "In the light of history, any attempt to assign the crucifixion of Jesus to 'the Jews' is absolutely absurd. The Jews in the first century, like any aggregation of people at any time, were divided into groups and individuals who thought, felt, and acted in varying ways. Responsibility for the trial and execution of Jesus belongs to those who had the responsibility of maintaining the peace in a frontier province of the Roman empire, a province seized by the Romans less than a century earlier and gradually incorporated into their empire. Though Jesus was not a Zealot of the group which later took the lead in rebellion against Rome, his mission could easily have been understood as pointing toward rebellion. Because this was so, the Sadducean high priest and his family—both Luke and John mention Ananus as well as Caiaphas—were eager to collaborate with the Roman prefect in getting rid of a potentially revolutionary leader. The political situation in both Galilee and Judaea was too dangerous for them to imagine doing anything else."

33. *Op. cit.*, p. 149.

34. *Op. cit.*, p. 498.

35. The part of the story which refers to the thirty pieces of silver Judas accepted as payment for the betrayal (Mt. 26:14–16; Mk. 14:10 f. and Lk. 22:3–5) was surely introduced in the attempt to provide a motive for Judas' act, and also to make the betrayal fulfill prophecy—especially since Matthew, who was eager to prove that Jesus had fulfilled all prophecy, is the one Evangelist who tells us about the payment and later explains: "The words of the prophet Jeremiah were then fulfilled: 'And they took the thirty silver pieces, the sum at which the precious One was priced by children of Israel, and they gave them for the potter's field, just as the Lord directed me'" (Mt. 27:9–10).

36. Farmer, *op. cit.*, p. 197. Cf. Brandon, *op. cit.*, p. 149.

37. Winter, *op. cit.*, p. 109; Brandon, *Jesus and the Zealots*, p. 1, and *The Trial of Jesus of Nazareth*, p. 141; Cullmann, *The State in the New Testament*, pp. 11 f., and *Jesus and the Revolutionaries*, p. 31; Cohn, *op. cit.*, p. 10; Jaubert, *op. cit.*, p. 113; Farmer, *op. cit.*, p. 197; Carmichael, *op. cit.*, p. 41; Morton S. Enslin, "The Temple and the Cross," p. 25; Josef Blinzler, *op. cit.*, p. 53; Gerard Sloyan, *op. cit.*, p. 62.

38. Brandon, *op. cit.*, pp. 81 ff.; also p. 174: "As Paul eloquently shows in I Cor. 1:22–23, the idea of a 'crucified Messiah' was a *skandalon* to the Jews." Cf. also Klausner, *op. cit.*, pp. 301–2.

39. Brandon, *op. cit.*, p. 6. Pierre Barbet, *A Doctor at Calvary*, Garden City, New York: Doubleday Image Books, 1963, pp. 2, 59, 209, writes of "the horror of the ancient world at the infamy of the cross," and notes that the first crucifixes did not appear (and then only rarely) until

the end of the fifth century almost two hundred years after the Emperor Constantine abolished crucifixion in the Empire (c. A.D. 315–330). It was not until the thirteenth century that devotion of the "Passion of Christ," that is, his crucifixion, was practiced.

40. Winter, *op. cit.*, p. 1.

41. Mt. 26:57 to 27:1; Mk. 14:53–72; Lk. 22:54–71; Jn. 18:13–27.

42. Winter, *op. cit.*, pp. 14, 154 (18). Cf. also Brandon, *The Trial of Jesus of Nazareth*, pp. 25 f.

43. Winter, *op. cit.*, p. 14.

44. Jeremias, *op. cit.*, p. 223: "The Sanhedrin, supreme assembly of post-exilic Judaism, grew out of the union of these non-priestly heads of families, representatives of the 'secular nobility,' with the priestly aristocracy," and pp. 229 and 229 (25): "Josephus' historical perspective confirms very convincingly these statements that the lay nobility consisted for the most part of Sadducees. He depicts, for example, the Sadducees as the most distinguished and important people in the entourage of King Alexander Jannaeus (103–76 B.C.), who held Sadducean ideas (*Ant.* XIII. 411; *War* I. 114) . . . It is true that followers of the Sadducees belonged to wealthy circles. Let us remember too that the Hellenistic influence was evident in the theology and philosophy of life of the Sadducees, and this also indicates the wealthy class since it was they who were most influenced by Hellenistic culture." In *Ant.* XIII. 298, Josephus writes: "the Sadducees having the confidence of the wealthy alone but no following among the populace."

45. Jeremias, *op. cit.*, p. 230. The book of Acts (5:17) shows the Sadducees as supporters of the High Priest.

46. Simon, *Jewish Sects at the Time of Jesus*, pp. 24 ff.

47. *Ibid.*, pp. 27 ff.

48. "A Literary Approach to the Trial," pp. 33 f.

49. *Op. cit.*, p. 63. Cf. Winter, *op. cit.*, pp. 120 ff.

50. *Op. cit.*, p. 50.

51. Winter, *loc. cit.*

52. *Op. cit.*, pp. 126 f.

53. *Ibid.*, pp. 17–18.

54. Paul Winter objects to the casting of the Sadducees as "collaborators." He says, "It would be wrong to make generalizing statements concerning the respective attitudes of Sadducees and Pharisees towards Rome. To label the former as 'collaborators' and the latter as 'patriots' is equally incorrect . . . in the year [A.D.] 66 it was the scion of a Sadducean family who sparked off the flame of revolt [*War* II. 409]. Although they disapproved of the extremism of the Zealots, Sadducees fought in the war against Rome, whereas the Pharisees were indifferent to political liberty and prepared to submit, provided that religious freedom was granted. Josephus' account of events during the revolt, and Josephus' own conduct, provide

evidence of occasional collusion, on the part of the Pharisees, with the Romans." *Op. cit.,* p. 209 (23).

55. Jeremias, *op. cit.,* p. 210.

56. Cohn, *op. cit.,* p. 16. The Catholic scholar Josef Blinzler is the chief exponent of this theory, according to which two separate charges are believed to have been made against Jesus: the Sanhedrin's charge of blasphemy and Pilate's adjudication on the charge of high treason, or sedition. Cf. Blinzler, *op. cit.,* p. 54.

57. Cohn, *op. cit.,* p. 17. For examples of this type of reasoning, see McRuer, *op. cit.,* p. 62: "The Hebrew trial had closed. Steeped as it was in illegality, it had been a mockery of judicial procedure throughout. Jesus was unlawfully arrested and unlawfully interrogated . . . The court was unlawfully convened by night. No lawful charge supported by the evidence of two witnesses was ever formulated . . . As he stood at the bar of justice he was unlawfully sworn as witness against himself. He was unlawfully condemned to death on words from his own mouth"; and Earl L. Wingo, *The Illegal Trial of Jesus,* New York: Bobbs-Merrill Co., Inc., Charter Edition, 1962, Ch. 12, who lists eighteen "errors" by which the Jews and Romans "raped the law and ignored the eivdence!" (p. 117) "A close study of this highly interesting subject—embraced by both the Hebrew and Roman trials—will establish, beyond question of doubt, that Jesus was not given even the remotest semblance of a legal trial; but, on the contrary, was made the victim of an unholy, mob-rule persecution which resulted in murdering their Victim!" (Preface) Jaubert, *op. cit.,* p. 166 (1), believes that the Sanhedrin met "in plenary session" to try Jesus: "The full Sanhedrin was composed of 71 members; but 23 members were sufficient to judge a capital case. Mark's expression would indicate a plenary session." Jaubert's interpretation of the Sanhedrin's meeting falls far short, however, of explaining the many incongruities and impossibilities in the New Testament accounts of the trial of Jesus. Cohn's conclusion seems to us the most plausible: that there was no convening of the Sanhedrin to try Jesus for blasphemy and that there was, therefore, no conviction or sentencing for blasphemy.

58. "A Literary Approach to the Trial of Jesus," pp. 32–33.

59. *Op. cit.,* pp. 29–30.

60. Winter, p. 162 (10). Cf. *Tractate Sanhedrin* 7. 4, 5, which calls for the death penalty only if the Sacred Name of God has been said aloud. *Sanhedrin* 6.4 requires that after the execution of a capital sentence for blasphemy—by stoning—the victim is to be hanged from a beam set in the ground, and that he had to be buried by nightfall. Cf. Brandon, *The Trial of Jesus of Nazareth,* pp. 188 (59) and 187 (53): "Jesus would not have been guilty of blasphemy for claiming to be the Messiah; but he would have been guilty if he had claimed to be the Son of Man." Contrast the above to McRuer, *op. cit.,* p. 60: "if he admitted his Messiahship the admission, no matter how obtained, would

have been interpreted as blasphemy and used to support a declaration that he was worthy of death"; and Wingo, *op. cit.*, p. 72: ". . . the final charge against Jesus, before the Sanhedrin, and upon which He was sentenced to be crucified by the Jews, was that of 'blasphemy.' "

61. Winter, *op. cit.*, pp. 129–30, cf. also p. 198 (7), and Carmichael, *op. cit.*, pp. 118 f. Cf. also Winter, *op. cit.*, p. 172 (10): "The charge of blasphemy (Mk. 14:64a), or the charge of threatening the Temple (Mk. 14:58), has been introduced into the Passion narrative by the Second Evangelist when he invented what we now read in Mark 14:53b, 55–64. Neither of these charges played any role in the arrest of Jesus or in his condemnation to death by crucifixion."

62. See n. 61 above.

63. Cf. Brandon, *Jesus and the Zealots,* pp. 281 ff.

64. Cohn, *op. cit.,* p. 30.

65. Winter, *op. cit.,* p. 135. Cf. also Carmichael, *op. cit.,* p. 39: ". . . in spite of the use of the word 'blasphemy' none of the specific charges laid against Jesus in fact involved blasphemy, and so did not concern the religious authorities. But the claim of Messiahship was, of course, very much the concern of the secular authority—the Roman procurator."

66. Winter, *op. cit.,* p. 40, translates this to read "If these things continue, the Romans will deprive us of our official position and of our statehood."

67. Carmichael, *op. cit.,* p. 198.

68. *The Trial of Jesus of Nazareth,* pp. 127–28.

69. Winter, *op. cit.,* p. 41: ". . . an intervention by the occupying power would be comprehensible if it were occasioned by reports as John 6:15 provides, namely, that it was the intention of certain Jews to make Jesus their king . . . behind John 11:47–53 there lies a report imparting information to the effect that the activities of Jesus—or the reaction of the people to Jesus' activities—caused the high-priest to express anxiety respecting the procurator's possible counter-measures. To the high-priest, as well as to the entire 'upper strata' of the nation, any agitation among the easily agitated masses constituted a threat to public order and especially to their own political privileges. An increase of unrest among the people could easily give a pretext for procuratorial interference with the rights of the Jewish Senate, and lead to diminution of such limited self-rule as the Sanhedrin still enjoyed."

70. Winter, *op. cit.,* p. 41, asserts the authenticity of a meeting before the trial of Jesus, as variously recorded in Mark 14:1, 2, 10, 11, and John 11:47–53: "If the Sanhedrin convened with the object of deliberating on the possibility of repercussions arising from Jesus' activities, repercussions likely to affect relations between the Jewish and Roman authorities, it would point to the fact that the high-priest—and the Sanhedrin as a whole—played a certain part in bringing Jesus to trial."

71. Winter, *op. cit.,* p. 42: "Whether Pilate knew of Jesus and whether

he was of the opinion that his preaching contributed to popular unrest, it is impossible to say. If he did, he might have demanded specifically that the high-priest should take charge of Jesus and put an end to his activities. If, as is more likely, Pilate's information about Jewish affairs was of a less definite character, he would merely have sent a warning to the local authorities instructing them, in general terms, to 'put their house in order.'"

72. Cf. Jn. 7:32–52; Mk. 11:18; 12:12; Lk. 19:47–48; 20:19; Mt. 21:45–46.

73. *Op. cit.,* pp. 87–88. Cf. Winter, *op. cit.,* p. 43: "Faced on one side by growing popular discontent and on the other side by an overwhelming foreign power, they tried to preserve what they could of the residue of Jewish self-rule. Their fears were real, and were justified. Whether their part in the arrest of Jesus was small or great, they acted from motives they considered to serve the best interests of the nation—and *the best interests,* as so often, happened to coincide with their own"; and Cohn, *op. cit.,* pp. 23–25: "There can . . . have been only one thing in which the Jewish leadership of the day can have been and was really and vitally interested: to prevent the execution by the Romans of a Jew (and a Pharisee) who happened to enjoy the affection and love of the people . . . While the Sanhedrin had thus to be watchful not to alienate such good will of the Roman authorities as it could still enjoy, the first and foremost condition for its survival and effectiveness was to retain the confidence and loyalty of the people . . . Nothing could have been further from their intentions, or more harmful to their purpose, than to arouse the discontent and disaffection of the people by lending a hand in the execution by the Romans of one in their midst; whereas any action on their part to prevent such execution would, if successful, have been likely to arouse popular applause and to reinstate the Sanhedrin in the eyes of the people as their natural and legitimate leaders."

74. Winter, *op. cit.,* p. 41; in considering the possibility of their being at the one extreme, an official convening of the Sanhedrin, and at the other, no meeting whatsoever, Gerard Sloyan, *op. cit.,* p. 66, concludes that "The truth probably lies somewhere in between, namely, that there existed in Christian circles an authentic tradition of an early morning inquisition of Jesus before some members of the Sanhedrin, complete with witnesses, which was not meant to be a judicial process." Cf. also Brandon, *op. cit.,* pp. 87, 186 (39). Cullmann, *Jesus and the Revolutionaries,* pp. 33–34, also views the Sanhedrin's session as an informal interrogation, but makes a clear distinction between the *moral* and *legal* responsibilities for Jesus' sentence: "Actually it was from the beginning the *Roman* cohort who arrested Jesus in Gethsemane. He was therefore the prisoner of the Romans. The preliminary hearing before the high priest was more of a moral interrogation which Pilate had wished in order to be certain that he would not

offend the Jewish authorities. The actual trial was the trial before Pilate, and hence a political trial. The *moral* responsibility therefore lay completely on the side of the high priest, the *legal* on the other hand entirely on the side of the Romans." Cf. William R. Wilson, *The Execution of Jesus,* New York: Charles Scribner's Sons, 1970, pp. 167 ff.

75. But cf. Brandon, *op. cit.,* p. 92: "the Sanhedrin was concerned that night to investigate Jesus' ideas and actions, in order to prepare a case for handing him over to Pilate. And that case was based upon the political, not the religious, significance of Jesus. Naturally, Judaism being what it was then, political and religious factors were inextricably intertwined, as we have seen in the ideals and aims of the Zealots. However, the Jewish leaders were primarily concerned with Jesus as one who menaced the existing social and political order, and not as a religious heretic. His activities in the last few days, especially his attack on the Temple establishment, convinced them that he was a subversive force, for whose suppression the Romans would hold them responsible." Cf. Sherwin-White, *op. cit.,* p. 45, who attributes the night trial to the Sanhedrin's haste because of the Passover—"there was every reason to hold the unusual night session if they were to catch the Procurator at the right moment" in the morning. Sherwin-White also reasserts the historical authenticity of the condemnation for blasphemy, pp. 46–47: "The trial before the Sanhedrin and the condemnation for blasphemy regain historical probability. There is nothing in the Roman background to make the older solution improbable: that the Jewish leaders, finding or knowing that Pilate was unwilling to confirm an execution for a purely theological offence, added or substituted an alternative charge of sedition, which Pilate ultimately accepted as the basis of his sentence. But it is equally possible, in Roman usage, that when Pilate refused a verdict on the political charge, they fell back on the religious charge, which Pilate finally accepted under the sort of political pressure that is indicated in a convincing technicality by John. The telling phrase—'If you let this man go, you are not Caesar's friend'—recalls the frequent manipulation of the treason law for political ends in Roman public life . . . the sentence of the Sanhedrin—is entirely within the scope of the procurator's *imperium.*" The author's work, rooted in his profound appreciation of Roman jurisprudence, nevertheless noticeably disregards the rabbinic sources concerning the functioning of the Sanhedrin under Jewish Law.

76. Cohn, *op. cit.,* pp. 23–26.

77. *Ibid.,* pp. 30–31. The "false witnesses" whom the High Priest had prepared to offer testimony before Pilate in Jesus' behalf, according to Cohn's theory, were included in the Gospel stories of the trial before Pilate, even though Jesus did not cooperate in the plan. The inclusion of the report of the "false witnesses" is part of what confuses the issue regarding the reason for Jesus' conviction.

78. *Op. cit.,* pp. 92 and 96.

79. *Ibid.,* p. 92.

80. *Op. cit.,* pp. 32–33.

81. Cohn, *op. cit.,* p. 8; William R. Wilson, *op. cit.,* p. 22. Cullmann, *The State in the New Testament,* p. 42, considers the question of the Jews' jurisdiction in capital cases a "side-track" because in the complicated discussion "centered exclusively on the juridical question of the right of the Jews to carry out capital punishment on their own authority . . . the principal question—whether Jesus was condemned by the Romans or by the Jews—was thus lost to view." Winter, *op. cit.,* p. 9, views Cullmann's charge as "indisputable"—yet still considers the question relevant to the study of Jesus' trial.

82. Cohn, *op. cit.,* p. 8. Winter, *op. cit.,* p. 74, who quotes Kingsley Barret and Robert Henry Lightfoot to the same effect, concurs: "Not before 70 CE [AD] was the Sanhedrin deprived of its right to administer capital punishment to persons it had tried and sentenced to death." Also cf. Winter, *op. cit.,* pp. 10, 88. Winter, pp. 156 (38), 162 (11), 180 (23), lists three actual cases in which individuals were tried and sentenced to death and executed: the stoning of Stephen (Acts 6:12; 7:58), the burning of the priest's daughter convicted of adultery (*Mishnah Sanhedrin* 7:2; *Tosefta Sanhedrin,* 9:11; *T. Y. Sanhedrin* 7:24b; *T. B. Sanhedrin* 41a), and the stoning of James (*Ant.* XX. 200). According to Jewish Law, had Jesus been sentenced to death and no new evidence been produced, he would have been executed immediately; cf. Acts 7:57–58. Talmudic sources (based on allegations by Christians against Jews that Jesus had been executed under Jewish Law) which state that Jesus was stoned to death testify, in Winter's opinion, to two things: (1) the rabbis' belief in the Sanhedrin's power to execute capital cases, and (2) the rabbis' acceptance of the allegation as fact and their subsequent presumption that he must have been executed as prescribed by their Law, that is, by stoning. For the contrary view, see Robert M. Grant, "The Trial of Jesus in the Light of History," p. 41, who says, "All the reliable evidence, therefore, shows that in the time of Jesus the high priest and his council did not possess the right to execute offenders against either Jewish or Roman law."

83. Re John's Gospel which states that the Sanhedrin required procuratorial concurrence to execute death sentences, Winter, *op. cit.,* p. 88, writes: "John 18:31b provides no evidence at all of the facts of history—the assertion denying the competence of Jewish law courts to administer capital punishment has its basis in the theological scheme devised by the Fourth Evangelist." Cf. also, Brandon, *op. cit.,* p. 91: "This comment reveals John's real intention in representing the Jewish leaders as declaring that it was not lawful for them to put any man to death. John was concerned to explain how Jesus had come to suffer crucifixion, which was not a Jewish punishment." Cohn, *op. cit.,* pp. 8–9, also believes no such clearance with the Romans was necessary. Winter, *op. cit.,* p. 73, states that in certain cases the Sanhedrin's sentence was "an academic pronouncement, the court lacking the power to put its verdict into effect." Winter's point has also been

made by Eisler, *op. cit.,* p. 523: "the rabbis for centuries consoled themselves for the Sanhedrin's loss of power to pronounce sentence of death.
Even in exile at Jabneh such sentences were believed to be still passed, the
penalty being inflicted by God himself. If the high court condemned any
one to stoning, a wall was supposed to collapse and fall upon him; if the
person was condemned to burning, he perished in a conflagration; and so
on." Brandon, *op. cit.,* p. 91, believes the Sanhedrin's competency to execute on a capital charge was upheld "subject to Roman confirmation."

84. Carmichael, *op. cit.,* p. 38. Cf. also Winter, *op. cit.,* p. 10: "As [Mark]
does not mention any legal impediment attaching to the Sanhedrin's authority, we have to presume that he knew of no such impediment."

85. Carmichael, *op. cit.,* p. 39. Cf. also Cullmann, *op. cit.,* p. 42. Sherwin-
White, *op. cit.,* pp. 34–37, 40–42, admits the logical force of this argument
but questions its validity. Sherwin-White believes the general line of reasoning is based on three false historical assumptions: (1) the belief that
Pilate would not have executed a Jewish sentence in the Roman fashion:
"If Pilate accepts a theological charge in his court, it would not occur to
him to give sentence in non-Roman terms"; (2) that Pilate was presented
with only one charge, instead of two, for if two charges had been presented
against Jesus before Pilate—as may have been the case—Pilate would have
been free to "proceed as he likes"; and, (3) that the Sanhedrin had jurisdiction in capital cases. Sherwin-White doubts the Court's capital jurisdiction, for such capital power "was the most jealously guarded of all the
attributes of government, not even entrusted to the principal assistants of
the governors," and "The general permission given to the Jews to follow
their own customs, in a series of decrees and edicts from the time of Julius
Caesar onwards . . . is very far from proving that the Sanhedrin was allowed capital jurisdiction." Moreover, "Turbulent Judea is the very last
place where we would expect any extraordinary concession." He rejects the
executions of Stephen and James and also the Temple's restriction upon
penalty of death against Gentile trespassers in its precincts as evidence of
capital jurisdiction, concluding that the Sanhedrin either lacked such powers
or that they were restricted to "police purposes in the Temple area and for
the maintenance of Jewish law." Capital cases, in Sherwin-White's argument, either belonged to the jurisdiction of the procurator or required his
sanction.

Doubt concerning the authority of the Sanhedrin in capital cases is
derived not only from the New Testament accounts, but also from Jewish
Talmudic references. These references apparently reflect the development
of the apologetic war which raged concerning the responsibility for Jesus'
death. The apologetic concern of the rabbis most intelligibly explains such
Talmudic sources as deny the Sanhedrin jurisdiction in capital cases: Cf.
Cohn, *op. cit.,* pp. 8–10: ". . . the talmudic dicta . . . were made during
the Christian era for apologetic reasons, in order to disprove the allegation that Jesus could have been tried and sentenced by a Jewish court," and

"there are reliable records to the effect that the Sanhedrin did in fact exercise capital jurisdiction during the forty years preceding the destruction of the Temple; and if the tradition were that such jurisdiction had already ceased forty years before the destruction of the Temple, there would be no point to the other (better) tradition that with the destruction of the Temple, capital sentences became obsolete . . . The dictum of Rav Nahuman bar Yitzhak [from which originated the tradition of the cessation of capital jurisdiction forty years before the fall of Jerusalem and destruction of the Temple, written about A.D. 350], and the spurious reason given therefor, are, however, easily explained if we bear in mind that it was exactly forty years before the destruction of the Temple that . . . Jesus had been tried and crucified . . . that in the fourth century, in which Rav Nahuman lived, the Christian religion had already become the official religion of the Roman emperors and the Jews had started to be accused of, and persecuted for, the death of Jesus; and that a Jewish religious and historical tradition to the effect that at the time of Jesus' death, Jewish courts no longer exercised capital jurisdiction, might have been a valuable weapon in the apologetic struggle, that the Jews could have had no hand in the trial and execution of Jesus."

86. Winter, *op. cit.*, p. 9: "Whatever the competence of the Jewish judicial authorities in capital cases might have been in the time of Jesus, it remains that Jesus was executed in the Roman fashion, as laid down by Roman law. The fact that this punishment was restricted to certain classes of persons—to which Jesus belonged—and was confined to certain categories of crimes—amongst which the charge laid against Jesus was included—makes the conclusion inevitable that the court whose sentence was carried out in this manner was a Roman court." Cf. also to Cohn, *op. cit.*, p. 8 quoted above in note 85, and Carmichael, *op. cit.*, p. 38: "Whether or not the Sanhedrin could inflict capital punishment for religious crimes, Jesus was not *in fact* condemned on a religious charge."

CHAPTER 12

The Crucifixion of a Rebel: King of the Jews

1. Colin Cross, *Who Was Jesus?* London: Hodder & Stoughton, 1970, p. 92.

2. A. N. Sherwin-White, *op. cit.,* pp. 5–6.

3. Sherwin-White, *op. cit.,* pp. 1, 5, speaks of the "unfettered quality" of the *imperium* which permitted "a tyrannical abuse of power" in the provinces.

4. *Ibid.,* pp. 13–14.

5. *Ibid.,* p. 23: "The form of judicial trial was the personal *cognitio* of the governor, who alone had the capital power, assisted by his *consilium,* which as its name indicates was more a body of assessors than of jurors." Cf. also Haim Cohn, *op. cit.,* p. 11: "The (armed or unarmed) insurrection inherent in the claim to be king, without being appointed or recognized as such by the Emperor, was an offence against the *Lex Julia Majestatis,* enacted by Augustus in the year 8 B.C. The offence was punishable with death. It was triable in the colonies by the 'procurators,' i.e., the governors who exercised in the colonies under their governorship the jurisdiction exercised in Rome by the Emperor. For this purpose the procurators were vested with the *jus gladii,* the right to pass and execute capital sentences."

6. Cohn, *loc. cit.*

7. *Op. cit.,* p. 67.

8. Cf. Lk. 23:1–5, and Brandon, *The Trial of Jesus of Nazareth,* p. 119.

9. Paul Winter, *op. cit.,* p. 14: "When Paul is accused in Corinth and the proconsul decides that it is a religious matter, he refuses to try the case; yet when the Apostle is accused of a political offense in Philippi, the praetor takes action."

10. *Annales* 15:44.

11. Sherwin-White, *op. cit.,* p. 24: "The account of this is generalized. In practice there must have been not more than two or three spokesmen."

12. *Loc. cit.:* "The charge is clearly indicated, not as a charge against a particular Roman law, but as a charge of particular undesirable actions on which Pilate is asked to adjudicate. Mark and Matthew merely hint at the nature of the charge giving Pilate the question: 'Are you a king of the Jews?' That this means 'a leader of the resistance' is shown by a parallel

from Josephus, who in his anti-resistance fashion remarks of the troubles after the death of Herod: 'as the several companies of the seditious lighted upon anyone to head them, he was created a king immediately, in order to do mischief to the public' (*Ant.* XVII. 285). Luke is explicit: 'we found this fellow disturbing our people, telling them not to pay tribute to Caesar, and calling himself a king.' This fits very well the workings of *cognitio*. The accusers allege offences and the judge decides what to make of them. Since there was no defence, Pilate had no option but to convict. That was the essence of the system." Cf. Cullmann, *Jesus and the Revolutionaries*, pp. 32 f.: "Other Zealot leaders were evidently viewed as kings of the future kingdom of Israel, which was identified with the kingdom of God . . . It is therefore not astonishing that for Pilate the case of Jesus was in the same category as the cases of the many Zealot leaders that he had to judge, indeed also in the same category as the case of Barabbas, who certainly was a Zealot . . ."

13. See Mt. 27:15–26; Mk. 15:6–15; Lk. 23:3–4, 13–25; Jn. 18:38–40; 19:1–16. For an example of an author who accepts the Gospels' presentation of Pilate uncritically, cf. McRuer, *op. cit.*, pp. 77 and 81, who writes, "As weak judges have done since the beginning of time, he equivocated— he temporized with justice and then compromised justice. Attempting to placate the emissaries of the Jews, he added a rider to his judgement . . ." and, later, regarding the sentencing, "What had up to this time been a retreat on Pilate's part turned into absolute surrender."

14. Cohn, *op. cit.* (quoting Winter), p. 11. Cf. also Joel Carmichael, *op. cit.*, pp. 40 f.; and Winter, *op. cit.*, p. 55.

15. Eisler, *op. cit.*, p. 42, writes that Professor Norden "rightly stressed the fact that Josephus 'found in his source a representation of Pilate's governorship as a series of "tumults." ' " Eisler lists the four tumults as the incident involving the emperor's standards, Pilate's expenditure of Temple funds for construction of the aqueduct and the resulting Jewish revolt, the expulsion of the Jews from Rome by order of Tiberius and the bloody repression of the Samaritan Messianic pretender.

16. Winter, *op. cit.*, p. 54: "Josephus informs us more fully than Philo on Pilate's rule in Judaea, recording several happenings that occurred during his term of office. They all supply ample illustration of the contemptuous manner in which Pilate dealt with the people of the province. What is of importance in assessing the trustworthiness of these reports is that Josephus also mentions Pilate's cruel behaviour towards Samaritans, a nation for whom Josephus had no particular fondness." Cf. Flusser, *Jesus*, p. 148 (220).

17. *Ibid.*, pp. 53 f.

18. Brandon, *op. cit.*, pp. 35–41 and 190 (100); and *Jesus and the Zealots*, pp. 68–80. Cf. also Sloyan, *op. cit.*, p. 67.

19. Cf. Mk. 15:15; Mt. 27:26; Lk. 23:25; Jn. 19:16. Winter, *op. cit.*, p. 56.

20. *Ibid.*, p. 59.

21. *Ibid.*, pp. 58, 182 (38).

22. *Ibid.*, pp. 60 f.: "Suddenly, in the fourth century, this development comes to an end. There is still, in the Gospel of Nicodemus, a belated echo of the tendency to accentuate Pilate's friendly disposition towards Jesus, and present him as a witness to the illegality of the latter's execution. But from Eusebius onward the current takes a sharp turn in the opposite direction, and Pilate's fortunes in Christian tradition enter upon a steep decline. The circle is closed. It only remains to read the portents.

"The historical conditions in which the Christian communities lived from the first to the fourth century are the background of Pilate's developing portrait; and it is they that help us to explain why, after such a promising beginning, the procurator's reputation started to go down in the fourth century. Pilate was cheated in his posthumous career by Emperor Constantine. Had it been one generation later, or perhaps two, when Christianity became a *religio licita*, Pontius Pilate would have been a saint to-day in Western Christendom as his wife is in the Greek Church . . .

"The process had begun before the Gospels. It ended after the battle at the Milvan Bridge. The upward trend in Pilate's reputation abruptly comes to an end—and this occasions no surprise when we consider that the inducement to describe the procurator as a witness to Jesus' innocence was no longer operative. All the restrictions imposed by Rome on Christian worship were now lifted; Constantine eventually became converted—and Pilate missed canonization." Cf. also Brandon, *op. cit.*, pp. 155–56.

23. Brandon, *op. cit.*, p. 201 (40).

24. "The Temple and the Cross," p. 30.

25. *Op. cit.*, p. 28.

26. *Ibid.*, p. 31.

27. *Ibid.*, pp. 31 f.

28. Mt. 27:15–26; Mk. 15:6–15; Lk. 23:13–25; Jn. 18:28b–40.

29. Winter, *op. cit.*, pp. 91 ff. But cf. Brandon, *op. cit.*, p. 99, who believes that Mark only *implies* that the Jews were given a choice of prisoners to be freed.

30. Cf. Winter, *op. cit.*, p. 94: "No doubt, the episode in Mark 15:7–15 is coloured by apologetic interest. The Evangelist throws the responsibility for the death of Jesus onto the Jews, making Pilate appear to have acted merely as an instrument of their heinous intention. The tendency is unmistakable—from the start, in Mark, and it grows with the advance of time after the composition of the Second Gospel"; Carmichael, *op. cit.*, p. 35: "The Barabbas episode in its present setting, in short, has a theatrical, tendentious effect, well in line with the general anti-Jewish and pro-Roman tendency of the Gospels but flagrantly contrary to probability"; and Brandon, *op. cit.*, p. 100: "[Mark's] purpose throughout the Barabbas episode is clearly twofold: to show that Pilate recognised the innocence of Jesus; and to exonerate Pilate from responsibility for the crucifixion of Jesus by repre-

senting him as compelled by the Jewish leaders and people to order the execution. Mark appears to invoke the episode, as a kind of desperate expedient, to explain away the intractable fact of the Roman cross after he had done all he could in emphasising the evil intent of the Jewish leaders."

31. C. Cross, *op. cit.*, p. 102: "There is nothing inherently impossible about such a scene but it must be remembered that the gospel narratives were written at a time when Christianity was separating from Judaism and was in conflict with it. It would be natural for the writers to stress the Jewish role in the crucifixion and to minimize the Roman responsibility"; Brandon, *op. cit.*, p. 115, observes, concerning Pilate's symbolic act of washing his hands: "This ritual ablution was a Jewish, not a Roman, custom, and its significance would have been understood by Matthew's Jewish Christian readers. Pilate's accompanying statement is clearly intended to be a formal and definitive repudiation of his responsibility for the death of Jesus . . ." For parallels of ritual ablution cf. Deut. 21:6 ff. and Ps. 26:6.

32. Italics ours. It is worth noting that John records a different charge from that listed above: here the Jews castigate Jesus, not for claiming to be the Son of God, but for pretension to kingship, the charge for which Jesus was in fact executed. Some scholars have accepted the report of the Jews' questioning Pilate's loyalty to Caesar as a reasonable explanation for Pilate's sentencing Jesus to death. Cf. Sherwin-White, *op. cit.*, p. 25. According to this reasoning, the prefect would not have dared release Jesus for fear of being charged with disloyalty to the emperor. The threat of the Jews to take the case to the emperor would have rendered Pilate's release of Jesus impossible. But this line of reasoning obviously would have applied with equal force to Pilate's releasing the rebel leader Barabbas whose identification with the forces of anti-Roman agitation was even more pronounced than Jesus'. Brandon, *op. cit.*, p. 137, on the other hand, considers the explanation that the Jews had threatened to take the case to the emperor "naïve in the extreme": "It ignores the practical difficulties that such an action, by a subject people against their accredited governor, would encounter; and it assumes that the Emperor would have accepted the Jewish report against that of his own Roman officer, whose ten years' tenure of office attests the trust that was placed in him. Further, it also overlooks the fact that Pilate would have been in far greater danger when the Emperor learned that he had released Barabbas, a rebel leader recently involved in a serious insurrection—that is, if such an incident did in fact ever occur. And there is one further aspect for comment. Like the authors of the Synoptic Gospels, John also presents the situation as one in which Pilate would have had to give an immediate decision. But, as we have already noted, Pilate would have had other ways open to him, if he had found the case too involved with the passions of the moment: he could, for example, have postponed a decision and called the case to Caesarea for further investigation." We feel Brandon's argument is the more convincing.

33. We have seen how the effort to shift responsibility for Jesus' death from the Romans to the Jews became exaggerated in the later Gospels, and how the theological interpretation imposed by the authors/compilers of the Gospels affected their portrayal of what actually occurred: for example, Matthew's inflated statements by the Jews who assume full and unequivocal blame for Jesus' death not only for themselves, but for their descendants as well. Cf. Winter, *op. cit.*, pp. 92 ff.

34. Brandon, *op. cit.*, p. 99.

35. *Op. cit.*, p. 67.

36. Winter, *op. cit.*, p. 57: "If the fact of a demonstration by the street-rabble is historically credible, its influence on a person of Pilate's domineering disposition belongs to the province of apologetics."

37. Cohn, *op. cit.*, pp. 12–14. Cohn also deals convincingly with those scholars who have suggested that "the priests claimed the release of Barabbas because the execution of a Jewish nationalist zealot might have caused a public uprising . . . as far as public sentiment was concerned, the same must be said of Jesus himself . . ." We have repeatedly shown that it was as a Zealot that Jesus too was tried and executed. Cf. also Brandon, *op. cit.*, p. 98: "When viewed thus, objectively, as a reported transaction between a Roman governor, who was supported by a strong military force, and native magistrates and a native mob, the whole account is patently too preposterous and ludicrous for belief."

38. Cf. Cohn, *op. cit.*, p. 13.

39. Brandon, *op. cit.*, p. 99: "Indeed, if Pilate had wanted to destroy Jesus instead of saving him, he could have devised no surer way—inevitably the crowd would ask for the release of the patriot Barabbas."

40. Cf. Winter, *op. cit.*, pp. 91, 94; Brandon, *op. cit.*, p. 101; Cohn, *op. cit.*, p. 14; Eisler, *op. cit.*, p. 474.

41. Cohn, *op. cit.*, p. 14: ". . . not only had the Procurator no right to pardon criminals, but the exercise by him of this Imperial prerogative would be a treasonable felony on his part." Cf. also to p. 11 (25) and to Eisler, *op. cit.*, p. 474: "But to pardon a known and condemned rebel was notoriously beyond the power of a Roman governor, and by doing so he would have been guilty of an invasion of the prerogative of the emperor such as the suspicious Tiberius would have been the last to tolerate."

42. See Shemuel Safrai, *Pilgrimage at the Time of the Second Temple*, Tel Aviv: Am Hassefer Publishers Ltd., 1965, pp. 159–60. Dr. Safrai makes reference to two articles in the *Journal of Biblical Literature* (*JBL*) that also cite this Talmudic source (*Mishnah Pesachim* B): C. B. Claivel's article, *JBL* LX, 1941, and Riggs' article, *JBL* LXIV, 1945. Cf. also Flusser, *Jesus*, p. 126. For the contrary opinion concerning this Talmudic source, see Winter, *op. cit.*, p. 91: "There is further evidence that Jews in Jerusalem who were discharged from prison on the eve of the Passover celebration were permitted to take part in the eating of the paschal lamb. This regulation [*Mishnah Pesachim* 8, 6] has not the slightest bearing on the case re-

ported in the Gospels. It refers to persons—unspecified in number—who were let out from jail too late to be present at the slaughtering of the lamb, yet in time to attend the evening meal. The stipulation provides for the admission of people to the festive table on the night of the fifteenth Nisan. The synoptic Gospels report that Barabbas was released after that night . . . it is clear that the ordinance refers to any number of people who happened to be discharged from prison in time to participate in the meal."

43. The authors are indebted to Professor David Flusser for calling the above to their attention. In Dr. Flusser's view, the fact that the Romans had no facilities for holding criminals other than debtors' prisons makes this Passover custom during Roman times even more credible.

44. *Op. cit.*, p. 67. Cf. also Cohn, *op. cit.*, p. 14: "If Pilate had, as he repeatedly said, found 'no fault in this man,' what cause was there to 'pardon' him? He could and would have set both Jesus and Barabbas free, the one on acquittal and the other on pardon."

45. Cullmann, *The State in the New Testament*, p. 47 (19), referring to M. Goguel, *op. cit.*, pp. 382 ff., who believes that the whole scene is unhistorical, states: "It is true that there are difficulties from the legal point of view, but they are not insurmountable." But, the Barabbas scene only becomes "less impossible" in Cullmann's view, if we accept "that Pilate and not the Jews passed judgment, and that the denunciation proceeded only from the Jewish upper class and not from the whole people."

46. Winter, *op. cit.*, p. 94.

47. Evidence for such a reading of Barabbas' full name is derived from various codices of the Gospels which give the name "Jesus" for Barabbas. It is believed that because the disciples would have been reluctant to associate the name Jesus with the rebel, manuscripts which read "Jesus Barabbas" are unlikely to be later Christian interpolation, and probably derive from an original tradition. Cf. Winter, *op. cit.*, p. 95; and Brandon, *op. cit.*, pp. 190 (113), 193 (42).

48. Winter, *op. cit.*, p. 97.

49. *Ibid.*, p. 99.

50. Eisler, *op. cit.*, p. 475: "It is inconceivable that the Roman governor could have liberated a rebel at the instance of the mob; but it is perfectly natural that he should be prepared to gratify the masses of pro-Roman supporters of the hierarchy, led by the high priests, by releasing to them at the feast one of their own number, the son of a learned rabbi, who had erroneously been arrested by his soldiers in the turmoil of the fray."

51. Brandon, *op. cit.*, p. 190 (113) lists scholars who accept the identification of "Jesus Barabbas" with an insurrection.

52. Cullmann, *The State in the New Testament*, p. 47; also, *Jesus and the Revolutionaries*, p. 33: "For Pilate the case of Jesus was in the same category as the cases of the many Zealot leaders that he had to judge, indeed also in the same category as the case of Barabbas, who certainly was a Zealot . . ."; Cohn, *op. cit.*, p. 13 (38): "Jesus himself was convicted and

executed by Pontius Pilate as a zealot, as Barabbas was"; Brandon, *op. cit.*, p. 190 (109); Klausner, *op. cit.*, p. 347; Driver, *op. cit.*, p. 246; Jeremias, *op. cit.*, p. 52: "According to John 18:40 Barabbas had been condemned to death as a robber, but the synoptic description of him as a revolutionary and murderer suggests that he belonged rather to the anti-Roman party of the Sicarii."

53. Brandon, *op. cit.*, p. 102.

54. Cf. Chapter 2 above on the religious motivation of the Zealots.

55. The Zealots held out in the Herodian Palace for three months after the Romans had captured the Temple and the fortress Antonia during the Revolt of A.D. 66. It occupied a commanding location overlooking the upper city of Jerusalem.

56. Brandon, *op. cit.*, p. 102.

57. *Ibid.*, p. 103.

58. *Ibid.*, p. 191 (118): "If a two-pronged attack had been made on the Temple and the Antonia, it would also explain why the Roman garrison in the Antonia did not intervene in the 'Cleansing of the Temple,' as they did in the fracas occasioned by Paul's arrest there (Acts 21:30 ff.)—they would have been fully engaged with the Zealot attack under Barabbas." Eisler, *op. cit.*, pp. 570 f., also accepts the notion of the insurrection in the city as a diversionary tactic. He believes the reference to Galileans whose blood was spilled by the destruction of the Siloam Tower was an allusion to the other part of the insurrection which complemented Jesus' assault on the Temple.

59. Bishop Pike thought it was at least possible that the crowd was shouting "release to us Jesus, Son of the Father," meaning *Jesus,* and that the Gospel writers invented a "Barabbas" ("son of the Father") to cover up the fact that in fact their wish had been denied and Jesus had been crucified as a rebel. He favored, however, the interpretation which follows.

60. See Chapter 9, n. 68 above.

61. Winter, *op. cit.*, p. 65; Cohn, *op. cit.*, p. 44.

62. Winter, *op. cit.*, p. 63. Cf. *War* II. 75; *Ant.* XVII. 295: Josephus relates how Quintilius Varus ordered the crucifixion of two thousand men; other examples are found in *Ant.* XX. 102, under Tiberius; *Ant.* XX. 129 and *War* II. 241, under Ummidius Guadratus; *War* II. 253 and *Ant.* XX. 161, under Antonius Felix; *War* II. 306, under Gessius Florus; *War* V. 449–51, under Titus Flavius.

63. As reconstructed by John M. Allegro, *Qumran Cave IV,* p. 39. The renowned Israeli archaeologist and Scrolls scholar Yigael Yadin indicated in a personal conversation with the authors that his work on the newly discovered Temple Scroll suggests that the reconstruction of the passage above should be "when he hangs men up alive *as was done* in Israel before-time." Usually scholars reconstruct it in the negative: *"as was never done* in Israel before-time." Professor Yadin bases his suggestion on what he believes to be an alternate, and more lengthy, ancient version of the Book

of Deuteronomy quoted at length in the Temple Scroll. Biblical scholarship has held that the words "Behold I am against thee says Yahweh of hosts," suggests an abhorrence of crucifixion—"hanging men up alive." If Professor Yadin is correct in his reconstruction of the above section from the Commentary on Nahum, the objection to crucifixion in the Masoretic text apparently in wide use at the time of Jesus, represents a humanitarian reform in penal measures adopted by the Jews. This reform would have been written into a "revised" edition of the book of Deuteronomy as part of the sacred Law. See note 80 below for further evidences of humanitarian reform in the penal procedures of Judaism.

64. Cullmann, *The State in The New Testament,* p. 42. See also Winter, *op. cit.,* p. 66: "Yet whereas the Romans crucified Jewish prisoners of war by the thousands—'there was not enough room for the crosses, nor enough crosses for the condemned' (*War* V. 451)—we know not a single instance in which the Jewish guerrillas, pitiless as they were in dealing with the enemy, resorted to the method of crucifixion in disposing of those who had fallen into their hands. Crucifixion was not a punitive measure used by Jews or adopted by Jewish judicial institutions at any time in history." The exception is Alexander Janneus, who, according to Josephus (*War* I. 97), executed fellow Jews during his high priesthood. It is significant to note, however, that Alexander was despised by his countrymen. So much so, in fact, that many scholars identify him as the "wicked priest" who is the object of the scorn of the literature of the Qumran sect. His unpopularity among his own people would seem not to contradict Winter's point. Nevertheless, see n. 63 above.

65. C. Cross, *op. cit.,* p. 87: "To the first Christians the crucifixion was an embarrassment which had to be explained away . . . It was not until the seventh century that the cross became the normal Christian symbol." The earliest picture of the crucifixion is found in the pagan art of the Roman catacombs. In this picture the figure on the cross has the head of a donkey, an obviously scornful reminder of what S. G. F. Brandon calls "the scandal of the cross." Cf. Brandon, *op. cit.,* p. 81.

66. C. Cross, *op cit.,* p. 113.

67. Brandon, *op. cit.,* p. 34: "The profession of Zealotism was dangerous: its founder Judas of Galilee, died for it, and two of his sons were later crucified by the Romans. Indeed crucifixion was a fate that every Zealot had to face."

68. *Jesus and the Zealots,* pp. 145, 344 f.: "When Jesus of Nazareth called upon his disciples to take up their cross, he uttered a grim challenge that every Zealot had to face for himself. The cross was the symbol of Zealot sacrifice before it was transformed into the sign of Christian salvation . . . it would seem inevitable that Jesus must have reckoned with the fact that his mission would ultimately bring him into conflict with the Roman government in Judaea. That he did foresee this seems to be attested by . . . the ascription to Jesus of a saying

which was probably of Zealot origin [quoted above] . . . Unless this saying is a prophecy *ex eventu,* which the Evangelists have assigned to Jesus, it means that Jesus foresaw that his mission was such that it could, or would, embroil him with the Romans and result in his dying the death which they inflicted on rebels." See also Brandon, *The Trial of Jesus,* p. 177 (59).

69. *Ant.* XII. 256. The parallel account to this incident in II Maccabees does not specify crucifixion—but lists execution by sword (5:24–26) and burning (7:4 f.) or undefined killings (6:9).

70. *War* I. 97. See n. 64 above.

71. *War* V. 446–52; *Ant.* XVII. 295; *War* II. 307–8; *War* VII. 190–209. Cf. Cohn, *op. cit.,* pp. 45 ff., who quotes Talmudic sources which prove that "Some of the Jewish sufferings on the cross even found an echo in Jewish law."

72. Winter, *op. cit.,* pp. 65, 185 (23): "There is no indication in the synoptic Gospels that Jesus was nailed to the cross. From John 20:25 we may draw the inference that the Fourth Evangelist wished to imply that Jesus had been nailed by his hands. The Gospel of Peter 6, describing how Jesus' body was taken down from the cross, also mentions the nails which were drawn from his hands. The Gospels nowhere state that Jesus' feet were nailed to the cross."

73. Barbet, *op cit.,* pp. 110 ff.

74. Winter, *op. cit.,* p. 65. Cf. also Josephus' *War* V. 451.

75. "Anthropological Observations on the Skeletal Remains from Giv'at ha-Mivtar," *Israeli Exploration Journal,* Vol. 20, Nos. 1–2, Jerusalem: Central Press, 1970. In this particular case, the nail driven into the victim's legs had bent in the upright post, apparently hitting a knothole, so that the body could be removed only after chopping off both legs. The skeletal remains therefore included the nail, plus fragments of the ash plaque and the olive wood cross which were still in the bones of the leg. It was only by this unusual circumstance that we have this new evidence. The skeleton was accidentally discovered in an ostuary (containing other bones as well) during excavations for a new housing project northeast of Jerusalem in 1968.

76. Cohn, *op. cit.,* pp. 44–45: "Crucifixion was characterized not only by the slowness of supervening death, but also by the preceding and accompanying acts of torture . . . The fact that the breaking of the legs [Jn. 19:31–34] was regarded as a sure way to accelerate death, indicates the measure of exhaustion and lack of resistance which is reached after hours of immobility and exposure. For the same cause, the vinegar which Jesus drank accelerated his death." Josephus records (*Life* 420) an incident where he persuaded Titus to remove three friends of his from crosses after three days, and that one of the three survived the ordeal. The similarity between Josephus' story and that of the New Testament concerning Jesus has often been pointed out.

77. Winter, *op. cit.*, p. 65, remarks that Jesus' scourging was apparently so severe that his executioners were forced to compel another man to carry the cross for him. Cf. Mk. 15:21.

78. *Ibid.*, p. 100, where Winter notes "no fewer than five descriptions of a scene containing basically the same motif . . . a maltreatment and mockery of Jesus . . . preceding his crucifixion." Each of the Evangelists places the beatings at different times and by different parties, adding his own flavor to it. Sherwin-White, *op. cit.*, pp. 27 ff., has observed that the Synoptic Gospels correctly distinguish between different gradations of beatings under Roman law. The severest form, that inflicted on Jesus prior to execution, was never a punishment in itself but accompanied other punishments. When in Luke 23:14–22, Pilate says that Jesus has done nothing to deserve the death penalty, and that he will release him after a "warning" (sometimes translated "beating") this refers to the mildest form of punishment, a "cautionary beating." "The synoptic writers thus get their technicalities right in this small matter—the severe beating accompanies the capital sentence, and the lighter whipping goes with the proposed act of *coercitio*."

79. Cohn, *op. cit.*, p. 31.

80. Cohn, *op. cit.*, p. 46. Cohn also shows how "talmudic reformers went so far as to discard modes of execution expressly prescribed by the Scriptures, only in order to replace them by modes that appeared to them lighter and more humane."

81. *Ibid.*, p. 31: "the frustration of those efforts and the impending and now unavoidable tragedy might well have deprived one or other of the more passionate among them of his last vestige of self-restraint."

82. Editor's note appended to W. F. Farmer's "The Palm Branches in John 12, 13," p. 66. Cf. Mt. 27:29; Mk. 15:17; Jn. 19:2, 5.

83. Brandon, *op. cit.*, pp. 103–4.

84. H. St. J. Hart, "The Crown of Thorns in John 19, 2–5," *Journal of Theological Studies*, N.S., Vol. III, Pt. 1, April 1952, pp. 66 ff.

85. Pictures of crowns woven from the palm branches, with their thorns providing the upthrusting rays, are provided in Dr. Hart's article (cf. n. 84 above), along with seven pictures of such crowns found on coins from the period from both Egypt and Syria—through which the thousands of Jewish pilgrims traveling to Jerusalem for Passover would have had to pass and whose coinage they would have been using and would have had in their possession upon arrival in Jerusalem. The meaning of the caricature would have been perfectly clear to the Jewish people.

86. James A. Pike, "Was the Crown of Thorns a Form of Torture?" *New Focus* [published by the Bishop Pike Foundation], Vol. I, No. 3, June–July, 1969, p. 5.

87. C. Cross, *op. cit.*, pp. 102–4; Cohn, *op. cit.*, pp. 46 f.

88. Cohn, *loc. cit.* Cf. Mk. 15:23; Lk. 23:27–28; and Mt. 27:47–48.

89. Cullmann, *Jesus and the Revolutionaries*, p. 50. Cf. *The State in the New Testament*, p. 48.

90. Cohn, *op. cit.*, p. 47; Sherwin-White, *op. cit.*, pp. 25–27.

91. A. Jaubert, *op. cit.*, p. 168 (28) has stated her preference for the Johannine version, as opposed to those of Mark and Matthew, which locates the "crown of thorns" incident during Jesus' appearance before Pilate. Jaubert also concurs with our conclusion concerning the "scourging": "the scourging must have taken place, in accordance with the normal practice, before the punishment."

92. Mk. 15:27; Mt. 27:38; Lk. 23:32, 39–43.

93. Winter, *op. cit.*, p. 50.

94. Eisler, *op. cit.*, p. 510.

95. Italics ours. Brandon, *The Trial of Jesus of Nazareth*, pp. 191 (122), 195 (118), and *Jesus and the Zealots*, pp. 339 (1), 351, 358; Cullmann, *The State in the New Testament*, pp. 47–48, and *Jesus and the Revolutionaries*, p. 66 (3); Driver, *op. cit.*, p. 246; Klausner, *op. cit.*, p. 347; Stendahl, *Peake's Commentary*, New York: Thomas Nelson & Sons, Ltd., 1962, p. 694.

96. The proper technical term for the inscription, *"titulus,"* is preserved in Jn. 19:19.

97. Cullmann, *The State in the New Testament*, p. 6.

98. *Ibid.*, pp. 42 f.

99. Cullmann, *Jesus and the Revolutionaries*, p. 34.

100. *Op. cit.*, pp. 107–9. Cf. also to Cohn, *op. cit.*, p. 10. Brandon, *The Trial of Jesus of Nazareth*, pp. 138, 149: "The placing of the *titulus* was in fact a proclamation of the Roman sentence of death . . . From our investigation of the Gospel accounts, it would seem that the main charge was that of the assumption of royal power as the 'King of the Jews,' with subsidiary charges of inciting the people to revolt and not to pay the Roman tribute." Cf. also, *ibid.*, pp. 191 (120), 198 (206); see Cullmann, *Jesus and the Revolutionaries*, p. 68 (11), for ancient evidences of Roman law concerning the public notice of the cause for execution; such as Eusebius' *Church History* 5.1.44, where "the martyrs [of Lyon] were required to wear signs stating the reason for their condemnation."

101. Cf. Mk. 15:24; Mt. 27:35; Lk. 23:34b; Jn. 19:23–24. Sherwin-White, *op. cit.*, p. 46.

102. Of course there is no way to establish the historicity of the "last words," though the words remembered in Aramaic seem to carry with them their own authority and authenticity. Nevertheless, all are consistent with the overall image of Jesus which emerges from the Gospel accounts, and we believe they can be accepted as plausible elements in the historical record.

103. Notice that the disciples are not mentioned. They had fled.

104. It is reported that after Jesus' death, Joseph of Arimathea, a respected member of the council, asked Pilate for the body of Jesus. Winter

believes that it was Joseph of Arimathea's "job" to guarantee proper care of the bodies of executed men. Cf. *op. cit.*, p. 180 (24), where he writes: "Joseph of Arimathea is a historical person. He was neither a member of the Great Sanhedrin—though the Third Evangelist made him such—nor was he a follower of Jesus. He was a member of a lower Beth Din (there were three Jewish courts in Jerusalem) whose duty it was to ensure that the bodies of executed persons were given decent burial before nightfall. He fulfilled this duty in accordance with Jewish law, and this act of piety was remembered." If this was the case, the elaborations by Matthew which indicate that Joseph of Arimathea made available his own unused tomb (Mt. 27:60) may have been added as a tribute to the man's kindness.

Flusser, *Jesus,* p. 119, cites the fact that Jesus was not buried in either of the two graves reserved for those executed by order of the Sanhedrin as further evidence that it was the Romans who condemned him to death.

CHAPTER 13

Not the Messiah, Yet Raised from the Dead

1. The full story of those experiences is told in *The Other Side,* by James A. Pike, Garden City, N.Y.: Doubleday, 1968; New York: Dell, 1969.
2. *The Jews in Their Land,* pp. 219 f.
3. *Loc. cit.*
4. Deut. 21:23. Cf. Gal. 3:13 and Chapter 13 above. See also Frend, *op. cit.,* p. 116: "Christianity came at a moment when the internal stresses affecting Judaism were already acute. These it exacerbated by offering the Jew a solution from which, however, he recoiled. The Cross was too great a scandal."
5. *Op. cit.,* p. 174.
6. *Ibid.,* pp. 152 f. Cf. Mt. 28:16; Mk. 16:10; Lk. 24:17b; Jn. 21:1–3.
7. There is one exception. In writing about a man named Shabbetai Zebi who arose among Jews in Europe as a potential Messiah in the seventeenth century, Abba Hillel Silver (*op. cit.*) makes the following observation: "Unlike all other Messianic movements since the time of Jesus, that of Shabbetai Zebi persisted even after his death; his followers spread Shabbetian doctrines, or those ascribed to him—some of them not without Trinitarian and Incarnation overtones—far and wide . . . Not even the death of Shabbetai Zebi put an end to the speculations. It was held that he would arise again and return to complete his work. In fact it was argued that the whole Jubilee period from 1640 to 1690 was the destined period of redemption. When the Jubilee ended in disappointment, the faithful continued to project still other but more remote dates" (pp. xiii, xiv).

The similarities of the Shabbetian movement to that of Jesus are remarkable. Terrible social conditions at the time of Shabbetai Zebi's appearance, particularly in Poland where Shabbetianism spread most rapidly, contributed to the eagerness of people for Messianic deliverance—as during the Roman period. Some of Shabbetai Zebi's followers sold all they owned (becoming voluntarily "poor") and left their homes, expecting redemption momentarily. Old Testament motifs were applied to the life of the pseudo-Messiah: the belief arose that because Moses had led the Jewish people for forty years in the wilderness before reaching the promised Land, Shabbetai Zebi would arise forty years after his first appearance in 1666 to accomplish the redemption of the Jews. Gematria (the interpretation of a word according to the numerical value of its letters) led the followers of Shabbetai Zebi to calculate and pinpoint the date of his "return" and of the redemption at 1675, 1680, 1686, 1692, 1706 and 1710, and the passing of these dates did not end the movement. Pseudo-prophets sustained the Shabbetian movement until the middle of the eighteenth century, and in the Slavic countries it persisted until the beginning of the nineteenth century. Silver, *op. cit.*, xv, 154–55, 158–61, 252. Thus many parallels between the Shabbetian movement and early Christianity can be seen. Otherwise, that a Messiah figure should continue to be followed after his death is unheard of in Judaism.

The authors are indebted to Mr. Stephen Kline, student at the University of California at Santa Cruz, for calling our attention to this similarity.

8. See Chapter 2, p. 25 above.

9. McLeman, *op. cit.*, p. 175. Cf. James M. Robinson, *op. cit.*, p. 35, who writes of the insight that "the Gospels are the devotional literature of the primitive Church" rather than histories, which marks the beginning of the twentieth-century study of the historical Jesus: "This insight, already at home in Old Testament research, was carried over to the New Testament . . . The Gospels are primary sources for the history of the early church, and only secondary sources for the history of Jesus."

10. Cf., for example, Morton Scott Enslin, *The Prophet from Nazareth*, New York: Schocken Books, 1968, who portrays Jesus as a prophet; McLeman, *op. cit.*, pp. 176 ff.; Martin Werner, *The Formation of Christian Dogma*, London: Adam & Charles Black, Ltd., 1957, pp. 18–21; Fuller, *op. cit.*, p. 130; cf. also James A. Pike, *What Is This Treasure*, pp. 60 f.

11. See Shlomo Pines, "The Jewish Christians of the Early Centuries of Christianity According to a New Source," The Israeli Academy of Sciences and Humanities, *Proceedings*, Vol. II, No. 13, Jerusalem: Central Press, 1966; and "'Israel, My Firstborn' and the Sonship of Jesus," *Studies in Mysticism and Religion*, Jerusalem, 1967.

12. Flusser, "Salvation Present and Future," *Types of Redemption*, R. J. Zwi Werblowsky and C. Jouco Bleeker, eds., Leiden: E. J. Brill, 1970, p. 51.

13. *Ibid.*, p. 52. Cf. Hans-Joachim Schoeps, *op. cit.*, pp. 55, 65 ff., who describes the faith of the Ebionites who believed that Jesus was the prophet like Moses prophesied in Deuteronomy 18. Jesus was understood by Ebionite Christianity to be a prophetic Messiah—the New Moses.

14. These questions have been dealt with at length by scholars. See, for example, Cullmann, *The Christology of the New Testament* and *The State in the New Testament;* Fuller, *op. cit.;* J. A. T. Robinson, *Jesus and His Coming;* Werner, *op. cit.;* Manson, *op. cit.;* W. G. Kummel, *Promise and Fulfillment*, London: SCM Press Ltd., 1966; etc.

15. Ch. Guignebert, *The Jewish World in the Time of Jesus*, London:

Kegan Paul, Trench, Trubner & Co., Ltd., 1939, pp. 134 f. See also McLeman, *op. cit.*, pp. 31 and 55 f.

16. Joachim Jeremias, *The Problem of the Historical Jesus*, p. 21, writes: "There is no parallel to the authority with which he [Jesus] dares to address God as *abba*. Anyone who admits merely the fact . . . that the word *abba* is an authentic utterance of Jesus, is, if he understands the word correctly, without watering down its meaning, thereby confronted with Jesus' claim to authority. Anyone who reads the parable of the Prodigal Son . . . is again confronted with the claim of Jesus to be regarded as God's representative, acting with authority . . . If with utmost discipline and conscientiousness we apply the critical resources at our disposal to the study of the historical Jesus, the final result is always the same: we find ourselves confronted with God himself." In this regard, Flusser ("Jesus in the Context of History") finds the scrolls particularly helpful, as they provide the only other example of "authentic utterances of charismatic Jewish leaders of Jesus' time," and, in the Thanksgiving Scroll, give evidence of "another Jewish religious personality in antiquity, besides Jesus, [with] a sublime realization of his own high place in the divine economy of the world" (p. 228). About Mt. 11:25–30, Flusser writes: "Here Jesus formulates his claim to be the sole repository and mediator of the divine mysteries expressing the relation between Father and Son. He claims to be God's son in other authentic sayings too. In the rabbinical literature, charismatic wonder-workers of Jesus' time are described as having access to God as a beloved son has it to his father" (pp. 228 f.). Hence Flusser sees rabbinic parallels to Jesus' "sonship"; but he sees even more striking similarities in the Scrolls' Teacher of Righteousness. Raymond E. Brown, "The Teacher of Righteousness and the Messiah(s)," *The Scrolls and Christianity*, has written of the Teacher of Righteousness: "He was evidently a man of deep personal piety . . . the hymns show him to have been profoundly conscious of his mission, aware of his weakness and dependence on God, but filled with trust in God's destiny for him. Speaking of God, he describes himself as one 'into whose mouth You have put doctrine and into whose heart You have put wisdom that he might open a fount of knowledge to all intelligent men' (Hymns 2:17–18) . . . 'You have made me a father to the pious' (7:20)" (p. 39). Brown notes that the impact of the Teacher on the sect was comparable to that of Jesus on his disciples: ". . . the Teacher set the basic pattern of the community's distinctive behaviour and thought. When the Qumran writings insist that the sectarians must observe the Law, they mean the Law as it was interpreted by the Teacher, who was also known as the Interpreter of the Law. In Com. on Hab. 7:2–3 the community is described as those 'whom God will deliver from the house of judgement because of their suffering and *because of their faith in the Teacher of Righteousness.*' Also the Teacher knew God's plan for the salvation of men, for God had revealed to him how the words of the prophets were being fulfilled in and through the Qumran community"

(Com. on Hab. 7:3–5; Brown, pp. 39–40. Italics his.). Flusser concludes, ". . . both Jesus and the sectarian author [of the Thanksgiving Scroll—the Teacher of Righteousness] were charismatic personalities, both thought that they had a central task in the final stage on the way to salvation, Jesus as the Messiah, and the sectarian author as a teacher of the eschatological community of the Sons of Light. Therefore we suggest that both Hymns 18:14–15 and Mt. 5:3–5 express the idea that the task of their author is the eschatological fulfilment of the prophecy predicting that in the Last Days there will be preached a blissful message to the meek and poor" (*Blessed are the Poor in Spirit*, pp. 10 f. and 10 [29]).

17. Flusser, "Jesus in the Context of History," p. 230.

18. *Loc. cit.*

19. J. A. T. Robinson, "The Most Primitive Christology of All?" *op. cit.*, p. 144; Neville Clark, *op. cit.*, p. 47.

20. Acts 2:41, 47; 4:13, 16, 31; 5:12–16; etc.

21. Eusebius, *Church History*, 3. 5. 2–3. Cf. S. G. F. Brandon, *Jesus and the Zealots*, pp. 208–17, esp. 209 (1), who doubts the authority of Eusebius' report of the flight of all the Christians to Pella before the Revolt. Brandon also argued against the authenticity of the Pella tradition in his work *The Fall of Jerusalem and the Christian Church*, pp. 168–73. Schoeps, *op. cit.*, pp. 22 ff., rejects as absurd the effort by Brandon and others to disprove the historicity of the Christian flight to Pella.

22. Cf. also Mt. 24:30–31; Mk. 13:26–27.

23. Cf. also Lk. 19:43–44; Mt. 24:2, 15–20; Mk. 13:2, 14–18.

24. Cf. also Mt. 24:1–51; Mk. 13:1–37; Lk. 21:5–28.

25. McLeman, *op. cit.*, p. 157; Clark, *op. cit.*, pp. 82 ff.

26. Clark, *op. cit.*, pp. 91 f.

27. *Ibid.*, p. 96.

28. McLeman, *op. cit.*, pp. 152 f. and 180; *The Interpreter's Bible*, Vol. VII, pp. 767 f.; Clark, *op. cit.*, p. 42.

29. Mt. 27:55–56; Mk. 15:40–41; Lk. 23:49; Jn. 19:25.

30. Though Passover was celebrated on Friday it was followed by the Sabbath, which meant the women could not have gone to the tomb until Sunday morning. Cf. Lk. 23:56b.

31. Cf. Mt. 28:1–7; Mk. 15:47; 16:1–8; Lk. 23:55; 24:1–12; Jn. 20:1–2. McLeman, *op. cit.*, p. 144; Ulrich Wilckens, "The Tradition-history of the Resurrection of Jesus," *The Significance of the Message of the Resurrection for Faith in Jesus Christ*, ed. by C. F. D. Moule, London: SCM Press Ltd., 1968, p. 73.

32. I Cor. 15:5; Lk. 24:34. Cf. also Willi Marxsen, "The Resurrection of Jesus as a Historical and Theological Problem," *The Significance of the Message of the Resurrection for Faith in Jesus Christ*, p. 33. McLeman, *op. cit.*, believes that Peter's confession of faith at Caesarea Philippi (Mt. 16:13–20; Mk. 8:27–30; Lk. 9:18–21) should be considered a post-crucifixion event, in the category of a resurrection appearance. As a result of

that experience, he contends, Peter was the first to become convinced that Jesus was indeed the Messiah and that it is on the basis of that "confession of faith" that he is regarded as the "rock" on which the Church is founded. "He may not have been alone in the conviction for long, but to him goes the honour of being the first to achieve and express [the faith that Jesus is Messiah]" (p. 190). See McLeman, *op. cit.*, pp. 180 ff. Cf. also Wilckens, *op. cit.*, p. 73.

33. Jn. 21:1–14; Mt. 28:16–17. Cf. McLeman, *op. cit.*, pp. 152 f.; Clark, *op. cit.*, p. 90; Wilckens, *op. cit.*, pp. 65 and 73.

34. Mt. 28:18–20.

35. Wilckens, *op. cit.*, pp. 73 f. It need not have been interpreted thus, as the Gospels themselves suggest. Cf. Mt. 28:11–15.

36. I Cor. 15:6–8. Cf. also Lk. 24:13–49; Jn. 20:19–29.

37. McLeman, *op. cit.*, pp. 143, 160, 202; Clark, *op. cit.*, p. 90; Wilckens, pp. 74 ff.

38. Marxsen, *op. cit.*, p. 31. Italics his. See also p. 34.

39. *What Is This Treasure*, p. 83.

40. *If This Be Heresy*, pp. 145 f.

41. Marxsen, *op. cit.*, p. 32.

42. McLeman, *op. cit.*, p. 164.

43. *Loc. cit.*

44. Clark, *op. cit.*, p. 51.

45. *Ibid.*, pp. 49 f. and 59; McLeman, *op. cit.*, pp. 81 ff.; Marxsen, *op. cit.*, p. 36.

46. McLeman, *op. cit.*, p. 84.

47. *Ibid.*, p. 97; Marxsen, *op. cit.*, p. 44.

48. Clark, *op. cit.*, pp. 38 and 46; Cullmann, *The Christology of the New Testament*, pp. 51 ff.; Dodd, *The Founder of Christianity*, pp. 112 ff.

49. Marxsen, *op. cit.*, pp. 49 f.; Fuller, *op. cit.*, pp. 142 ff. David Flusser, on the other hand, in his article "Jesus in the Context of History," p. 228, maintains that higher Christological conceptions were applied to Jesus soon after his death and that they were not the result of the passage of time and the delay of Jesus' coming "in power." Flusser refers to the Book of Revelation, the writings of Paul, and the Dead Sea Scrolls as evidence that Christology with its inflated notions of Jesus' standing in the divine economy of the world was not a pagan invention of the Hellenistic Christian communities which developed with the passage of time. Rather, the high Christological conceptions applied to Jesus after his death were current in the thought of Palestinian Judaism at that period.

50. Cf. *What Is This Treasure*, pp. 61 ff.

51. Marxsen, *op. cit.*, pp. 34 and 48.

52. Pike, *If This Be Heresy*, pp. 69 ff.

53. Cf. for example, Sheila Ostrander and Lynn Schroeder, *Psychic Discoveries Behind the Iron Curtain*, Englewood Cliffs, N.J.: Prentice-Hall, Inc., 1970; Sir Alister Hardy, *The Divine Flame, Natural History and*

Religion, London: Collins Publishers, 1966, and *The Living Stream,* New York: Harper & Row, 1965.

54. Cf. accounts of other similar appearances, e.g., Swami Paramahansa Yogananda's description of the "bodily" resurrection of his teacher Sri Yukteswar in *The Autobiography of a Yogi,* Los Angeles: Self-Realization Fellowship Publishers, 1969, pp. 413 ff., and numerous accounts gathered and analyzed by Robert Crookall in *The Supreme Adventure,* London: James Clarke & Co., 1961.

55. See I Cor. 15:35–50.

SELECTED INTRODUCTORY READINGS

We suggest the following books to any of our readers who would like to read further about the Dead Sea Scrolls and the historical Jesus, and who are "beginners" in this field. For full citations, see the bibliography.

THE HISTORICAL JESUS (GENERAL)

Cross, Colin. *Who Was Jesus?*
A journalist's report of the findings of modern scholarship, including those resulting from the study of the Dead Sea Scrolls, with regard to understanding the historical Jesus.

Flusser, David. *Jesus.*
A Jewish New Testament scholar's sensitive assessment of the historical Jesus.

Klausner, Joseph. *Jesus of Nazareth.*
Perhaps the first modern objective portrait of the historical Jesus by a Jewish scholar.

Schonfield, Hugh J. *The Passover Plot.*
Though the final thesis is highly controversial and difficult to take seriously, a basically sound book scholastically which makes fascinating reading.

Schweitzer, Albert. *The Quest of the Historical Jesus.*
The classic work which set the stage for the twentieth-century study of the historical Jesus. Difficult reading at times but well worth the effort.

JESUS AS A REVOLUTIONARY

Brandon, S. G. F. *Jesus and the Zealots.*
A scholarly and fascinating book which, while not easy reading, is a must for those interested in Jesus' relationship to the revolutionary movements of his day.

Cullmann, Oscar. *Jesus and the Revolutionaries.*
A noted Christian scholar's attempt to portray Jesus against a realistic political backdrop.

Farmer, W. R. *Maccabees, Zealots and Josephus.*
A thorough discussion of Jewish Nationalism in the Greco-Roman period, giving background for understanding Jesus in the context of that movement.

THE DEAD SEA SCROLLS (GENERAL)

Allegro, John. *The Dead Sea Scrolls.*
A colorful, easy-to-read, general discussion of the discovery of the Scrolls and of their importance.
Vermes, G. *The Dead Sea Scrolls in English.*
A paperback edition of a very readable translation of the major Dead Sea Scrolls.
Wilson, Edmund. *The Dead Sea Scrolls 1947–1969.*
A fascinating, journalistic account of the discovery of the Scrolls, the study of them, and their implications as seen by scholars.
Yadin, Yigael. *The Message of the Scrolls.*
The full story of the discovery of the Scrolls and of their contents told by an Israeli archaeologist.

THE SCROLLS AND CHRISTIANITY

Black, Matthew. *The Scrolls and Christian Origins.*
An investigation of the origins of Christianity in the light of the Dead Sea Scrolls from both historical and theological perspectives.
Cross, Frank M. *The Ancient Library of Qumran.*
A short, but comprehensive survey of the findings resulting from ten years of study of the Dead Sea Scrolls, including a comparison of the Qumran community and the early Christian Church.
Daniélou, Jean. *The Dead Sea Scrolls and Primitive Christianity.*
A discussion of the implications of the Dead Sea Scrolls for our understanding of the early followers of Jesus.
Davies, A. Powell. *The Meaning of the Dead Sea Scrolls.*
The story of the discovery of the Dead Sea Scrolls, with an interpretation of their relationship to the Bible and to the origins of Chistianity.
Stendahl, Krister. *The Scrolls and the New Testament.*
A collection of articles by some of the best-known Scrolls scholars dealing with particular areas in which the Scrolls have had an impact on our understanding of Jesus and the New Testament faith.

OTHER

Simon, Marcel. *Jewish Sects at the Time of Jesus.*
A concise and readable description of the various sects of Judaism at the time of Jesus.
Steinmann, Jean. *Saint John the Baptist.*
An easy-to-read description of John the Baptist and the Desert Tradition.

BIBLIOGRAPHY

Albright, W. F. "The Names 'Nazareth' and 'Nazoraean.'" *Journal of Biblical Literature,* Vol. LXV, 1946.

Albright, W. F. and Mann, C. S. "Qumran and the Essenes: Geography, Chronology, and Identification of the Sect." *The Scrolls and Christianity.* Matthew Black, ed. London: S.P.C.K., 1969.

Allegro, John. *The Dead Sea Scrolls.* Baltimore: Penguin Books, 1966.

————. "Further Messianic References in Qumran Literature." *Journal of Biblical Literature,* Vol. LXXV, 1956.

————. *Qumran Cave 4: I (4Q158–4Q186).* London: Oxford University Press, 1968.

Barbet, Pierre. *A Doctor at Calvary.* Garden City, N.Y.: Doubleday Image Books, 1963.

Black, Matthew. *The Dead Sea Scrolls and Christian Doctrine.* London: The Athlone Press, 1966.

————. *The Scrolls and Christian Origins.* New York: Thomas Nelson & Sons, Ltd., 1961.

————, ed. *The Scrolls and Christianity.* London: S.P.C.K., 1969.

————. "The Dead Sea Scrolls and Christian Origins." *The Scrolls and Christianity.* Matthew Black, ed. London: S.P.C.K., 1969.

Blinzler, Joseph. "The Trial of Jesus in the Light of History." *Judaism,* Vol. 20, No. 1, Winter 1971.

Bowman, J. "Early Samaritan Eschatology." *Journal of Jewish Studies,* Vol. 6, No. 2, 1956.

Brandon, S. G. F. *The Fall of Jerusalem and the Christian Church.* London: S.P.C.K., 1957.

————. *Jesus and the Zealots*. New York: Charles Scribner's Sons, 1967.

————. "The Messiah." The Manchester *Guardian*. Feb. 25, 1971.

————. "The Trial of Jesus." *Judaism*, Vol. 20, No. 1, Winter 1971.

————. *The Trial of Jesus of Nazareth*. New York: Stein & Day, 1968.

Brown, Raymond E. "The Qumran Scrolls and the Johannine Gospel and Epistles." *The Scrolls and the New Testament*. Krister Stendahl, ed. New York: Harper & Brothers, 1957.

————. "The Teacher of Righteousness and the Messiah(s)." *The Scrolls and Christianity*. Matthew Black, ed. London: S.P.C.K., 1969.

Brownlee, W. H. "John the Baptist in the Light of Ancient Scrolls." *The Scrolls and the New Testament*. Krister Stendahl, ed. New York: Harper & Brothers, 1957.

————. *The Meaning of the Qumran Scrolls for the Bible*. New York: Oxford University Press, 1964.

Bruce, F. F. "The Dead Sea Scrolls and Early Christianity." *Bulletin of the John Rylands Library*, Vol. 49, No. 1, Autumn 1966.

————. "Jesus and the Gospels in the Light of the Scrolls." *The Scrolls and Christianity*. Matthew Black, ed. London: S.P.C.K., 1969.

————. *Second Thoughts on the Dead Sea Scrolls*. London: The Paternoster Press, 1966.

————. *The Teacher of Righteousness in the Qumran Texts*. London: The Tyndale Press, 1957.

Bucke, Richard Maurice. *Cosmic Consciousness*. New York: E. P. Dutton & Co. 1964.

Bultmann, Rudolf. *Theology of the New Testament*. New York: Charles Scribner's Sons, 1951.

Burrows, Millar. *The Dead Sea Scrolls*. New York: The Viking Press, 1955.

————. *More Light on the Dead Sea Scrolls*. London: Secker & Warburg, 1958.

Carmichael, Joel. *The Death of Jesus*. New York: The Macmillan Co., 1962.

Carmignac, Jean. *Christ and the Teacher of Righteousness*. Baltimore: Helicon Press, Inc., 1962.

Charles, R. H., ed. *The Apocrypha and Pseudepigrapha of the Old Testament*, Vols. I and II. London: Oxford University Press, 1963.

Clark, Neville. *Interpreting the Resurrection*. London: SCM Press Ltd., 1967.

Cohn, Haim J. "Reflections on the Trial and Death of Jesus." *The Israel Law Review*. Jerusalem: *Jerusalem Post* Press, 1967.

————. "Reflections on the Trial of Jesus." *Judaism*, Vol. 20, No. 1, Winter 1971.

————. *The Trial and Death of Jesus*. New York: Harper & Row, 1971.

Crookall, Robert. *The Interpretation of Cosmic and Mystical Experiences*. London: James Clarke & Co., 1969.

————. *The Supreme Adventure*. London: James Clarke & Co., Ltd., 1961.

Cross, Colin. *Who Was Jesus?* London: Hodder and Stoughton, Inc., 1970.

Cross, Frank M. *The Ancient Library of Qumran*. Garden City, N.Y.: Doubleday & Company, Inc., 1961.

Cullmann, Oscar. *The Christology of the New Testament*. Philadelphia: Westminster Press, 1963.

————. *Jesus and the Revolutionaries*. New York: Harper & Row, 1970.

————. "The Significance of the Qumran Texts for Research into the Beginnings of Christianity." *The Scrolls and the New Testament*. Krister Stendahl, ed. New York: Harper & Brothers, 1957.

————. *The State in the New Testament*. New York: Charles Scribner's Sons, 1956.

Daniélou, Jean. "Christianity as a Jewish Sect." *The Crucible of Christianity*. Arnold Toynbee, ed. London: Thames & Hudson, 1969.

————. *The Dead Sea Scrolls and Primitive Christianity*. New York: The New American Library, 1962.

————. *The Work of John the Baptist*. Baltimore: Helicon Press, 1966.

Davies, A. Powell. *The Meaning of the Dead Sea Scrolls*. New York: The New American Library, 1956.

Davies, W. D. *Paul and Rabbinic Judaism*. New York: Harper & Row, 1967.

―――. *The Setting of the Sermon on the Mount*. Cambridge, England: Cambridge University Press, 1964.

Dodd, C. H. *The Founder of Christianity*. New York: Macmillan Co., 1970.

―――. *Historical Tradition in the Fourth Gospel*. Cambridge, England: Cambridge University Press, 1965.

Driver, G. R. *The Judaean Scrolls*. Oxford: Basil Blackwell, 1965.

Drower, E. S. *The Mandaeans of Iraq and Iran*. Leiden: E. J. Brill, 1962.

―――. *The Secret Adam*. London: Oxford University Press, 1960.

Dupont-Sommer, A. *The Dead Sea Scrolls*. Oxford: Basil Blackwell, 1956.

―――. *The Essene Writings from Qumran*. Oxford: Basil Blackwell, 1961.

Edersheim, Alfred. *The Temple: Its Ministry and Services As They Were at the Time of Jesus Christ*. Grand Rapids, Mich.: W. B. Eerdmans Publishing Co., 1965.

Eisler, Robert. *The Messiah Jesus and John the Baptist*. New York: Lincoln Macveagh, The Dial Press, 1931.

Elliott-Binns, L. E. *Galilean Christianity*. Chicago: Alec R. Allenson, Inc., 1956.

Enslin, Morton Scott. *The Prophet from Nazareth*. New York: Schocken Books, 1968.

―――. "The Temple and the Cross." *Judaism,* Vol. 20, No. 1, Winter 1971.

Farmer, William Reuben, ed. *The Great Jewish War*. New York: Harper & Brothers, 1960.

―――. *Maccabees, Zealots and Josephus*. New York: Columbia University Press, 1958.

―――. "The Palm Branches in John 12, 13." *Journal of Theological Studies,* N.S., Vol. III, Pt. 1, April 1952.

Flusser, David. "Blessed are the Poor in Spirit." *Israel Exploration Journal,* Vol. 10, No. 1. Jerusalem: Central Press, 1960.

————. "The Dead Sea Sect and Pre-Pauline Christianity." (Aspects of the Dead Sea Scrolls.) *Scripta Hierosolymitana,* Vol. IV. Jerusalem: Hebrew University, 1958.

————. *Jesus.* New York: Herder and Herder, 1969.

————. "Jesus in the Context of History." *The Crucible of Christianity.* Arnold Toynbee, ed. London: Thames & Hudson, 1969.

————. "A Literary Approach to the Trial of Jesus." *Judaism,* Vol. 20, No. 1, Winter 1971.

————. "Salvation Present and Future." *Types of Redemption.* R. J. Zwi Werblowsky and C. Jouco Bleeker, eds. Leiden: E. J. Brill, 1970.

Frend, W. H. C. *Martyrdom and Persecution in the Early Church.* New York: New York University Press, 1967.

Fuller, Reginald H. *The Foundations of New Testament Christology.* New York: Charles Scribner's Sons, 1965.

Gartner, Bertil. *The Temple and the Community in Qumran and the New Testament.* Cambridge, England: Cambridge University Press, 1965.

Gaster, Moses. *The Samaritans.* London: Oxford University Press, 1925.

Gaster, Theodore H. *The Dead Sea Scriptures in English.* A translation. Garden City, N.Y.: Doubleday Anchor Books, 1964.

Goguel, Maurice. *Jesus and the Origins of Christianity,* Vols. I and II. New York: Harper & Brothers, 1960.

Grant, F. C. *The Economic Background of the Gospels.* London: Oxford University Press, 1926.

Grant, Robert M. "The Trial of Jesus in the Light of History." *Judaism,* Vol. 20, No. 1, Winter 1971.

Guignebert, Ch. *The Jewish World in the Time of Jesus.* London: Kegan Paul, Trench, Trubner & Co., Ltd., 1939.

Haas, N. "Anthropological Observations on the Skeletal Remains from Giv'at ha-Mivtar." *Israel Exploration Journal,* Vol. 20, Nos. 1–2. Jerusalem: Central Press, 1970.

Hardy, Sir Alister. *The Divine Flame, Natural History and Religion*. London: Collins Publishers, 1966.

――――. *The Living Stream*. New York: Harper & Row, 1965.

Harrison, R. K. "The Rites and Customs of the Qumran Sect." *The Scrolls and Christianity*. Matthew Black, ed. London: S.P.C.K., 1969.

Hart, H. St. J. "The Crown of Thorns in John 19, 2–5." *Journal of Theological Studies*, N.S. Vol. III, Pt. 1, April 1952.

Hennecke, Edgar, ed. *New Testament Apocrypha*, Vols. I and II. Wilhelm Schneemelcher, ed. Philadelphia: Westminster Press, 1963.

Interpreter's Bible, The. 12 Vols. New York: Abingdon Press, 1951.

James, M. R., tr. *The Apocryphal New Testament*. Oxford, England: The Clarendon Press, 1963.

Jaubert, Annie. *The Date of the Last Supper*. Staten Island: Alba House, Society of St. Paul, 1965.

Jeremias, Joachim. *The Eucharistic Words of Jesus*. London: SCM Press, Ltd., 1966.

――――. *Jerusalem in the Time of Jesus*. Philadelphia: Fortress Press, 1969.

――――. *The Problem of the Historical Jesus*. Philadelphia: Fortress Press, 1964.

Jervell, Jacob. *The Continuing Search for the Historical Jesus*. Minneapolis: Augsburg Publishing House, 1965.

Jews in Their Land, The. David Ben-Gurion, ed. London: Aldus Books, 1966.

Johnson, Raynor C. *The Imprisoned Splendour*. New York: Harper & Row, 1953.

――――. *Nurslings of Immortality*. New York: Harper & Brothers, 1957.

Klausner, Joseph. *Jesus of Nazareth*. Boston: Beacon Press, 1964.

Kollek, Teddy and Pearlman, Moshe. *Jerusalem, Sacred City of Mankind*. Jerusalem: Steimatzky's Agency Limited, 1968.

Kraeling, Carl Hermann. *John the Baptist.* New York: Charles Scribner's Sons, 1951.

Kuhn, K. G. "The Lord's Supper and the Communal Meal at Qumran." *The Scrolls and the New Testament.* Krister Stendahl, ed. New York: Harper & Brothers, 1957.

Kummel, W. G. *Promise and Fulfillment.* London: SCM Press, Ltd., 1966.

Leaney, A. R. C. *The Rule of Qumran and Its Meaning.* London: SCM Press, Ltd., 1966.

McLeman, James. *Resurrection Then and Now.* London: Hodder & Stoughton, 1965.

McRuer, J. C. *The Trial of Jesus.* London: Blandford Press, 1965.

Manson, T. W. *The Servant-Messiah.* London: Cambridge University Press, 1966.

Marxsen, Willi. "The Resurrection of Jesus as a Historical and Theological Problem." *The Significance of the Message of the Resurrection for Faith in Jesus Christ.* C. F. D. Moule, ed. London: SCM Press, Ltd., 1968.

Mauser, Ulrich W. *Christ in the Wilderness.* London: SCM Press, Ltd., 1963.

Montefiore, Hugh. "Revolt in the Desert? (Mk. 6:30 ff.)." *New Testament Studies,* 8, 1961–62.

Moule, C. F. D., ed. *The Significance of the Message of the Resurrection for Faith in Jesus Christ.* London: SCM Press, Ltd., 1968.

Oesterley, W. O. E. *A History of Israel,* Vol. II. Oxford, England: The Clarendon Press, 1945.

Ostrander, Sheila and Schroeder, Lynn. *Psychic Discoveries Behind the Iron Curtain.* Englewood Cliffs, N.J.: Prentice-Hall, Inc., 1970.

Peake's Commentary. Matthew Black and H. H. Rowley, eds. New York: Thomas Nelson & Sons, Ltd., 1962.

Pike, Diane Kennedy. *Search.* Garden City, N.Y.: Doubleday & Company, Inc., 1970; New York: Pocket Books, 1971.

Pike, James A. "Christianity in Retreat." *Look,* Vol. 24, No. 26, December 20, 1960.

———. *If This Be Heresy.* New York: Delta Publishing Co., Inc., 1969.

———. *The Other Side.* Garden City, N.Y.: Doubleday & Company, Inc., 1968; New York: Dell Publishing Co., Inc., 1969.

———. *A Time for Christian Candor.* New York: Harper & Row, 1964.

———. "Was the Crown of Thorns a Form of Torture?" *New Focus* [published by the Bishop Pike Foundation], Vol. I, No. 3, June–July 1969.

———. *What Is This Treasure.* New York: Harper & Row, 1966.

Pines, Shlomo. " 'Israel, My Firstborn' and the Sonship of Jesus." From *Studies in Mysticism and Religion.* Jerusalem: 1967.

———. "The Jewish Christians of the Early Centuries of Christianity According to a New Source." The Israel Academy of Sciences and Humanities, *Proceedings,* Vol. II, No. 13. Jerusalem: Central Press, 1966.

Ploger, Otto. *Theocracy and Eschatology.* Oxford: Basil Blackwell, 1968.

Pryke, John. "Eschatology in the Dead Sea Scrolls." *The Scrolls and Christianity.* Matthew Black, ed. London: S.P.C.K., 1969.

Rabin, Chaim. "The Dead Sea Scrolls and the History of the Old Testament Text." *Journal of Theological Studies,* N.S., Vol. VI, Pt. 2, October 1955.

Rengstorf, Karl Heinrich. *Hirbet Qumran and the Problem of the Library of the Dead Sea Caves.* Leiden: E. J. Brill, 1963.

Robinson, James M. *A New Quest of the Historical Jesus.* London: SCM Press, Ltd., 1966.

Robinson, John A. T. *Jesus and His Coming.* London: SCM Press, Ltd., 1967.

———. *Twelve New Testament Studies.* London: SCM Press, Ltd., 1965.

Roth, Cecil. *The Dead Sea Scrolls: A New Historical Approach.* New York: W. W. Norton & Co., Inc., 1965.

―――. *A History of the Jews.* New York: Schocken Books, 1961.

Rowley, H. H. *The Dead Sea Scrolls and the New Testament.* London: S.P.C.K., 1964.

―――. "The History of the Qumran Sect." *Bulletin of the John Rylands Library,* Vol. 49, No. 1, Autumn 1966. Manchester, England.

―――. "The Qumran Sect and Christian Origins." *Bulletin of the John Rylands Library,* Vol. 44, No. 1, September 1961. Manchester, England.

Russell, D. S. *The Method and Message of Jewish Apocalyptic.* Philadelphia: Westminster Press, 1964.

Safrai, Shemuel. *Pilgrimage at the Time of the Second Temple.* Tel Aviv, Israel: Am Hassefer Publishers Ltd., 1965.

Schoeps, Hans-Joachim. *Jewish Christianity: Factional Disputes in the Early Church.* Philadelphia: Fortress Press, 1969.

Schonfield, Hugh J. *The Passover Plot.* New York: Bantam Books, 1967.

Schubert, Kurt. "The Sermon on the Mount and the Qumran Texts." *The Scrolls and the New Testament.* Krister Stendahl, ed. New York: Harper & Brothers, 1957.

Schweitzer, Albert. *The Kingdom of God and Primitive Christianity.* London: Adam & Charles Black, 1968.

―――. *Pilgrimage to Humanity.* New York: Philosophical Library, 1961.

―――. *The Quest of the Historical Jesus.* New York: The Macmillan Co., 1968.

Scobie, Charles H. H. "John the Baptist." *The Scrolls and Christianity.* Matthew Black, ed. London: S.P.C.K., 1969.

Sherwin-White, A. N. *Roman Society and Roman Law in the New Testament.* London: Oxford University Press, 1963.

Silver, Abba Hillel. *A History of Messianic Speculation in Israel.* Boston: Beacon Press, 1959.

Simon, Marcel. *Jewish Sects at the Time of Jesus.* Philadelphia: Fortress Press, 1967.

————. *St. Stephen and the Hellenists in the Primitive Church.* London: Longmans, Green and Co., 1958.

Sloyan, Gerard S. "The Last Days of Jesus." *Judaism,* Vol. 20, No. 1, Winter 1971.

Steinmann, Jean. *Saint John the Baptist.* New York: Harper & Brothers, 1958.

Stendahl, Krister, "Hate, Non-Retaliation and Love." *Harvard Theological Review,* Vol. 55, 1962.

————, ed. *The Scrolls and the New Testament.* New York: Harper & Brothers, 1957.

Stringfellow, William and Towne, Anthony. *The Bishop Pike Affair.* New York: Harper & Row, 1967.

Sutcliffe, Edmund F. *The Monks of Qumran.* London: Burns & Oates, 1960.

Tart, Charles T., ed. *Altered States of Consciousness.* New York: John Wiley & Sons, Inc., 1969.

Taylor, Vincent. *The Life and Ministry of Jesus.* Nashville: Abingdon Press, 1955.

————. "The Life and Ministry of Jesus." *The Interpreter's Bible.* Vol. VII.

Thackeray, H. St. J., tr. *Josephus: The Jewish War, Jewish Antiquities, The Life, Against Apion.* 9 vols. Cambridge: Harvard University Press, The Loeb Classical Library edition, 1966.

Toynbee, Arnold, ed. *The Crucible of Christianity.* London: Thames & Hudson, 1969.

Underhill, Evelyn. *Mysticism.* London: Methuen & Co., Ltd., 1967.

Vermes, G., tr. *The Dead Sea Scrolls in English.* Baltimore: Penguin Books, 1966.

Werblowsky, R. J. Zwi and Bleeker, C. Jouco, eds. *Types of Redemption.* Leiden: E. J. Brill, 1970.

Werner, Martin. *The Formation of Christian Dogma.* London: Adam & Charles Black, Ltd., 1957.

Wilckens, Ulrich. "The Tradition-history of the Resurrection of Jesus." *The Significance of the Message of the Resurrection for Faith in Jesus Christ.* C. F. D. Moule, ed. London: SCM Press, Ltd., 1968.

Williamson, G. A., tr. *The Jewish War.* Baltimore: Penguin Books, 1967.

————, tr. *Eusebius: The History of the Church from Christ to Constantine.* Baltimore: Penguin Books, 1965.

Wilson, Edmund. *The Dead Sea Scrolls 1947–1969.* New York: Oxford University Press, 1969.

Wilson, William R. *The Execution of Jesus.* New York: Charles Scribner's Sons, 1970.

Wingo, Earl L. *The Illegal Trial of Jesus.* New York: Bobbs-Merrill Co., Inc., Charter Edition, 1962.

Winter, Paul. "Magnificat and Benedictus—Maccabaean Psalms?" *Bulletin of the John Rylands Library,* Vol. 37, No. 1, September 1954. Manchester, England.

————. *On the Trial of Jesus.* Berlin: Walter de Gruyter & Co., 1961.

Yadin, Yigael. *Masada.* New York: Random House, 1966.

————. *The Message of the Scrolls.* New York: The Universal Library, Grosset & Dunlap, 1962.

————. "The Temple Scroll." *The Biblical Archaeologist,* Vol. XXX, No. 4, December 1967.

Yogananda, Paramahansa. *Autobiography of a Yogi.* Los Angeles: Self-Realization Fellowship Publishers, 1969.

Zeitlin, Solomon. *Josephus on Jesus.* Philadelphia: The Dropsie College for Hebrew and Cognate Learning, 1931.

INDEX